CW00732664

# THE
# PICTS
## AND THE
# SCOTS
## AT WAR

## NICK AITCHISON

SUTTON PUBLISHING

First published in the United Kingdom in 2003 by
Sutton Publishing Limited · Phoenix Mill
Thrupp · Stroud · Gloucestershire · GL5 2BU

Copyright © Nick Aitchison, 2003.

All rights reserved. No part of this publication may be reproduced, stored
in a retrieval system, or transmitted, in any form, or by any means,
electronic, mechanical, photocopying, recording or otherwise, without
the prior permission of the publisher and copyright holder.

Nick Aitchison has asserted the moral right to be identified as the author
of this work.

British Library Cataloguing in Publication Data
A catalogue record for this book is available from the British Library.

ISBN 0-7509-2556-6

---

*In memoriam*
Theresa Ford
1938–2002

---

Typeset in 10/12 pt New Baskerville.
Typesetting and origination by
Sutton Publishing Limited.
Printed and bound in England by
J.H. Haynes & Co. Ltd, Sparkford.

# Contents

# Acknowledgements

Any work of synthesis owes an enormous debt to preceding generations of scholars and this is no exception. I hope that my gratitude to those many archaeologists, historians, editors and translators is adequately reflected in the Notes and the Bibliography and apologise to any whose views I have subconsciously absorbed along the way and whose contribution is not acknowledged specifically. However, any interpretations or errors attached to the evidence presented here are mine alone.

One site is more responsible than any other for sparking and maintaining my interest in the Picts and Scots at war and, indeed, in early medieval Scotland in general. It is therefore a pleasure to express my thanks to my parents, Norma and Jim, who first took me to visit Dunadd, the hillfort and presumed royal fortress and inauguration place of the Scots of *Dál Riata*, while on a family holiday in 1972. I am very grateful to Dr Alan Lane of the School of History and Archaeology, Cardiff University, who gave me the opportunity to participate in his excavations at Dunadd in 1981, a stimulating experience that provided many unique insights. My thanks are also due to Dr Stephen T. Driscoll of the Department of Archaeology, University of Glasgow, for inviting me to accompany him on an aerial reconnaissance flight over Dunadd in 1987, which provided me with a new perspective on the hillfort within its landscape.

I am very fortunate to have received encouragement and support from two successive senior commissioning editors at Sutton Publishing, firstly Jane Crompton and latterly Christopher Feeney. I am extremely grateful to them for the flexibility and patience they have demonstrated so consistently as this project mutated over time and successive deadlines came and went. I would also like to thank Alison Miles for her very helpful and thorough work at the editorial stage. I wish to record my thanks to the institutions and individuals, appropriately credited in the relevant figure captions, that gave permission to reproduce copyright material. In addition, I would like to thank Kristina Johansson of the National Monuments Record of Scotland, Royal Commission on the Ancient and Historical Monuments of Scotland, and Helen Nicoll of the National Museums of Scotland, for identifying and providing illustrations in such a helpful and timely manner. I am also grateful to the staff of the British Library and Glasgow University Library for their assistance, particularly with some of my more obscure queries and requests. I also wish to thank my parents for providing a convenient base from which the final stage of research was conducted.

Lastly, but by no means least, I owe an enormous debt to my wife Karen for the patience she has demonstrated so consistently while this project was in progress; to her my loving thanks are due.

# Introduction

In addition to a plethora of books on Scottish battles, the past decade has witnessed a growing interest in wide-ranging aspects of the many and varied Scottish experiences of war.[1] Regardless of this, very little attention has been focused on the wars, warfare and weapons of early medieval Scotland and their study remains largely neglected. Regardless of the steadily increasing number of publications on the Picts and Scots, little effort has been devoted to the study of these peoples at war. Indeed, previous studies of the Picts and Scots have been criticised for including insufficient and/or inadequate coverage of warfare[2] and warfare is absent from the only published research strategy concerning the Picts.[3] Moreover, only a single early medieval battle, Dunnichen, features in those many books on Scottish battles and, even then, only in some. This situation is in marked contrast to the study of other periods of Scottish history and of the neighbouring peoples of the Picts and Scots, notably the Anglo-Saxons and Vikings,[4] in which battles, warfare and weapons feature prominently. This probably reflects the greater availability of both artefactual evidence and documentary sources relating to the warfare of other areas and periods. However, this does not negate the importance of warfare among the Picts and the Scots, although it does make their study more challenging.

The apparent lack of interest in the Picts and the Scots at war is particularly surprising given the prominence attached to this subject in contemporary documentary sources and that the early medieval period was the most formative one in the emergence of the medieval kingdom of the Scots. Indeed, warfare is central to the study of early medieval Scotland. From the earliest recorded references to the Picts and Scots, where they appear as raiders attacking late Roman Britain, these peoples were engaged in a series of struggles, internally, against each other and with neighbouring peoples over the following centuries. This is reflected in a wide range of source material. From at least the mid-sixth century, when the earliest contemporary historical records begin, warfare – in the form of battles, raids and sieges – features more frequently and prominently than any other subject in early medieval references to the Picts and Scots.

One of the enduring stereotypes of 'Dark Age' warfare is that of hordes of marauding barbarians engaged in a frenzied free-for-all of violence and looting, whether on or off the battlefield. But such perceptions are misleading and even a cursory glance at the evidence reveals that early medieval armies and navies displayed considerable organisation and were capable of some impressive achievements. This was also the case among the Picts and the Scots. More fundamentally, warfare was not simply a means of defending territory from aggressive neighbouring peoples, but underpinned the very fabric of society. Social and political institutions were shaped by the requirements of warfare. Although the evidence is patchy, military obligation was an integral part of those economic and social relations of dominance and dependency that existed between a king and his lords and, in turn, between a lord and his clients. That the Picts and Scots were capable of fighting and winning battles, raising sizeable fleets and mounting campaigns by land and/or sea against both neighbouring and overseas kingdoms, attests not only an impressive degree of military organisation and discipline, but also the existence of extensive social and economic mechanisms required to levy, equip and supply warbands and armies.

Warfare itself presented a multitude of opportunities for reinforcing those social relationships both on and off the battlefield, in the organisation and conduct of the army, in acts of heroism in combat and through the appropriation and distribution of booty seized from the enemy. Arms and armour also played a central role in the social dimension of warfare. Elaborate swords, decorated shields, horses on which to ride into battle and possibly chain mail were all the preserve of high-status warriors, symbols of prestige to impress subjects and enemies alike in both war and peace. Regardless of their stereotyped portrayal in late Roman and early British sources, the Picts and Scots at war were not simply ravaging savages.

Warfare is one of the central themes in the history of the Picts and Scots and yet has received surprisingly little attention. This book attempts to redress that imbalance by identifying and introducing the main themes, from military obligations and organisation to the battle-dead and contemporary attitudes to warfare. In between, it examines Pictish and Scottish arms and armour, warriors and warfare, fortifications, naval warfare and the spoils of war. But it makes no pretence at providing a definitive account. Specifically, further research is required on Pictish and Scottish attacks on later Roman Britain, Roman frontier policy and the campaigns mounted in response to those northern incursions, as well as on hillforts and early medieval battles. In particular, the absence from this book of a discussion specifically on the battles fought by the Picts and Scots might seem puzzling. However, with only the possible exception of Dunnichen, battles of the Picts and Scots are very poorly recorded.

Contemporary references to battles, where they exist, usually reveal little, if anything, of military significance. Instead, these terse accounts frequently present a range of problems concerning the names, locations and dates of many battles and even the identities of the warring sides and the outcome of the battle often remain obscure. This makes the thematic approach adopted in this study even more appropriate and references to specific battles are incorporated under the themes covered. This is more realistic than attempting to impose a chronological structure on information when, for the purposes of this study, precise historical contexts are not of great importance.

The period covered by this study begins in the early centuries AD, with the prehistoric ancestors of the Picts and the Scots. But the main focus is on the period from the mid-sixth century, when the earliest contemporary historical documents begin, while most of the sculptural evidence dates from the eighth and ninth centuries. There is no obvious or universally accepted end date for the early medieval period in Scotland. The year 843, when the Picts were traditionally believed to have been conquered by the Scots, is, like this interpretation itself, no longer accepted and a date of *c.* 900 is now generally considered more appropriate for the disappearance of most aspects of Pictish life and culture. But, as there is nothing to indicate dramatic changes in war or warfare at this time, this study includes evidence from as late as the mid-tenth century where it seems relevant.

## NAMES, DATES AND NOTES

The names of early medieval population groups, kingdoms and territories pose considerable potential for ambiguity and confusion because they often changed in meaning and/or form over their frequently long histories. This necessitates a brief definition of some of the names used in this book. The people of *Dál Riata* are referred to throughout as Scots in preference to Gaels (*Goidíl*), which is also the Irish name for themselves, or awkward anglicisms such as 'Dalriadans'. The Scots, for the purposes of this study, are the Scots of *Dál Riata*. The Pictish name for their own territory is unknown. In the absence of a clearly established contemporary name used by a neighbouring people, Pictland is employed throughout this study, in preference to the Latinised *Pictavia*, which only appears in medieval sources. *Alba*, the Gaelic equivalent of Latin *Scotia*, refers to the kingdom north of the Forth that was forged from the merger of Pictland and *Dál Riata* by *c.* 900. But Scotland provides a convenient and readily understood geographical unit and is used in this sense throughout the book.

Personal names pose problems of a different type. There is very little consistency of spelling in either primary or secondary sources. Pictish names are particularly problematic, reflecting the scarcity of Pictish documents,[5] and are recorded mostly in Irish/Gaelic forms in Irish and medieval Scottish documents. However, the current trend is to use original name forms where these are known or can be inferred. As a compromise, the original Pictish and Gaelic names are used here where these can be established but their anglicised and (for Pictish names) Gaelic equivalents are included in parentheses where they first appear in the text.

Dates are easily as controversial and complex. There is often some uncertainty about the precise year in which many events occurred during the early medieval period, as a result of discrepancies between documentary sources. This study avoids being drawn into lengthy and complex chronological debates and relies upon (corrected) dates derived from the *Annals of Ulster* (AU). This is one of the most reliable annalistic sources and incorporates entries made on Iona that are contemporary with the events recorded.[6] Events not recorded in the Irish Annals are often less precisely dated and some can only be assigned to a particular reign. This should not hinder this study, which is structured thematically, rather than chronologically.

All dates given are AD unless stated otherwise and all dates given for kings are regnal dates. In accordance with established archaeological practice, uncalibrated radiocarbon dates are expressed in the form years AD or BC.

The end notes give Harvard-style short references, the expansions for which may be found in the Bibliography. These notes are intended to provide guidance to both the primary and secondary sources used and to assist those wishing to pursue their own study of the Picts and Scots at war. They are not essential to the understanding of the text and may be ignored by the more casual reader.

## The Pictish Arts Society

The Pictish Arts Society, a charity registered in Scotland, was founded in 1988 to affirm the importance of Pictish culture in Scotland's past. In addition to holding a lively programme of lectures, conferences and field trips, the Society also publishes an influential journal, the principal forum for new ideas and information about all aspects of the Picts. For further information and details of membership contact: The Pictish Arts Society, c/o Pictavia, Haughmuir, by Brechin, Angus DD9 6RL, Scotland.

## CHAPTER ONE

# The Picts and the Scots

The Picts and the Scots were the most powerful and warlike peoples of northern Britain in the period between late Roman Britain and the arrival of the Vikings from the late eighth century.

Both the Picts and the Scots had a ferocious reputation among their neighbours. From their earliest recorded appearance, the Picts and the Scots were recorded as aggressors by a succession of southern neighbours and widely portrayed as violent peoples, feared for their raiding, plundering and destruction. The Picts and the Scots were often associated with each other in their earliest recorded attacks, on the province of later Roman Britain. In 360 the 'savage peoples' (*gentium ferarum*) of the *Picti* and *Scotti* broke a treaty with Rome and ravaged those areas of Roman Britain beside the frontier defences.[1] In the fifth century, St Patrick criticised the Picts as 'utterly iniquitous, evil and apostate' for buying Irish slaves from the Strathclyde Britons.[2] Gildas,[3] a British monk writing *c.* 540, described them as 'two exceedingly savage overseas nations', 'foul hordes of Scots and Picts, like dark throngs of worms who wriggle out of narrow fissures in the rock when the sun is high and the weather grows warm . . . in perfect accord in their greed for bloodshed'. These Picts and Scots, according to Gildas, inflicted 'the cruellest massacres' on the Britons, in which 'the pitiable citizens were torn apart by their foe like lambs by the butcher'. In the seventh century, Wilfrid, first Bishop of Hexham castigated the 'warlike Picts' (*feroces Pictos*), famously referring to them as 'the bestial peoples of the Picts with savage minds' (*populi bestiales Pictorum feroci animo*).[4] Even the Venerable Bede,[5] abbot of Monkwearmouth–Jarrow and who is generally more sympathetic to the Picts, repeats Gildas' account of the bloody exploits of the Picts and Scots.

Warfare was an important aspect of both Pictish and Scottish society. But the stereotype of the Picts and the Scots as belligerent barbarians reflects biases in the evidence caused by the scarcity of documentary records and historians' dependency on external sources. Most of this evidence originates among the neighbours of the Picts, peoples who were themselves periodically hostile to the Picts and therefore tend to portray them in a negative light. Eddius Stephanus, for example, was referring to a war against the Picts in 671–3 but, writing in the early eighth century, must have been influenced by the overwhelming Northumbrian defeat by the Picts in the battle of Dunnichen in 685. Eddius conveniently overlooked the fact that, on both occasions, the Picts were fighting in defence of their own kingdom, on their own soil and against Northumbrian overlordship and invasion. The Picts and, to a lesser extent, the Scots have had a bad press.

Nevertheless, warfare was clearly important to the Picts and the Scots. In a society in which power was drawn from the command and redistribution of natural resources, the struggle for access to more and better resources inevitably led to ambitions of territorial expansion. Similar aspirations among the other peoples of early medieval Scotland resulted in a dynamic, even volatile, political situation in which the fortunes of kingdoms ebbed and flowed. Phases of territorial expansion and political primacy almost inevitably culminated in over-extension and were followed by periods of decline and eclipse. Warfare and its associated institutions were integral to these processes. But before examining these, who were these warlike peoples, what do we know about them, and how?

## THE PICTS

The Picts are traditionally the most enigmatic of the early medieval peoples who inhabited what is now Scotland. Although much of the modern appeal of the Picts lies in the mystery surrounding them, considerable progress in their study has been made since the publication of the seminal *The Problem of the Picts* in 1955.[6] The growing contribution of archaeology in particular has ensured that the Picts are now the best understood and certainly the most extensively researched people of early medieval Scotland.[7]

The Picts were traditionally believed to be immigrants from Scythia, a tale first recorded in the eighth century.[8] Later interpretations sought to explain the perceived peculiarities of the Picts, especially their distinctive symbols and strange names, from their origins among the pre-Celtic inhabitants of Britain, who supposedly spoke a non-Indo-European language. More recently, the Picts have been accepted as a Celtic people, or at least one that spoke a Celtic language. The Pictish language belongs to the P-Celtic or Brythonic branch of Celtic languages,[9] which also includes Breton, Cornish and Welsh. P-Celtic languages were common across Britain and Gaul when the Romans invaded in the first centuries BC and AD and, although their origins and mechanisms of introduction are unclear, they were probably spoken from the mid-first millennium BC.

The linguistic evidence indicates that the Picts originated among the native peoples of the Scottish Iron Age.[10]

The indigenous origin of the Picts is also apparent from documentary sources. The earliest recorded reference to the Picts is in the anonymous *Panegyric of Constantius Caesar* of 297,[11] formerly but mistakenly attributed to Eumenius. This refers to the *Picti* and *Hiberni* (Irish) as being accustomed to fighting the *Britanni* (Britons). In 364, the Picts, *Scotti*, Saxons and the enigmatic *Attacotti* 'were harassing the Britons with constant disasters'.[12] The aggressors included the '*Picti* divided into two peoples, *Dicalydones* and *Verturiones*'.[13] The latter peoples have such similar or even identical names to the *Caledonii* and *Verturiones*, peoples of north-east Scotland recorded by the Greek geographer Ptolemy in the second century, that they must be closely related. This reveals that the Picts originated among the native population of Iron Age Scotland and probably represented a coalescence of smaller peoples into a larger and more powerful socio-political unit. The social and political processes involved are obscure, but were probably facilitated, if not stimulated, by Roman Britain. This arose partly from the need to mount an effective defence against periodic Roman campaigns in Scotland. Moreover, the proximity of Rome's northernmost frontier and the wealthy province beyond it provided an incentive for raiding and, in the wealth plundered there, the means of supporting socio-political élites, the development of emergent kingdoms and a society organised for war.

Pictland comprised most of what is now northern Scotland and its limits are recorded by contemporary commentators. Its southern boundary was marked by the Firth of Forth and, before the Scots extended their settlement into this area, the Firth of Clyde.[14] To the south-east lay the North British kingdom of *Gododdin* until its collapse *c.* 640, when the Angles of Northumbria extended their territory as far north as the Forth.[15] To the south-west lay the Strathclyde Britons, although their fortified royal centre at Dumbarton Rock stood on the north bank of the River Clyde. The western boundary of Pictland was marked by what contemporary sources refer to (in Irish and Latin respectively) as *Druim Alban* or *Dorsum Britanniae*, the 'Ridge of Britain',[16] the south-western extension of the Grampian mountains. Beyond *Druim Alban* lay the kingdom of the Scots of *Dál Riata*. From the Forth–Clyde isthmus, Pictland extended north and west to include the Outer Hebrides and the Northern Isles.

This extensive territory is unlikely to have comprised a single kingdom, at least for much of the history of Pictland. The Grampian mountains form a natural barrier across Pictland, imposing a distinction between north and south. This feature is traditionally referred to as the Mounth, after Gaelic *monadh*, 'mountain'. Bede[17] refers to the Northern and the

Southern Picts and, although he provides no geographical contexts, the Mounth probably formed the boundary between them. The Picts north and south of the Mounth were clearly recognised by contemporary commentators as belonging to the same people and therefore probably shared the same or very similar culture and language. However, some cultural differences are suggested by the distribution of types of sculpture and the symbols occurring on them. Moreover, the Southern Picts, according to Bede, had been converted to Christianity by St Ninian long ago, although the Northern Picts were still pagans.

Northern Pictland and Southern Pictland probably comprised separate kingdoms, although there is little hard evidence. The political heartland of the Southern Picts was the fertile valleys of Strathearn and Strathtay, where their political and religious centres of Forteviot and Scone were later adopted by the Scots. During his mission to convert the Northern Picts to Christianity, Columba arrived at the fort of King Bridei (Brude) son of Maelchor near Inverness, where Bridei held a sub-king of Orkney as a hostage.[18] This suggests a northern kingdom, probably that of the Northern Picts, centred around the Moray Firth but which stretched as far as Orkney.[19]

Pictland comprised several provinces, each probably ruled by its own sub-king under the overlordship of the king of the Northern or Southern Picts. Seven provinces were traditionally inferred from later sources, although the reliability of this approach is now queried because not all these provinces are recorded in contemporary sources.[20] References to provincial kings are even rarer, although Orkney was presumably a province under the overlordship of the King of the Northern Picts, while a king of Atholl was a brother of the King of the (Southern) Picts.[21] The province recorded most frequently in contemporary sources is *Fortriu. Although not subsequently used here, the asterisk indicates that the name is a hypothetical form, inferred from the title rex Fortrenn, 'King of Fortriu'.[22] The prominence of Fortriu in the sources reflects its status as the most powerful province of Southern Pictland, the location of its political heartland. The King of Fortriu was not only the most powerful in Southern Pictland but, by the reign of Bridei son of Bile (Brude son of Bili) (671–92) at the latest, the kingship of Fortriu also appears to have been synonymous with the kingship of Southern Pictland.

## THE SCOTS

Tracing the origins of the Scots of Dál Riata in the documentary sources is hindered by the fact that Roman commentators referred to the Irish as

*Scoti* or *Scotti*. But some also refer to the Irish more specifically as *Hiberni*, suggesting that *Scotti* may have been a general name applied by the Romans to raiders from the north and west who spoke the same language and were neither Britons nor Picts. The earliest references to the *Scotti* are in the 360s, when they were one of the peoples who attacked Roman Britain in the 'Barbarian Conspiracy' of 367, together with the *Attacotti*, who were probably also from either Ireland or the Western Isles, as well as the Picts and Saxons. The Scots of *Dál Riata* also had their own origin myth. According to the *Senchus fer nAlban* (*History of the Men of Scotland*), under King Fergus Mór mac Eirc, the first Scots crossed from Ireland to what is now western Scotland, where they settled and founded the kingdom of *Dál Riata*.[23] This event is traditionally dated to *c.* 500.

The historical veracity of this tradition appears to be corroborated by the fact that the Scots of *Dál Riata* shared a common language with the Irish, from which Scots Gaelic developed. Moreover, the kingdom of *Dál Riata* that they founded shares its name with a kingdom in north-eastern Ireland, with which it had close political connections. It is also supported by analogy in the form of Irish settlements in western Britain during the mid-first millennium.[24] But archaeologists point out that, if the Scots were really Irish migrants, they must have travelled without luggage because there is no archaeological evidence to support such a population movement. There were certainly strong contacts and influences, but this could be accounted for by trade, religious activity and perhaps even a ruling class asserting its authority over a neighbouring people.[25] The Scots, like their Pictish neighbours, are increasingly thought to be descended from the indigenous inhabitants of the region.[26] The origin myth of *Dál Riata* is not a statement of historical fact, but seeks to establish the legitimacy of the kings of *Dál Riata* with reference to a constructed past. This is seen most clearly in the genealogical passages in the *Senchus*, which trace the descendants of Fergus Mór. These were added to this seventh-century document in the tenth century in an attempt to strengthen the claims of one lineage for the Scottish kingship.[27]

The kingdom of *Dál Riata* corresponds approximately with Argyll and Bute. Its borders were defined by the Firth of Clyde to the south, *Druim Alban* to the east and probably the mountains of Lochaber to the north. *Dál Riata* was initially divided into thirds, each with its own royal kindred or *cenél*: *Cenél nOengusa* ruled Islay, *Cenél nGabráin* held Kintyre and *Cenél Loairn* possessed northern Argyll, giving their name to the district of Lorne.[28] It is unclear which royal kindred held mid-Argyll, with its important royal fortress and probable inauguration place of Dunadd.[29] Control of this area may have shifted to *Cenél Loairn* as the power of

*Cenél nGabráin* waned. A fourth kindred, *Cenél Comgaill*, emerged by
*c.* 700, probably as a result of the weakened power of *Cenél nGabráin*. *Cenél Comgaill* held the eastern part of *Dál Riata*, probably including the Isle of Bute, and gave its name to Cowal. Each *cenél* was subdivided, probably among cadet lines of the main royal kindred. Not all these lesser *cenéla* are recorded, but *Cenél Loairn* was divided into three, according to the *Senchus*, although it names four.[30]

The territory of *Dál Riata* was severely restricted, both in terms of its limited area and the poor quality of its land, comprising mostly rugged mountain and moorland terrain on islands and peninsulas. That the kingdom of *Dál Riata* thrived to become so powerful is testament to its vigour and its extensive connections with Ireland, Pictland and the Church.[31] The Scots exerted considerable influence on Pictland from an early date and this is detectable in the growing political links that originated from the intermarriage of the Pictish and Scottish royal kin groups, as well as linguistically. But there were also periods of warfare between the Picts and Scots, including occasions when either the Picts or the Scots held the upper hand. By the ninth century, Scottish kings were jointly ruling both *Dál Riata* and Pictland.[32] From this, it was only a step to the two kingdoms combining under a single kingship and this occurred during the reign of Cináed mac Ailpín (Kenneth mac Alpin). Traditionally interpreted as the Scottish 'conquest' of the Picts and dated to 843,[33] this is now viewed as the culmination of a long and largely peaceful process of cultural interaction and political assimilation. The Picts, their language and culture have disappeared as recognisable entities by *c.* 900 and the sources then refer to *Alba* or *Scotia*.[34] This, one of the earliest nation states in Europe, and comprising Scotland north of the Forth, was the forerunner of the medieval kingdom of the Scots.

The availability of more documentary evidence concerning the Scots than the Picts has strongly influenced studies of the Scots of *Dál Riata*.[35] Much analysis has focused on St Columba, his cult and monastic community on Iona,[36] reflecting the enduring influence of Adomnán's *Life of Columba*. But, in contrast to the Picts, much less has been published, either as general accounts or specialised studies, on the Scots.[37]

## SOURCES OF EVIDENCE

Sources of evidence concerning the Picts and Scots are many and varied, in both nature and provenance, but are invariably limited in their coverage. Knowledge of the Picts and Scots at war must be pieced together from these disparate and frequently difficult to interpret sources. The evidence falls into three main categories: documentary sources, the archaeological record and, to a lesser extent, placenames. Each of these presents specific challenges not only of interpretation but also concerning the identification and acquisition of data in the first place. The fragmentary nature of the evidence requires that any wide-ranging study of the Picts and/or Scots must be multi-disciplinary in nature. By integrating the analysis of different types of evidence, a multi-disciplinary approach potentially makes a greater contribution to the understanding of the Picts and Scots, one that is greater than the sum of its constituent parts.

## Documentary Sources

The importance of a multi-disciplinary approach is emphasised by the meagreness of the documentary record, particularly that of the Picts.[38] This lack of evidence presents a considerable obstacle to their study and has, more than any other single factor, resulted in the stereotyped perception of the Picts as both enigmatic and problematic. Indeed, the Picts are perhaps described more accurately as a proto-historic people; they are referred to in the textual records of neighbouring peoples but have left scarcely any of their own. But this reflects the poor preservation of documents, rather than implies that the Picts did not keep any. The Picts, their language and probably many of their records disappeared by *c.* 900 and other early documents were lost or destroyed during the Middle Ages.[39] The only surviving textual source of Pictish origin, the king list formerly known as the *Pictish Chronicle*, is preserved in several manuscript copies that are no earlier than the mid-fourteenth century.[40]

Nevertheless, detailed analysis occasionally yields new sources on the Picts. For example, an otherwise lost Pictish source, a contemporary or near-contemporary chronicle of the mid-eighth century, has been identified recently.[41] This is preserved in the *Historia Regum Anglorum* of Symeon of Durham, which was compiled from earlier sources in the twelfth century. The lengthy and complex processes of textual recording, transmission and copying involved here may explain why some battles are recorded only in late sources.

As documentary sources on the Picts are almost wholly dependent on those of neighbouring peoples, these reflect an external perspective. These sources may therefore be biased, as the quotations above reveal, or simply inaccurate and must be used with care. Independent corroboration is occasionally provided by other sources, but usually only for more notable events, such as large or decisive battles. Classical texts, particularly the panegyrics of Claudian,[42] provide the only documentary evidence on the early Picts and Scots. But although they refer to Pictish and Scottish attacks on later Roman Britain they are ambiguous and contain little detail.[43] Most later textual sources on the Picts are Irish, Scottish or Northumbrian. In contrast, a range of Scottish documents survive, mostly preserved in later Irish sources, while Irish and Northumbrian sources also contain references to the Scots.

The most important group of sources used in this study are the Irish annals (*see* Plate 1). These comprise a sequence of entries made either contemporaneously with the events recorded or annually. Some Irish annals display a close interest in Scottish and Pictish affairs because they incorporate entries from a contemporary, and therefore probably accurate, chronicle kept on Iona until *c.* 740. The date from which the 'Iona Chronicle' was compiled is disputed but falls sometime between the foundation of the monastery of Iona by St Columba in 563 and the 680s.[44] The earliest recorded warfare between the Picts and Scots, when the Pictish King Bridei son of Maelchon routed a Scottish army in 558 or 560,[45] may mark the start of annalistic recording on Iona. These entries in particular, and the Irish annals in general, are a primary source of information about battles, raids and sieges, providing laconic but unparalleled insights into the Picts and Scots at war.

The annalistic entries originating on Iona are restricted in their coverage, both geographically and chronologically. Understandably, they are primarily concerned with events in *Dál Riata*. The only events in neighbouring kingdoms they record are noteworthy ones, such as the more significant battles or sieges, mostly involving the Scots, and some internal battles among the Picts. More remote from Iona and the Irish centres of annalistic recording, events in Northern Pictland are rarely recorded. As a result, this is a particularly poorly documented region. Events in both *Dál Riata* and Pictland become obscure after *c.* 740, when the recording of annals on Iona appears to have stopped. Transferred to Ireland, the 'Iona Chronicle' became the common source of several Irish annalistic compilations. There, the tradition of annalistic recording continued, although with fewer entries concerning *Dál Riata* and Pictland. Despite their frequency, only a small proportion of battles and sieges involving the Picts and Scots, those that came to the attention of the annalists and that they considered to be significant in some respect, are probably recorded.

The annals also present problems of interpretation. In particular, the Iona entries can be difficult to identify. Although many are distinguishable from their references to people and/or places in *Dál Riata* or Pictland, others are not, with the result that it is sometimes unclear whether a battle or siege occurred in Ireland, *Dál Riata* or Pictland. This problem is exacerbated by the terseness of individual entries, which frequently omit even the most basic information required for understanding the event recorded, such as the opposing sides in a battle or siege. However, sometimes their contents may be augmented with information from parallel entries in other annals or, occasionally, from other sources. The annals inevitably record events from an Iona or Irish perspective, occasionally introducing doubts about their interpretation, terminology and reliability. In addition, there are sometimes uncertainties about the contemporaneity of annalistic entries. Most Irish annals survive only in much later manuscripts and the lengthy processes of copying and recopying occasionally resulted in entries being corrupted, duplicated or misplaced. A peculiarity of the dating employed in the *Annals of Ulster*, one of the most important annalistic compilations for the study of *Dál Riata* and Pictland, is that all entries between *c.* 480 and 1012 are ante-dated by one year. For this reason, dated annalistic entries are usually cited in the notes *sub anno* (s.a.), under the year in which they are given, with the corrected calendrical year being given in the text. Moreover, annalistic entries do not always appear in chronological order under a specific year,[46] sometimes creating problems in interpreting a sequence of events. Despite these difficulties, the 'Iona Chronicle' and the Irish annals are still among the most important textual sources on the Picts and Scots.

Another important Iona source is Adomnán's *Life of Columba*, written in the 690s. Although Adomnán, a successor of Columba as Abbot of Iona, was primarily concerned with recording the saintliness and miraculous powers of his predecessor, he provides unique insights into warfare in some incidental references. The *Senchus fer nAlban*[47] comprises a mixture of genealogical tracts, civil survey and military assessment and is of exceptional importance for our understanding of military obligation in *Dál Riata* (*see* Plate 2).[48] Later Scottish sources include what historians have traditionally known as the (*Old*) *Scottish Chronicle*, for which the title the *Chronicle of the Kings of Scotland* or *Alba* has also been proposed.[49] This records events under regnal rather than calendar years, or sometimes just lists them under a reign, introducing some imprecision about the dates concerned.

In contrast to the Irish annals, the *Anglo-Saxon Chronicle* (ASC), with its predominantly southern focus, contains disappointingly few references to the Picts and Scots. Other Anglo-Saxon sources are more useful. Northumbria was one of the most powerful Anglo-Saxon kingdoms during the seventh and eighth centuries and its great ecclesiastical centres were the focus of a 'golden age' of art and literature.[50] The most important of these writings are by Bede, Abbot of the monastery of Monkwearmouth-Jarrow (Co. Durham), who combined a northern perspective with a wide-ranging interest in historical and political issues and access to contemporary sources. As a result, his *Historia Ecclesiastica Gentis Anglorum (Ecclesiastical History of the English People)* (HE), completed in 731, and his *Life of Cuthbert* both contain important information on the wars between Northumbria and the Picts and Scots. Another valuable Northumbrian source is the *Life of Bishop Wilfrid* by Eddius Stephanus.

One of Bede's more questionable sources was *De excidio et conquestu Britanniae (Concerning the Ruin and Conquest of Britain)* by Gildas, a British monk writing *c.* 540.[51] Gildas portrays the Picts and Scots as bloodthirsty barbarians and blames them for precipitating the calamity that befell the Britons in the fifth century. When the Roman defence of Britain from Pictish and Scottish attacks ended, claims Gildas, the Britons had to recruit Anglo-Saxon mercenaries from the Continent who then turned on their hosts, invited their Germanic kinsfolk to invade and seized all of south-eastern Britain. But Gildas' evident hatred of the Picts and Scots suggests that he was influenced by more recent and immediate events, probably his own experience of Pictish 'piracy'.[52] Although the reliability of Gildas as a source is doubtful and his florid style of Latin is both obscure and off-putting, *De excidio* is important because of the scarcity of evidence concerning Pictish and Scottish attacks on later Roman Britain.

British sources are less informative about the Picts and Scots than Anglo-Saxon or Irish ones. This reflects the poor survival of texts originating among the North British kingdoms of what is now southern Scotland, the southern neighbours of the Picts and Scots. Some events of interest are recorded in the Welsh annals, which probably received their information from the North British kingdom of Strathclyde, although the Strathclyde Britons themselves remain obscure. The exceptional North British source is *The Gododdin*, composed *c.* 600. This epic poem celebrates the army of the kingdom of *Gododdin* and their heroic but disastrous attack on Northumbria. Although only containing passing references to Picts who fought alongside the North Britons, *The Gododdin* is a key source on the heroic ethos and military organisation of the period. A later British text, the ninth-century *Historia Brittonum*, traditionally attributed to 'Nennius' but compiled from various sources, also contains some references to the Picts and Scots.

Although many relevant texts containing references to the Picts and Scots have been studied since at least the nineteenth century, advances in their critical analysis are still adding to our understanding of them, their sources, compilation and transmission. In many cases, however, modern editions and translations, with full critical apparatus, are still required.

## Placenames

As a record of how the landscape was used and perceived, placenames provide unique insights into past societies. The study of Pictish placenames is particularly challenging.[53] The few placenames in Pictland that are recorded before the Pictish language disappeared already exhibit Gaelic influence. Pictish placenames were then supplanted by first Gaelic or Norse and latterly by Scots and/or English placenames. Partly as a result of this, and of the difficulty in attributing surviving Gaelic placenames to the early medieval period, placenames play only a limited role in this study. However, they enable some of the places mentioned in the sources to be identified as forts and sometimes allow the locations of recorded forts and battles to be identified.[54] Placenames have other uses. The Pictish chronicle preserved in Symeon of Durham's *Historia Regum Anglorum* was identified from two Pictish names, including a placename.[55] As knowledge of Pictish placenames expands, other Pictish sources fossilised in later texts may be identified.

## Archaeology

Archaeology, the study of past societies from the material remains they have left behind them, lends itself to the study of 'everyday life'. Archaeological survey and excavation of domestic, fortified and funerary sites have made a substantial contribution to our knowledge of Pictish and, to a lesser extent, Scottish agricultural, manufacturing, trade and ritual activities. The sites concerned are 'Pictish' or 'Scottish' in the sense that they date to the early medieval period and are located in the areas known to have comprised historic *Dál Riata* and Pictland. But, reflecting the status of the Picts and Scots as essentially historical phenomena, it is often difficult to identify archaeological sites or artefacts as distinctively 'Pictish' or 'Scottish' on material grounds alone.

However, the contribution made by archaeology to the study of the Picts and Scots is uneven, reflecting variations in archaeological survival and the patchy nature of archaeological discovery, excavation and research. Most excavation has been conducted on a piecemeal basis, largely on sites threatened by coastal erosion, quarrying, development or ploughing. This has included a small number of forts, notably the hillfort at Clatchard Craig (Fife) (*see* Plate 3),[56] the coastal promontory fort at Portknockie[57] and the twin ringforts at Aldclune (Perthshire).[58] Little excavation has been conducted within the framework of research strategies designed to address specific questions or problems and although Pictish and Scottish forts have featured prominently in this, excavation has only occurred on a small scale. Professor Leslie Alcock's exploratory excavations on early medieval royal centres in Scotland that are referred to in contemporary sources included the Pictish and Scottish forts of Dundurn (*see* Plate 4), Dunollie, Dunottar and possibly Urquhart Castle,[59] while Dunadd (*see* Plates 5 and 6) has also been subjected to limited but important excavations.[60]

The archaeological potential of individual sites varies according to their state of preservation. Sites revealed by cropmarks have already been damaged by the plough, often resulting in the disappearance of old land and floor surfaces and with only 'negative' features – those cut into the ground, such as ditches, pits and post-holes – surviving to show in the ripening crops above them. The preservation of organic material, including artefacts and environmental evidence, is largely dependent on soil conditions. Organic remains rarely survive in acidic soils, but can be exceptionally well preserved in anaerobic conditions, where there is no oxygen to assist processes of natural decay. This occurs in waterlogged contexts, typically in peat bogs, although similar conditions may occur on archaeological sites. Excavations on the summit of Dundurn unexpectedly revealed waterlogged occupation deposits containing well-preserved organic material, including artefacts and environmental evidence.[61] This hints at the rich potential of archaeology for illuminating our knowledge of the Picts.

Identifying archaeological evidence of warfare is less straightforward. This is most likely to come from forts, several of which are recorded as having been besieged, destroyed or burned.[62] These events may be archaeologically detectable and a phase of destruction at Dundurn is probably associated with the siege recorded in 683.[63] However, the imprecision of both conventional and scientific dating techniques in archaeology makes it difficult, if not impossible, to link conclusively an archaeologically defined 'event' with a historically recorded one. It is also very difficult to prove that the burning of a fort was a result of enemy action or an accident. The only exception might be if human remains showing signs of deliberately inflicted injuries, and possibly still associated with the weapons that killed them, were found *in situ* within a fort or in an associated grave. Weapons are a very tangible manifestation of warfare and a society organised for warfare and, although rare, have been found during excavation and as stray finds.

The Picts are best known for their sculpture, particularly the enigmatic symbol stones.[64] Of greater interest here are the secular scenes on the reverse of Pictish 'Class II' stones, cross-slabs carved in relief and associated with Pictish symbols. Hunting and occasionally battle scenes portraying Pictish aristocrats and warriors, including details of their dress, weapons and equipment, contain a wealth of information and provide a unique insight into Pictish warfare. Yet, apart from isolated studies, the wider potential of this source has not been exploited. This book seeks to integrate this sculptural evidence within the wider archaeological and historical study of the Picts and Scots at war.

Recent advances demonstrate that archaeology presents an enormous and still relatively untapped potential for expanding our knowledge of the Picts and Scots. Although other disciplines will always have a role to play within a multi-disciplinary approach, the nature of the surviving evidence indicates that archaeology will have the primary role in contributing to our understanding of the Picts and Scots at war in the future.

## CHAPTER TWO

# Military Obligation

A fundamental prerequisite for successful warfare is the ability to mobilise sufficient numbers of suitably equipped and trained men – warfare is historically a predominantly male pursuit – and deploy them in the right place and at the right time. In the shifting political and territorial situation that prevailed in early medieval Scotland, an effective means of raising an army was essential to the well-being, even the survival, of the kingdoms of the Picts and the Scots. Yet early medieval kings had no standing armies, of professional and permanently available soldiers, other than the warband that acted as their personal bodyguard.[1] Throughout the early Middle Ages, armies were composed mostly of common foot soldiers whose normal occupation was working the land. These armies were not recruited in the modern sense but were levied from among those elements of society that owed military service. This necessitated means of assessing and raising military service, of mustering the men levied and deploying them in the field.

Military obligation concerns those duties of armed service owed by someone of inferior social standing to his superior, for example, by a free client to his lord and by a lord to his king. This was part of a wider personal relationship of dominance and dependency between client and lord found throughout the Celtic peoples of early medieval Britain and Ireland. Although freely entered into by both parties when the client submitted to his lord, the two sides were of unequal status and power. A client received physical and legal protection, land and perhaps seed and breeding stock from his lord. In return, the client was required to pay dues and tribute in the form of livestock and agricultural produce, hospitality, and labour and military service. The institution of clientage is very poorly documented in northern Britain, but is recorded in detail in the early Irish laws.[2]

Military obligations and institutions form the essential background to the study of early medieval warfare but, despite its importance, are little studied. Perhaps understandably, most attention has focused on the more dramatic or tangible aspects of warfare, such as battles, fortresses and weaponry. This tendency is assisted by the fact that military obligations and institutions are difficult to study. Most documentary references to early medieval warfare concern 'events' – usually battles, sieges and killings – rather than administrative, organisational and social aspects, which were perceived to be more mundane and therefore less noteworthy. Nevertheless, one text provides detailed information about the military obligations of *Dál Riata*. This may be augmented by incidental references in other sources and with parallels drawn from apparently similar but better documented practices among neighbouring and later peoples. From these varied sources a general understanding of Pictish and, in particular, Scottish military obligation may be constructed.

## ASSESSING MILITARY OBLIGATION

A means of assessing the military service owed by clients to their lords is central to the effectiveness of any system of military obligation. What form and length of military service was owed, by and to whom, how often and where? Without an agreed and established system for establishing these points, it would have been more difficult to raise an army when it was required.

Although the social organisation and institutions of the peoples of early medieval Scotland are poorly documented, one exceptional source provides a unique insight into the military obligations of the Scots of *Dál Riata* and their assessment.[3] This is the *Senchus fer nAlban* (*see* Plate 2). The *Senchus* survives only in late manuscripts, but the form of Gaelic used indicates that it is derived from texts that were compiled and added to in the tenth century, while its contents reveal that these originated *c.* 650–700.[4] The *Senchus* includes a civil survey, providing rich insights into the socio-political organisation of *Dál Riata*. However, it is as a detailed record of the assessment of those military and naval obligations owed by the three main *cenéla* or royal kindreds of *Dál Riata* that the *Senchus* is of primary interest here. The assessment of naval service is considered separately.[5] This assessment may represent a legacy of the vigorous military campaigns that the Scots engaged in during the reign of Aedán mac Gabráin (574–?608).[6] Alternatively, the military obligations recorded in the *Senchus* may have been prompted by the increasing pressure that *Dál Riata* and the other peoples of northern Britain were coming under from the expansion of Northumbrian power during the mid-seventh century.[7]

The *Senchus* reveals the principles by which military obligation was assessed and military service was levied by the Scots. The basic unit of assessment used in the *Senchus* is the *tech*, 'house'.[8] This was not simply a dwelling but the social unit used for assessing and collecting dues or tribute, from a household. This comprised the occupants of a house, probably an extended family and its dependants, who paid rent or tribute to their lord for their accommodation and its associated landholding. The link between military obligation and landholding is expressed explicitly in a late sixth-century preface to *Amra Coluimchille*, an elegy to St Columba, which states that 'military service always goes with the soil'.[9] The extent of these landholdings varied in size, as the *Senchus* records that 'small are the lands of the houses of *Cenél nOengusa*'.[10]

The *Senchus* presents problems of interpretation. Fundamentally, there are internal discrepancies between the number of men raised from, and the number of houses in, each of the three *cenéla*. The *Senchus* records the total number of houses of each kindred: *Cenél nOengusa* had 430, *Cenél nGabráin* had 560 and *Cenél Loairn* had 420. However, a separate passage records the 'expeditionary strength of the hostings' (*fecht airmi slógad*) of *Cenél nOengusa* as 500 men, that is, foot soldiers, that of *Cenél nGabráin* as 300 men, and that of *Cenél Loairn* as 700 men, including 100 from *Airgialla*, an Irish kingdom.[11] Not only is it unclear how many men could be levied from each house, but the size of the armies levied are also incompatible with *Cenél nGabráin*'s historically attested position as the dominant kindred within *Dál Riata*. Moreover, the *Senchus*, as it now survives, does not include a civil survey of *Cenél nGabráin*. There are also anomalies with the total number of houses recorded for each *cenél*. A civil survey of *Cenél nOengusa* records the number of houses in each district of Islay,[12] but its total of only 350 houses is demonstrably incomplete and contrasts with the 430 given elsewhere in the *Senchus*. Similarly, the survey of *Cenél Loairn* records that two kindreds of *Cenél Loairn* each had 30 houses. As *Cenél Loairn* comprised three kindreds, and four are actually named, this implies a total number of houses of either 90 or 120, in marked contrast to the 420 houses recorded elsewhere in the *Senchus*. It is unclear how these inconsistencies arose, but they were presumably introduced during the transmission of the manuscript, the long process of copying and recopying texts that ensured the survival of the *Senchus*.

The solution to this problem lies within the text of the *Senchus* itself. By comparing the military and naval service levied by each *cenél*, in total numbers of (infantry) men and oarsmen, the number of men raised by *Cenél nGabráin* and *Cenél nOengusa* are confirmed as underestimates. As a result, it is necessary to adjust the figures given in the *Senchus* to compensate for this.[13] This may be done by referring to the naval obligations recorded in the *Senchus*. For each *cenél*, the *Senchus* records this as 'two seven-benchers', crewed by 30 men from every 20 houses.[14] If the same levy, of 1.5 men per house, is used to calculate the military obligation of *Cenél Loairn* this gives a total of 630 men, which correlates closely with the recorded 'expeditionary strength' of 600 men. The difference is explained by the practice of rounding military strengths recorded in the *Senchus* to the nearest hundred. If the ratio of 1.5 men per house is applied to the total number of houses recorded for the other *cenéla*, *Cenél nGabráin* would have raised 840 men and *Cenél nOengusa* 645 men. Significantly, these figures correlate closely with the recorded size of armies in early medieval Ireland. The late seventh- or early eighth-century Irish law tract *Uraicecht Becc* (*Little Grammar* or *Small Primer*)[15] records that the lowest grade of Irish king could raise 700 men from his *túath* or petty kingdom. As inferred from the *Senchus*, the numbers of men in each *cenéla* that owed an obligation of military service are comparable with, and indeed straddle, this figure.

When its figures are corrected, the *Senchus* implies that the total military strength of *Dál Riata* in the seventh century was 2,115 men. Remarkably, this tallies almost exactly with the size of the warband of Aedán mac Gabráin ('Gauran mab Aedan' in the text) given in the Welsh triads, which is recorded as 2,100 strong.[16] However, the fact that the triads give an identical strength for all 'three faithful warbands of the Island of Britain', suggests that this represents a literary convention and that little significance should be attached to the figure.

These figures provide only a minimum estimate of the numbers of men liable for military service in *Dál Riata*. Obligations to do naval service may have been even higher than the figures used above to correct military obligations recorded in the *Senchus*. Ships may have carried one or two relief crews in wartime[17] and this has considerable implications for the scale of military obligation among the Scots. On the basis of a ship's complement of 45 men, rather than 15, each group of 20 houses would have been obliged to raise 90 men for a sea expedition, an average of 4.5 men from each house. If this is also applied to military obligation across *Dál Riata*, this gives totals of 1,890 men for *Cenél Loairn*, 2,520 for *Cenél nGabráin* and 1,935 for *Cenél nOengusa*, a total strength of 6,345 men. The burden of military service levied on the Scots was higher than those of other early medieval peoples. Each *tech* of *Dál Riata* was obliged to raise a minimum of 1.5 men, and possibly as many as 4.5. In contrast, only 1 man was levied from every 5 hides, the equivalent unit in late Anglo-Saxon England.[18] With a military obligation of between 7.5 and 20 times greater than that of the Anglo-Saxons, the Scots were organised for war on a major scale. Indeed, it has been suggested that *Dál Riata* was unique in its ability to raise large armies.[19] The capacity to levy large numbers of men for military service may have been achieved by making all free grades within society liable for military service. Although Bede[20] implies that Northumbrian peasants were not obliged to do military service, this is unlikely to have been the case in *Dál Riata*.[21]

The *Senchus fer nAlban* is one of the outstanding documentary sources of early medieval Britain. The earliest known civil survey in Britain, it pre-dates the *Domesday Book* by almost five centuries. Despite the problematic nature of its contents, the *Senchus* provides a unique insight into the social organisation and military obligation of *Dál Riata* during the seventh century. In addition, as military obligation was calculated within each kin group of *Dál Riata*, this was clearly the basis on which armies were levied and organised. But the *Senchus* attests a higher level of military organisation, that the forces of all three *cenéla* could be combined under the leadership of the king of *Dál Riata*. As a formal record of the number of fighting men that the king could expect to levy from each *cenél*, the *Senchus* reveals a sophisticated level of military planning that reinforced the ability to raise an expeditionary force, whether by putting an army in the field or a fleet to sea. The *Senchus* attests a powerful centralised authority, capable of assessing and levying military service throughout the kingdom of *Dál Riata*.

Unfortunately, there is no Pictish equivalent of the *Senchus fer nAlban*. Indeed, there are no documentary references to, and therefore no direct evidence of, Pictish military obligation. Nevertheless, the Picts may be assumed to have had a means of levying military service. This is clear from their military capability, which included raising armies and navies and fighting battles, sometimes on a large scale.[22] It may also be concluded from the fact that the other peoples of early medieval Britain had systems for levying armies. In the absence of first-hand evidence, the fundamental principles of Pictish military obligation may be inferred from the practices of neighbouring peoples and from later sources.

Among the Picts, as with their neighbours, free commoners were probably obliged to undertake military service. This would have been an integral element of those dues or renders of agricultural products and labour obligations owed by clients to their lord under the terms of the relationship they had entered. The Pictish unit of assessment is unrecorded but may have been the house, as in *Dál Riata*, or a unit of land-holding, perhaps analogous to the hide of Anglo-Saxon England.[23] If Pictish military obligation was assessed according to landholding, the obvious candidate for the unit of assessment is the *\*pet(t)*. This was literally a 'piece' or share of land, probably belonging to a dependant estate, where the free commoners who worked them had entered a relationship of clientage by submitting to their lord. These lands are attested by *Pit-* placenames in north-east Scotland, of which over 300 still survive, such as Pitlochry (Perthshire) and Pittenweem (Fife).[24]

Landholding formed the basis for assessing military obligation in north-eastern Scotland after the eclipse of the Picts and the creation of the kingdom of *Alba*, *c.* 900. As many of the institutions of *Alba* are believed to have been inherited from the Picts,[25] this provides the best line of enquiry into the nature of Pictish military obligation. Despite their later date, some medieval sources record apparently archaic practices and refer to obligations that were already of great age. These may be derived from, and closely related to, Pictish practices of military obligation, enabling some details of Pictish practices to be inferred. The principal source here is the *Book of Deer*, a ninth-century illuminated gospel book.[26] This is chiefly of interest for six late eleventh- and early twelfth-century *notitiae* or notes recorded, in Gaelic, in its margins.[27] These record grants of land made at an earlier, but uncertain, date to the monastic community of Old Deer (Aberdeenshire) by local lords and refer to the secular obligations attached to those lands, particularly those duties of military service owed. One note in the *Book of Deer* claims that the *mormaer* who granted the lands on which the monastic church of Deer was founded had granted 'freedom until Domesday from *mormaer* and *toísech*'.[28] *Mormaer* and *toísech* were ranks of noble and war leader[29] who played an important role in levying military obligations. In support of its claim, the *Book of Deer* cites precedents for the 'quenching' from secular obligations of lands granted by laymen to the Church.[30]

The *Book of Deer* implies that military obligations were attached to and levied from all lands, with the result that every landowner or tenant was liable for military service. This included monastic communities that had not been granted the immunity claimed in the *Book of Deer*. These monasteries would have been responsible for raising armed men for military service from among their tenants, and perhaps those tenants from their peasants, according to the lands they held. At some stage, this obligation was probably commuted to payments in goods and discharged by paying in kind for the army, probably in victuals or other supplies. Only later, after the introduction of currency in the mid-twelfth century, were those dues converted into a monetary payment and the revenues diverted to non-military uses.[31] Although the *Book of Deer* post-dates the disappearance of Pictland, its evidence probably offers a close parallel to the nature of one of the highest, provincial levels of military obligation among the Picts.

Another unit of landholding that may have been used in the assessment of military obligation is the *dabhach* (Scotticised as 'davach' or 'davoch'). A term for a unit, and therefore holding, of arable land, the *dabhach* was the normal basis of assessment for levying dues or renders in the form of agricultural produce and military obligation during the

19

medieval period.[32] The *dabhach*, from a Gaelic word meaning 'tub' or 'vat', was a unit of measure, the area of land that could be sown with a tub of seed granted by a lord to his client or, more probably, that produced a tubful of grain. The *dabhach* was therefore a measure of the dues or renders of agricultural produce that a lord could expect from a client's landholding. Although these food renders would normally have been consumed by the lord, his family and entourage as they progressed around their territory, some may have been used to supply armies. Bede[33] implies that, at least in Northumbria, food was delivered by peasants to soldiers on the battlefield. In some Highland areas, such as Loch Broom (Ross and Cromarty), the *dabhach* retained its significance as a unit of landholding until after the 1745 Jacobite Rebellion.[34] Remarkably, the role of the *dabhach* as a unit of military obligation also survived into the modern period. Men were listed in the muster roll of the Eastern Company of the Strathspey Volunteers according to the davochs of the parish as late as 1772.[35]

The distribution of the *dabhach*, as reflected in both documentary sources and placenames, is restricted to north-eastern Scotland, the former territory of Pictland. Although its name is of Gaelic origin, both the distribution and use of the *dabhach* reflect archaic landholding practices; there is 'something inescapably Pictish' about the *dabhach*.[36] Supporting this, an element of continuity between the *pet(t)* and the *dabhach* is indicated by placename evidence in the form of several davochs with *pet(t)* names, such as *Petcarane*, now Tullochcurran, in Strathardle (Perthshire).[37] Despite this, the *dabhach* is now believed to be of Scottish origin and to date to the period after the founding of *Alba*.[38] Nevertheless, the *dabhach* offers a useful model or parallel for practices of Pictish landholding and military obligation.

Military obligation was widespread among the Scots and, by inference, the Picts. But although levied upon free commoners and probably peasants who worked the land, the basis of assessing Pictish and Scottish military obligation appears to have differed. In *Dál Riata*, the unit of assessment was social – the household. The landholding of houses varied and this probably suited the relatively rough terrain, where only small pockets of land were cultivatable. In contrast, military assessment in Pictland was probably based on administrative territorial units, as the prominence of firstly the *pet(t)* and later the *dabhach* indicates. Among the Picts, military service was owed according to the land held and was proportionate to its extent. This parallels the mechanism of levying armies throughout Europe before the introduction of feudalism and was probably better suited to the generally more fertile lands of much of Pictland. This distinction has, potentially, considerable implications.

## MILITARY SERVICE AND STRENGTHS

The military strengths of *Dál Riata* and Pictland would have been determined by the effectiveness of their systems of military obligation, combined with wider demographic and geographical factors, influencing their ability to raise and mobilise troops. There may have been a gap between the capabilities of the Picts and Scots here. Under a territorially based system of assessment, as the Picts appear to have had, the number of men that could be levied for military service would have been limited by the area of land held and worked. However, the system employed in *Dál Riata* would have been capable of accommodating greater demands. With the assessment of military obligation on a social basis, the manpower raised would have increased in direct relation to the population as it expanded. This may explain how *Dál Riata* shouldered a considerably heavier burden of military service than Anglo-Saxon England. The *Senchus* not only implies that the Scots had a much greater and more effective capability for raising military service than their neighbours,[39] but reveals a society organised for war, presumably in response to considerable threats or stresses. The *Senchus* indicates that the Scots were on a permanent war footing.

Among the Scots, the obligation of military service was known as *fecht*, 'army service', or *slógad*, 'hosting'. Although there is no direct evidence concerning the Picts and Scots, sources record the existence of different types of hosting in early medieval Ireland. *Críth Gablach* ('Branched Purchase'),[40] an Irish law tract of *c.* 700, defines the three types of *slógad* for which military service could be levied: a hosting within the border to repel an invading army, a hosting to the border to guard against invasion and a hosting across the border against a rebellious subject kingdom. Military service was probably levied among the Picts and Scots in similar circumstances. The 'expeditions' referred to in the *Senchus* denote foreign service, in campaigns beyond the borders of *Dál Riata*, and, consistent with this, the Scots are recorded conducting long-range military operations, from Orkney to Ireland to the Scottish Borders.[41]

The size of the army raised may have varied according to circumstances. A hosting would not necessarily require men from throughout *Dál Riata*, but would have depended on the location, nature, scale and immediacy of the military objective. When *Dál Riata* itself was threatened, a higher levy may have been imposed in order to muster more men in defence of the homeland. However, where an aggressor had the advantage of surprise, there may not have been enough time to muster and deploy all the men eligible for military service. This was probably also the case in Pictland and may be paralleled by military obligation in medieval Scotland, where men could be mobilised throughout the kingdom for its defence.[42] This contrasted with *servitium forinsecum* or 'forinsec', literally an additional obligation to that due to the immediate lord and usually denoting foreign military service. This was levied on a smaller scale and was not necessarily imposed on all provinces of the kingdom but might require only a limited number of men from each unit of assessment.

Despite its inconsistencies and problematical interpretation, the *Senchus* displays the nature and extent of the military obligations levied on the Scots during the seventh century. It also enables the potential size of the army that could be mustered from throughout *Dál Riata* to be calculated. Taking the internal discrepancies of the *Senchus* into account, the minimum total force available within *Dál Riata* was about 2,115 men, but could have been three times that. Without a Pictish equivalent of the *Senchus*, estimating the size of the fighting force that the Picts could levy is very difficult. Pictish military strength cannot be extrapolated from the figures given for the Scots in the *Senchus*. The *cenéla* of *Dál Riata* could each muster around 700 men. On the traditional, but questionable, basis that there were seven provinces in Pictland[43] and approximating each province to a *cenél* of *Dál Riata* would give a minimum total Pictish strength of around 4,900 men. To this must be added the additional forces that could be raised from the Pictish periphery, Orkney, Shetland and the northern Hebrides, each perhaps the equivalent of a province. However, a total force of around 7,000 men cannot be sustained. While *Dál Riata* occupied only the area of modern Argyll, Pictland comprised the rest of what is now Scotland north of the Forth–Clyde isthmus. The territory occupied by each *cenéla* was therefore less than that of most, if not all, Pictish provinces. Moreover, much of Pictland comprised better quality land than the rugged terrain of *Dál Riata* and could therefore support a greater population. While this might result in a considerable underestimate for the number of men that the Picts could potentially levy, the onerous nature of the military obligation recorded in the *Senchus* should be recalled. This is not comparing like with like and the unquantifiables involved mean that any results from this approach should be handled with great care.

Another method of estimating the potential military strength that the Picts could levy is to calculate it from the size of the Pictish population. Eighteenth-century accounts from the Highlands and Isles record that males capable of bearing arms ranged from around 12 or 14 to 40 or 45 years of age and give ratios of 1:5 and 1:6 for the proportion of males within the overall population capable of bearing arms.[44] As this information pre-dates the breakdown of the clan system, the Highland clearances and the Industrial Revolution, these ratios are probably broadly applicable to earlier periods. But this approach is limited by uncertainty about Pictish population figures. The traditional estimate of around 40,000[45] has been revised upwards, to a 'conservative estimate' of 80,000.[46] But even this is too low, as it omits 'peripheral' Pictland. Assuming a population of 100,000 and an equal proportion of males and females, the ratios give an estimated potential military strength of around 7,000 to 10,000 men. The Picts were theoretically capable of raising a very sizeable fighting force, totalling several thousand men. However, a distinction must be drawn between the total number of men theoretically liable for military service and those actually mobilised. The latter figure may have been diminished by several factors, including, for example, physical or mental incapacity.

## MUSTERING WARRIORS

The only reference to a muster is the colourful description by Eddius Stephanus[47] of Pictish warriors as 'swarms . . . gathered from every cranny of the north . . . a vast army hidden in the hills'. Terse though this is, it suggests an extensive muster. However, Eddius was more concerned with literary effect than accurate recording and his intention was to praise the action of Ecgfrith, King of Northumbria, whose 'little band' defeated this superior Pictish force in 672 in the battle of the Plain of Manau, a district of Gododdin whose name is preserved in Clackmannan and Slamannan.[48]

The physical and political geographies of *Dál Riata* and Pictland must have been important factors in determining the ability to muster forces on a large scale. In particular, the territorial extent of Pictland would have presented considerable logistical difficulties for any general muster. As a result, a muster in one part of Pictland need not imply a call-up in another simply because of the considerable distances involved and the time taken to travel them. Moreover, the combined effects of physical and political geography, with the rugged terrain of the Mounth separating the kingdoms of Northern and Southern Pictland, may have made any general muster of troops from throughout Pictland unlikely. However, in areas where military obligations were owed but actual service was not practical, the obligation may have been levied in other forms. These may have included more mobile naval forces or supplies of arms, foodstuffs or horses, with the result that one area of Pictland would have been supporting or subsidising an army from another. The much smaller area of *Dál Riata* and its coastal character would have assisted the extensive but still relatively swift mustering of its forces. Not surprisingly, naval obligations feature prominently in the *Senchus*.[49]

As a result of these factors, obligations of military service are more likely to have been levied at a local or regional level. This is implicit in the territorial and social bases of obligation and assessment. In particular, the *Senchus* demonstrates that military obligation in *Dál Riata* was assessed at the level of the *cenél*, of which there were then three. The regional character of armies in *Dál Riata* is supported by a reference in *The Gododdin*[50] to an 'array [of troops] that came from Kintyre'. Kintyre was the territory of the ruling *Cenél nGabráin*, to which King Domnall Brecc, who led the army, belonged. That military obligation was assessed in a similar manner by the Picts is indicated by the apparently provincial character of at least some Pictish armies.[51] These factors presumably enhanced the effectiveness of a muster and, therefore, the capability and readiness of the Picts and Scots to respond to a military threat or opportunity. Moreover, local loyalties and knowledge would have improved the morale and military effectiveness of an army.

It is unclear how men owing military service were mustered. The right to call a muster probably lay with kings in normal circumstances. This was the case in early medieval Ireland, where the abuse of this right may be inferred from the legal definition of the three types of hosting for which a king could legitimately levy military service.[52] But military service was owed by a tenant farmer to his landlord, a superior grade of freeman or a noble, rather than to the king directly. This suggests that the call to arms would have been cascaded down the social hierarchy, giving musters a strong local character. This is supported by the *Senchus*. Some 20 houses was the basic unit of fiscal assessment employed in the *Senchus*, which assesses the districts of Islay (*Cenél nOengusa*) and the property of *Cenél Loairn* in subdivisions of 5 and multiples of between 1.5 (30 houses) and 6 (120 houses). It is no coincidence that the assessment of naval obligations is based on a unit of 20 houses, which must, at some time, have represented the average number of houses in a typical administrative district of *Dál Riata*.

Paralleling the assessment of military obligations in *Dál Riata*, Pictish and Scottish armies were likely mustered on a regional basis, presumably *cenéla* in *Dál Riata* and provincial kingdoms in Pictland. The locations at which armies were mustered are also uncertain, but probably included royal fortresses.[53] These were centres of royal authority from which the king's call to arms may have been sounded. That the Picts were familiar with this form of muster is indicated by *The Gododdin*, which describes the presence of some Pictish warriors in the warband that assembled in the fortress at *Eidyn* (Edinburgh) and drank and feasted before it departed to do battle with the Angles of Northumbria. This suggests that Pictish warbands were mustered in a similar manner. Moreover, as royal forts and their occupants were also key targets for enemy forces, their status as muster points may have been partially defensive in function. This may also explain why several battles occurred near royal centres and fortresses.[54] As each *cenél* of *Dál Riata* appears to have had its own principal royal fortress, these were probably the muster points for their respective armies.

Alternatively, established assembly places such as local administrative centres may also have functioned as muster points. Likely candidates include court or moot hills, at which justice was dispensed. Many of these sites are now identifiable only from placenames, often a variant of 'cuthill', from Gaelic *cómhdháil*, 'assembly, meeting'.[55] In all probability there were different levels of assembly and muster, local and regional, with their corresponding locations. Assemblies would have been held in the open air and, if used as muster points, have probably left little, if any, detectable archaeological traces. However, some assembly places were associated with mounds, either earlier burial monuments, or other artificial structures such as the Moot Hill at Scone (Perthshire).[56] Established locations of power that were the scene of other royal business, such as law courts or inauguration places, may also have been obvious muster places.

Armies were predominantly composed of men who were probably normally engaged in agricultural or related craft activities. As a result, musters and hostings may have been a seasonal activity, planned – where possible – to avoid the all-important agricultural seasons of sowing, in spring, and harvest time, in late summer and autumn. A date or month is recorded for only five battles fought by the Picts or Scots, but these demonstrate a wide seasonal range: Dunnichen on 20 May 685, *Druimm Derg Blathung* on 12 August 729,[57] *Finnglen* on 13 September 719,[58] *Ard Nesbi* on 6 October 719[59] and Strathcarron, 'at the end of the year, in December' 642.[60] But the battle of Dunnichen reveals that the timing of a muster was dictated by military necessity. This may have applied equally to offensive warfare, where the objective was to exploit an enemy's weaknesses, including by surprise attack where possible.

## CHAPTER THREE

# Military Organisation

Levying and mustering troops were the fundamental precursors to putting an army in the field. But other factors were equally important in contributing to a successful outcome on the battlefield. How were those troops organised and led? To maximise their chances of success, war fighters need to act not as individuals but as a unified force, requiring their organisation into units of predetermined size and function. This demands organisation, motivation, training, leadership and discipline. It is these qualities, above all, that make a successful army and the difference between victory or defeat on the battlefield, often outweighing any advantages conferred by numerical or technological superiority.

Military organisation forms an essential background to the study of early medieval warfare. But, like military obligation, military organisation is poorly documented and remains a challenging and relatively neglected subject. Here again, the evidence is very sparse because contemporary sources tend, not surprisingly, to concentrate on the outcome of battles rather than the preparations for them. Unfortunately, there is no equivalent to the *Senchus fer nAlban* recording Pictish or Scottish military leadership or organisation. Nevertheless, the obscurity of this subject is in inverse proportion to its importance, not only for the manner in which warfare was conducted by the Picts and Scots, but also for providing a socio-political context. As discussed in the previous chapter, military obligations were owed to lords and kings, and military organisation was closely linked to this.

Despite the difficulties encountered in its study, some information concerning Pictish and Scottish military organisation may be gleaned from occasional references.

## WARBANDS

The basis of military organisation among the peoples of early medieval Britain was the *comitatus*.[1] This Latin word means 'escort, retinue, company', but in an early medieval context it usually applies to a warband. The *comitatus* was primarily the personal bodyguard of a king or lord, a retinue of usually noble and mounted 'professional' warriors.

Attending their king on a permanent basis, members of a *comitatus* lived and slept in the royal hall inside the king's fortress, and were fed, equipped and horsed by the king. The *comitatus* therefore comprised not just a group of warriors but a military and social élite, emphasising the aristocratic nature of military obligation and organisation. The warband was the fundamental military unit in early medieval warfare.

The size of a *comitatus* depended on the power, status and wealth of the person it was responsible for protecting. But, reflecting the status of its warriors, the *comitatus* was normally a small and select unit. This royal bodyguard would have formed the core of a larger army, mustered to mount an attack or counter a threat as required. This may have blurred the distinction between a *comitatus* and the army as a whole. Indeed, the *comitatus* can also be interpreted more broadly, as the body of armed men that a king or lord could muster from his territory. For example, inferring from the naval obligations recorded in the *Senchus fer nAlban*, thirty foot soldiers were levied from each unit of twenty houses in *Dál Riata*. This would have comprised a warband, raised and led by its lord, to whom it owed an oath of loyalty as well as an obligation of military service. The identity, morale and team spirit of a warband would have been reinforced by its local connections and probably the kinship ties of some of its members.

The origins of the *comitatus* probably lie in Iron Age social and military organisation. In what may be the earliest appearance of the warband in Britain, small raiding parties overran Roman Britain during the 'Barbarian Conspiracy' of 367.[2] These are not specifically described as Pictish or Scottish and are perhaps more likely to have comprised roving bands of deserted slaves or Roman auxiliary troops. Nevertheless, these groups may represent the predecessors of the early medieval warband and were ideally suited to raiding and low-intensity warfare over long distances.

Although there are few references to the *comitatus* among the Picts and Scots, the North British epic poem *The Gododdin*[3] provides unique confirmation of the Pictish *comitatus* with its reference to 'the warband from over the Firth [of Forth]'. *The Gododdin*[4] also gives an indication of the size of such a warband with its reference to a Pictish warrior who 'used to lead a hundred men'. Although no further information is revealed, this must have been a Pictish warband, as the Pict concerned was now fighting for the *Gododdin*. References to units of 100 men recur throughout *The Gododdin*,[5] where the word *cintrann*, literally 'centurions', is used for war leaders.[6] However, *The Gododdin*'s predilection for other units of 100, including 'a hundred chieftains' and, most implausibly, an army of 'a hundred thousand',[7] suggests that this represents a poetic ideal or convention. These warbands, Pictish and North British, should not be accepted literally as being 100-men strong, although this is of the right order of magnitude and may be approximately correct.

The *comitatus* was not just a military unit but a social institution, the life of which centred around heroic deeds on the battlefield and their retelling in the royal hall. Its members were under a powerful social obligation to their king, whose life they pledged to defend with their own, an ideal also found in Anglo-Saxon society.[8] The *comitatus* and its ethos of mutual loyalty, personal honour, martial prowess and fear of dishonour are central to concepts of an early medieval 'heroic society' and feature prominently in epic literature.[9] This heroic mentality is evident in *The Gododdin*, which vividly describes the assembly of a North British warband or army in the hall of the king of *Gododdin*, in his royal fortress at *Eidyn*. There they feasted for a year, drinking mead and wine, before embarking on their ill-fated expedition against the Angles of Northumbria and their annihilation in battle at *Catraeth*, probably Catterick (North Yorkshire), *c.* 600.

*The Gododdin* provides a unique insight into the character and social context of the warband among the North Britons, the southern neighbours of the Picts and Scots. Rather than carefully planning their expedition for a year,[10] there are more plausible interpretations for the lengthy feast that the warriors of *Gododdin* indulged in. It would have given the army or warband time to assemble, particularly as it included warriors not only from *Gododdin* itself, but also Pictland and as far away as Wales. At the same time, this would have enabled a bond of loyalty and a competitive rivalry to develop between the warriors. It would also have assisted the army's mental, if not physical, preparation for battle, including by listening to epics about the heroic exploits of celebrated warriors. The heroic ethos of the mead hall, with its emphasis on honour, bravery and the glory won by death in battle, pervades the poem. Indeed, each stanza of *The Gododdin* honours an individual warrior who was killed in action, or the army as a whole. Alternatively, the year-long feast may represent a poetic convention, intended to emphasise the heroic ideals of hospitality, hard drinking and comradeship among warriors.

The absence of comparable sources to *The Gododdin* makes the characteristics of the *comitatus* more difficult to trace among the Picts and Scots. Nevertheless, conveying the bond of loyalty that existed between a *comitatus* and its lord, the Welsh triads refer to the warband of Aedán mac Gabráin, King of *Dál Riata*, as one of the 'three faithful war-bands of the Isles of Britain'.[11] The only other explicit reference to a Scottish *comitatus* provides an insight into the aristocratic milieu and social obligations of the warband. According to Adomnán,[12] Columba arranged for Tarain, an exiled member of 'a noble family of the Picts' (*de nobili Pictorum genere*), to 'live in Feradach's *comitatus*, as one of his friends' and under his protection. But Feradach, a 'rich man', and therefore presumably a noble, of Islay, soon had Tarain killed. Columba's reported outrage at this 'monstrous crime' may be attributed to his betrayal by Feradach. But it was probably also because Feradach had broken the bond of loyalty and protection that existed between a lord and members of his *comitatus*; Feradach had violently and blatantly breached a fundamental social convention.

The passage reveals other interesting details, although it is unclear if they are typical of Pictish and/or Scottish practices. Tarain joined Feradach's *comitatus* on Columba's personal recommendation, perhaps in a process analogous to that of entering a foster relationship. Although the reason for Tarain's exile is not stated, this incident implies that the *comitatus* could provide a refuge for social and/or political outcasts of noble birth. This may have been because they had nowhere else to turn or because it provided them with a chance to redeem themselves through loyal military service to their new lord. In addition, service in a foreign *comitatus* may have provided additional opportunities for warriors seeking adventure, glory and plunder. This may also explain the presence of Pictish warriors in a North British warband, particularly as they joined specifically to participate in an expedition.

*The Gododdin*[13] celebrates two fallen heroes, Llifiau son of Cian and Bubon or Bufon, who may be identified as Picts from their places of origin. These warriors are described as coming 'from the Stone of the *Venicones*', which is 'beyond *Bannawg*', north of the Bannockburn Hills, and 'beyond the Sea of *Iuddew*', north of the Firth of Forth, respectively. Both locations are in Pictland.[14] Moreover, the composer of *The Gododdin* describes Llifiau as his 'foster brother'.[15] This may be a poetic reference and need not imply that Llifiau, unlike Tarain, was actually fostered. However, this still conveys the very close relationship that existed between this Pictish warrior and his North British comrades.

That Pictish warriors served in Scottish and North British warbands indicates that language and culture were no barrier to military service among a neighbouring people. This probably reflects the universal concept of the *comitatus* and its ideals and practices among the peoples of early medieval Britain. Although there is no evidence of Scottish or North British warriors serving in Pictish warbands, Irish and Northumbrian contingents are recorded fighting for *Dál Riata*. A 'Saxon' prince, Osric, and many of his people, presumably his warband, were slain fighting alongside the Scots in the unidentified battle of *Fid Eóin* in Ireland in 629.[16] Osric was one of the sons of King Aethelfrith who had sought exile in Pictland and Ireland when Edwin seized the kingship of Northumbria in 617.[17]

An Irish kingdom is of particular interest in this context. *Airgialla* was an over-kingdom, comprising a group of small kingdoms in mid-Ulster subject to the Northern *Uí Néill*.[18] In a manifestation of the close relationship that existed between *Dál Riata* and the Northern *Ui Néill*, the *Senchus fer nAlban* records that the *Airgialla* provided the seventh-hundred of the expeditionary force of *Cenél Loairn*.[19] It is in this context that they are recorded in 727, when 'some men of the *Airgialla*' were killed in the battle of *Irros Foichnae* between Selbach of *Cenél Loairn* and the 'family' of Eochaid of *Cenél nGabráin*.[20] Although opinion varies about whether this battle was fought in Scotland or Ireland,[21] the political context indicates that it occurred in *Dál Riata*. The identification of the *Airgialla* referred to with the Irish over-kingdom of the same name has been queried[22] and it has been suggested that the *Airgialla* concerned had settled in *Dál Riata*.[23] But, confirming their Irish identity and the strength of this relationship, the *Airgialla* were still providing military support to *Dál Riata* over a century later when, in 836, 'Gofraidh mac Ferghusa, ruler (*toísech*) of *Airgialla*, went to *Alba* to reinforce *Dál Riata* at the request of Cináed mac Ailpín'.[24] The precise nature of the relationship between *Dál Riata* and *Airgialla* is unclear, but it endured for over two centuries.

There is no evidence that warriors serving in foreign warbands were mercenaries in the accepted sense of being paid for military service. This appears to be inconsistent with the social context and ideals of the *comitatus*. Instead, warriors sought their reward in the form of glory and honour, although the prospect of plunder must also have been a motivating factor.[25] But mercenaries did exist in Ireland, leading to claims that Scottish armies involved in battles there were fighting in that capacity. A contemporary account describes the Scottish warriors defeated in a battle in *Inis hOinae*, either Inishowen or an island in the River Bann, as mercenaries (*amhsaibh*).[26] But this reference is unique and may represent the views of a hostile annalist. And although suggested that Domnall Brecc, a future king of *Dál Riata*, was acting as a mercenary when he fought in the battle of *Cend Delgthen* in Meath in 622,[27] his participation is attributable to the close relationships that existed between *Dál Riata* and various Irish kingdoms.

## ARMIES

References to Pictish and Scottish armies are rare and those that do exist tend not to be very informative. Exceptionally, two Pictish armies are referred to in a reference to the battle of *Monid Carno* fought near *stagnum Loogdae*, possibly Lochán na Bì near Tyndrum (Perthshire),[28] in 729.[29] This was fought between the army (*exercitus*) of Unuist son of Uurguist (Óengus son of Fergus, 'Óengus I') (729–61) and the hosts (*hostes*) of Nechtan son of Derelei (Derile) in their struggle for the Pictish kingship. It is unclear whether the use of two different terms here has any significance or if the annalist was simply avoiding repetition. The 'men of *Fortriu*' (*firu Fortrenn*), who fought two battles in 839 and 904,[30] probably refers to a provincial army, the 'common army' of *Fortriu* or of Southern Pictland as a whole. The only other references to Pictish armies are in later texts, although these probably draw on earlier sources. The large army (*exercitu magno*) led into battle on the Plain of *Merc*, possibly Mercia, by the later Unuist son of Uurguist (820–34) is mentioned in the foundation myth of St Andrews[31] and a Pictish army (*slúagh Cruithnech*) in *The Prophecy of Berchán*.[32] There are few more references to Scottish armies. The *Senchus fer nAlban* records the 'expeditionary strength of the hostings' of each *cenél* of *Dál Riata*,[33] denoting an army for external service. Examples of this are the 'army of Aedán [mac Gabráin]' (*exercitu Aidani*) that defeated the *Miathi* in an unnamed battle in 574X97,[34] the 'raiding army' (Anglo-Saxon, *here*) defeated by the Northumbrians at *Degsastán* in 603[35] and the 'array that came from Kintyre' but was defeated by the Strathclyde Britons at Strathcarron in 642.[36] Fighting inside *Dál Riata*, a Scottish *exercitus* was defeated by the Picts in the battle of *Cnoc Cairpri* in 736.[37]

Armies would normally have comprised two main elements. The core of any army consisted of the royal warband, the personal retinue or bodyguard of a king. This was supplemented by the warbands of his nobles. Together, these formed a military and social élite of well-armed and mounted professional warriors who had joined forces in a common cause under the king's command. In effect, each army was an agglomeration of small units fighting under the command of, and loyal to, individual commanders or nobles. But the bulk of an army's strength would have been made up of a king's able-bodied subjects, men who owed their lord an obligation of military service but were probably normally engaged in agricultural or related craft activities. These were 'common armies', made up of levied free commoners and probably also including peasants,[38] raised in troops by their lords.

The composition of armies may have varied according to their function. Raiding armies, such as the Scots' 'expeditionary strength of the hostings', required greater mobility, because of the greater distances they needed to cover to attack enemy territory. Although its Latin equivalent, *expeditio*, implies an army campaigning on foot, these warriors would have been mounted and, therefore, were mostly nobles. While relatively small in size, such an army may have made up for in experience, weaponry and mobility what it lacked in numbers. This is the type of warfare portrayed so vividly in *The Gododdin*. In contrast, a defensive army would not have needed to be so mobile because it was defending its own territory and a larger, more static army would have enabled a heavier levy of military service to be placed on the common folk. This may parallel the distinction that existed in the twelfth century between the burdens of *communis exercitus*, for homeland defence, and *expeditio*, owed to the king.

There is very little information on the sizes of Scottish armies, and even less about Pictish ones. Exceptionally, the *Senchus fer nAlban* records the 'expeditionary strength of the hostings' of each *cenél*. When adjusted to compensate for internal discrepancies, the *Senchus* gives total strengths of 630 men for *Cenél Loairn*, 840 men for *Cenél nGabráin* and 645 men for *Cenél nOengusa*, giving *Dál Riata* a total military strength of 2,115.[39] An additional insight into the size of a Scottish army is provided by a reference to the loss of 303 men in a battle against the *Miathi* in 574X97.[40] The *Miathi*'s name is cognate with that of the earlier *Maeatae*, which is preserved in the placenames Dumyat and Myot Hill (Stirlingshire), indicating that their territory included the area around the head of the Firth of Forth.[41] Although the body count appears in a prophecy made by Columba *before* the battle, Adomnán's point in relating this episode was presumably to illustrate the accuracy of the saint's prediction. Moreover, as a senior Scottish cleric with close links to the kingship of *Dál Riata*, Adomnán would have had no motive for exaggerating losses sustained by his own side. If accurate, the Scots lost the equivalent of about half the army that could be levied from a single *cenél*. But, significantly, the Scots still won the battle despite their losses. This suggests that their army was substantially larger than the number of their warriors killed. This is also supported by the Scots' ability to mount attacks on neighbouring peoples within a few years, notably at *Degsastán*,[42] possibly Dawston in Liddesdale (Roxburghshire).[43] That the Scots could absorb such heavy losses and yet still win the battle attests the scale of their mobilisation and the size of their army. Although even its approximate size remains unclear, this battle reveals that the Scots were capable of mustering and fielding an army that must have been at least several hundred men strong. This may reflect the heavy burden of military service within *Dál Riata* that the *Senchus* records and the high level of mobilisation that the many, often long-range, campaigns of Aedán mac Gabráin imply.[44]

Although Adomnán would have had no reason to exaggerate Scottish casualties, the figure of 303 dead cannot be accepted literally. It is uncannily close to the size of the warband or army celebrated in

*The Gododdin*, which is variously referred to in the text as 300, 'more than 300'-, 330- or 363-men strong.[45] Figures of 303 dead and 300, 330 or 363 warriors are idealised. Reflecting literary conventions, these numbers are deliberately, and perhaps artificially, based on units of three, in hundreds, scores and ones. But although these exact figures cannot be taken at face value, they are probably of the right order of magnitude and possibly even close.[46] This is supported by the only other casualty figure recorded: 500 men were killed in battle against the Vikings in 904.[47] Early medieval armies probably comprised several hundred men.

*The Gododdin*'s reference to an army of 'a hundred thousand'[48] is clearly fanciful but is a useful reminder that some sources inflate the size of armies for literary effect, to stress a point or to impress an audience. Northumbrian sources habitually overestimate the size of opposing armies. Likening them to 'swarms' of ants, Eddius Stephanus[49] relates how 'innumerable peoples' (*innumeras gentes*) of the Picts mustered to form a 'vast army' (*hostem . . . immensam*), which was defeated by Ecgfrith's 'troop of horsemen' (*equitatui exercitu*) in the Plain of *Manau* in 672. Similarly, the Scottish force defeated by Northumbria at *Degsastán* is described as 'a large and powerful army' (*inmenso et forti exercitu*),[50] while a 'very large' Scottish army (*cum innumerabili multitudine*) was defeated by a 'very small army' (*paucitati militum*) of Northumbrians in the battle of Mundingdene, near Norham (Northumberland), in 883X96.[51]

There is no direct evidence about the size of Pictish armies, although there is no reason to assume that they differed substantially from those of neighbouring peoples. Adomnán's[52] reference to a Pictish *cohors* implies a sizeable force and the fact that he refers to a warband (*comitatus*) and army (*exercitus*) elsewhere[53] indicates that he is making a deliberate distinction between these various units. 'Cohort' is an unusual word in an early medieval context, reflecting the Latin learning of ecclesiastical writers, but is also used to describe the units (*cohortes*) deployed by Ecgfrith, King of Northumbria, against the Picts in 672.[54] The distinction Adomnán was trying to convey may have been one of size and/or status. A Roman *cohors* was around 600-men strong, but the Pictish unit concerned is unlikely to have been as large as this, as a force of this size would have qualified as an army in an early medieval context.

Adomnán's reference to a *cohors* does not imply the survival of Roman influences or traditions in Pictish military organisation, as has been claimed.[55] Instead, it attests the enduring legacy of Roman military organisation within heroic ideal and literary convention. Another manifestation of this are the references in *The Gododdin* to war leaders as 'centurions'. More prosaically, Adomnán, who was writing in Latin, may simply have selected what he considered to be the closest Latin equivalent term to a Gaelic or Pictish word for the military unit concerned. The meaning that was probably intended was that this body of troops was larger than a *comitatus* but smaller than an army. This may reflect the status of the person it served, and the *cohors* may represent the larger than normal warband of a senior noble or king. This is also reflected in the leadership of the unit.[56]

## WARRIOR KINGS

Military leadership was inextricably linked with those systems of military obligation and organisation used by the Picts and Scots. Men had a personal obligation to do military service for their lord, those lords would have been responsible for raising troops of warriors from their estates or provinces, while the army as a whole was mustered under the overall command of a senior noble or the king himself. As a result, there were tiers of military leadership within Pictish and Scottish armies. These various levels of command, and their roles, are recorded in contemporary sources only in a very patchy manner. Not surprisingly, the most senior, and therefore royal, level of leadership features most prominently.

Pictish and Scottish kings were ultimately war leaders. A king would normally have led his army into battle and was expected to do so, unless he was too old or infirm. The king not only provided leadership but his presence on the battlefield also boosted the morale of his army. This may have had a religious dimension as a result of the close links that existed between kingships and the Church.[57] The strength of the link between kingship and warfare among the Picts and Scots is a consistent feature of contemporary sources, primarily in the many records of battles fought by kings. Other sources are equally revealing in their references to the association of kings and warfare. The Pictish King Drest son of Uirp (Drust son of Erp) is claimed to have reigned for 100 years and fought 100 battles.[58] This is obviously exaggerated, and both king and battles are presumably mythical. Nevertheless, by making an explicit link between the length of a reign and the number of battles fought, it demonstrates that kingship and leadership in battle were perceived to be closely associated, even mutually dependent. In contrast, and reflecting the rarity of the absence of warfare in *Dál Riata*, the reign of Comgall mac Domangairt (*c.* 507–38) was reportedly 'without strife'.[59]

It was not enough for kings simply to fight battles. They also had to win. Without success on the battlefield, kings and their kingdoms were nothing. Pictish and Scottish kings were guarantors of the security of their kingdom, land and people, and, as war leaders, were expected to demonstrate their bravery and martial prowess if they wanted to retain their kingship. This is part of a wider early medieval phenomenon and is particularly prominent in early Irish concepts of kingship.[60] Cowardice in battle reduced a king's honour-price, the compensation payable by a guilty party to someone who was injured. *Críth Gablach*[61] states that a king wounded in the back of the neck while fleeing the battlefield is entitled only to the payment due to a commoner but points out that, if the wound was received after breaking through the enemy ranks, he is entitled to the payment due to a king. A king's defeat in battle was perceived as a sign of the injustice of his rule. Another early Irish law tract records that defeat resulted in the loss of the king's honour-price and therefore, in theory at least, his kingship. But despite the unambiguous legal evidence, historians cannot point to a single Irish king who lost his kingship as a result of defeat in battle, except, of course, where the king was killed. There are occasional hints of these attitudes and practices among the Picts and Scots.

As in early medieval Ireland, victory in battle was probably central to Pictish and Scottish concepts of kingship. A link between defeat on the battlefield and loss of kingship is sometimes implied. Aedán mac Gabráin, king of *Dál Riata*, may have abdicated or been overthrown after his disastrous defeat by the Northumbrians at *Degsastán* in 603. One late source refers to his expulsion and another states that he was no longer king when he died, possibly in 608.[62] The Picts under Nechtan son of Derelei were heavily defeated by the Northumbrians in 711 in another battle fought between the rivers Avon and Carron in the Plain of *Manau*.[63] This may have raised doubts about Nechtan's kingship and signs of stresses within the royal kin group soon emerged, with the killing of one of Nechtan's brothers and Nechtan holding another brother captive in 713.[64] Although the circumstances are unknown, these incidents attest problems within the royal kin group, perhaps evidence that Nechtan's defeat prompted his brothers to challenge his kingship.

Clearer evidence of the link between defeat in battle and loss of kingship is provided by another case. The Picts were heavily defeated by the Strathclyde Britons in 750 at a battle which is recorded variously in Irish and Welsh annals as *Catoic, Maes-ydawc, Metgadawc, Moce-tauc, Mygedawc* and *Ocha*,[65] possibly Mugdock (Stirlingshire).[66] The dead included two brothers of the Pictish king, Unuist son of Uurguist, at least one of whom was a provincial king and war leader. Under the same year, the annals also record the 'end of the reign' or 'ebbing of the sovereignty' of Unuist.[67] The occurrence of these two events in the same year implies that Unuist's defeat weakened his power to such an extent that he lost the kingship. This could, of course, have resulted from the invasion or occupation of Pictland by the North Britons, but there is no evidence of this. Instead, Unuist's expulsion from the kingship may be attributed to internal processes.

The heavy casualties sustained in the battle probably deprived Unuist of the support of a social, political and military élite of kinsmen and nobles that maintained him in power. Rather than Unuist being removed from the kingship as a result of an immediate and direct reaction to losing the battle, the outcome may have left him more susceptible to subsequent challenges. A king who was not an effective and successful war leader did not retain the kingship for long. However, in this case, the situation was reversible because Unuist not only survived to fight another day but also regained the Pictish kingship and held it until his death in 761.[68]

The loss of a king in battle was more serious. This heralded defeat and disaster, not just for his army, but also for his subjects and kingdom. This theme is expressed symbolically in the record of the Scots' defeat by the Vikings in a battle, probably at Inverdovet (Fife) in 877, in which Causantín mac Cináeda (Constantine son of Kenneth, 'Constantine I'), King of Alba, and many of his men fell. Conveying the extent of the calamity, the source adds ominously, 'That was the occasion when the earth gave way under the men of Alba.'[69]

The role of Pictish and Scottish kings as war leaders is amply attested by records of their achievements on the battlefield. These include, among many entries:

The flight of the Scots before Bridei son of Maelchon, king of the Picts. (560)[70]

The battle of Srath Ethairt [was won] by Talorcan son of Eanfrith, king of the Picts. (654)[71]

The exploits in battle of some Pictish and Scottish kings are also recorded in surviving fragments of praise poems.[72]

Reinforcing the status of kings as war leaders, Pictish and Scottish armies are sometimes referred to by the king commanding them. The Miathi were defeated in 574X97 by 'Aedán's army' (exercitu Aidani), after Aedán mac Gabráin, King of Dál Riata.[73] The Scots were defeated by the Picts in the battle of Cnoc Cairpri in 736, where 'Ainfchellach's son', that is, Muiredach, King of Dál Riata, and 'his army' were routed.[74] Pictish armies are referred to similarly: the battle of Monid Carno, between rivals for the Pictish kingship, was fought in 729 between the 'army of Unuist' (*exercitum Oengusa*) and the 'hosts of Nechtain' (*hostem Nectain*).[75] Indeed, so strong were the bonds – geographical and social – between kings and their armies that the Scottish army routed in the battle of *Glenn Mairison* or *Glenn Muiresan*, possibly Glen Moriston (Inverness-shire),[76] in 638 is referred to as the 'family' (Latin, *familia*; Irish, *muinntir*) of Domnall Brecc, King of *Dál Riata*.[77] But armies and their victories could legitimately be referred to as a king's because of the royal authority invested in them and without implications for the king's presence on the battlefield. That kings were not only present at battles but also fought in them is strongly suggested by the cumulative weight of entries referring to kings and battles and confirmed by the deaths of several kings in battle.[78] In most annalistic records of battles the army is simply implied and only the kings leading them or the kingdom to which they belonged are referred to.

The preoccupation of the Irish annalists with battles and other notable events gives a distorted impression of the character of Pictish and Scottish kingship. Kings were not only war leaders, but also had important administrative, legislative, judicial and religious roles. Nevertheless, several Pictish and Scottish kings emerge from these sources as particularly capable and ambitious war leaders, their military achievements distinguishing them as bold strategists and shrewd tacticians. The best documented example of this is the defeat of a superior Northumbrian army by the Picts under their king, Bridei son of Bile, at Dunnichen in 685.[79] But two kings in particular stand out from the annals and may justifiably be described as 'warrior kings'. That one is Pictish and the other Scottish, one belonging to the sixth century and the other to the eighth, demonstrates that this is no isolated phenomenon. In both cases, their reigns are characterised by their expansionist ambitions, their willingness and ability to conduct campaigns against several enemies and to take the war to them in a succession of battles over considerable distances.

Aedán mac Gabráin (574–?608) was one of the most vigorous kings of *Dál Riata* and pursued an aggressive and ambitious expansionist policy.[80] Aedán may have been challenged soon after his reign began. Many followers of the sons of Gabráin were killed fighting an unidentified, possibly internal, Irish or Pictish, enemy in the battle of *Delgu* or *Teloch* in Kintyre in 576.[81] But Aedán was soon conducting long-range military operations. He led at least one campaign to Orkney in 580 and/or 581 and then, striking as far south as he had north, won a battle on the Isle of Man in 582 or 583.[82] This rapid succession of campaigns may be the cause of the evident confusion among the sources about the number of battles fought by Aedán.[83] Aedán also fought the battle of *Leithrig* in 590,[84] although its outcome is unrecorded and its location remains unidentified. In 574X97, Aedán's army lost 303 men and his sons Artuir and Eochaid Find were killed in a victory over the *Miathi*,[85] a North British or possibly Pictish people whose territory lay at the head of the Firth of Forth. Aedán's reign culminated in his defeat in a series of far-flung battles, in which more of his sons were killed. Aedán lost the battle of *Círcenn*, the Pictish province comprising the Mearns (Kincardineshire), in which his sons Bran and Domangart were slain, in 596.[86] Attesting some confusion among the sources, Domangart's death is also recorded in a battle that Aedán lost in England.[87] This may have been the battle of *Degsastán*, in which Aedán and his army were comprehensively defeated in 603. This appears to have marked the end of Aedán's campaigning, and possibly his kingship.[88]

Unuist son of Uurguist is probably the most notable Pictish warrior king.[89] He seized the Pictish kingship in 729 after defeating the previous king, Nechtan son of Derelei, in the battle of *Monid Carno*.[90] Unuist soon embarked on an ambitious strategy to assert Pictish dominance over northern Britain. As the Picts lacked the capability to achieve this by military strength alone, they concluded a peace treaty with the Angles of Northumbria, which was in place by 731.[91] Having neutralised the other most powerful nation in northern Britain, the Picts had a free hand to attack their weaker neighbours. Unuist wasted no time in mounting a series of campaigns in which he inflicted a rapid succession of defeats on the Scots.[92] He routed *Dál Riata* in an unnamed battle in 731, seized Pictish opponents from exile in *Dál Riata*, caused the Scottish king Dúngal mac Selbaich to flee to safety in Ireland and destroyed a Scottish fortress in 734, and defeated the Scots in the battle of *Cnoc Cairpri*, laid waste to *Dál Riata* and took hostages, seizing one fortress and burning another in 736. The Picts may also have overcome the Scots in the battle of *Forboros* in 741 and the annals record 'The smiting (*percutio*) of *Dál Riata* by Unuist son of Uurguist' the same year.

The alliance with Northumbria had collapsed by 740, when the Picts and Northumbrians were at war.[93] But, having asserted his authority over *Dál Riata*, Unuist's ambition was to do the same to the North British kingdom of Strathclyde. His campaign had begun by 744, when the Picts and Britons fought a battle, although its location and outcome are unrecorded.[94] But Unuist's fortunes had turned. Unexpectedly, the Strathclyde Britons were more formidable opponents than the Scots. In 750, the Picts were defeated decisively at a battle that remains unlocated.[95] The dead included Unuist's brother, Talorgan, who had led the army that defeated the Scots in 736. Indeed, so heavy was this defeat that Unuist lost his kingship temporarily[96] and, although he later recovered the throne, his military ambitions appear to have been checked. Certainly, there is no further record of his campaigns, although his second period in the kingship falls after the decline in the Scottish entries in the Irish annals.

It is worth emphasising that these are just the events that were recorded. Given the paucity of documentary sources concerning the Picts in particular, the reigns of Aedán, Unuist and many other Pictish and Scottish kings were probably even more turbulent than they appear.


MILITARY LEADERSHIP

Kings were not the only war leaders. Other members of the royal kin group held important positions within the gift of the king, including provincial kingships and lordships. These individuals also played a key role in military leadership, although this is scarcely visible because even the most senior participants in a battle are rarely recorded. This is compounded by the limited genealogical evidence available, particularly for the Picts, which makes it difficult to identify kin relationships even when battle casualties are recorded. A notable exception is Aedán mac Gabráin, who lost at least four sons in three battles,[97] although the sources are confused about which son fell in which battle. Similarly, Fáilbe and Rígullán, brother and cousin respectively of Connad Cerr, King of *Dál Riata*, were killed with their king in the battle of *Fid Eóin* in Ireland in 629.[98] Close members of the Pictish royal kin group held similar positions and the nature of the relationship is revealed on one occasion. In a Pictish attack on *Dál Riata* in 736,[99] the Pictish king, Unuist son of Uurguist, and his brother, Talorgan, appear to have led separate armies or units. Talorgan's army defeated the Scots in battle at *Cnoc Cairpri* and Unuist's ravaged *Dál Riata* and seized its royal centres.[100] Another of Unuist's war leaders was his son, Bridei, who defeated Talorgan mac Congusso in an unnamed battle in 731.[101] Although kings themselves were war leaders, they sometimes relied upon their closest and presumably most trusted relatives to fulfil critical roles as subordinate commanders.

Intermediate levels of military leadership were filled by nobles, although the evidence is limited. Some of the individuals whose obituaries sometimes accompany annalistic records of battles were presumably nobles but are referred to only by name. On the rare occasions where their ranks or offices are given, either a generic Latin term or the Latin equivalent of a native title is usually used, with the result that Pictish and Scottish noble ranks of war leader remain obscure. Emphasising the aristocratic status of Pictish war leaders, *The Gododdin*[102] refers to 'A foreign horseman of most refined nature, / the noble hero used to lead a hundred men'. This illustrates the function of lords in early medieval warfare. Lords, too, owed obligations of military service to their king or superior noble and would have acted as war leaders on their behalf. This would have involved raising and perhaps also training and equipping a *comitatus*, comprising either a band of horsemen or a company of foot soldiers, and leading them into battle as part of a wider army under the overall command of the king. However, sources such as those recording that 'many of the noblest of the Picts fell' in battle against the Scots in 834,[103] appear to be influenced by later traditions concerning the Scottish takeover of Pictland by killing the Pictish ruling class.[104] Pictish sculpture provides graphic confirmation of aristocratic involvement in warfare.[105]

The *mormaer* is of potential relevance to Pictish military leadership. *Mormaers* were powerful territorial magnates and their extensive provinces comprised the primary level of royal administration in *Alba* during the tenth and eleventh centuries.[106] This rank was probably of Pictish origin[107] and its name is derived from a Pictish title meaning 'great officer' or similar.[108] The office of *mormaer* probably originated in the provincial kingships of Pictland. Its Pictish origins are supported by the distribution of recorded *mormaer*-doms, which are confined to north-eastern Scotland, the former territory of Pictland. However, the earliest recorded reference to a *mormaer* is not until 918, when an unspecified number of *mormaers* fought alongside their king, Causantín mac Áeda (Constantine son of Aed, 'Constantine II'), against the Vikings at the River Tyne, probably the Haddington Tyne (East Lothian).[109] Emphasising their role in warfare, three named Scottish *mormaers* accompanied two Irish kings on a raid in 976[110] and the *mormaer* of Mar was killed in the battle of Clontarf, near Dublin, in 1014.[111] The prominence attached to the rank of *mormaer* in the notes in the *Book of Deer*[112] amply attests the authority of this rank of noble in levying military service. *Mormaers* were powerful warlords, responsible for raising an army from their province and for leading the warriors they levied into battle.

The office of *mormaer* appears to have been unknown in *Dál Riata* and its equivalent is unclear. Indeed, the smaller size and apparently more centralised political authority of *Dál Riata* may have meant that there was no direct equivalent. In both *Dál Riata* and *Alba*, as in Ireland, the *toísech*, 'lord' or 'leader', was a royal official with a military role. Perhaps significantly, this is the only rank of noble other than *mormaer* recorded in the *Book of Deer*.[113] The *toísech's* authority to levy military obligations is also referred to in the *Book of Deer*, implying that this noble rank was also a war leader. This appears to be confirmed by an entry recording that Conall mac Comgaill, *toísech* of *Dál Riata*, led a raid on Seil and Islay in 566.[114] But *toísech* could also mean 'prince' and Conall was actually King of *Dál Riata*.

Some Latin sources use the title *comes*, literally 'earl', as the Latin equivalent of *mormaer*. The St Andrews foundation legend records that the ninth-century Unuist son of Uurguist was accompanied on the Plain of *Merc* by 'seven of his most friendly [and, therefore, presumably trustworthy] *comites*' (*cum septem comitibus amicissimis*),[115] the number of war leaders reflecting the size of his 'great army'. The same title is also recorded in *Dál Riata*. But although 'a number of nobles (*comites*)' were killed in a naval battle fought by Scottish factions at *Ard Nesbi* in 719,[116] *comes* is simply the Latin equivalent of a native title that remains obscure. Less specifically still, 'many nobles' (*multi nobiles*), most of whom, presumably, were on the defeated Scottish side, were killed in the battle of *Cnoc Cairpri* in 736.[117]

Lower levels of military leadership may have been performed by royal officials. Inevitably, their lesser status means that their presence or death in battle is recorded only rarely. Indeed, no Scottish and only a single Pictish royal official appear in accounts of battles. The Pictish official concerned is the *exactor*, 'collector of dues', three of whom (*exactatores*) were killed in the battle of *Monith Carno* in 729.[118] That all three of Nechtan's tax collectors are named in the annalistic entry indicates that they were men of status. Their presence may not have been typical but was possibly related to the circumstances of the battle, which occurred during a struggle for the Pictish kingship. This suggests that Nechtan was attempting to collect tribute in an unsuccessful bid to enforce his overlordship on Unuist, his contender for the kingship.

Nevertheless, the existence of other royal officials and their involvement in warfare may be inferred. Adomnán[119] describes the baptism on Skye of Artbranán, 'a certain pagan old man', whose identification as a Pict is supported by Columba's need for a translator during the ceremony. Providing the only evidence of a Pictish official specifically concerned with warfare, Artbranán is described as 'leader of the cohort of (?)Geon' (*Geonae primarius cohortis*). 'Geon' is unidentified and may be a person rather than a place, possibly the king or lord who appointed Artbranán to head his personal retinue and presumably reflecting Artbranán's status and experience as a warrior. Artbranán's position as the leader of a warband is paralleled among the Scots.

Adomnán[120] refers to 'a grasping chief . . . among the governors of thy district'. Although the standard translation gives the impression that these are civil or administrative offices, the Latin words used, *primarium*, 'leader' and *praepossitís*, 'commanders', are military in character. The Gaelic equivalent of at least one of these terms was probably *toísech*.[121]

## MILITARY OBJECTIVES

Military organisation and leadership inevitably leads to the issue of military objectives. Why were the Picts and Scots so warlike, or at least were perceived to be so by their neighbours? And what were they trying to achieve through warfare? The study of military objectives is hampered by the limitations of the sources, which do not record the intentions of the belligerents but take the necessity of warfare for granted. However, the motives involved sometimes may be identified from the historical and/or geographical context in which a battle was fought. This, understandably, becomes more difficult for those battles that remain unlocated or where the warring parties are unidentified. Nevertheless, a broad consistency is detectable among the motives behind many of the battles fought by the Picts and the Scots.

Most battles appear to have been fought for the control of resources and the most readily identifiable objectives are territorial and political. Territorial battles were both offensive and defensive in character, as the opposing sides attempted to acquire or hold territory. The aggressor is sometimes difficult to identify, particularly if a battle remains unlocated, but is obvious in other cases. For example, the Picts were defending their independence against Northumbrian overlordship at the battle of Dunnichen. In such cases, the aggressor's motive was probably to expand its territory by conquering an adjacent area belonging to a neighbouring people, or to extend its sphere of influence by reducing their enemy to subject status and imposing the collection of tribute on them. Three key elements of such warfare were the plundering of portable goods, the laying waste of enemy territory and the taking of slaves and hostages.[122] But these were also key elements of the raids mounted on enemy territory, brief incursions not involving any attempt to conquer territory but aimed solely at seizing portable spoils and inflicting destruction. Not surprisingly, many of the battles fought by the Picts, the Scots and their neighbours occurred on or near their borders, which explains the concentration of early medieval battlefields across central Scotland. But other battles, fought deep inside hostile territory, are unlikely to have been intended to conquer new lands and may have had more strategic objectives. For example, the battles of *Degsastán* and at *Catraeth* were apparently similar responses by *Dál Riata* and the *Gododdin* respectively, intended to check the Northumbrian expansion northwards at the end of the sixth and start of the seventh centuries.

Battles and wars with political motives are easily identified, at least when they involve warfare among the same people, primarily between rival royal kin groups. Wars fought for possession of the kingship can sometimes be linked to the start of a new reign or the political background may be recorded in the Irish annals, as with the struggle for the Pictish kingship in 724–9. But other political motives may be more difficult to identify. And, of course, an attempt by one king to impose his overlordship on another king of the same people also has a territorial dimension. Another motive behind some battles may have been revenge, where an attack may have been mounted in retribution for actual or perceived defeats, insults or injustices committed by the enemy in the past. This may help to explain the apparently tit-for-tat nature of the sieges of Dunadd and Dundurn, two of the principal royal fortresses of *Dál Riata* and *Fortriu* respectively, in 683.[123] But, in many cases, battles and wars probably involved a combination of motives. The balance between these different objectives may have varied according to the circumstances of the battle and its participants. Indeed, even combatants fighting on the same side may not have had shared the same priorities and motives, which probably varied according to the circumstances and social status of warriors.

## CHAPTER FOUR

# Arms and Armour

The study of arms and armour can reveal much about the nature of warfare, as well as wider artistic, social and technological issues. Unfortunately, the study of both Pictish and Scottish arms and armour is severely constrained by the small number and limited range of surviving examples. In marked contrast to Anglo-Saxon mortuary practices, the Picts and Scots do not appear to have buried their dead with grave goods. There is no Pictish or Scottish equivalent of Sutton Hoo, the Anglo-Saxon royal ship-burial in East Anglia with its spectacularly rich grave goods.[1] Moreover, with only one possible exception, there are no Pictish or Scottish parallels to the many more mundane, but still highly informative, Anglo-Saxon weapon burials.[2] These weapon burials have traditionally, though increasingly controversially,[3] been interpreted as the graves of warriors, buried with the weapons that were intended to accompany them to the afterlife. The problem is exacerbated by the relatively small number of Pictish and Scottish sites excavated, the limited scale of those excavations and the poor survival of ironwork in most soil conditions. As a result, it is impossible to produce for the Picts and Scots the detailed studies of weaponry that exist for the Anglo-Saxons.[4]

Also in contrast to Anglo-Saxon England,[5] the documentary record is similarly unproductive, with no descriptions or illustrations of Pictish or Scottish arms or armour in any sources. Textual references to weapons are rare and, where they do occur, ambiguous. For example, Cassius Dio[6] records simply that the *Caledonii* and *Maeatae* had daggers, but may mean short swords. The Roman panegyrist Claudian[7] referred to a *tela . . . Scottica*, a 'Scottic javelin', but this could also apply to a dart, shaft or missile generally, a sword or simply a weapon. Where more detail is given, as with Gildas'[8] account of the Picts pulling Britons from Hadrian's Wall with barbed spears, there is no evidence to support the use of such weapons by the Picts. Gildas[9] also refers metaphorically to 'the claws of their [the Picts' and Scots'] sword-points'. Other literary references to weapons, notably in Adomnán's *Life of Columba*, concern their use in acts of casual violence rather than in battle. This meagre literary evidence may be supplemented by the more plentiful references to weapons in *The Gododdin*. This evidence is referred to where it provides useful parallels but is not analysed in detail here, partly because of limitations of space but also because it is more appropriate to the study of weapons and warfare among the North Britons.

Nevertheless, some Pictish and Scottish weapons and their decorative fittings have survived. Although some items of weaponry have been recovered as stray finds, such as the sword pommel from the Culbin Sands, most have been found during archaeological excavation. Excavations at the Scottish royal fortress of Dunadd[10] in 1904–5, 1929 and 1980–1 proved exceptionally productive, yielding a total of 2 possible sword fragments, 7 spearheads, at least 24 spear ferrules and 4 arrowheads or crossbow bolts. The only other weapons found in *Dál Riata* are a spearhead and several arrowheads from Dunollie, although apparently pre-dating the fortifications there.[11] Pictish forts are also potentially rich sources of weapon finds, as a frustrating case demonstrates. When the ramparts of the promontory fortress of Burghead were levelled in the early nineteenth century, 'the many . . . battle-axes and spear-heads then found were given to any English tourist who came that way'.[12] The most detailed descriptions of what appears to have been a large and important assemblage of weaponry simply refer to the discovery of an iron axe and a bronze spearhead at Burghead.[13] The best known weapon finds, and the most highly accomplished artistically, are the sword fittings found during the excavation of an early ecclesiastical site on St Ninian's Isle (Shetland). The only other Pictish weapons found during excavations are two spearheads, one from the ringfort at Aldclune (Perthshire), the other from post-broch occupation levels at Upper Scalloway (Shetland).

As a result of the rarity of surviving examples, our knowledge of Pictish arms and armour is largely dependent on the evidence available from sculpture. Pictish warriors are portrayed, often in hunting and occasionally in battle or other scenes, on the reverse of many Pictish cross-slabs. These scenes contain a wealth of information about Pictish weaponry, occasionally portraying them in use. The relevance of this evidence has been queried on the grounds that many of these scenes were not original Pictish compositions but were derived from illuminated manuscripts, presumably from outside Pictland.[14] But the details found in Pictish sculptural scenes, specifically the clothing and weapons of the figures portrayed, have long been recognised as native to Pictland.[15] Despite this, they have received little attention, amounting to one brief survey[16] and short studies of shields, crossbows and the Aberlemno battle scene.[17] Recently, attention has focused not on the artefacts depicted, but on their use for dating the sculpture on which they appear.[18] Although some Pictish symbols are claimed to represent arms or armour there are serious doubts about such interpretations. Sculpture in *Dál Riata* belongs to a different tradition, of Irish origin and influence. Warriors are rarely depicted and there are no comparable secular scenes to those found widely in Pictish sculpture. The evidence for Pictish and Scottish arms and armour is therefore largely complementary. While more literary references and actual weapons survive from *Dál Riata*, the sculptural evidence is overwhelmingly Pictish.

Two remarkable sculptures deserve introduction at this point. The battle scene on the reverse of the eighth-century Pictish cross-slab in Aberlemno churchyard (Angus) (*see* Plate 8) is of particular value because it provides an insight not only into the weapons, but also the tactics and formations used by Pictish warriors.[19] The other famous, and much more extensive, battle scene is on the reverse of the monumental cross-slab known as Sueno's Stone, on the outskirts of Forres (Morayshire) (*see* Plate 7). However, this remarkable and impressive monument, which stands over 6.5 m high, poses considerable problems of interpretation. Sueno's Stone is badly weathered, reducing most of the ninety-eight warriors portrayed to little more than ghostly outlines. Its significance is further obscured by the fact that it is not closely dated and is the subject of divergent traditions and interpretations.[20] Although often claimed as Pictish, Sueno's Stone probably dates to the tenth century, after the eclipse of the Picts, and records a historical confrontation between the armies of a king of *Alba* and a *mormaer* of Moray, possibly the battle in which King Dubh (Duff) was killed in 966.

The use of sculptural evidence poses both practical and methodological problems.[21] The greatest difficulty encountered in studying the weapons depicted in Pictish sculpture is caused by the worn and weathered condition of many stones after exposure to the elements for over a millennium, now exacerbated by the corrosive effects of environmental pollution. As a result, the detail no longer survives on many Pictish stones, although old engravings or photographs may help to clarify their form, as may examining stones in different lighting conditions or using digital recording techniques. Even when details are visible, the sculptor's perceptions, intentions, competency and artistic licence are all potential factors affecting the accuracy of the images. The weapons depicted in Pictish sculpture are accepted here as accurate on the following grounds. First, many weapons are portrayed consistently on several Pictish stones, but with enough minor variations to reveal that they were not simply copied slavishly from a pattern book. Second, the meanings – artistic, religious and socio-political – of Pictish sculpture were derived in part from the stones' association with real people, the powerful patrons who commissioned and are portrayed on them. This indicates that their weapons were also based on real examples. Third, the accuracy of some sculptural representations is confirmed by the few surviving weapons and their fittings.

The weapons most frequently depicted in Pictish sculpture are the sword, spear and shield. These were the principal arms of Pictish warriors and, almost certainly, this was also the case among the Scots. Most of this chapter therefore concerns swords, spears and shields, although their use in battle will be examined in more detail in the next chapter. Although other weapons, notably the axe, crossbow and knife or dagger, are portrayed occasionally in Pictish sculpture, it is unclear whether these were used in warfare or were primarily for hunting or craft activities. But in all cases they possess a potential for offensive use and therefore are considered here.

## SWORDS AND SCABBARDS

Swords were highly prized weapons. Unsurprisingly, few swords or their fragments and fittings survive from early medieval Scotland. They would have been discarded only rarely, complete swords being handed down to heirs or seized by victorious enemies, while the components of broken swords would have been recycled. For the few early medieval swords that are known from Scotland, the absence of comparative examples has tended to result in them being classed and dated by Petersen's typology and chronology of Viking swords, which survive in greater quantities.[22] As a result, these swords tend to be identified as Viking. However, as similar types of sword also occur in Anglo-Saxon England, it is clear that these are of wider currency and that their attribution to the Vikings is doubtful.

Two early medieval swords survive from Pictland. Both are straight-sided and double-edged with rounded tips, intended for single-handed use. A sword from Gorton (Moray) is assumed to be Viking on account of its form.[23] This has a slightly curved, oval-shaped crossguard and tri-lobate pommel with a more pronounced curve.[24] The other sword, from Harvieston (Clackmannanshire) has curved upper and lower crossguards[25] and is also similar to types of Viking sword. The evidence from *Dál Riata* is even more limited, with no complete swords and only two possible fragments recorded. A fragment of an iron sword blade, 40 mm wide, was found during the early excavations at Dunadd.[26] The 1980–1 excavations recovered a fragment of a double-sided blade, 30 mm wide, possibly from a small sword.[27] Although the tip of a sword blade was also believed to have been found at Dunadd during the 1929 excavations, this artefact was later identified as a spearhead.[28] The only other surviving swords of early medieval date from Scotland are from Torbeckhill (Dumfriesshire)[29] and a fragmentary blade, tapering towards the tip, from Carronbridge (Dumfriesshire).[30] The latter is possibly of ninth- or tenth-century date and, again, has been claimed as probably Anglo-Saxon or Viking.[31]

As a result of the scarcity of surviving examples, the technology of sword production among the Picts and Scots is unclear, but there is no reason to believe that it differed substantially from that of their neighbours. Both the Picts and Scots were accomplished metalworkers, as a wide range of ornate metalwork reveals. Evidence of fine metalworking and ironworking at Dunadd was revealed by excavation, indicating the royal control of raw materials and finished products,[32] possibly including weaponry. Surviving Pictish sword pommels have parallels with Anglo-Saxon examples and, in addition to stylistic traits, technical expertise in blade production was probably exchanged between the Picts and their neighbours. The only contemporary reference to the manufacture of bladed weapons is Adomnán's[33] description of how a blessing bestowed by Columba on one implement was extended to others: 'skilled monks softened the metal of that dagger in a hot fire, and distributed it by welding it onto all the iron tools of the monastery'. The reference to 'skilled monks' attests the specialised nature of this activity. Reflecting the importance and status of metalsmiths within Pictish society, theirs is the only specialist trade or occupation represented among the extensive repertoire of Pictish symbols. Regardless of their symbolic meaning, the metalworkers' tools of the trade – anvil, hammer and tongs – are readily identifiable in Pictish sculpture.[34]

Although widely claimed to represent swords, some Pictish sculpture presents problems of interpretation. These include the symbol usually described as a 'tuning fork' and extensively interpreted as a broken sword.[35] Instead, this is actually a stylised representation of a smith's tongs, an identification confirmed by its association with the anvil and hammer symbols.[36] A symbol incised on outcropping rock at Trusty's Hill, Anwoth (Kirkcudbrightshire)[37] is often interpreted as a Pictish sword or dagger.[38] Although it occurs beside a characteristically Pictish double-disc and Z-rod symbol, these carvings lie far outside Pictland. Moreover, the 'sword' is unparalleled and too stylised to be interpreted with confidence. Reflecting this, it has also been described as a whetstone and a 'triskele-headed' stick pin.[39] Last, a Pictish symbol stone at Newton of Lewesk (Aberdeenshire) bears a secondary carving of a sword with a simple pommel and crossguard.[40] However, it is so crudely executed and partially obscured by what appears to be a rectangular shield that it is of little value in the study of Pictish swords.

Most of the swords depicted on Pictish cross-slabs remain in their scabbards. The only exceptions are in the Aberlemno battle scene, where a foot soldier and mounted warrior both wield swords, the duelling warriors on the Shandwick (Easter Ross) cross-slab and the mounted hunter on the St Andrews (Fife) sarcophagus[41] (*see* Plates 8, 9 and 10). These reveal that Pictish swords were short, with broad, straight-sided and probably double-edged blades. A possible sword on the Meigle 2 cross-slab[42] differs from this form and resembles an angle-backed, single-edged Anglo-Saxon *seax*, although it could be a club or a stake. The tips of the drawn swords are either obscured or eroded, but they appear to have been rounded or possibly angular. These swords were intended for single-handed use and would have been ideal in close-quarter battle, for either slashing or stabbing.

All the swords depicted are similar in style, but some variations are detectable in their fittings.[43] Most swords have either short and straight crossguards, as on the Fowlis Wester 2 (Perthshire), Inchbrayock 1 (*see* Plate 11) and Kirriemuir 2 cross-slabs (both Angus), or crossguards that curve out from the hilt, as in the Aberlemno battle scene (*see* Plate 8) and on the possible sword on the Nigg cross-slab.[44] A hybrid form, also depicted in the Aberlemno battle scene, has a straight lower crossguard, at the top of the blade, and a slightly curved upper guard, at the top of the hilt. Pommels are either domed, as with the swords on the Fowlis Wester 2, Kirriemuir 2 and Nigg cross-slabs, or button-shaped, as on Samson's sword on the Inchbrayock 1 cross-slab. Both straight and curved crossguards are readily paralleled in Anglo-Saxon swords,[45] the former dating to the seventh and eighth centuries and the later from the mid-ninth century onwards. Attempts have been made to use the swords depicted in Pictish sculpture to date the stones on which they appear.[46] However, given the paucity of comparative material from within Pictland and the broad dating brackets assigned to most Anglo-Saxon swords, little confidence can be attached to this approach currently.

Although no complete Pictish swords survive, some decorative metalwork fittings do. All but one of these are from a hoard of eighth-century Pictish silverwork, buried below the floor of what was probably a Pictish church on St Ninian's Isle, Dunrossness (Shetland), and excavated in 1958.[47] The St Ninian's Isle hoard includes a silver-gilt sword pommel resembling the 'cocked hat' type, so-called from its shape[48] (*see* Plate 12). Finely decorated with symmetrically interlaced beasts, their bodies picked out with *pointillé* (punched dot) decoration, this clearly belonged to an elaborate sword. The pommel shows some similarities with the pommel of the drawn sword on the St Andrews sarcophagus and both are closely related to Anglo-Saxon examples of the eighth century.[49]

Another pommel, this time of bronze, was discovered in the Culbin Sands (Morayshire).[50] With a curved back and flat underside, from which two pins project to attach it to the hilt, this pommel is decorated with double-stranded interlace dated to the late sixth or early seventh century and has sockets that once held settings of glass or precious stones. In the absence of comparative examples from Pictland, both the Culbin Sands and St Ninian's Isle pommels have been identified as Anglo-Saxon,[51] although neither have exact parallels. However, both pommels are now widely accepted as Pictish on account of their distinctive decoration, discovery within Pictland and, in the case of the St Ninian's Isle pommel, its association with identifiably Pictish metalwork.

Silver sword and scabbard components are also claimed to have been present in the hoard of Pictish silverwork found in or near a burial mound known as Norrie's Law, Largo (Fife) in or around 1819.[52] Although most of the hoard was dispersed and melted down by jewellers soon afterwards, it reputedly included 'a small sword hook . . . the mouth-piece and tip of a very large sword-scabbard – an ornamented circular plate', although 'no parts or relics of the blade were discernible'.[53] These were interpreted as belonging to 'a large cross-hilted weapon, such as were commonly used with both hands'.[54] However, these artefacts were in a crushed condition when found and were soon recycled, while the descriptions were made from memory some twenty years after the hoard was discovered. The only surviving item, the mount with raised scroll ornament, was soon rejected as a scabbard fitting.[55] Moreover, the illustration accompanying this account[56] (see Plate 13), also drawn from memory, is completely anachronistic, depicting a cross-hilted sword of late or post-medieval form. As a result, little credence can be attached to the reported discovery of a sword, or sword components, in the Norrie's Law hoard.

Metalwork fittings were probably the preserve of only the most elaborate swords. The majority of swords likely had fittings manufactured from organic materials. Wooden and bone sword pommels are known from Iron Age Scotland and Ireland[57] and some Pictish swords probably incorporated components made from these materials. The only recorded example of this is a whalebone crossguard, found in early medieval levels during the excavation of a post-broch settlement at Upper Scalloway.[58]

The stylistic variations evident in sculptural depictions of Pictish swords may be interpreted in different ways. Dr Isabel Henderson[59] suggests that the swords of the Old Testament figures portrayed in Pictish sculpture – Jonah (Fowlis Wester), Samson (Inchbrayock 1) and the unidentified horseman on the St Andrews sarcophagus (*see* Plates 11 and 10) – differ in form and function from those used by the Picts who erected these monuments. But Henderson does not identify these differences, or the period or area from which the 'biblical' swords originated. In contrast, the swords shown in Pictish sculpture are consistent in form, with some stylistic variations in their crossguards and pommels, and related to Anglo-Saxon and Viking swords. Moreover, as conscious expressions of Pictish social order,[60] sculpture would have incorporated contemporary references, including both the appearance and weapons of the warriors portrayed. The swords depicted, therefore, were contemporary, at least in use if not also manufacture, with the monuments on which they appear. Differences between sword styles simply reflect the range of artistic influences operating within Pictland and the time-span over which these sculptures were erected, as fashions in sword fittings changed.

Sword scabbards were probably of wood and/or leather and have not survived. On the Inchbrayock 1 cross-slab (*see* Plate 11), a raised line running the length of the mounted warrior's scabbard may represent a seam in the leather or a strengthening mid-rib. Several scabbards depicted in Pictish sculpture have chapes, a scabbard mount or guard intended to protect the scabbard end and sword tip from damage and the warrior and his horse from accidental injury. Two types of chape are shown. Samson's scabbard on the Inchbrayock 1 cross-slab is protected by a contoured chape, a U-shaped band of metal wrapped around the edges of the tip of the scabbard. The expanded or crescentic form of chape appears more frequently in Pictish sculpture, but this may be because it is readily identifiable from the bulbous terminal of scabbards. More detailed examples, such as the scabbards of the horsemen on the Benvie and Meigle 3 cross-slabs[61] (*see* Plate 14), depict this as a horseshoe-shaped feature, indicating that it was a separate fitting, mounted on the end of these scabbards.

The bulbous form of sword chape may be paralleled directly by the only surviving Pictish examples, confirming the reliability of Pictish sculpture as a source of information on weapons. The St Ninian's Isle hoard includes two expanded chapes, one of silver, the other silver gilt, both decorated with animal-headed terminals in a style probably dating to the eighth century[62] (*see* Plate 15). The gilded chape bears a Latin inscription on each side: INNOMINEDS on the front and RESADFILISPUSSCIO on the reverse. The former is readily recognisable as *in nomine d[ei] s[ummi]*, 'in the name of God the highest'. But the interpretation of the inscription on the reverse is more controversial. Taking its theme from the first, this has been expanded as the second half of an inscription beginning on the other side of the chape: *res ad fili sp[irit]us s[an]c[t]io*, 'property of the son of the holy spirit'.[63] Alternatively, the inscriptions have been combined and expanded to read *In nomine d[eu]s Resad fili sp[irit]us s[an]c[t]i*, 'In the name of God, of the son, of the Holy Spirit, Resad', although this must dismiss the final letter o as a scribal error.[64] More straightfordly, and plausibly, it has also been read as *resad fili spusscio*, '[Property of] Resad son of Spusscio', an ownership inscription,[65] although both names are otherwise unattested. Ownership inscriptions and Christian dedications are sometimes found on Anglo-Saxon sword-blades and scabbards,[66] while the dedicatory inscription on the Anglo-Saxon helmet from Coppergate, York,[67] provides a parallel.

Three silver-gilt cone-shaped hollow mounts from the St Ninian's Isle hoard may also be sword or scabbard fittings. These vary slightly in size and are decorated in different styles, one with interlaced beasts, another with panels of spirals and zoomorphic interlace and the third with interlocking spirals.[68] A pair of slots in the baseplate of each mount would have enabled them to be suspended from cords or straps and signs of wear on the tips of the cones supports this interpretation. The function of these mounts remains unclear but they may have decorated a sword belt or harness, or functioned as belt adjusters or fasteners.[69] Alternative, though less probable, interpretations of the mounts' function include buttons and shield fittings.[70] More controversially, the sword and scabbard fittings from the St Ninian's Isle hoard are claimed to have had ecclesiastical functions, the sword pommel and mounts as fittings from a *flabellum* or liturgical fan and the chapes as strap ends from a cleric's vestments.[71] But this interpretation has not been accepted widely.

The pommel, chapes and mounts from the St Ninian's Isle hoard are superb examples of craftsmanship and their presence in this peripheral part of Pictland only hints at the rich weaponry that must have existed in the Pictish heartland. Their quality emphasises that, in addition to being lethal instruments of war, swords were also potent symbols of status. Not every Pictish warrior would have owned a sword, certainly not of the richness consistent with the fittings in the St Ninian's Isle hoard. The expertise and resources, in precious materials and skilled labour, required to produce such weapons and their fittings ensured that their possession was restricted to members of a warrior élite. Few artefacts attest the close links that must have existed between the Pictish nobility and warfare as vividly as elaborately decorated swords. Swords were weapons of prestige, well suited to the symbolic display of status both on and off the battlefield. Adomnán[72] reveals that elaborately ornamented swords were also used to conduct social transactions in the form of gift-giving, describing how an Irish layman was presented with 'a sword decorated with shaped pieces of ivory' by Columba to offer to his lord as a gift for his freedom.

SPEARS

The arms of the common Pictish and Scottish foot soldier were the spear and shield and each commoner liable for military service was probably required to supply his own or they may have been provided by his lord. Reflecting their widespread possession, Adomnán[73] records separate incidents in which spears were used in acts of casual violence. The spear is a simple weapon to manufacture and use, comprising a long, straight wooden shaft tipped with a spearhead. Adomnán[74] describes a man scraping the bark from a wooden spear shaft ([h]astili) with a small knife. At its simplest, a stout wooden shaft with a fire-hardened point makes a serviceable improvised weapon. However, in the early medieval period spearheads were of iron, socketed to enable them to be mounted on the shaft and often secured with a rivet and/or binding.

The spear is a versatile, multi-purpose weapon. It makes an excellent thrusting weapon for foot soldiers engaged in close-quarter battle against either infantry or cavalry. This function is described by Adomnán:[75] 'a strong man's powerful thrust of a very sharp spear' was mistakenly believed to have transfixed his intended victim. A spear can also be used underarm, as a lance, by mounted warriors. Here, its effectiveness relies solely on the momentum of the charging cavalryman. Alternatively, spears may be thrown overarm, as javelins, by either mounted or foot soldiers, enabling them to attack from a distance. Adomnán[76] refers to all three types of weapon: spear (*hasta*), lance (*lancea*) and javelin (*iaculum*). The Aberlemno battle scene depicts cavalrymen using spears in two of these ways, as lances and javelins.[77]

These different functions were probably reflected in the forms of the spears themselves. A smaller, lighter projectile head would be better suited for a javelin, while a larger, heavier spearhead would be more appropriate for thrusting. Different types of spear may be depicted in a scene on a Pictish symbol stone from the Brough of Birsay[78] (*see* Plate 16), an important Pictish political centre in Orkney.[79] The first in a line of three warriors carries a spear comprising a long, stout shaft tipped with a large leaf-shaped blade. This is the usual form of spearhead depicted in Pictish sculpture and would have made an ideal thrusting weapon. A constructional detail, comprising a line running the length of this spearhead, probably represents a mid-rib or possibly a corrugated blade. Both features give greater longitudinal strength to a spearhead, increasing its effectiveness at piercing shields and armour. The men behind the leading warrior carry spears with slightly shorter, more slender shafts and smaller, narrower spearheads, suggesting that they were intended for throwing rather than thrusting. But it is unclear whether the Brough of Birsay stone displays a genuine distinction between spears and javelins or if it symbolises differences in the status of the soldiers portrayed, as the leading warrior is clearly of higher rank.[80]

Several Pictish and Scottish spearheads survive. This probably reflects their more common possession and use, in contrast to the more socially restricted ownership of swords. Moreover, the relatively solid mass of at least the larger spearheads assists their survival, as well as their retrieval and identification during excavation. The most productive site is the Scottish fortress of Dunadd, where excavations yielded seven spearheads[81] (see Plate 17), while Dunollie produced a single spearhead.[82] Pictish royal fortresses also possess potential for yielding weapons, as the reported discovery of 'many . . . spear-heads'[83] during the nineteenth-century excavations at Burghead reveals. However, the bronze spearhead reportedly found there[84] is probably not Pictish but is more likely to date to the late Bronze Age (c. 1200–c. 700 BC). As none of the spearheads from Burghead were recorded or kept, their form and date are unknown.

Fortunately, a small number of spearheads have been found during the excavation of other Pictish sites. A leaf-shaped spearhead, apparently socketed but with most of the socket missing, was found on the Brough of Birsay.[85] Excavation of a pair of ringforts at Aldclune (Perthshire) also yielded a spearhead thought to be associated with Pictish occupation of the site.[86] A well-preserved leaf-shaped iron spearhead, a spear socket, possibly from the same spearhead, and a ferrule, with wood still preserved in its socket, were found at Upper Scalloway.[87] More unusually, the only weapon known to have been found in a Pictish grave was a fragment of an iron socket, all that survived of a spearhead. This was discovered in 1854 at Dunrobin (Sutherland), in a slab-lined grave containing two adult males and covered with a Pictish symbol stone.[88]

These surviving spearheads vary in form, perhaps reflecting their different functions. Most have contiguous sockets, but those with extended sockets would have helped to prevent the spearhead from breaking or being chopped off its spearshaft in close-quarter battle. The leaf-shaped spearheads from Dunadd and Upper Scalloway belonged to heavier weapons, their broad blades, heavy mid-ribs and long and wide sockets indicating that they were intended for thrusting, but making them less suitable for throwing, particularly with accuracy over distance. The spearheads from Dunadd also include a more slender and angular example, its lighter and more aerodynamic form suggesting that it was designed for throwing. Its short socket and slender neck indicate that it represents an *angon*, a native adaptation ultimately derived from the Roman *pilum* or javelin. This is similar to the two smaller spearheads depicted on the Brough of Birsay stone. The forms of the few surviving

1. *The Annals of Ulster (Trinity College Library, Dublin, MS 1282, fol. 29v). The lower paragraph includes the first and the start of the second entries made under the year 735 (for AD 736), which record a series of defeats inflicted on the Scots by the Picts under King Unuist son of Urguist, including the devastatio of Dál Riata, capture of Dunadd and the battle of Cnoc Cairpri. (Copyright: The Board of Trinity College Dublin.)*

2. *The* Senchus fer nAlban *(Trinity College Library, Dublin, MS 1298, cols 68–9), originally compiled in the seventh century as a civil survey of* Dál Riata *and recording the military and naval service that could be levied from each kindred of* Dál Riata. (Copyright: The Board of Trinity College Dublin.)

3. *Clatchard Craig, Fife. An oblique aerial view showing the multiple ramparts of the Pictish hillfort.* (Crown Copyright: Royal Commission on the Ancient and Historical Monuments of Scotland.)

4. *An oblique aerial view of the hillfort at Dundurn, Perthshire. This Pictish royal fortress defends upper Strathearn, effectively blocking any Scottish incursions from the west. The scree-strewn hillsides are not the result of natural processes, but comprise collapsed rampart material.* (Crown Copyright: Royal Commission on the Ancient and Historical Monuments of Scotland.)

5. *Dunadd, Argyll. An oblique aerial view of the hillfort and probable inauguration place of the kings of Dál Riata. The River Add, with its numerous oxbows, meanders past the hill on the right towards Crinan Bay, one of the best natural harbours on the west coast of Scotland.* (Copyright: Dr **Stephen T. Driscoll.**)

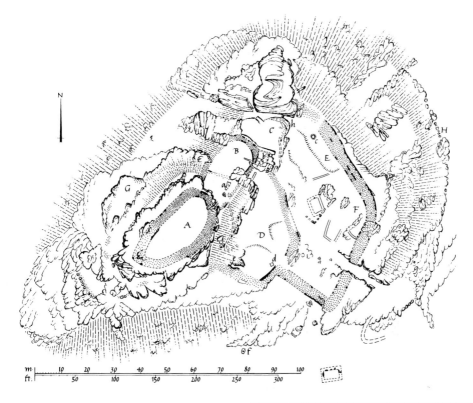

N

| m | 10 | 20 | 30 | 40 | 50 | 60 | 70 | 80 | 90 | 100 |
| ft. | 50 | 100 | 150 | 200 | 250 | 300 | | | | |

6. *A plan of the hillfort, Dunadd, showing the hilltop 'citadel' and the fortified lower terraces.* (Crown Copyright: Royal Commission on the Ancient and Historical Monuments of Scotland.)

7. *One of four panels from the extensive battle scene on the reverse of Sueno's Stone, Forres, Morayshire. This massive cross-slab, standing over 6.5 m high, probably dates to the tenth century and records a historical confrontation between the armies of a king of* Alba *and a* mormaer *of Moray.* (Crown copyright: Historic Scotland.)

8. *The Aberlemno battle scene on the reverse of the cross-slab in Aberlemno kirkyard, Angus. This scene is widely believed to depict the Battle of Dunnichen, in which the Picts defeated the Northumbrians in 685.* (Copyright: Tom and Sybil Gray Collection.)

9. *The hunting scene (panel 3), including duelling swordsmen (lower left) and a crossbowman (lower right), on the reverse of the cross-slab at Shandwick, Ross and Cromarty.* (Copyright: Tom and Sybil Gray Collection.)

10. *The hunting scene with, right, the biblical David rending the jaws of a lion on the side panel (stone 1) of the St Andrews sarcophagus, Fife.* (Crown Copyright: Royal Commission on the Ancient and Historical Monuments of Scotland.)

11. *The biblical Samson and a mounted warrior on the reverse of the Inchbrayock 1 cross-slab, Angus.* (Copyright: Tom and Sybil Gray Collection.)

Pictish and Scottish spearheads therefore reflect the range of functions recorded by Adomnán.

A distinctive feature of the spearhead from Dunadd is its cleft or split-sided socket, also found in the spear socket from Upper Scalloway. This enabled the spearhead to be secured on the spearshaft by hammering the sides of the socket tightly together around the end of the spear shaft. As with Anglo-Saxon examples, the attachment of the spearhead on the shaft may have been strengthened with one or two iron rivets, an iron binding ring around the socket or with twine, although no traces of these are detectable on surviving Pictish or Scottish spearheads. Split-sided sockets are claimed to be characteristic of Anglo-Saxon spearheads.[89] But this type of spear socket occurred more widely than Anglo-Saxon England, the extent of its distribution obscured by the few examples found further afield.

The other end of the spear shaft, the butt, is also significant. Spear shafts were sometimes tipped with a ferrule, a simple cylindrical or conical iron binding. Ferrules are not detectable on the spears shown in Pictish sculpture but at least twenty-four socketed and pointed iron ferrules, probably from spear shafts, have been found at Dunadd.[90] The narrow diameter of their sockets, between 11 and 16 mm, suggests that they belonged to slender spear shafts. The weapons concerned were therefore probably javelins, supporting the interpretation of some of the spearheads from Dunadd. However, the narrow diameter (10 mm) of four similar artefacts from Dunollie led the excavators to query their interpretation as spear ferrules and propose that they are arrowtips instead.[91]

In contrast to small ferrules, the Classical historian Cassius Dio[92] describes how, during the emperor Septimius Severus' campaigns in Scotland in 208 or 209 to 210,[93] the *Caledonii* and *Maeatae* fought with 'a short spear with a bronze apple attached to the end of the spear-shaft, so that when it is shaken it may clash and terrify the enemy'. By beating the spearbutt against their shields they could produce a deafening noise to intimidate their enemies. But a knobbed spearbutt had more than just a psychological impact. It was also a clubbing weapon and may have helped to balance the spear, although a spear with a weighty butt is unlikely to have been intended for throwing. Bronze spearbutts of the distinctive 'doorknob' type described by Cassius Dio, and the clay moulds in which they were cast, occur widely in Scotland and Ireland.[94] These take the form of a large, spherical or sub-spherical basal knob of cast bronze, from which extends a cylindrical or funnel-shaped socket (*see* Plate 18). Knobbed spearbutts occur in archaeological contexts dating from the first century BC to the second or third centuries AD.[95] Cassius Dio's account confirms that the knobbed spearbutt survived in Scotland into at least the third century. But it is now claimed that knobbed spearbutts are more securely dated to the third to fifth centuries,[96] suggesting that they were used by the early Picts and certainly by their late Iron Age ancestors.

No traces of butts of any type are visible on the spears depicted in Pictish sculpture. The resemblance of the Z-rod component of some Pictish symbols to a broken spear with a knobbed butt is sometimes noted.[97] But although the ball-ended feature of the Z-rod is reminiscent of a knobbed spearbutt, the resemblance is superficial and is attributable to the twin curlicues or tendril-like decorations that adorn this symbol, while the other end is also decorated with a set of floriations or curlicue-like features. These features are not easily compatible with the interpretation of the Z-rod as a broken spear and alternative interpretations have been proposed.[98] Even if the Z-rod was ultimately modelled on a spear, it is now so stylised that it reveals nothing about Pictish spears. More fundamentally, the Z-rod never occurs by itself, but only in combination with a very limited range of symbols, superimposed on the double-disc, notched rectangle and snake. The Z-rod therefore has no meaning by itself[99] and, as a result, is unlikely to represent a spear.

Although knobbed spearbutts do not appear on Pictish symbol stones or cross-slabs, two examples occur on a less easily categorised form of sculpture. The incised figures on the Newton of Collessie (Fife) and Rhynie 3 (Aberdeenshire) stones both carry spears with knobbed spearbutts[100] (*see* Plate 19). The date(s) of these carvings are uncertain, but they are widely believed to be Pictish. Both are associated with simple horseshoe symbols, an early Pictish symbol.[101] The similar appearance of the Collessie and Rhynie 3 warriors, and a less well preserved one at Westerton of Balgavies (Angus)[102] suggests that they represent the same figure. The figure depicted has been interpreted as an ancient hero or mythical being, possibly a Pictish warrior god. This supposedly explains the archaic form of his shield and spear, which are claimed to be anachronistic representations, based on Iron Age forms.[103] More plausibly, these sculptures date from a period preceding the transition from shields and spears of styles that are characteristic of the late Iron Age to those that are more familiar from sculpture of the eighth and ninth centuries. Although not closely datable, this suggests an early date for the Collessie and Rhynie 3 carvings, perhaps no later than the fifth or sixth centuries.

## SHIELDS

One item of military equipment common to most mounted and foot soldiers portrayed in Pictish sculpture is the shield. Indeed, Pictish warriors are rarely portrayed without their shields and, when they are, it is in hunting rather than battle scenes. Every Pict and Scot eligible for military service probably had a shield and would have been unlikely to attend muster or go on campaign without it. Despite their widespread use, no Pictish or Scottish shields or their fittings are known to survive, probably reflecting their construction from mostly organic materials.

The only possible exceptions to this are from the Norrie's Law hoard. This reputedly included a shield measuring 16 inches by 10 inches (406 mm by 254 mm) that was 'heart-shaped and had upon it the figure of a man on horseback'.[104] However, both this description and an illustration[105] (*see* Plate 13) were made from memory, twenty years after the discovery of the hoard. Anachronistically, the illustration shows a shield of a style belonging to the high Middle Ages, decorated with a mounted figure based on the artist's knowledge of equestrian scenes in Pictish sculpture.[106] As a result, the description and illustration of the Norrie's Law 'shield' cannot be accepted as reliable.

Despite this, the surviving contents of the Norrie's Law hoard may still contain the only known remains of a Pictish shield. Up to twenty-six fragments of scrap silver from the hoard belong to a circular plate, 440 mm in diameter, decorated with a border of *repoussé* (raised) squares around its cut rim.[107] This plaque bears the impression of two smaller roundels, each of which was fastened at the centre by means of a perforation in the plaque. Although neither roundel is still attached, a compressed boss in the hoard matches one impression and another boss in the hoard may also have adorned a shield.[108] The plaque has been interpreted as the silver covering or mount for a leather or wooden shield.[109] Although this silver cover would have provided little or no protection against attack, this shield would not have been for use in battle, but for display on ceremonial occasions. This is supported not only by the parallel of ceremonial shields in Bronze Age and Iron Age Britain but also by sculptural evidence for such shields among the Picts.[110] Like the silver sword and scabbard fittings from St Ninian's Isle, a silver shield cover would have been a striking symbol of power.

In the absence of surviving examples, the study of Pictish shields is wholly dependent on sculptural evidence. The many shields depicted reveal much about their form, from which their construction and use[111] may be inferred. The shields depicted in Pictish sculpture are either round or square/rectangular in form. Round shields are by far the most common and are carried by mounted and, occasionally, foot soldiers. However, the preponderance of circular shields may be due to the greater number of mounted warriors, who are shown using only circular shields, portrayed in

Pictish sculpture. Round shields occur widely throughout early medieval Europe and may have been copied by the Picts from their neighbours.

Square or rectangular shields are only carried by foot soldiers in Pictish sculpture, their angular form making them unsuitable for horsemen. Although claimed that square and rectangular shields were modelled on Roman prototypes or inspired by illustrations in Continental manuscripts,[112] they probably originated in indigenous Iron Age designs. The Roman distance slabs from the Antonine Wall at Bridgeness (West Lothian) and Summerston (Lanarkshire), dating to 139–42, portray Iron Age warriors with rectangular shields with a round central boss[113] (*see* Plate 20). An undated but probably Iron Age shield of this form survives from Ireland.[114] The rectangular shields carried by the figures on the Collessie and Rhynie 3 stones are similar to Iron Age examples, although the latter shield lacks a boss. A secondary carving of a rectangular shield with a roughly circular central boss on a Pictish symbol stone at Newton of Lewesk[115] suggests that this form of shield survived into the early medieval period. But the absence of rectangular shields from Pictish relief sculpture indicates that they had fallen out of use by the eighth century.

Square shields appear less frequently than round examples in Pictish sculpture, possibly reflecting the smaller number of foot soldiers portrayed. The best example is provided by a group of three warriors, carved in relief on a symbol stone from the Brough of Birsay (*see* Plate 16). Although foot soldiers were usually commoners, the noble status of these warriors is apparent from their appearance[116] and the swords hanging from their belts. All three soldiers carry square shields of the same size, although one is more highly decorated than the others.[117] Their decoration suggests that these were 'parade shields', intended for display on ceremonial occasions rather than for use in battle. This is supported by the warriors standing in line, as if in procession. A possible ritual procession is also depicted on the Fowlis Wester 1 (Perthshire) cross-slab,[118] where a cow is led by one person and followed by a line of six men, two of whom hold what appear to be square shields. However, the sculpture is very eroded and the square shapes may represent other artefacts, perhaps buckets.[119]

Although a ceremonial function seems likely, the Brough of Birsay shields exhibit the same constructional details apparent on round shields, including a shield boss and reinforced edges.[120] Moreover, the Brough of Birsay warriors are also armed with the foot soldier's usual equipment of shield and spear. Lastly, the functional nature of at least some square shields is demonstrated by the duelling swordsmen carrying roughly square shields, although with slightly concave upper and lower edges, on the Shandwick stone and by warriors on the Aberlemno 3, Eassie and Nigg cross-slabs.[121]

A rare variant of the rectangular shield has distinctively indented or notched upper and lower (shorter) edges, producing an H-shaped form. Although widely considered to be a characteristically Pictish form of shield,[122] the only example in Pictish sculpture is on the St Andrews sarcophagus, dating to *c.* 800–850[123] (*see* Plate 10). The only other recorded example occurs on a ninth-century cross at Ardchattan (Argyll),[124] which is also the only shield depicted in sculpture from *Dál Riata*. This reveals that indented shields were also used by the Scots, unless the Ardchattan cross portrays a Pictish warrior, and indicates that Scottish shields were similar in form and construction to Pictish examples.

The dates of these sculptures suggest that the indented shield represents a late development in shield design. This contrasts with claims that it originated in the Iron Age.[125] The Iron Age prototypes claimed from Deal (Kent) and Salisbury (Wiltshire),[126] which probably date to the second or first centuries BC, are unconvincing because these 'hide-shaped' shields are essentially oval, not rectangular, in form, with convexly bowed long sides and concavely bowed short upper and lower ends. Moreover, the Deal and Salisbury shields are far removed, in both space and time, from those of Pictland. The indented shield is unparalleled, suggesting that it may have been a short-lived form or that the sculptors of both monuments were working from a common model.[127] As a result, it remains of enigmatic origin, cultural association(s) and significance.

Although Pictish shields vary in size, they tend to be relatively small, indicating that they were intended to protect only the face and upper body in light and mobile warfare. However, some shields are exceptionally small. The indented shield on the St Andrews sarcophagus is so small that it covers only the hunter's hand (*see* Plate 10). Square or rectangular shields of comparable size are represented on the Eassie and Kirriemuir 2 cross-slabs (both Angus).[128] In addition, two round shields held by a figure on the Nigg cross-slab[129] are unusually small. All these shields cannot have offered much protection in the thick of battle and would have been no use in forming a shield wall. Instead, these are bucklers or 'fist-shields', specifically intended for use in single combat.[130] This is exactly what is portrayed on the Shandwick cross-slab, where two men fight with swords, their fist-shields raised, ready to parry any sword-blows (*see* Plate 9).

As no shields or shield fittings survive, our knowledge of their construction is also dependent on sculptural evidence. Several constructional features are detectable. Both round and square shields appear to be of simple construction. Anglo-Saxon parallels[131] suggest that they were probably of wooden board or planks, perhaps covered with leather. This technique for manufacturing small, round shields, known as targes or targets, survived in the Highlands until the Jacobite Rebellion of 1745. The edges of several Pictish shields, both round and square, are defined by two closely set lines, as on the round shields on the Inchbrayock 1 and Kirriemuir 3 cross-slabs[132] (*see* Plate 11). This represents leather or metal binding strips, U-shaped in section, which would have secured the leather covering to the underlying board and strengthened the shield rim. The objective of this was to minimise the principal weakness of a wooden shield, that it could be split in two with a well-aimed sword or axe blow, leaving a warrior defenceless.

But not all Pictish shields were of flat boards. As in Anglo-Saxon England,[133] both flat and convex shields appear to have been used by the Picts. Several circular shields bear a roundel design of concentric circles, as with those on the Benvie and Menmuir 1 cross-slabs[134] (*see* Plate 14). This may represent their construction from laminated wood or leather, with the shield being of greater thickness towards its centre. This is supported by side views of shields in the Aberlemno battle scene (*see* Plate 8) and on the Murthly (Perthshire) panel.[135] These are shown in cross section, their crescentic form suggesting that round shields were domed rather than flat. This would be more difficult, though not impossible, to produce in wood, indicating that they were of leather pressed on a wooden mould. Although the Pictish crescent symbol is claimed to represent a side view of a small circular shield,[136] the absence of a boss argues against this interpretation.

The external face of round shields is often depicted with a centrally set circular feature (*see* Plates 11, 14 and 21). This is a conical or pointed boss, as revealed by those shields shown in profile (*see* Plate 8). Metallic shield bosses would have been secured to the shield with a flange around their outer rim, as with Anglo-Saxon examples.[137] But the absence of flanges, which might have been represented by a double line in sculptural representations of shields, suggests that Pictish shield bosses were of leather or wood instead. The boss also provided a secure feature to which a short strap or handle grip could be attached to the inside of the shield and protected the warrior's hand when holding the shield. This is shown by the warrior in the front rank in the Aberlemno battle scene (*see* Plate 8).

Pictish shields were also fitted with a *guige*, a long cord or strap with two main functions. This enabled shields to be suspended when not in use, either slung across the back when warriors were not under threat or from the walls of a hall when warriors were not on campaign. A shield could also be hung around the neck by a *guige*, as shown on the horsemen on the Benvie cross-slab and Burghead 8 fragment and the foot soldiers on the right side of the Dupplin cross[138] (*see* Plates 14 and 21). The purpose of this was to leave both hands free to hold the reins and/or a weapon, while still deriving protection from the shield by suspending it across the upper body. This is clearly visible in the Aberlemno battle scene[139] (*see* Plate 8).

Of the many round shields depicted in Pictish sculpture, not one has a square boss.[140] However, other forms of shield boss are portrayed in Pictish sculpture. Just as round shields have round bosses, the square shields on the Brough of Birsay stone have square ones (*see* Plate 16), although this could also represent a decorative panel. Unusually, the indented shield on the St Andrews sarcophagus has a round boss with a depressed centre. The arrangement of the paired circles on either side of the central boss on two shields on the Brough of Birsay stone suggests that these were rivets securing either the shield boss to the shield itself or the hand-grip to the inside of the shield. The use of rivets indicates that these bosses may have been metallic, perhaps in keeping with their ceremonial character and the high status of their owners. Arrangements of what appear to be studs occur on either side of, and across, the central boss on the round shields shown on the Dull and Murthly panels respectively.[141] These are probably the bosses of board rivets. Although their symmetrical arrangement is decorative, they would also have strengthened a shield by securing the leather covering to the wooden board beneath. Alternatively, these rivets may have secured two arm straps, enabling a larger, heavier shield to be carried on the arm.[142] Although none of the shields concerned are held by horsemen, arm straps would have freed their left hands to hold the reins, while gripping a spear or sword in the right hand.[143]

Overtly decorative features also appear on Pictish shields. The leading warrior on the Brough of Birsay stone carries a shield bearing a possibly foliate design. This could have been painted, carved or burned onto the surface of the shield or, alternatively, may comprise metalwork fittings. Several geometric and zoomorphic metalwork appliqués from Anglo-Saxon shields survive, notably in the Sutton Hoo ship burial,[144] although no comparable Pictish or Scottish examples are recorded. No known items of Pictish metalwork appear to have been shield fittings. The crescentic bronze plaque from Laws, Monifieth (Angus) is decorated on both sides, indicating that both were visible, while it and the plaques from Norrie's Law[145] have no means for securing them to a shield. The surviving contents of the Norrie's Law hoard include a broken sub-oval disc with a central rectangular hole, decorated with three, originally four, *repoussé* snail-shell spiral bosses.[146] This is suggestive of the spiral decorations on the shield of the leading warrior on the Brough of Birsay stone and may be a decorative fitting from a ceremonial shield. But the disc appears to have been cut from a larger artefact and, without knowledge of its original form, its function is unclear.

Most Pictish shields, if decorated at all, would have borne simpler decoration. If not a constructional feature, the distinctive roundel design shown on many circular shields may be decorative, perhaps representing painted bands. Limed, waxed and white-painted shields are mentioned in *The Gododdin*[147] and in the poem *The Birth of Aedán mac Gabráin*[148] of *c.* 1060, suggesting that shields were usually painted white. More unusual, but obviously decorative, the round shield on the Dull stone bears a quartered design, indicating that it was painted in different colours. Distinctively painted shields could have assisted identification on the battlefield, either of individual warriors, those under the command of the same noble and/or in the same warband or army.

## BOWS AND CROSSBOWS

Evidence for archery in Scotland begins remarkably early, with a surviving bow dated to *c.* 3800 BC.[149] But there is little evidence of archery among the Picts and Scots. This may parallel the situation in Anglo-Saxon England,[150] although the bow is now thought to have played a more significant role in Anglo-Saxon warfare than previously.[151] Nevertheless, crossbows are shown on four Pictish stones: St Vigeans 1 (the 'Drosten Stone') (Angus), Shandwick (Ross and Cromarty) (*see* Plate 9), Glenferness (Nairnshire) and the lost Meigle 10 panel (Perthshire).[152] In addition, a fifth crossbowman is sketched on a stone from Jarlshof (Shetland).[153]

The weapons depicted are clearly crossbows and not simple bows.[154] Either ready or preparing to fire at a target, the crossbowmen hold the stock or tiller and not the bow itself. But in each case the crossbow is shown in plan, at right angles to the position in which it would have been held when firing. This is artistic licence, enabling the sculptor to portray a clearly identifiable crossbow, which it would not have been if shown in profile. The stock, across which the bow was attached, would have had a groove in which the bolt rested and a simple mechanism, comprising a notched nut for holding the tensed bowstring and a trigger for releasing it. These crossbows are all of an early form and would have been spanned or cocked by hand. Without a foot stirrup at the end of the stock, which is characteristic of crossbows of the high Middle Ages, the crossbowman would simply have stood on the bow and pulled back the bowstring. There is no evidence for crossbows in *Dál Riata*, although it would be surprising if they were not used there.

The crossbow would have been effective on the battlefield, its bolt probably capable of penetrating armour or shields. Despite this, all crossbowmen depicted appear in hunting rather than battle scenes. This may simply reflect the fact that hunting scenes are much more common than battle scenes in Pictish sculpture but it casts some doubt on whether the crossbow was used in Pictish warfare. This is paralleled by the absence of evidence for its use in warfare by the Anglo-Saxons and Vikings.[155] Crossbows have one great weakness, limiting their effectiveness in battle. They are slow to span and (re)load, giving them a much slower rate of fire than the simple bow. This left crossbowmen vulnerable to attack and would have reduced their success in mobile warfare. Crossbowmen also needed both hands to span and fire their weapon and, without the protection of a shield, were even more exposed to attack. However, crossbows may have been useful in more static warfare, such as sieges.

The only sculptural evidence of archery in early medieval Scottish warfare is on Sueno's Stone (*see* Plate 7), although this is too weathered to distinguish whether the two warriors concerned hold bows or crossbows. Although simple bows are much easier and quicker to use than crossbows, there is also no evidence of their use in warfare by the Picts. A claim that Pictish sculpture depicts the use of longbows in warfare[156] is unsupported by the evidence and the longbow is anachronistic, belonging to warfare of the high Middle Ages. Pictish symbols have also been cited as evidence for the bow. The V-rod component of Pictish symbols, usually superimposed on a crescent, is claimed to be an (apparently broken) arrow,[157] although the crescent does not appear to represent a bow. A unique symbol on the Congash 2 (Inverness-shire) stone[158] is frequently, if tentatively, identified as a bow and arrow,[159] but is too stylised to interpret confidently.[160]

Could the conventions and values surrounding Pictish warfare have deterred the use of bows and crossbows in battle? Single combat and/or close-quarter battle were of great importance to a society that valued martial prowess and the courage, strength and leadership that it required.[161] Distanced from their targets, archers and crossbowmen had fewer opportunities to display these qualities and, as a result, may have been perceived as inferior. By possibly contravening the heroic ideals of hand-to-hand combat, bows and crossbows may not have been favoured weapons. A related factor here may have been the absence of any effective defence against the great penetrative power of the crossbow, a concern during the high Middle Ages that led to the Lateran Council of 1139 banning the use of the crossbow in warfare.

Not surprisingly, as their components were largely organic, no Pictish bows, crossbows or their fittings survive. A lathe-turned crossbow nut of antler found in an unstratified context during excavations at Urquhart Castle (Inverness-shire) appears to be medieval or later in date.[162] Similar nuts were probably used in Pictish crossbows and certainly occur elsewhere in early medieval Scotland, as an example from Buiston crannog (Ayrshire) proves.[163] Iron projectile heads are more likely to survive. Socketed iron arrowheads and simple conical arrowtips have been found at Dunadd (four arrowheads) and Dunollie (one arrowhead and four 'arrowtips').[164] Arrowheads and crossbow bolts can sometimes be distinguished by their form. Those from Dunadd include a simple, socketed head with a leaf-shaped blade with mid-rib, which appears to be an arrowhead. In contrast, a square-sectioned projectile head with a slender circular-sectioned stem and socket, measuring 95 mm in overall length, probably belongs to a crossbow bolt. This is closely paralleled by three bolts from Buiston crannog.[165]

## AXES

The axe was a favoured weapon among the Anglo-Saxons and the Vikings[166] and was well suited for close-quarter battle, particularly against armoured opponents. But, despite claims that the Picts used axes in warfare,[167] the evidence is slight. Axes are depicted being used as weapons in only one scene in Pictish sculpture, in a single combat on the Glamis Manse (Glamis 2) (Angus) stone[168] (*see* Plate 22). In addition, a man holds an axe in an aggressive stance on the stone from Barflat, Rhynie (Rhynie 7) (Aberdeenshire)[169] (*see* Plate 23). And on the Golspie (Sutherland) stone,[170] a man with an axe in his right hand and a knife or dagger in his left apparently defends himself from a dog or wolf, although the animal's proximity may be coincidental. That the figures concerned are not shown with shields suggests that they are not soldiers. These are not battle scenes. As a multi-purpose and commonly available domestic implement, axes would have been readily available for use in either self-defence, against man or beast, or in acts of casual violence. For example, Columba prophesied that a noble would die on a threshing floor after being struck by an axe.[171] This parallels the reported tendency of the Irish to use their axes as weapons in the heat of the moment.[172]

Casting further doubt on the use of the axe in warfare by the Picts, axes are usually associated with hybrid mythological creatures in Pictish sculpture. Centaurs carry axes on the Aberlemno 3, Gask 1A, Glamis Manse and Meigle 2 cross-slabs.[173] Bird-headed men are depicted with axes on the Glamis 1 and Rossie Priory (Perthshire) cross-slabs, while the arms of a bird-headed warrior on the Murthly panel terminate in a shield and an axe or club.[174] In addition, two creatures with human bodies, heads and arms but the beaks and legs of a bird both hold axes on the cross-slab from Papil, Island of Burra (Shetland).[175] Another fantastic creature, a dog- or wolf-headed man on the Mail (Shetland) stone also holds an axe.[176] These scenes reveal that the axe was associated with mythological beings and otherworldly violence, the Pictish equivalent of Odin's hammer in Norse mythology. This has implications for the interpretation of the scenes on the Glamis Manse, Golspie and Rhynie 7 stones. These do not refer to everyday life and the unusual axe-wielding figures portrayed are probably not ordinary men but mythological characters or gods.

Three types of axe are depicted in Pictish sculpture. The axes wielded by the warriors on the Glamis Manse stone and by the Rhynie man have narrow heads and short blades, consistent with their function as axe-hammers, and also have long handles. Although described as battle-axes,[177] these lack the broad, curving blades characteristic of Anglo-Saxon, Viking and later weapons. Other axes, such as those carried by the centaur on the Glamis Manse stone, have broader blades and triangular or square heads. But most distinctive is the short-handled and broad-bladed T-shaped axe held by the man on the Golspie stone, while a centaur on the Aberlemno 3 cross-slab holds two T-shaped axes. Although claimed to be a weapon of the Picts,[178] the T-shaped axe is a woodworking tool, used widely throughout early medieval Europe.[179]

Few Pictish or Scottish axes survive. Although 'many . . . battle-axes' and an iron axe or axehead were reportedly found during excavations at Burghead in the late nineteenth century[180] these were soon lost. These were probably interpreted as battle-axes simply because they were found within a fort. In *Dál Riata*, a T-shaped axehead was found in a seventh- to tenth-century context within the fort at Dunollie.[181]

The axe was not a normal weapon of war among the Picts. Although it is possible that axes were used in combat by the Picts and Scots, there is no evidence for this or for the existence of specialised battle-axes. The function of the battle-axe was primarily to penetrate chain mail or other armour. In the absence of evidence for their use among the Picts or Scots,[182] it is unlikely that battle-axes were also used.

## KNIVES AND DAGGERS

The knife was an even more versatile and universal artefact than the axe. Reflecting this, small domestic or craft knives have been found on various sites, including Dunadd, where forty-nine examples or fragments have been found.[183] These implements were unsuitable for use in warfare, probably accounting for their rarity in Pictish sculpture. The only knife-wielding figure, the man on the Golspie stone, was discussed above. Knives could also be used in the manufacture of some weapons and Adomnán[184] describes the use of a small knife (*cultellus*) to scrape the bark from a spear shaft.

Daggers are more obviously offensive in character and, like swords, are also a convenient medium for expressing status. Although no daggers are detectable on the horsemen portrayed on Pictish cross-slabs, this may be due to Pictish sculptural convention, in which riders appear in profile, viewed from the left. A warrior's shield and sheathed sword, potent symbols of his status, therefore feature prominently. In contrast, his dagger would have been suspended from his belt on the opposite, right-hand, side, which is rarely shown. This is supported by the only dagger depicted in Pictish sculpture, which is worn on the right-hand side of the biblical David portrayed on the St Andrews sarcophagus. This is a long, angle-backed or curved dagger with a small crossguard and a domed pommel, held in a sheath decorated with interlace and a bird's head, suggesting that the lipped projection at its tip represents a stylised beak (*see* Plate 10).

This dagger is of a type known as a *seax* in Anglo-Saxon England and on the Continent, where it has seventh- to ninth-century parallels as a high-status weapon and a holy relic.[185] The sheath represented is paralleled by surviving examples thought to be of Anglo-Saxon manufacture and tenth- or eleventh-century date,[186] illustrating the divergent dates proposed for some early medieval weapons. Although probably not of Pictish manufacture, the dagger on the St Andrews sarcophagus may have been modelled on one owned by a Pictish king or kept in a Pictish monastery and which probably reached Pictland as a diplomatic gift[187] or as plunder. While the style and quality of this dagger may have been unusual or even exceptional in Pictland, the prominence accorded to it on the St Andrews sarcophagus strongly suggests that daggers were important symbols of status for Pictish kings and nobles.

## SLINGS, SLINGSHOTS AND STONES

Slings and stones were important weapons among the peoples of Iron Age Europe and to the Romans but their use appears to have declined during the early Middle Ages, when they were used mostly for hunting. Nevertheless, Mongan mac Fiachnai Lurgan died in Kintyre in 625 after a Briton, or possibly a Pict,[188] struck him with a stone.[189] However, the circumstances are unclear and there is no evidence that this incident occurred in battle or that a sling was used; the stone could simply have been thrown.

Quartzite pebbles, painted with a range of simple designs of dots and curving lines, have been found in Caithness, Orkney and Shetland.[190] These are imprecisely dated but occur on settlement sites ranging from *c.* 400 to 900 and are therefore believed to be 'Pictish'. It has been suggested that these stones are slingshots, their designs being tribal in nature or messages intended to ensure that they hit their target.[191] However, a ritual interpretation, for example as charmstones to ward off evil spirits or treat illness, or as gaming counters, seems more likely.[192] The largest assemblage of painted pebbles from a single site is from the Pictish settlement at Upper Scalloway, which also yielded groups of small rounded pebbles.[193] Although sometimes referred to as slingstones, these are both lighter and rounder than slingstones found on Iron Age sites in southern England and may be gaming pieces instead.

## ARMOUR

Armour does not appear to have been used widely by the peoples of later Iron Age Scotland. Referring to the Severan campaigns against the *Caledonii* and *Maeatae*, Herodian[194] records that the *Britanni* 'are not familiar with the use of breast-plates and helmets, considering them to be an impediment to crossing the marshes'. In keeping with this, the only archaeological evidence for armour during this period is a fragment of chain mail from the first- or second-century metalwork hoard found in Carlingwark Loch (Kirkcudbrightshire).[195] Chain mail was also used during the early medieval period, particularly by the Anglo-Saxons[196] and, as *The Gododdin*[197] records, the North Britons. But the wearing of chain mail is unlikely to have been widespread because its production was a skilled and labour-intensive process, ensuring that mail shirts were restricted to a warrior élite. This is reinforced by the only surviving Anglo-Saxon mail shirt or hauberk, which was found in the Sutton Hoo royal ship burial.

Despite its use by neighbouring peoples, there is no evidence that Pictish or Scottish warriors wore chain mail or any other form of armour. Adomnán[198] refers to 'a coat of well-fortified and impenetrable armour' (*munitissima et inpenetrabilis lurica*), but this is a metaphor for something conferring divine protection. No surviving examples of armour from *Dál Riata* or Pictland are recorded. The only possible exception is the Norrie's Law hoard, which reputedly included 'part of a rich coat of scale-armour, the pieces of which consisted of small-sized lozenge-shaped plates of silver, suspended loosely by a hook from the upper corner'.[199] This is suggestive of *lorica squamata*, Roman scale armour,[200] the silver scales revealing that it was probably parade armour. But, in the absence of any surviving plates, this interpretation remains uncertain. If this was a suit of Roman scale armour, it presumably represents plunder[201] and therefore does not comprise evidence for the manufacture and use of armour by the Picts. But it is worth recalling the claim that both Anglo-Saxon and British warrior-kings mimicked Roman parade dress in the clothes they wore into battle.[202] This may also have been the case among the Picts.

Only one warrior portrayed in Pictish sculpture appears to be wearing armour, possibly a chain-mail hauberk, with split sides to facilitate movement. However, this warrior, in the Aberlemno battle scene, is not a Pict but an Anglo-Saxon, as his helmet reveals.[203] In contrast, there is no sculptural evidence that the Picts themselves wore any form of armour. Instead, the highly mobile character of warfare fought by the Picts and Scots suggests that their warriors were unarmoured. Still, protective battle shirts, known as byrnies or hauberks, could have been made from other materials, including padded fabric or leather. Foot soldiers are usually depicted wearing knee-length tunics, as in the Aberlemno battle scene (*see* Plate 8). In contrast, the tunics worn by the spearmen on the Brough of Birsay stone (*see* Plate 16) are long, almost ankle length, and may be a form of *aketon* or quilted armour, stiffened or padded to protect the bodies and legs of its wearers. These worked by helping to absorb the force of blows from weapons, distributing them over a wider area of the body.[204] These garments may reflect the unusual, perhaps ceremonial, nature of this scene and/or the high status of the warriors portrayed.

## HELMETS

Helmets were not only a specialised item of armour, but were also very visible symbols of office and power in many early medieval societies. This was certainly the case among the Anglo-Saxons, although only three helmets, from Benty Grange, Coppergate (York) and Sutton Hoo, survive.[205] But despite claims that some Pictish warriors wore helmets, and the presence of helmeted Pictish 'chieftains' in some reconstruction drawings,[206] the evidence is weak. No Pictish helmets or helmet components are known to survive. Like the shield and armour also allegedly found there, claims that the Norrie's Law hoard of Pictish silverwork included a helmet of unspecified type[207] are unsubstantiated. These claims may be dismissed as unreliable and the object concerned may have been a crushed silver plate instead.[208] Some fragments of silver from the hoard have been compared to the bronze or silver plates from late Roman helmets of a type ancestral to the early medieval European *spangenhelm,* a helmet constructed from several segments, usually around an iron frame.[209] However, this remains doubtful. Fragments of gilded copper plate decorated with vinescroll, found in Dumfriesshire, were also identified as belonging to a *spangenhelm.*[210] Although the absence of a frame construction led to this identification being rejected in favour of a related form of helmet,[211] it now seems doubtful that these plates belonged to a helmet at all.

Helmeted warriors are depicted on at least one Pictish stone and their prominence on the Aberlemno battle scene has influenced the debate. Although cited as evidence that the Picts wore helmets in battle,[212] the warriors concerned are identifiable as Northumbrian. The helmets depicted are closely paralleled by the Anglo-Saxon helmet from Coppergate[213] and are used in the scene to distinguish Northumbrian warriors from their Pictish opponents.

Other sculptural scenes are claimed to portray Pictish warriors wearing helmets,[214] but may be countered by alternative interpretations.[215] The lower warrior on the Benvie (Angus) cross-slab[216] (*see* Plate 14) is said to be wearing a helmet with a nasal guard,[217] but this effect is produced simply by the combination of his cowled cloak and prominent, block-like nose, a recognised element in Picto-Scottish sculpture.[218] The upper warrior on this stone has a similar nasal feature and yet his ringleted hair is clearly visible, revealing that he is bare-headed. The figure on the West Balblair (Inverness-shire) stone[219] has also been described as helmeted[220] and his 'helmet' claimed to have a crest and visor.[221] However, the latter feature is anachronistic. The only comparable type of helmet is a Continental *bascinet* with a *hounskull* visor, with a pointed nose and hinged sides, dating to the late fourteenth century.[222] Instead of a helmeted warrior, this is a mythological bird-headed warrior similar to those portrayed on the Glamis 2, Murthly, Rossie Priory and Papil stones.[223] Lastly, the symbol on the Congash 2 stone[224] has been identified tentatively as a crested helmet with nasal guard.[225] But there is nothing to corroborate this and it has also been interpreted as a bow and arrow[226] or, more plausibly, an abstract symbol.

That no helmeted Picts can be identified in Pictish sculpture is fundamental to the debate about the existence of Pictish helmets. Their absence is claimed to reflect their rarity rather than imply that the Picts did not wear helmets.[227] If the Picts did have helmets then these, like other items of elaborate metalwork, would have been the preserve of high-ranking war leaders. Members of this warrior élite appear prominently and frequently in Pictish sculpture. That Pictish warriors are so consistently portrayed without helmets confirms that they were not worn. In the absence of any evidence that Scottish warriors wore helmets, this also appears to have been the case in *Dál Riata*.

## CHAPTER FIVE

# Warriors, Weapons and Warfare

Having examined the arms and armour of the Picts and Scots, their implications for the nature of Pictish and Scottish warfare may now be considered. How much can we tell about the manner in which these weapons were used in combat and the warriors who were armed with them? Historians would normally seek eye-witness accounts while archaeologists would examine weapons for signs of use and human remains for evidence of trauma consistent with wounds sustained in battle. However, the limitations of both the documentary evidence and the archaeological record mean that this is not possible. As a result, the study of Pictish and Scottish warfare is restricted largely to the secular scenes depicted in Pictish sculpture. Examination of these enables some conclusions to be drawn concerning the warriors involved, the types of forces to which they belonged, their use of weapons and the tactics they deployed on the battlefield. The reliance on sculptural evidence inevitably means that this discussion is heavily biased towards Pictish warriors, weapons and warfare.

## WARRIORS' APPEARANCE

The traditional image of Scottish and particularly Pictish warriors is as savage barbarians, distinguished not only by their brutal behaviour but also their uncivilised appearance. This enduring stereotype originates in Classical accounts of the Celtic peoples of Britain going into battle naked and exposing their painted bodies.[1] The earliest account of this practice is by Julius Caesar,[2] writing of his second invasion of Britain, in 54 BC: 'All the *Britanni* dye their bodies with *vitrum* [possibly woad (*isatis tinctoria*)],[3] which produces a blue colour, and this gives them a more terrifying appearance in battle.'

These practices survived among the Iron Age peoples of northern Britain, including the ancestors of the Picts. The native warriors on the Bridgeness distance slab, erected *c.* 142, are portrayed as naked (*see* Plate 20). Referring to the *Caledonii* and *Maeatae*, against whom the Severan campaigns of 208 or 209 to 10 were directed, Herodian[4] (*fl.* 235) records that the *Britanni* 'tattoo their bodies with various patterns and pictures of all sorts of animals' and 'do not wear clothes, so as not to cover the pictures on their bodies'. Their warriors were 'protected only by a narrow shield and a spear, with a sword slung from their naked bodies'. The *Britanni* were described as 'accustomed to fight still half-naked' in 297,[5] implying that the practice had declined by then. Although frequently, but mistakenly, thought to refer to the Picts, this panegyric simply refers to the Picts as an enemy of the Britons. Nevertheless, the early Picts may also have gone into battle naked. Gildas,[6] writing in the mid-sixth century, describes Pictish and Scottish raiders as 'readier to cover their villainous faces with hair than their private parts and neighbouring regions with clothes'. But although Bede[7] describes how the routed Picts and Saxons escaped naked after the 'Alleluia victory' of 429,[8] they could have lost their clothes in the turmoil of battle and the ensuing rout.

Tattooing was explicitly associated with the Picts. Writing in 400–2 of the Roman general Stilicho's suppression of a rebellion by the Picts and Scots, the poet Claudian personifies Britannia as a woman with 'her cheeks tattooed' and, in the earliest explicit reference to this practice among the Picts, refers to 'the strange devices tattooed on the faces of the dying Picts'.[9] Claudian was referring to permanent body decoration, tattooing, rather than less permanent forms of body painting. This is apparent from his use of the phrase 'iron-marked' (*ferro picta/ferroque notatas*), which presumably refers to the use of a sharp point to pierce the skin, allowing coloured dyes to be injected. Anachronistically attributing the practice to the earlier *Caledonii*, Jordanes (*fl.* 550) also claimed that they had 'iron-painted bodies'.[10]

Although possibly influenced by Classical traditions, later sources record that the Picts continued to tattoo themselves into the early medieval period. According to Isidore of Seville[11] (*fl.* 620): 'The race of the Picts has a name derived from the appearance of their bodies. These are played upon by a needle working with small pricks and by the squeezed-out sap of a native plant, so that they bear the resultant marks according to the personal rank of the individual, their painted limbs being tattooed to show their high birth.' As late as 787, Bishop George of Ostia criticised the pagan practice of disfiguring their bodies with 'hideous scars' and 'this injury of staining' or dyeing.[12] George was then in Northumbria but, as there is no evidence that the Anglo-Saxons practised tattooing, his comment may have been prompted by tattooing among the neighbouring Picts.[13] These various accounts have led to speculation that the Picts decorated their bodies with the distinctive symbols that now survive only in sculpture and metalwork.[14]

No tattooed figures are detectable in Pictish sculpture, although this is unsurprising given the difficulty of representing tattoos in this medium and the weathered condition of most Pictish stones. But some decorated figures, including warriors with blue- or green-coloured bodies and a man covered with interlaced ornament are illustrated in the *Book of Kells*,[15] of *c.* 800.[16] Their long, pointed beards give these figures a distinctly Pictish appearance and, although the provenance of the *Book of Kells* remains controversial, it displays some Pictish artistic influences. The illustrators of the *Book of Kells* were probably at least aware of, if not familiar with, the Picts. However, even if these are Picts, these illustrations may not confirm that the Picts tattooed and/or painted their bodies but may simply represent a visual pun on the Picts' name.[17] Moreover, the illustrations need not be of Picts, as references to tattooing in early medieval Ireland[18] indicates that the practice was not confined to the Picts.

The debate concerning Pictish tattooing is intimately linked to that surrounding the name of the Picts.[19] In the earliest reference to the name's etymology, Claudian refers to 'the well-named Picts' (*noc falso nomine Pictos*).[20] The Irish text *Lebor Bretnach* also records that 'From their tattooing their fair skins / Were they called *Picti*.'[21] The name *Picti* was long believed to mean 'the painted ones' and to have originated in a nickname bestowed by Roman soldiers on account of the Picts' painted bodies. This is now interpreted as a pseudo-learned etymology without linguistic basis, with the name being of native origin instead. However, these two interpretations need not be mutually exclusive and the debate continues.

Were the Picts painted? The accumulated literary evidence for the Pictish tradition of body decoration is very persuasive. Nevertheless, one school of thought[22] maintains that the inconsistencies between accounts and the absence of first-hand supporting evidence suggests that they should not be accepted at face value. In particular, early medieval accounts of Pictish body painting or tattooing are uncorroborated by better informed contemporary sources such as Adomnán and Bede, both of whom display an interest in Pictish customs but say nothing about the practice. But the consistency of the evidence over several centuries is more convincing than the minor differences in detail between sources. And Adomnán and Bede may not have felt it necessary to explain such a well-known custom, particularly if they and their contemporaries were aware of the meaning of the name *Picti*.[23]

Perhaps understandably, the name *Picti* and Classical descriptions of painted or tattooed Picts have been treated with suspicion because of their ideological nature. Body decoration was associated in the Classical world with savagery and was one of the characteristics that defined 'barbarian' peoples. This *topoi*, a stock literary description in Classical accounts, signified the barbaric character of the ancient Britons in general and, latterly, the Picts in particular. But this need not mean that it was inaccurate. Instead, its widespread currency points to its basis in reality. Mirroring this, Elizabethan illustrations of tattooed Pictish warriors perpetuated Classical perceptions of the Picts, using body decoration to distinguish them as barbarians, but were actually influenced by the first British contacts with the native inhabitants of North America[24] (see Plate 24). Traditions that the inhabitants of what is now Scotland were painted and/or hirsute have a long currency. Such prejudices persisted among the English into the high Middle Ages and are vividly expressed in the fourteenth-century *Luttrell Psalter*, where the Scots are depicted as beasts with hair-covered bodies and blue-faced human heads.[25] The latter stereotype resurfaced in the film *Braveheart* (1994), where the blue and white face paint worn by the Scottish patriot Sir William Wallace (*c.* 1270–1305), played by Mel Gibson, was transformed into an expression of national identity, allegiance and defiance. And, bizarrely, face painting has undergone a modern revival among followers of those sporting substitutes for warfare, football and rugby.

There is one way in which the debate surrounding Pictish tattooing may be settled conclusively. Human bodies from various periods have been found preserved in peat bogs in north-western Europe.[26] These bodies and the peat adhering to them can be tested for indigotin, the colourant in woad, and examined for traces of tattoos using infra-red photography.[27] These techniques were employed, although without result, on the famous Lindow Man (Cheshire), possibly dating to the third century BC. But an excess of metallic elements in the skin of Lindow Man is attributed to the residue of clay-based mineral-rich pigments applied to the skin.[28] This indicates that the body of Lindow Man was painted. Copper and iron provided the basic colourants in these pigments, although the colours produced could have been black, blue, green or red depending on which oxide was used. Several bodies have also been discovered in bogs in northern Scotland, although all appear to be medieval or post-medieval in date.[29] Given the right environmental conditions, Pictish bog bodies may also survive and, if discovered, could be examined for evidence of body decoration.

The only depictions of naked warriors in native sculpture are on the Newton of Collessie and possibly the Westerton of Balgavies stones (*see* Plate 19).[30] The shaved faced and knotted hairstyle of the Collessie man, together with his knobbed spearbutt,[31] differ markedly from the appearance of Pictish warriors on later cross-slabs, presumably reflecting the early date of the Collessie Stone and changing fashions since it was carved. In contrast to these early figures and Classical accounts, Pictish sculpture does not depict warriors as naked, indicating that the Picts had abandoned the practice of going into battle naked by the eighth century at the latest.

Although clothed, the warriors portrayed in Pictish sculpture still vary considerably in appearance, reflecting their social status and the activities in which they were engaged. Pictish sculpture provides graphic testimony of aristocratic involvement in warfare. As élite art, many Pictish cross-slabs portray, usually in hunting or battle scenes, the nobles they presumably commemorate and whose graves they probably marked. As a result, these images may reflect the values of those who erected the stones, thereby revealing Pictish perceptions rather than social realities. However, Pictish sculpture consistently expresses the elevated status of its subjects with specific attributes of nobility. Noble warriors are distinguished by several features. Most obviously, they are usually depicted on horseback and possess a sword, in contrast to ordinary foot soldiers.[32] Other distinguishing features associated with Pictish nobles include their more elaborate clothing and hairstyles. This is most readily apparent when used to convey a distinction in status between figures in the same scene. For example, the leading warrior on the Brough of Birsay stone not only has a larger spear and more highly decorated shield,[33] but also sports an elaborate hairstyle, with ringlets on top, a long, curly pony tail and a goatee beard (*see* Plate 16). His clothing, a long tunic with a wide decorated or fringed hem, also sets him apart from the warriors behind him, who have no ringlets, shorter pony tails and tunics with narrower and undecorated hems, while one warrior is beardless. This does not mean that they are commoners, simply that they are of lesser status than the man in front of them. Indeed, all three are dressed similarly, in ankle-length *aketons*, tunics of padded or quilted armour. The stature, appearance and weapons of the warriors on the Brough of Birsay stone vividly convey that these are men of power and influence. Unusually, the elaborately pleated clothes worn by all three figures on the St Andrews sarcophagus[34] (*see* Plate 10) may reveal external, possibly Classical, artistic influences.

These indicators of nobility occur widely in Pictish sculpture. Several mounted warriors are portrayed with curly locks, including the upper horseman on the Benvie cross-slab (*see* Plate 14), or pony tails, as on the Kirriemuir 3 stone (both Angus).[35] That these do not simply reflect Pictish artistic conventions is suggested by their occurrence in contexts other than the formal scenes on cross-slabs. A graffito of a cloaked figure from the Broch of Burness (Orkney) also incorporates the curled hair and the cloak's decorative border.[36] In addition, a graffito from Jarlshof (Shetland) of a man with a row of curls from his forehead to his neck, a goatee beard and a neatly trimmed moustache was traditionally thought to be Viking but is now believed to be Pictish.[37]

Several stones, such as the Kirriemuir 3 and Meigle 4 cross-slabs (both Angus),[38] include figures with goatee beards of various sizes. The horsemen on the Aldbar and Benvie cross-slabs (both Angus) (*see* Plate 14) and the horseman and two of the foot soldiers on the Dupplin cross (Perthshire) are distinguished by their impressively long, drooping moustaches.[39] Facial hair is an indicator of high status, with moustaches perhaps identifying specific grades.[40] In the absence of Pictish symbols on these stones, these mustachioed warriors have been identified as Scots rather than Picts,[41] raising the intriguing possibility that Pictish and Scottish nobles could be differentiated by their contrasting styles of moustache. Instead, these portraits attest changing fashions in facial hair. The recently discovered inscription on the Dupplin cross commemorates 'Custantin filius Fircus', who is identifiable as Causantín son of Uurguist (Causantín mac Fergusa), King of Pictland (789–820) and *Dál Riata* (810–20).[42] This inscription occupies the same position on the west face of the Dupplin cross as the horseman on the east face, leaving little doubt that this portrait is of the king. Uniquely in Pictish sculpture, a figure may be identified with a named individual, confirming both the high status of the horsemen portrayed and providing an insight into the appearance of Pictish kings in battle.

Early medieval warfare was not an exclusively élite activity. Although horsemen predominate in images of Pictish warriors, this reflects the aristocratic milieu of Pictish sculpture rather than the composition of Pictish armies. Pictish sculpture, like the heroic literature of neighbouring peoples, reflects the interests and concerns of a warrior élite. But, as with other early medieval peoples, commoners would have formed the bulk of an army and the great majority of them would have fought on foot. In contrast to their war leaders, ordinary foot soldiers are portrayed rarely in Pictish sculpture. Nevertheless, these few scenes contrast with earlier accounts that the Picts went into battle naked and are important to the study of the appearance of warriors.

Where common foot soldiers are portrayed, they lack the stylistic details in appearance and dress normally found on noble warriors. Their hairstyles are virtually indistinguishable, although their low status is reflected in their lack of facial hair. On the St Andrews sarcophagus, for example, the warrior hunting on foot is clean-shaven, in contrast to Daniel and the horseman, who are both bearded (*see* Plate 10). The clothes of foot soldiers are simple, comprising short tunics, presumably over breeches. The foot soldiers in the Aberlemno battle scene wear plain tunics that reach the knee or just below it, although no details are apparent (*see* Plate 8). This appears to be the standard dress for Pictish men. Although not warriors,[43] the figures on the Golspie cross-slab and Rhynie 7 stone[44] (*see* Plate 23) wear single-piece, long-sleeved tunics that reach just above the knee and are gathered at the waist with a belt. The Rhynie tunic is very plain, although the Golspie tunic has an upturned collar, a plain hem and lines suggesting seams or possibly quilting.

Overgarments are depicted occasionally. The warrior on the Rhynie 3 stone is claimed to be 'wearing a cloak and something like a ball-ended necktie',[45] the latter possibly for fastening the cloak, although the stone is now too eroded to be confident about these features. Four foot soldiers on the Eassie Priory (Angus) cross-slab[46] (*see* Plate 25) wear distinctive kite-shaped cloaks that could easily be mistaken for late Anglo-Saxon or Norman shields, but the warrior on the front of the cross-slab also carries a small square shield. The cloaks' stiff appearance suggests that they were of leather. Such cloaks may have had double-peaked hoods such as those worn by the crossbowmen on the Glenferness, St Vigeans and Shandwick cross-slabs. Britain was famous for such outer garments, reflecting its climate. A hooded waterproof cloak known as the *birrus Britannicus* is one of two British woollen products mentioned in Diocletian's price-fixing edict of 301, indicating that these had acquired a reputation throughout the Roman Empire, and British cloaks were still valued in European markets in the eighth century.[47]

## COMMUNICATIONS

Reliable communications are fundamental to the command and control of any military force and can make the difference between defeat and victory. This is particularly true in fast-moving mobile warfare, such as that fought during the early medieval period. Nevertheless, communications were probably rudimentary, particularly once battle was joined. Banners, flags or standards may have been used to give signals on the battlefield, although there is little evidence of their use by the Picts or Scots. Interestingly, none are detectable in the extensive battle scene on Sueno's Stone. The only reference to such a standard suggests that they may have had a ritual or totemic significance. The men of *Alba* are said to have taken with them a holy relic, a crozier known as the *Cathbuaid* or 'Battle Triumph' of Columba, into every battle at the head of their army as their battle standard.[48] By raising them aloft, distinctively decorated or coloured shields could also have been used to give basic signals or simply indicate the whereabouts of its owner on the battlefield, although not without some risk to the warrior concerned.

Effective sound communications needed to be loud enough to be heard above what Adomnán[49] describes as 'the terrible crashings of battles' and distinctive enough not to be confused with the enemy's. Pictish sculpture and the archaeological record both provide some clues. A horseman on the Dunkeld 1 stone holds a spear in one hand and raises a horn to his lips with the other.[50] Although interpreted as a drinking horn,[51] its mouth points away from the horseman. The rider is therefore sounding a blast horn, a simple musical instrument producing a limited range of notes.[52] The Dunkeld horseman is thought to belong to an unfinished hunting rather than a battle scene,[53] an interpretation perhaps influenced by the pairs of long horns being sounded in the hunting scenes on the Aberlemno 3 and Hilton of Cadboll cross-slabs.[54] However, in another reminder that hunting provides good preparation for warfare, horns could also have been used on the battlefield for giving signals and intimidating the enemy. This is depicted on Sueno's Stone, where three men are shown sounding long horns (*see* Plate 7).

The association of horns with élite activities such as hunting and warfare is supported by the only surviving fragment found in a Pictish or Scottish context. A decorative rim mount from a ninth-century Anglo-Saxon blast horn is one of very few finds to survive from the early excavations within the Pictish fortress at Burghead.[55] Its craftsmanship reveals that this was a prestige item, probably owned by a noble or king. But it was also functional and its loop for a carrying strap, enabling it to be hung over the shoulder, emphasises that it was intended to be used on the move. Whether it reached Burghead as a result of trading, raiding or as a diplomatic gift, the blast horn and its findspot attest its association with a social élite and imply its use in hunting and warfare.

## CAVALRY

Did the Picts and Scots have cavalry? Despite the large number of mounted warriors portrayed in Pictish sculpture, only the Aberlemno battle scene shows mounted Picts engaged in combat (*see* Plate 8). It is unclear, therefore, whether mounted warriors actually fought on horseback or simply rode to the scene of battle, where they dismounted and fought on foot. Were horses used as fast-moving weapon platforms or simply for transport? This parallels a long debate concerning warfare among the Anglo-Saxons and Britons,[56] although *The Gododdin* confirms that both used cavalry in battle.[57] *The Gododdin* also refers to a Pictish warrior who joined the army of the *Gododdin* on its expedition to *Catreath* as a 'foreign horseman'.[58] Although not conclusive, this strongly suggests a Pictish mounted warrior fighting alongside his North British counterparts. The situation among the Scots is less clear. Like the *Gododdin*, the Scots' ability to fight far beyond their own borders, from *Círcinn* (Kincardineshire) to *Degsastán* (somewhere in the Scottish Borders), confirms their use of horses, at least to mount expeditions. Given that the neighbouring Picts, Angles and North Britons all used cavalry, it would be surprising if the Scots did not.

But the best evidence for Pictish cavalry comes from the many secular scenes on Pictish cross-slabs. The horsemen depicted in Pictish sculpture are engaged in typical aristocratic pursuits, usually riding into battle or hunting. The specialist arms and equipment required, principally a horse, bridle gear and sword, indicate that these mounted warriors were of noble status and this is confirmed by their dress and appearance. As Pictish horses have been the subject of several recent studies,[59] they are not considered here. However, the quality of both the horses and horsemanship depicted in Pictish sculpture supports the use of cavalry in warfare.

Lightly armed for mobile warfare, horsemen are usually portrayed in Pictish sculpture with a spear, sword and round shield. The spear is always held in the warrior's right hand, the shield in his left. Many of these horsemen are shown riding into battle. This is apparent from their combat-ready stance, each warrior holding his spear in an underarm grip. Supported by the length of the warrior's forearm, this enabled the spearshaft to be held behind its point of balance, providing a tighter grip with which to parry enemy thrusts and enabling a greater reach to be achieved with the weapon. This indicates that Pictish mounted warriors used their spears for thrusting rather than for throwing, as lances rather than javelins. This may explain why Pictish horsemen are only portrayed with a single spear, while it would have made sense for them to have been armed with more than one if they were to be used as javelins. This is supported by the angular spearhead on the weapon carried by the horseman on the Meigle 3 stone, which would have been too heavy, and not aerodynamic enough, to have tipped an effective projectile.

Battles probably began with a cavalry charge. In this, mounted warriors used their spears and the momentum behind them to unseat their opponents as they charged forward. On locking battle with the enemy, spears would have been used as thrusting weapons in close-quarter battle. The importance attached to cavalry and their role at the start of battle is supported by the Aberlemno battle scene (*see* Plate 8). This illustrates a sequence of events from the battle of Dunnichen,[60] including two phases in an engagement involving Pictish and Northumbrian warriors fighting on horseback.[61] In the first, depicted in the lower register of the scene, two mounted warriors charge at each other with spears ready. A Pictish horseman, his spear held in an underarm grip with his right arm drawn back fully, ready to thrust or throw it, and his shield raised to protect his head and upper body, advances towards a Northumbrian warrior who holds his spear aloft in an overarm grip, ready to throw.

Once thrown or lodged in an opponent's shield or body, spears could not easily be retrieved and may have been broken in any case. Warriors, therefore, would have either withdrawn from the field, possibly to rearm and/or regroup, or, more probably, drawn their swords and fought on at close quarter. The sword is usually depicted in its scabbard against the warrior's left-hand thigh, presumably suspended from a belt around his waist (see Plates 8, 11, 14 and 16). The sword was drawn with the warrior's right hand, across his body and behind his shield, which protected him during this potentially vulnerable manoeuvre. The swords depicted were for single-handed use and would have been ideal in close-quarter battle, for either slashing or stabbing. The Aberlemno battle scene also depicts this next stage of the battle, in the top register. Their spears thrown, two horsemen have drawn their swords, the Pictish warrior brandishing his upright in front of him. But his Northumbrian opponent has been driven from the field and, routed, has discarded his sword and shield, which lie on the ground behind him.

The opening cavalry charge has implications for the composition of armies and the casualties sustained in battle. Mounted warriors, largely or exclusively nobles, probably formed the front rank of an army, the vanguard. This, as The Gododdin confirms,[62] was a position of honour. It presented nobles with an opportunity to acquire or reinforce their heroic reputation by leading the initial assault on the enemy and, if they survived that, of becoming involved in the thick of combat. Not surprisingly, the casualties among kings, members of the royal kin group and nobles could be high.[63] This also explains why, in a battle against the Vikings at the River Tyne in 918, a Scottish army lost 'neither king nor mormaer', despite being attacked in the rear and slaughtered.[64]

Despite the vivid portrayal in Pictish sculpture of horsemen in action, cavalry were probably of only limited effectiveness and nobles rode into battle as much to convey their status as for military reasons. The biggest limitation to the effectiveness of early medieval cavalry was the absence of the stirrup, which was not introduced to Britain until the late first millennium. There is no evidence for the use of the slipper stirrup, a saddlecloth with pockets at the front corners into which the rider could place his feet and use his weight to guide the horse by leaning in the direction in which he wanted to travel. Although the feet of Pictish horsemen are sometimes shown touching the front corners of the saddlecloth, this appears to be coincidental. As the riders' boots are clearly visible, slipper stirrups were not used in these cases.[65] Without stirrups, riders lacked stability. Unable to rise in the saddle, they would have found it difficult to put much force behind a sword blow or spear thrust. Indeed, Pictish and Scottish horsemen also lacked saddles, explaining why they are often depicted sitting very low on their horses, an effect exaggerated on the St Madoes (Perthshire) cross-slab.[66] Pictish riders are usually portrayed sitting well forward on their horses and with their legs sticking forward rather than dangling at the horse's side. By resting their legs over the horse's shoulders, riders could use their weight to control the horse more effectively, partially compensating for the absence of stirrups. Although lacking saddles and stirrups, other horse fittings are clearly visible on several stones. Bridles, bridle bits, cruppers, reins and harness-rings are all shown on the Benvie, Inchbrayock 1 and St Madoes cross-slabs[67] (*see* Plates 11 and 14).

The impact of a cavalry charge may have been as much psychological as military. The great noise generated by a body of galloping mounted warriors ensured that the psychological impact was felt before the armies actually locked in combat. A successful cavalry charge could intimidate and demoralise an opposing army, breaking up infantry formations and leaving the enemy more susceptible to the following infantry attack. It could also rout the enemy before the foot soldiers had an opportunity to enter the fray or possibly even before any combat had actually occurred. Horsemen may have dismounted in order to engage the enemy on foot after the opening cavalry charge, suggesting that nobles could have fought as both cavalry and infantry in different phases of a battle. At its most effective, a cavalry force could defeat a larger army comprising mostly foot soldiers. Although there is clearly some exaggeration in the account, a 'vast army' of Picts was defeated by Ecgfrith's 'little band' of Northumbrian cavalry in the Plain of *Manau* in 672, when 'host upon host' of the Picts were killed.[68]

But a cavalry charge was not invincible and could be stopped or even broken up. If bows and crossbows were used in warfare by the Picts and Scots,[69] advancing horsemen could have been brought down before they had the opportunity to engage their enemy. Conducted effectively, this may have inflicted sufficient casualties to break up or repel an enemy cavalry charge. This is depicted on Sueno's Stone, where two archers or crossbowmen at the head of a group of foot soldiers are shown targeting a group of six fleeing horsemen (*see* Plate 7). The other defence against a cavalry attack was the ranked infantry formation.[70] Successfully repulsing a cavalry attack would have had powerful psychological and practical consequences for both sides because the leading ranks would have included many royal and noble war leaders. A skilful opening move on the battlefield could effectively leave an opposing army leaderless and the death or flight of a king probably ensured the defeat of his army, so pivotal was the figure of the king in early medieval warfare.[71]

## CHARIOTS

Whether the Picts or Scots had war chariots is of relevance to the role of cavalry in battle. The chariot is popularly perceived as one of the classic features of Celtic warfare,[72] epitomised by the statue of Boudicca astride a chariot with scythed wheels on the Thames Embankment. The terminology is controversial. Many archaeologists now use the more neutral 'carriage', 'cart', 'wagon' or even 'wheeled vehicle', in preference to the more value-laden 'chariot', with its perceived associations with warfare.[73] This also overcomes the problem that different types of wheeled vehicle are often indistinguishable archaeologically. Nevertheless, the use of chariots in warfare by the Celts is recorded by several Classical historians. War chariots remained in use in northern Britain after they had disappeared from the Continent and southern Britain. Tacitus[74] famously describes their presence at the battle of *Mons Graupius* in 84, although they appear to have been used more for the display of status and bravado and in an attempt to intimidate the enemy before the battle rather than in combat itself. Writing of the Severan campaign of 208 or 209 to 10, Cassius Dio[75] records that the *Caledonii* and *Maeatae* 'go into battle in chariots, and have small, swift horses; there are also foot-soldiers, very swift in running and very firm in standing their ground'. This is the latest recorded historical reference to the use of chariots in warfare in western Europe.

The presence of chariots in late Iron Age Scotland is indicated by their metallic fittings, particularly lynch pins, terrets and pairs of horse bridles.[76] Terrets, rein-guiding rings that would have been mounted on the yoke, pole or chariot itself, include a distinctive 'massive' type, dated to between the late first and possibly the fourth centuries.[77] These have been found throughout Britain but their distribution is concentrated in north-east Scotland – hence their alternative name, 'Donside' – which appears to have been their centre of production. The recent discovery of a chariot burial at Newbridge (Midlothian),[78] the first in Scotland, confirms the existence of chariots in Iron Age Scotland.

The documentary and archaeological evidence demonstrates that the Iron Age ancestors of the Picts had chariots and used them in warfare. But what about the historical Picts and, for that matter, the Scots? Here the evidence is much more limited. Adomnán[79] refers to the 'carriage' (*currus*) as a form of transport for high-status clerics in Ireland, where there is both documentary and sculptural evidence for their use by kings and senior ecclesiastics,[80] although overshadowed by the war chariot of early Irish epic literature.[81] In contrast, when Columba was too infirm to travel around Iona, his modest transport was a wagon or cart (*plaustrum*).[82] But there is also literary evidence for the use of chariots in secular contexts, perhaps including warfare. Columba prophesied that an Irish king would escape the battlefield on a chariot (*currus*) after his defeat and an Irish king was killed in his chariot in 558.[83] However, the exact circumstances are unclear in both cases and neither source records the actual use of chariots in warfare. Similarly, the *Amra Coluimchille* of c. 597 mentions 'chariots of battle', but in a metaphor for salvation.[84] *The Gododdin*[85] refers to a 'champion in a war-chariot', although this may be a deliberate archaism, harking back to a heroic age, as in the great Irish epic *Táin Bó Cuailnge* (*The Cattle Raid of Cooley*).

Some Pictish symbols are claimed to represent chariots. The divided or notched rectangle symbol is sometimes interpreted as a chariot with two ponies, the double-disc symbol as the wheels from a dismantled chariot and the wheel symbol as a chariot wheel.[86] But the notched rectangle and double-disc symbols are too abstract to be interpreted confidently and their meanings remain obscure. Although the wheel symbol is readily recognisable, it occurs only twice, at Knockando 1 (Moray) and Ardjachie (Ross and Cromarty),[87] and its significance is unclear. There is no evidence that the wheels depicted belonged to a chariot or, indeed, any other type(s) of vehicle. The wheel may have expressed some deeper symbolic meaning instead and the widespread association of the wheel with Celtic solar symbolism[88] provides a plausible alternative interpretation. These symbols are not reliable evidence that the Picts had chariots.

The only firm evidence for the use of chariots by the Picts is two sculptures, both now lost. A cross-slab at Newtyle (Angus) included a scene showing 'ane goddes . . . in ane cairt', according to a source of 1569.[89] The Meigle 10 (Perthshire) panel is better recorded, in five illustrations made during the eighteenth and nineteenth centuries.[90] These depict a two-wheeled vehicle, each wheel with twelve spokes, drawn by a pair of horses. Behind a seated driver, the carriage superstructure has open sides with a balustraded rail and a frame supporting a canopy over two passengers. The occupants are unarmed and the vehicle's awning would have made it an unsuitable fighting platform, revealing that this is not a war chariot but a form of prestige transport. Classical or biblical influences and/or interpretations, notably the ascension of Elijah,[91] have been claimed for this scene.[92] But it seems more probable that, like the many ecclesiastical and secular scenes on Pictish cross-slabs, it depicts a scene from contemporary Pictish life. However, the stone is not recorded in sufficient detail, or was already too eroded, for the passengers to be identified as either clerics or laymen.

There is no evidence that the Picts used chariots in warfare, although two-wheeled vehicles may have been used as both a mode of transport and a status symbol by members of the Pictish ecclesiastical and/or secular élites.

## INFANTRY

Despite the prominence accorded to mounted warriors in Pictish sculpture, both Pictish and Scottish armies would have been composed mostly of foot soldiers. Together with the apparent significance of the opening cavalry charge, this raises questions about how infantry and cavalry belonging to the same side operated together on the battlefield. Common foot soldiers would have owed loyalty and obligations of military service to their mounted lord, who would have led them into battle, possibly after an opening cavalry charge. This is depicted in Pictish sculpture, where one or more riders, representing a king or lord with or without his *comitatus* of mounted warriors, is accompanied by a band of foot soldiers. At least six foot soldiers precede at least two mounted warriors on the (broken) Dull panel and four foot soldiers are shown below at least two horsemen on the (damaged) Dunkeld 2 cross-slab (the 'Apostles' Stone').[93] Below the mounted warrior identified as King Causantín on the Dupplin cross are four ranked spearmen, flanked by another two on an adjacent panel on the right-hand side of the cross, their impressive moustaches and decorative hems on their tunics revealing their noble status (*see* Plate 21).[94]

The warrior scenes on the Dupplin cross have been interpreted as evidence that only the king rode into battle and that his senior commanders fought on foot.[95] But this is more likely to be attributable to sculptural convention, emphasising the king's elevated status and reflecting the limited space available on these stones. Nevertheless, it leaves unresolved the issue of whether common foot soldiers followed their lord in the initial cavalry assault or joined him afterwards, perhaps as the horsemen regrouped for the next phase of battle. But dispelling any doubts that these scenes depict genuine Pictish military formations in battle, the prostrate and, in one case, decapitated bodies of the dead are shown beneath the warriors on the Dunkeld 2 stone.

Among the Picts and their neighbours, the arms of the common foot soldier were the spear and shield.[96] These were typically employed in the classic infantry formation of early medieval warfare, the shield wall.[97] To create a shield wall, warriors formed a tight rank by standing, perhaps side-on to the enemy, in a line close enough to hold their shields so that they overlapped, typically by a width of up to half a shield, so that they were 'boss to rim'. Warriors in the shield wall held their spears in the 'ready' position, facing their opponents, each warrior helping to cover the person on either side of him. A shield wall could be formed from one or more ranks of foot soldier. The shield wall may explain the design of the indented or notched shield.[98] When used in this formation, indented shields may have given a shield wall a crenellated appearance, perhaps mimicking the wooden breastworks that topped fort ramparts. The effect here may have been symbolic, the formation drawing psychological strength from its resemblance to a fort's battlements and, at the same time, intimidating the opposing army. The upper notch on the shield may also have had practical uses in a shield wall, perhaps enabling a spear to be rested and guided on top of the shield without risk of it obstructing the warrior on either side.

The formations and tactics adopted by a shield wall probably varied according to topography and circumstances, particularly whether it was fighting offensively or defensively. The shield wall operated as a unit and, when used successfully, formed a mobile but solid barrier that could withstand enemy attack, mounted or on foot, and crush an opposing army by advancing against it and breaking the opposing shield wall. Assisted by occupying higher ground than the enemy and advancing downhill, the objective of the shield wall was, typically, to advance in line, building up momentum as it went but without wavering or fragmenting. The shield wall then hit the opposing army with sufficient weight of numbers and force to break through the enemy's shield wall and press home their advantage, attacking the enemy from behind. At its most effective, such an attack would smash an opposing shield wall and overwhelm its ranks, either trampling the enemy troops underfoot or routing them.

Shields not only had a defensive function in a shield wall. The central boss projecting from a shield's external face made the shield an offensive weapon that could be used in a thrusting manner to drive back or crush opponents in close-quarter battle. The boss could also catch a sword blow, potentially throwing the attacker off balance and/or leaving him exposed to a counter-thrust. Shields were expendable. Intended to deflect or absorb blows, shields would often have been damaged or destroyed in battle. Once lodged in a shield it would have been difficult either to extract a spear or continue to use the shield, requiring warriors to discard their shields. This deprived warriors of their principal arms and armour, which is why horsemen and some foot soldiers were also armed with swords. Depending on the nature and intensity of the engagement, both shields and spears may have been lost when armies first locked in combat, leaving warriors to fight on with swords. *The Gododdin*[99] describes a shield after the battle: 'As much as his hand could grip / there did not return of it': the warrior was left holding only that part of the shield attached to the hand grip. As evidence of prowess in battle, a heavily damaged shield was a mark of honour.

In what may be the only depiction of a shield wall in Pictish sculpture, the Dupplin cross portrays a closely formed rank of four foot soldiers on its east face and two on its right-hand side (*see* Plate 21). Each warrior is armed with a spear and a small circular shield and although the spears are held upright rather than in the 'ready' position, this may be artistic licence, being easier for the sculptor to depict in the limited space available. The Brough of Birsay stone and the Eassie cross-slab both depict a line of three foot soldiers, each armed with a spear, and the Brough of Birsay warriors also carry shields. Most of the fighting would have been done with spears, both as armies advanced and in close-quarter battle. That spears had different functions is indicated by the variety of forms among surviving spearheads and in sculptural depictions.[100] This suggests the existence of more complex formations of troops than simple shield walls. The three warriors on the Brough of Birsay stone may portray a ranked battle formation of foot soldiers. Warriors in the front rank, each armed with a heavy spear for thrusting, may have provided cover for the middle and rear ranks, who were armed with lighter spears, javelins, for hurling over the heads of those in the front rank. Larger spears may have been wielded with two hands, but this would have left the spearman exposed to attack and was therefore unsuitable for warriors in the front rank, as the Aberlemno battle scene illustrates.[101] Although armed with swords, these remain in their scabbards at the warriors' sides, presumably until after their spears have been used. Sueno's Stone depicts ranks of two-, three- and four-deep foot soldiers, although three-deep predominate. These include both spearmen and warriors with their swords drawn (*see* Plate 7).

The number of warriors shown in close formation in Pictish sculpture is usually three. This may be an artistic convention, intended to symbolise a larger number of foot soldiers. But the Aberlemno battle scene provides evidence for the existence of a three-deep rank of warriors, suggesting that this represents a standard Pictish infantry formation. But, in contrast to the other sculptures, it depicts warriors in the 'ready' position, prepared to engage the enemy. The warrior in the front rank of the Aberlemno battle scene stands in the 'ready' position, his sword drawn and raised in his right hand, ready to slash at an advancing

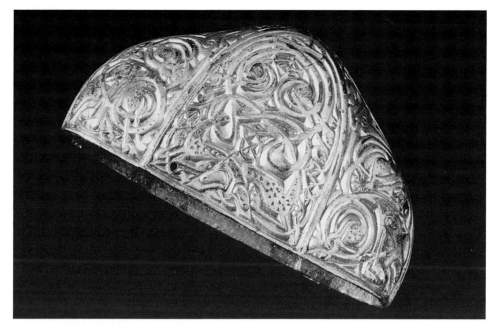

12. *The silver sword pommel from the St Ninian's Isle hoard, Shetland.* (Copyright: Trustees of the National Museums of Scotland 2002.)

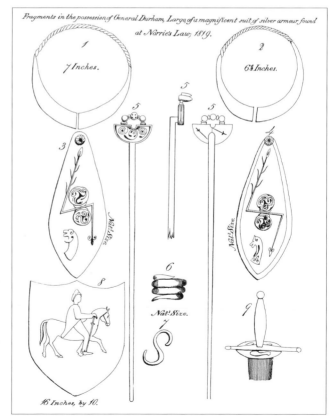

13. *Some of the contents of the Norrie's Law hoard, Fife, discovered in about 1819. The 'shield' and 'sword' were drawn from memory, some twenty years after their discovery and destruction. This image has been reproduced at 40 per cent of the original.* (From George Buist's *Report on the Silver Fragments in the Possession of General Durham, Largo, Commonly Called the Silver Armour of Norrie's Law,* 1839.)

14. *Two mounted warriors depicted on the reverse of the cross-slab at Benvie, Angus.* (Copyright: Tom and Sybil Gray Collection.)

15. *One of two sword chapes, this one of gilded silver, with zoomorphic terminals from the St Ninian's Isle hoard, Shetland. The first part of the inscription, INNOMINEDS, which may be expanded to read* in nomine d[ei] s[ummi], *'in the name of God the highest', is visible (the rest is on the reverse).* (Copyright: Trustees of the National Museums of Scotland 2002.)

16. *Three warriors on foot, depicted on the lower panel of a stone from Brough of Birsay, Orkney.*
(Copyright: Trustees of the National Museums of Scotland 2002.)

17. *Two spearheads and an arrowhead, found in excavations within the hillfort at Dunadd, Argyll.* (Copyright: Trustees of the National Museums of Scotland 2002.)

18. *A late Iron Age spearbutt of 'doorknob' style in cast bronze, from Crichie, Inverurie, Aberdeenshire.* (Copyright: The British Museum.)

19. *The Collessie warrior, incised on a monolith at Newton of Collessie, Fife.* (Copyright: Tom and Sybil Gray Collection.)

20. *Native warriors, naked and defeated, being ridden down by a Roman cavalryman, as depicted in the central panel of the Roman distance slab from the Antonine Wall at Bridgeness, West Lothian.* (Copyright: Trustees of the National Museums of Scotland 2002.)

21. *A mounted warrior and his accompanying formation or shield wall of four foot soldiers on the lower panels of the east face of the Dupplin Cross, Perthshire. The horseman is almost certainly the Pictish King, Causantín son of Uurguist (789–820), who is commemorated by an inscription on the opposite face of the cross.* (Crown Copyright: Royal Commission on the Ancient and Historical Monuments of Scotland.)

horseman. But he also maintains a defensive posture. His left arm is raised, extending his shield towards the approaching Northumbrian cavalryman, who holds his spear aloft in an overarm grip, ready to throw. The Pictish foot soldier is increasing the protection his shield provides to his head and upper body by holding it away from him. In skilled hands, wooden and/or leather shields would have deflected a sword blow or absorbed the impact from a spear, but they did not offer complete defence. By attempting to block his opponent, this warrior is making himself the smallest possible target behind his shield and, at the same time, minimising the risk of being wounded by a projectile penetrating his shield.

The warrior in the second rank covers the man in front of him. This warrior holds, in both hands, a long spear at the ready in a horizontal position. The stout shaft is longer than the spearman is tall, enabling its large spearhead to project beyond the warrior in the front rank. This is a thrusting, not a throwing weapon and the spearman is braced, ready to unseat the attacking rider with it. The spearman wears his shield across his upper body suspended on a *guige* around his neck or shoulders, its lower edge resting on his wrist. This arrangement frees both the warrior's hands, which are needed to support the weight of his spear. As he is unable to parry blows with it, his shield is therefore larger than that of the warrior in the front rank in order to provide added protection. Resting at an oblique angle, his spear is in the ideal position for deflecting thrown spears.

A warrior with his spear held upright brings up the rear of the ranked formation. He performs the important role of protecting the more vulnerable rear of the formation. But he is also ready to step forward and assist the middle or front ranks, if required, by closing up any gap that emerged in the formation as it took casualties or advanced over uneven ground. Alternatively, the role of the rear rank may have been to hurl spears over the heads of the front ranks in an attempt to thin the ranks of the approaching enemy formation before the armies locked in close-quarter battle. The objective here was to open up gaps in the opposing shield wall, which could then be penetrated more easily. Supporting the latter role, the shorter and lighter spear held by the warrior in the back rank appears to be for throwing rather than thrusting. The use of javelins by the Picts and their lethal effect is confirmed graphically elsewhere in the Aberlemno battle scene by a prostrate Northumbrian warrior, a spear lodged in the crown of his helmeted head (*see* Plate 8). That this projects upwards from the crown of his head indicates that the projectile was thrown, apparently in a high trajectory, although it is unclear if the aggressor was a mounted or foot soldier.

The Aberlemno battle scene illustrates a cross section of a classic battle formation of close-ranked infantrymen, familiar from the schiltron (or schiltrom), the 'shield troop' employed by medieval Scottish armies against English cavalry. Protected behind a wall of shields and a bristling thicket of spears, this formidable, hedgehog-like formation formed an impenetrable barrier, providing defence-in-depth with each rank covered by the rank behind. When stationary or withdrawing, this formation offered defence against attack from more heavily armed and mobile cavalry or a stronger infantry force. But it could also be used offensively by an advancing formation to penetrate enemy ranks or drive back or crush a weaker opponent. It may have been this manoeuvre that enabled a Pictish army to defeat an apparently numerically superior Northumbrian force at Dunnichen in 685[102] by advancing down Dunnichen Hill and pushing the Angles back into the bog that gave the battle its alternative name, Nechtanesmere.

Whether fighting or manoeuvring, the ranked infantry formation required not just all ranks, but every foot soldier making up those ranks, to operate in concert. The impression created is of an organised fighting force executing a pre-arranged and well-rehearsed tactical manoeuvre requiring training, coordination and discipline. This suggests that Pictish foot soldiers drilled, with implications for the nature and frequency of military obligation. Pictish military obligation and organisation clearly involved more than just getting men onto the battlefield and may not have been confined to wartime. Paradoxically, Eddius'[103] contemptuous description of Pictish warriors as 'swarms . . . gathered . . . like ants in summer sweeping up an earthwork to protect their home from ruin' conveys an impression of order and teamwork on a large scale, a sizeable battle formation in which everyone had their own role. The Picts were not simply the naked, tattooed and marauding barbarians of popular imagination.

## THE ROUT

The primary objective of a successful charge, whether by cavalry or a shield wall of infantry, was to rout the enemy. If accomplished in the opening or early stages of battle, this potentially enabled the battle to be won more by show of force than actual combat, not only driving the enemy from the field but also ensuring that they made a rapid retreat for their own self-preservation. Although the course of events that preceded them are unrecorded, several battles involving the Picts and/or Scots culminated in a rout, suggesting that this tactic was sometimes successful. For example, 'the family [i.e. army] of Domnall Brecc [King of *Dál Riata*] was put to flight', probably by the Picts, in a battle in *Glenn Mairison* or *Glenn Muiresan* in 638.[104] And, in an internal power struggle within Pictland, (the army of) Bridei son of Unuist, son of the Pictish king, routed (the army of) Talorgan son of Congus in an unnamed battle in 731.[105]

As the defining or concluding episode of a battle, routs were regarded as significant. Indeed, such was the prominence attached to them that one rout, in 558 or 560, is even recorded without any reference to the battle or its location: 'Flight of the Scots before Bridei son of Maelchon, King of the Picts'.[106] Also reflecting the importance of the rout, Adomnán[107] describes how Columba had a vision of the Scots under Aedán mac Gabráin defeating the *Miathi* in a battle, fought in 574X97, in which 'the barbarians are turned to flight; and the victory is yielded to Aedán'. Its appearance in a saintly vision suggests that a rout was perceived to be the most desirable outcome for a battle. But Aedán and his army were themselves routed on another occasion. Aedán 'was defeated and fled with very few, having lost almost his entire army' in the battle of *Degsastán* against the Angles of Northumbria in 603.[108] This was probably the 'rout of battle' in England in which Domangart, one of Aedán's sons, was killed.[109] But a routed army was not always annihilated. The army of Elpín, King of the Picts, was routed in a battle for the Pictish kingship at *Monid Craebe* or *Monidhcrobh*, probably Moncreiffe Hill (Perthshire), in 728 but evidently regrouped, as it was routed again in a battle at the unidentified *Castellum Credi* or *Caislén Credi* later the same year.[110]

The most detailed and remarkable account of a rout involving the Picts concerns their earliest recorded battle, the location of which is unknown. In 429, a combined force of Picts and Saxons, both of whom were still pagans, were ambushed by an inexperienced British army, led by Germanus, Bishop of Auxerre.[111] But this was no ordinary encounter and the pagans clearly underestimated their opponents. When the Picts and Saxons were in the right position, Germanus raised his standard and on this predetermined signal: 'The bishops three times shouted, "Alleluia!" The whole army joined in this shout, until the surrounding hills echoed with the sound. The enemy column panicked, thinking that the very rocks and sky were falling on them, and were so terrified that they could not run fast enough. Throwing away their weapons in headlong flight, they were well content to escape naked.'

The 'Alleluia victory' is a good example of the use of noise to intimidate an enemy. The Picts and Scots probably also practised this, producing noise by shouting war cries or insults and/or by beating their spears against their shields, as the *Caledonii* and *Maeatae* reportedly did.[112] Horns need not have been used just for sending orders within an army.

A battle was not necessarily over even with the rout of one side. In its panic and chaos, a routed army presented the opposing force with an opportunity to inflict even heavier losses. As a routed army's structure and discipline collapsed, war leaders may have become separated from their *comitatus*, leaving them particularly vulnerable. The capture and/or killing of a defeated king and his nobles may have been a prized objective of this stage of a battle. After defeating the Scots in the battle of *Cnoc Cairpri* in 736, Talorgan, the Pictish war leader and brother of the Pictish king, went 'in pursuit of Ainfcellach's son [i.e. Muiredach, King of *Dál Riata*] who had taken flight with his army'.[113] Routed warriors would have discarded anything that impeded their flight, including shields, spears and swords, as Bede describes in the 'Alleluia victory' and the Aberlemno battle scene depicts (*see* Plate 8). This left them even more vulnerable to attack. Exposed and defenceless, common soldiers would have accounted for the bulk of the casualties sustained, the victims of the 'great slaughters' recorded in the sources. And, in its desperation to flee the battlefield, a routed army was sometimes exposed to other dangers, notably drowning in nearby lochs or rivers.[114]

CHAPTER SIX

# Forts and Fortresses

Fortified sites were an integral element of the settlement patterns of both Pictland and *Dál Riata*. As such, forts were not simply of military significance, but performed a wide range of economic, social and political functions. They were domestic settlements, the fortified residences of members of the aristocratic class, their extended families, followers and retainers. Forts were intimately linked to a large hinterland, acting as centres of agricultural, artistic and craft production and storage. Reflecting the high social status of their occupants, forts were probably also centres for the assessment, collection and redistribution of dues and tribute, comprising mostly agricultural products. At the top of the social scale, a small number of fortresses were heavily fortified centres of royal power, royal residences and courts, closely associated with rituals of royalty in the form of pagan or Christian religious centres and royal inauguration sites. There were no single seats of power or 'capitals'. Instead, early medieval kingship was peripatetic and kings would have travelled between their power centres while on progress around their kingdom, demonstrating their status and asserting their authority through the dispensing of justice and the levying and consumption of taxes in the form of food renders.

Despite their many functions, Pictish and Scottish forts also possessed a military role. This is apparent from the naturally defended locations selected, the ramparts and ditches that comprise their most prominent features and visible remains and from documentary references to the warfare associated with forts. As a result, the military role of forts is pre-eminent in both the archaeological record and documentary sources. This chapter concentrates on the military aspects of forts and particularly their association with warfare. But before looking at hillforts in action, it is necessary to consider the hillforts themselves.

## HILLFORTS AND PROMONTORY FORTS

By the earliest recorded references to the Picts and Scots, the long tradition of constructing and occupying fortified sites in Scotland stretched back almost a millennium through the Iron Age and into the late Bronze Age.[1] With at least 1,500 hillforts recorded in Scotland,[2] this causes problems for the identification and study of early medieval hillforts. While it was traditionally presumed that the great majority of hillforts in Scotland belong to later prehistory, it is now claimed that around 50 per cent of them are of early medieval date in either their construction or some phase of their use.[3] As a result of the reoccupation and/or refortification of later prehistoric hillforts during the early medieval period, Pictish or Scottish hillforts cannot be identified from surface form or appearance alone. Indeed, there may be nothing uniquely or characteristically 'Pictish' or 'Scottish' about hillforts and this is paralleled by the artefacts found within them, which display a wide range of artistic and cultural influences.[4] The attribution of hillforts as 'Pictish' or 'Scottish' is used here simply as a term of convenience to denote early medieval forts that are located within Pictland and *Dál Riata* respectively.

A more conclusive means of identifying early medieval hillforts is through the retrieval of datable material, preferably from a secure archaeological context during the course of excavation. Suitable dating material may comprise either artefacts identifiable to the period or material that can be dated using scientific techniques. For example, carbon-14 dates from the hillfort of Craig Phadraig (Inverness-shire) indicate that its ramparts were constructed in the fourth century BC, but a secondary occupation level within the interior of the hillfort revealed a phase of early medieval activity. This secondary horizon contained a mould for a hanging bowl escutcheon and sherds of Class E imported pottery and also yielded a carbon-14 date of 410±85 AD, giving a calibrated date range between the late fourth and early sixth centuries.[5] However, it is unclear if the ramparts at Craig Phadraig were refurbished during the early medieval period. Some of the best evidence of Pictish hillforts and their associated activities has come from sites that were believed to be of Iron Age date before excavation. Clatchard Craig (Fife) (*see* Plate 3), for example, was assumed to be an Iron Age hillfort before carbon-14 dating revealed that at least three of its multiple ramparts were built during the early medieval period.[6]

Documentary references are of particular interest as a potential means of identifying and dating Pictish and Scottish forts, as well as linking the archaeological record with historically recorded events. The very fact that these places were recorded implies their importance, probably as royal fortresses. Several words are used to describe these fortifications.[7] Their names, recorded in the Irish annals and/or preserved in placenames, often incorporate the Gaelic/Irish word *dún*, 'fort, fortress': *Aberte* (Dunaverty, Argyll), *Dún Att* (Dunadd, Argyll), *Dún Durn* (St Fillan's Hill,

Perthshire), *Dún Fother* (Dunottar, Kincardineshire), *Dúncalden* (Dunkeld, Perthshire) and *Dún Ollaigh* (Dunollie, Argyll).[8] Other fortified sites recorded in the annals, *Dún Baitte, Dún Deauae Dibsi* and *Dún Leithfinn*,[9] remain unidentified but appear to be Pictish or Scottish because they belong to the same stratum of entries in which the identifiable forts are recorded. But the claimed identifications of *Dún Baitte* and *Dún Deauae Dibsi* as Dunbeath (Caithness) and Dundaff (Stirlingshire) respectively[10] are unconfirmed.

Some more unusual terms are also used to refer to fortified sites. These include *caisel* (Irish) or *castellum* (Latin), as in the 'fortress of Créde';[11] *munitio*, the fortress of Bridei son of Maelchon, King of the Northern Picts,[12] and *rath*, 'enclosure', possibly referring to an earthwork fortification[13] and used of the unidentified *Rithe* and *Rathinveramon*, Inveralmond (Perthshire).[14] *Op[p]idum*, 'town', is used instead of *dún* in one reference to Dunottar,[15] indicating its political importance rather than its size or function. Other places, such as *Aberte* (Dunaverty, Kintyre), *Cluana* (Clunie, Perthshire) and *Tairpert Boitter* (Tarbert, Loch Fyne, Argyll), are not named as fortifications in the sources but are referred to in contexts that suggest they were fortresses. This is supported by placename and archaeological evidence in some cases.[16] The methodological issues associated with historical references to forts were explored in Professor Leslie Alcock's programme of excavations on power centres in early medieval Scotland, conducted between 1974 and 1984.[17]

Archaeology provides the best source of evidence, but has so far yielded only a tantalising glimpse of what this resource has to offer. Only a very limited amount of excavation has been devoted to a small number of Pictish and Scottish forts in recent decades, and with very mixed results. While trial excavations at Dundurn amply demonstrated the archaeological potential of the site, traces of early medieval activity were not detected at Urquhart Castle (Inverness-shire) and Dunottar, possibly because of their burial beneath, or disturbance by, later periods of fortification.[18] Moreover, not all excavations of early medieval forts have been fully published, with the absence of a definitive report on those at Craig Phadraig comprising a particular gap. There are also very few published general[19] or regional[20] surveys of forts in Pictland. Even less attention has been devoted to the hillforts of *Dál Riata*. Although a comprehensive and detailed inventory of the many forts of Argyll is available,[21] what little analysis there is focuses on the Iron Age.[22] Only two early medieval hillforts on Argyll, Dunadd and Dunollie, have been excavated and, even then, only a small proportion of their overall areas.[23]

Archaeological evidence suggests that there were two main phases of hillfort construction in Scotland, one during the latter half of the first millennium BC and another beginning in the seventh century AD. The latter has been interpreted as a reflection of growing tensions between the Picts and Scots.[24] But this assessment is based on a tiny sample, the limited proportion of the very small number of forts excavated. Further excavation, together with greater use of scientific dating techniques, may close this apparent gap. Although the construction or occupation of forts may not have continued in areas held by, or accessible to, the Romans during the early centuries AD, other areas may have responded to the Roman threat with increased fort building.

DEFENCES

Hillforts derive their strength from combining naturally defensive locations with man-made fortifications in the form of ramparts (banks or walls) and ditches. But Pictish and Scottish hillforts vary greatly in terms of location, layout, size and defences, influenced by the topography of the locations they occupy and possibly by any earlier fortifications they reused or refurbished. Most forts occupy either prominent and isolated hills or coastal promontories. Some early medieval hillforts are located at lower altitudes. Inland examples include Dunadd (Argyll) and Dundurn (Perthshire),[25] which occupy isolated crags rising from the floors of the Add valley and Strathearn respectively (*see* Plates 4 and 5), and Aldclune (Perthshire),[26] on a gravel ridge in Glen Garry. These locations provide not only tactical defensive advantages, but also strategic control of the surrounding natural resources and communication routes, variously dominating valleys, passes or fords. Dundurn, for example, is located near the head of Strathearn, ideally placed for controlling a major east–west communication route between *Dál Riata* and *Fortriu*, thereby protecting the Pictish heartland from Scottish attacks and/or providing a forward base from which to mount attacks on *Dál Riata*. Other early medieval hillforts occupy lofty hilltops, as at Craig Phadraig and possibly Dunsinane (Perthshire).[27]

Early medieval hillforts in Scotland were traditionally classified by their layout. This distinguished between simple ringforts, 'citadel forts' comprising a free-standing central hill-top enclosure within outer defences and 'nuclear forts', where a central fortified citadel is linked to a series of ramparts enclosing lower terraces.[28] Although the type of site used to define the 'nuclear fort', Dalmahoy (Midlothian), lies south of the Forth, hillforts in both *Dál Riata* and Pictland, notably Dunadd and Dundurn (*see* Plate 6), were assigned to this category. However, hillforts are frequently more complex than their surface appearance indicates and the relationships between different components can only be determined by excavation. Rather than representing unitary structures, hillforts may comprise several phases of construction, with excavation suggesting that hillforts begun in the fifth or sixth centuries did not reach their full extent until the ninth century.[29] The absence of any obvious diagnostic features shared by early medieval hillforts, and which might enable them to be identified by surface features, reinforces the importance of archaeological and documentary dating evidence.

Although they are no longer widely accepted as valid classifications, the concepts of 'citadel' and 'nuclear' forts highlight the hierarchical use of space. The rocky bosses favoured for the siting of many early medieval hillforts (*see* Plates 4 and 5) offered only very limited areas for habitation or other activities, with the result that the hillforts concerned frequently comprise a small summit enclosure with one or more outer enclosures or annexes. This is not simply dictated by the topography but also reflects social and political factors, the exclusivity of access to the 'citadel' emphasising the high social status of the forts' occupants.[30] The siting of an early medieval 'citadel' within the area enclosed by the rampart(s) of an earlier hillfort, as perhaps at Moncreiffe Hill,[31] emphasises this hierarchy of space, making the approach to the summit stronghold all the more impressive and difficult. This also has a military significance, providing defence-in-depth to the summit enclosure, which can be reached only after storming the outer ramparts and overwhelming their defenders. Even if earlier ramparts were not refortified, they would still offer some defence to a determined group attempting to hold the fort against assault.

Promontory forts exploit the strong natural defences provided by coastal headlands, the narrow landward necks of which were strengthened with artificial defences. Coastal promontory forts offered not only tactical defence but, through their association with natural harbours or landfalls, probably played a strategic role in naval warfare.[32] Archaeological evidence for early medieval forts has a mostly coastal distribution[33] and this may reflect the importance of maritime communications and trade as well as naval warfare. Nevertheless, few of the many promontory forts around the coasts of *Dál Riata* and Pictland, have been dated to the early medieval period although many others may do so.[34] Of those that have, most are located on the Moray and Buchan coasts of north-eastern Scotland.[35]

The most impressive of these coastal promontory forts was the great fortress of Burghead (Moray). Although now largely obliterated by the harbour and planned town constructed in 1809, a plan of the fort survives (*see* Plate 27) and nineteenth-century excavations provide a tantalising glimpse of the fort's rich structural remains and occupation layers.[36] That this was a site of great importance, probably a royal fortress, is revealed by its three massive ramparts across the neck of the promontory and its large size. With an internal area of 2 hectares, Burghead is the largest fortified site in early medieval Scotland by a factor of three. Unusually for a promontory fort, Burghead also displays a hierarchical use of space, with an upper 'citadel' and a lower annexe, and is fully enclosed, with ramparts around the seaward sides. Although the landward defences are undated, artefactual evidence and carbon-14 dates from timbers in the seaward ramparts suggest that Burghead was constructed and occupied between the fourth and tenth centuries.[37]

Inland promontory forts of the early medieval period are less common, although this may reflect the fact that few have been excavated and the absence of dating evidence from some that have, such as Hopewell Lodge, Aberdeenshire.[38] However, a small post-Roman example occurs at Inchtuthil (Perthshire).[39]

Islands may also have provided strong defensive locations for forts. The construction of two 'island fortresses' are recorded in the annals, *Ailén Daingen* in 703 and *Ailén mac Craich* in 725.[40] Although the islands concerned are unidentified, these entries belong to the same stratum of annalistic entries concerning Pictish and Scottish forts. Some crannogs, loch dwellings constructed on natural or artificial islets,[41] were certainly occupied by the Scots, as the example in Loch Glashan (Argyll) attests.[42] The defensive role of crannogs is illustrated by an incident in the *Tale of Cano mac Gartnáin* in which Aedán mac Gabráin killed Gartnan son of Aed mac Gabráin in the crannog of *Inis-meic-Uchen* in Skye, and would have killed Cano mac Gartnan, had Cano not escaped with his followers in currachs.[43]

Forts in the northern and western isles are likely to have differed from those on the mainland. Although offering an abundance of easily fortified promontories,[44] the relative scarcity of timber supplies and the long tradition of drystone building in these areas suggests that most early medieval forts were small, stone-built structures. And, as on the mainland, some earlier forts there may have been reoccupied or refurbished. For example, excavations at the 'blockhouse fort' of Scatness (Shetland) yielded radiocarbon dates indicating limited use of the site into the late first millennium.[45] Although these forts are perceived to have been associated with 'ritual' warfare between competing champions,[46] this may reflect the absence of documentary references to forts in the isles. Where forts on the Pictish mainland are recorded it is usually through their involvement in acts of 'real' warfare.

The defences of Pictish and Scottish hillforts display various constructional techniques. The simplest of these comprise simple dump ramparts of earth and stone and of stone-faced ramparts with rubble cores.[47] Where rampart sequences are detectable, the trend is for the defences to become more complex and massive over time. For example, a substantial timber stockade, set in rock-cut grooves, defended the upper terrace at Dundurn during the late sixth or early seventh century. This was succeeded by a massive stone and possibly timber-laced rampart, 8 m wide, and accompanied by the fortification of the hill-top 'citadel' with a timber-laced stone rampart, 4 m wide.[48] It is the collapsed remains of these fortifications, not natural erosion, that account for the apparently scree-strewn slopes of the hill (*see* Plate 4). These defences are comparable in scale with the western rampart of the upper fort at Burghead, which was up to 8.5 m thick and its inner face still survives to a height of 3 m,[49] suggesting that it was originally considerably higher.

The ramparts at Burghead, Dundurn and Portknockie were timber-laced. Their stonework incorporated a timber frame for greater stability and strength, a constructional technique that was particularly well suited for constructing substantial fortifications on uneven or sloping surfaces. This type of rampart is sometimes referred to as *murus Gallicus* from Julius Caesar's[50] description of its use by the Iron Age Gauls, but it was clearly employed more widely, in both space and time. This fortification technique was used in Scotland from as early as the eighth or seventh centuries BC and accounts for the large number of vitrified forts, where the firing of a timber-framed rampart produced such high temperatures that the rampart core melted or partially melted, giving its stones a glassy or slag-like appearance.[51] Although vitrified forts are usually assumed to be Iron Age in date, the use of timber-lacing in some Pictish fortifications suggests that a proportion of vitrified forts may belong to the early medieval period. This is supported by thermoluminescence dating of the ramparts of Finavon Fort (Angus), long believed to belong to the Iron Age or even late Bronze Age, but which produced a date of 640±130 AD.[52] Exceptionally, the internal rampart timbers at Burghead and Dundurn were secured with iron spikes and nails respectively.[53] The spikes at Burghead were some 200 mm long and had possibly been augered, rather than driven, into the timberwork. This level of complexity, and the amounts of resources in both labour and raw materials required, reveals that these fortifications were the preserve of a powerful socio-political élite. Indeed, as the use of nails or spikes offers little or no structural advantages, these ramparts were as much symbols of power as defensive fortifications and this probably applies to hillforts in general.

The symbolic significance of the defences of some Pictish forts is also implied by their reuse of masonry from abandoned Roman forts. The massive inner rampart of the possibly multi-period promontory fort at Inchtuthil incorporated dressed Gourdie stone from the rampart of the nearby Roman legionary fortress.[54] But the Roman masonry reused in the ramparts at Clatchard Craig and Dundurn[55] must have been carried a much greater distance and uphill, requiring considerable labour. These cases indicate that the reuse of Roman masonry was not simply utilitarian in motivation but, by manufacturing a tangible link with the past, was also of great symbolic power. This may have been used by Pictish socio-political élites to derive prestige or legitimise their power by either emphasising their descent from those who defeated the Romans or possibly even by casting themselves as the inheritors of Roman imperial power.[56] The possible identification of *Rathinveramon*, where kings Domnall mac Ailpín died in 862 and Causantín mac Cuilén was killed in 997,[57] with the reoccupied Roman fort of Bertha[58] (Perthshire) is of particular interest here.

The weakest point in the defences of any fort was usually the entrance, which is why most early medieval forts have either restricted access and/or only a single entrance. Entrances usually take optimum defensive advantage of the topography, sometimes spectacularly so, as at Dunadd, where the hillfort is entered through a natural cleft in the rock. The entrance was a very significant component of any fort and it is interesting that the gateway features so prominently in Adomnán's[59] account of Bridei's fortress (*munitio*), where Columba found his way barred on his arrival. Although the fortifications themselves are not described, the entrance through them comprised a double-leaved gate secured with bars.

## FORTS AS TARGETS

Pictish and Scottish forts occupied positions of both tactical and strategic strength. They were also centres and symbols of power and wealth, holding concentrations of portable property, particularly metalwork, livestock, slaves and agricultural produce. It is hardly surprising, therefore, that forts in general and royal fortresses in particular were attractive targets for hostile forces intent on seizing goods, power and/or territory. Indeed, Pictish and Scottish forts are recorded in documentary sources primarily as a result of their association with warfare. But attacks on hillforts were recorded as notable events in their own right and the wider military and political significance of these actions often remains obscure. As a result, it is usually unclear whether an assault on a hillfort was the sole objective or if this simply formed one element, of either tactical or strategic significance, in a more extensive campaign.

Attacks on royal fortresses in particular may have had various objectives, both military and political, and were probably also of symbolic significance, the capture and destruction of an enemy's royal centre perhaps symbolising that of the kingdom itself. In some cases this may have resulted in a battle being fought near a fort that was the aggressor's target and/or the defender's rallying point. Despite the difficulties in identifying early medieval battlefields, the association of some battles with forts is revealed by placename evidence. The name given by the Irish annals[60] to the battle fought between the Picts and Northumbrians in 685, *Dún Nechtain*, 'Nechtan's Fort', is of particular interest here. This battle presumably took its name from the fort on Castle Hill, the southern shoulder of Dunnichen Hill, overlooking the battlefield.[61] This may be a Pictish hillfort and its name certainly incorporates a Pictish personal name, Nechtan,[62] although the fort may already have been ancient when it acquired this name. Damaged, if not obliterated, by quarrying, Nechtan's Fort is likely to remain shrouded in mystery.

Battles near forts are also a feature of internal power struggles. Royal centres, particularly inauguration sites, fulfilled a symbolic function, their possession conferring or symbolising a claimant's possession of the kingship itself, with the result that they became a focus of battles for the kingship. This appears to have been the case during a war for the Pictish kingship, when rival contenders fought two battles at or near forts in 728. The first battle occurred at *Monid Craebe* or *Monidhcrobh*, probably Moncreiffe Hill.[63] Strategically located between the rivers Earn and Tay, Moncreiffe Hill is crowned by the multi-period hillfort of Moredun.[64] This may be a Pictish fort in at least one of its phases, although excavation is required to test its suggested identification as 'one of the royal fortresses of *Fortriu*'.[65] The same opponents also fought a battle at the unidentified *Caislén Credi* or *Castellum Credi*, the 'fortress of Créde', traditionally but mistakenly identified with the possible Pictish royal centre and inauguration site at Scone.[66] The association of both forts with battles indicates that they were of strategic significance, perhaps because of their proximity to Scone, only 7 km from Moncreiffe Hill. Although neither battle was fought at Scone, the royal centre may still have been the intended prize.

In all these cases, the nature of the relationship between the battle and the fort from which its name is derived is unclear. In the case of forts that were well-known or prominent landmarks, the battle may have occurred some distance away. Other battles fought at or near forts are examined in the case studies below, where the availability of more evidence provides insights into the military significance of the forts concerned.

The three main methods of attack employed against fortifications during the early medieval period were burning, direct assault and siege, or any combination of these. Although the Irish annals provide most of the evidence for attacks on forts, the relevant entries are even less informative than those concerning most battles. The burning (*combustio*), destruction (*distructio*) and siege (*obsessio*) of forts feature prominently in the Scottish entries in the Irish annals. But these entries are characteristically laconic and formulaic, simply naming the fort concerned and rarely recording its location or the identities of the combatants, presumably because they were obvious to those compiling the annals. Even the circumstances in which a fort was burned or destroyed and the outcomes of sieges usually go unrecorded. This need not imply that these sieges were unsuccessful, simply that the siege itself was the most noteworthy event. The actual seizing of a fort was presumably commonplace, it was the manner in which it occurred and the outcome that were of interest. Despite the dearth of information, some of the forts concerned are identifiable from their names and/or the historical context in which they are recorded, enabling the combatants to be inferred. Other forts remain unlocated and, like some battles, it is even unclear whether some were in Scotland or Ireland. But, as all the identifiable sieges occurred in Scotland, it seems probable that the others also did and that all the relevant annalistic entries originated on Iona.

The extensive use of wood in their construction, including gateways, stockades, timber-laced ramparts and internal buildings, made forts particularly vulnerable to fire. Firing was a simple and common means of attack in early medieval warfare. Fire breached defences and either killed defenders or drove them from the security of their fort, forcing them to flee or fight in open field, while posing only minimal risks to the aggressors. Fire was also a weapon of last resort, where a frontal attack or siege failed or was not practicable. Bede records such an event in Northumbria, when Penda, King of Mercia, attacked the royal fortress of Bamburgh: 'As he could not capture it by assault or siege, he attempted to set it on fire. He pulled down all the steadings which he found in the neighbourhood of the town and brought thither a vast heap of beams, rafters, walls of wattles, and thatched roofs, and built them up to an immense height around that side of the city which faced the land; then when a favourable wind arose, he set it on fire in an attempt to burn the town.'[67] Bamburgh and its inhabitants were saved by divine intervention when the wind changed direction. Such attacks may account for entries recording the death by fire of individuals, such as the 'burning of the son of Iarndodb mac Gartnait' in 643.[68] The destruction by fire of such important and prominent forts must have been spectacular sights, as well as having perhaps far-reaching military and political implications.

The burning of several Pictish and Scottish forts are recorded in the annals: Dunollie in 685 and 698 and *Tairpert Boitter* in 712 and 731.[69] Although none of these burnings are attributed to military action, all the entries belong to an annalistic horizon recording attacks on Pictish and Scottish forts. Another entry from the same annalistic stratum records the burning of *Creich* by the Picts in 736 during a campaign in *Dál Riata* in which they also seized Dunadd[70] (*see* Plate 1). *Creich* was probably another fort in mid-Argyll but remains elusive, despite its claimed identification with places of the same name,[71] and may be related to *Ailén mac Craich*. Dunblane was burned by the Strathclyde Britons during the reign of Cináed mac Ailpín (Kenneth mac Alpin, 'Kenneth I') (843–58).[72] The name means 'the fort of [St] Blane' and this may have been the location of a fortress,[73] possibly the substantial ditched enclosure recently discovered by aerial reconnaissance.[74] However, the relevance of Dunblane's modern name is questionable, because it appears in the text as *Dulblain*, 'the hill-meadow of [St] Blane'.[75] The Scots mounted similar attacks and the presumably fortified Northumbrian royal centre of Dunbar (East Lothian) was seized and burned during one of Cináed's raids.[76] The Strathclyde Britons were equally vulnerable to such attacks and their royal fortress at Dumbarton Rock was burned on 1 January 780,[77] although by whom is not recorded.

Consistent with the documentary sources, there is archaeological evidence of extensive burning at some forts. The burned rampart core at Burghead marks the swift and catastrophic end of the fortress by fire, in what is claimed to have been a Viking attack.[78] Excavation revealed that the earliest timber-laced rampart enclosing the citadel at Dundurn had been destroyed by fire and radiocarbon dates obtained from these defences are probably consistent with their destruction in a siege recorded in 683.[79] In addition, the many vitrified forts, particularly in north-east Scotland, attest the destruction of timber-laced ramparts by fire and some of these may date to the early medieval period. Archaeology offers great potential for studying the role of forts in early medieval warfare. But, in practice, it is always extremely difficult to distinguish between the accidental and deliberate destruction of hillforts and it cannot be confirmed that the burning of either Burghead or Dundurn was a result of military action.

In contrast, the destruction of forts is clearly attributed to military action in contemporary sources. Dunollie was destroyed in an internal power struggle within *Dál Riata* in 701[80] and *Dún Leithfinn* by the Picts in 734.[81] As the annals appear to make a distinction between burning and destruction, the implication may be that these forts were destroyed by being physically dismantled. But it is uncertain whether the forts were destroyed during the assault itself or if they were demolished after their capture, perhaps to prevent them from being reused by the enemy and/or to emphasise the completeness of their occupants' defeat. Curiously, there are no annalistic entries recording the storming (*expugnatio*) of Pictish or Scottish forts, in contrast to warfare in early medieval Ireland. This suggests that the direct assault of forts was not favoured among the Picts and Scots, who may have preferred to fire or besiege forts, presumably entering only once their defenders had fled, surrendered or were incapacitated.

## *OBSESSIO*: SIEGE WARFARE

Sieges were a prominent element of Pictish and Scottish warfare. Indeed, most annalistic references to Pictish and Scottish forts record sieges: *Rithe* in 641, *Dún Baitte* in 680, Dunottar in 681, Dunadd and Dundurn in 683, *Dún Deauae Dibsi* in 692, Dunottar again in 694, *Rithe* again in 703 and Dunaverty in 712.[82] The besieging of a person, Alpín mac Croip, presumably in a fort, is also recorded in 742.[83] Although the records of the second sieges of Dunottar and of *Rithe* are claimed to be scribal errors repeating earlier entries,[84] the identical wording of the entries is more probably attributable to their formulaic nature. These multiple entries attest the importance of the forts concerned and both the political instability and prevalence of siege warfare during this period. Nevertheless, recorded sieges probably represent only a small proportion of those in which the Picts and Scots were involved, those that came to the attention of the Iona chroniclers. As a result of Iona's location, most of the sieges recorded in the annals are of fortresses in *Dál Riata* and Southern Pictland.

These entries prove that forts played an active role in warfare. At least some attacks were resisted as occupants attempted to defend their forts. With the defences frustrating initial assault, the only option for the aggressors was to besiege the fort concerned. The nature and duration of these siege operations are uncertain. There is no evidence, archaeological or documentary, for the construction of any form of siege works or engines, such as those commonly used in Classical and medieval siege warfare. Instead, the attacking force probably laid siege to a fort by encamping on the plain or adjacent hills around it, beyond the range of the defenders' missiles. Indeed, the Vikings who besieged Dumbarton Rock for four months in 870 are described simply as 'camping against' the Strathclyde Britons.[85] In this case the Vikings would have had the advantage of their ships, which carried provisions and provided shelter, but other forms of 'camping' would have been more basic and are unlikely to have been sustainable over a prolonged period. There they would attempt to isolate the defenders until their food, water or will to fight were exhausted, compelling them to surrender.

These outcomes are illustrated by accounts of two sieges of Dumbarton Rock. The Britons were forced to submit when confronted by a superior allied force of Picts and Northumbrians in 756: 'King Eadberht [of Northumbria] . . . and Unuist, King of the Picts, led an army to the city of Alcwith [i.e. *Alt Clut*, Dumbarton]. And hence the Britons accepted terms there, on the first day of the month of August.'[86] In contrast, it took a siege lasting four months before the Dublin Vikings took Dumbarton Rock in 870, only attacking when the defenders were weakened by lack of food and water.[87] This is the only occasion on which the length of a siege is recorded, presumably because it was considered exceptional. In what may be remarkable archaeological corroboration of this siege or its aftermath, the pommel of a Viking sword and a Viking lead weight were found during excavations on Dumbarton Rock.[88] Although there are no recorded instances of sieges being raised, it would be surprising if this did not occur, for example, when the attacking force exhausted its own supplies or will to fight or was counterattacked by either the occupants of the fort besieged or an allied force coming to its relief.

Although booty was a major motivation in besieging royal forts, as it was in warfare generally,[89] the sources remain curiously reticent about the plundering of forts. Only two examples are recorded, both concerning Dumbarton. The taking of Dumbarton by Aedán mac Gabráin (574–?608) features in the 'Three Unrestrained Ravagings of the Island of Britain' (*Teir Drut Heirua Ynys Brydein*) listed in the Welsh triads: 'Aedán the Wily came to the court of Rhydderch Hael at *Alclud*; he left neither food nor drink nor beast alive'.[90] And, when Dumbarton Rock fell in 870, the Vikings not only 'destroyed and plundered it',[91] but 'took all the goods that were inside. A great host was taken out into captivity.'[92] This, presumably, was a major source of the Britons enslaved by the Vikings, who 'returned to Dublin from *Alba* with 200 ships, bringing away with them in captivity to Ireland a great prey of Angles and Britons and Picts' the following year.[93] Indeed, so significant were Aedán's plundering and the Viking siege of Dumbarton Rock that either or both of these events were probably the theme of two Irish tales, the 'Plundering of Dumbarton' (*Argain Atha Cliath*) and the 'Plundering of Strathclyde' (*Argain Sratha Cluada*), although only their titles survive.[94]

Medieval siege warfare was regulated by a series of conventions and laws of ancient origin covering the conduct of sieges, surrender terms, the treatment of captives and looting.[95] Although there is no evidence of this among the Picts and Scots, it would be surprising, given the apparent frequency of sieges in early medieval Scotland, if some form of (unwritten) code of conduct was not employed in siege warfare. What form any conventions may have taken is obscure, although the absence of references to the storming of forts is suggestive. Lack of familiarity with, or even rejection of, such conventions by the Vikings may have led to the exceptional length of their siege of Dumbarton Rock and the large numbers enslaved once the fortress fell.

Sieges were more numerous than pitched battles in medieval warfare.[96] Although there is no evidence that this was the case among the Picts and Scots in general, there were brief periods when recorded sieges outnumbered recorded battles. For example, no pitched battles between the Picts and Scots are recorded during the period between 680 and 694, in contrast to the siege and/or destruction of six Pictish and Scottish forts. When battles that take their names from forts – indicating that they were fought at or near the forts named – are also taken into account, it becomes apparent that forts played a prominent role in the wars of the Picts and Scots between the late seventh and mid-eighth centuries. This coincides with the last half-century of annalistic composition on Iona, when the annals display a more detailed interest in Scottish affairs. The prominence of warfare involving forts at this time may therefore reflect the circumstances of annalistic recording rather than any differences in the warfare of the period, suggesting that the besieging and burning of forts were just as numerous at other times.

## FORTS IN ACTION

### Wars between the Picts and the Scots

The heaviest concentration of recorded sieges of Pictish and Scottish forts occurred between 680 and 683, with four sieges in as many years. These sieges have been attributed to Bridei son of Bile, King of the (probably Southern) Picts.[97] Although there is no direct evidence of his involvement, Bridei was campaigning actively during this period, as his destruction of Orkney in 682 and victory in the battle of Dunnichen in 685 attest.[98] Indeed, the burning of Dunollie is recorded in the same annalistic entry as the battle of Dunnichen,[99] although this may be a corrupt entry.[100]

The locations of the forts besieged, where identifiable, indicates the identities of the warring parties. Dunadd and Dundurn were both besieged in 683,[101] the only case of two sieges being recorded in the same year. Moreover, the recording of both sieges in the same annalistic entry indicates that they were linked, perhaps occurring during the same campaign. This suggests the ebb and flow of military fortunes as warfare was waged across *Druim Alban*, with a Pictish siege of Dunadd perhaps provoking a Scottish counter-offensive that included the siege of Dundurn. This entry also implies the equivalent status of Dunadd and Dundurn, as royal fortresses of the kings of *Dál Riata* and *Fortriu* or Southern Pictland respectively, if not in terms of the actual sieges then at least in the annalists' perception of them as events worth recording. This seems more plausible than the attribution of these sieges to an internal Scottish dispute and a presumably unrelated border skirmish, neither with any special significance.[102] The sieges of Dunadd and Dundurn hint at the cyclical nature of violence between the Picts and Scots, with military actions, whether sieges, battles or raids, perhaps triggering later attacks to seek revenge or regain honour.

Although no sieges are recorded, forts also feature prominently in the campaigns of Unuist son of Uurguist, King of the Picts, against *Dál Riata* in the 730s. In 734, the Picts destroyed *Dún Leithfinn*,[103] an unidentified and apparently royal fort. This involved a struggle, perhaps even a battle, because it occurred 'after the wounding of Dúngal', King of *Dál Riata*. The Picts may have attacked or besieged another fort in *Dál Riata* the same year, as Talorcan son of Drostan, one of Unuist's Pictish opponents, was captured 'near Dunollie'.[104] Forts were also targeted when Unuist invaded *Dál Riata* again in 736. After his brother Talorgan defeated a Scottish army at *Cnoc Cairpri* at Ederline, only 10 km north of Dunadd, Unuist laid waste to *Dál Riata*, seized Dunadd and burned *Creich*[105] (*see* Plate 1). Unuist also 'bound in chains two sons of Selbach, i.e. Dúngal and Feradach'.[106] Although the annals do not state explicitly that they were captured at Dunadd or *Creich*, the implication is that forts were a good source of royal hostages who could then be ransomed or held to ensure the compliance of a subject kingdom and its payment of tribute.[107]

Within the interior of the hillfort of Dunadd, a unique group of carvings, now covered by a fibreglass replica for their protection, occupies a bedrock shelf below the summit and just outside the entrance to the citadel[108] (*see* Plate 28). Some of these carvings are traditionally believed to be Pictish and interpreted as evidence of the hillfort's capture by the Picts, probably in 736.[109] Indeed, so confident was the Royal Commission on the Ancient and Historical Monuments of Scotland of this interpretation that they pronounced 'a Pictish origin for the artist seems certain'.[110] An incised wild boar or, less probably, domestic pig[111] (*see* Plate 29), was considered similar to Pictish examples at Clune and Knocknagael (both Inverness-shire).[112] In addition, an inscription in ogam script, comprising short strokes off baselines provided by natural fissures in the bedrock, was claimed to be Pictish because, like examples in Pictland, it was allegedly unintelligible.[113]

Superficially, both the sculpture and inscription appear to be outlying examples of those found exclusively or predominantly in Pictland. But the Dunadd boar has no uniquely 'Pictish' features, lacking both the elaborate joint scrolls that are characteristic of Pictish animal sculpture and precise parallels in Pictland, where animal sculpture occurs predominantly on monoliths and in conjunction with Pictish symbols. Instead, the Dunadd boar belongs to a widely occurring style of early medieval insular animal art, examples of which are also found in the *Book of Kells* and the *Lindisfarne Gospels*.[114] Pictish sculpture appears to be the closest parallel to the Dunadd boar because it is also naturalistic and also in stone, but that does not make the Dunadd carving Pictish. More categorically, recent advances in the study of ogam scripts reveal that the Dunadd inscription displays no Pictish characteristics but is instead Irish in form and can be read partially to give a personal name.[115]

Both the boar carving and the ogam inscription may be associated with other features on the same rock surface (*see* Plate 28). In particular, a rock-cut basin and a carved human footprint, to which may be added the more recently discovered pecked outline of another footprint, have long been interpreted as evidence of Dunadd's status as the inauguration site of the kings of *Dál Riata*.[116] The Dunadd carvings are now generally accepted as Scottish, not Pictish, and as evidence that the rock platform was a focus of ritual activity, probably royal inauguration rituals.[117] If Dunadd was the inauguration site of the kings of *Dál Riata* between the late seventh and mid-eighth centuries, this underlines the political and symbolic importance of the fort as a target for Pictish attacks.

Two areas of doubt remain about the Dunadd carvings. The basin may be a prehistoric cup-mark[118] while the incised head and shoulders of a hatted or crowned man smoking a pipe below the inscription 'KING FERGUS' was added sometime between 1904 and 1928, when a protective glass plate was installed. These emphasise that the Dunadd carvings range widely in date. Although the boar carving and ogam inscription are early medieval in date, they need not be contemporary with each other or with the other features on the rock surface. As a result, some uncertainty remains about their interpretation.

A widely cited argument against the traditional attribution of the carvings to the Picts is that they would have been erased when the Scots regained control of Dunadd.[119] But what successive commentators have overlooked is that the Dunadd boar *has* been defaced, at least partially. The boar's back, probably with its original and characteristic crest of dorsal bristles, and the top of its head are scarcely visible (*see* Plate 29). Although this damage has been attributed to natural weathering,[120] this seems improbable given that adjacent areas of the same carving, incised on the same rock, have been affected to a much lesser degree. Instead, this part of the boar carving has been deliberately obliterated by pecking out an area of rock. This indicates that the boar had sufficiently negative associations for someone to attempt to remove it, but who may have been interrupted in the process or had insufficient time to erase it completely. Instead of the boar carving being of Pictish origin, it may instead have been the Picts who defaced a Scottish carving during one of the occasions on which they captured, and probably destroyed, Dunadd.

## Trusty's Hill

Another sculpture found inside a hillfort has also been interpreted as evidence of Pictish military activity. Incised on an outcropping rock inside the entrance to the small fort on Trusty's Hill, Anwoth (Kirkcudbrightshire), are a serpent-like creature and sword-like carving,[121] both of which are unparalleled, a human head with antennae or horns and a double-disc and Z-rod symbol of unmistakably Pictish form.[122] These carvings are widely interpreted as Pictish and as evidence of the fort's capture by a raiding party of Picts.[123] If this was the case, these carvings provide unique evidence of a Pictish attack deep into Galloway, almost to the Solway Firth. This has wider implications. It emphasises that, other than those concerning *Dál Riata*, Pictish campaigns and attacks on forts are poorly recorded in documentary sources. Moreover, if it demonstrates a Pictish predilection for leaving a carved calling card in seized hillforts, the Trusty's Hill symbol may support the interpretation of the Dunadd boar as evidence of that fort's capture by the Picts.

But the Trusty's Hill carvings remain controversial. First, the double-disc and Z-rod symbol is of a stylistically late form. It is similar to those found on Class II stones, cross-slabs bearing Pictish symbols in relief, and therefore probably dates to the mid-eighth century or later.[124] This rules out any link with the historical context usually claimed for the symbol, the Pictish advance into southern Scotland after their victory over the Northumbrians in the battle of Dunnichen in 685. Moreover, the fort on Trusty's Hill is unlikely to have been besieged by the Picts because it is later prehistoric in date. Excavation yielded no evidence of early medieval activity,[125] although only a small area was excavated. And although the hill's name appears to be related to the Pictish name Drosten (also Drest or Drust), it is more probably derived from a related

British name, Tristan, which may not have been attached to the hill until after the fort was abandoned.

The authenticity of the Trusty's Hill carvings has been questioned:[126] they have been described as 'dubious',[127] while 'the possibility that we are dealing with relatively modern forgeries should not be discounted'.[128] Nevertheless, the double-disc and Z-rod symbol is indisputably Pictish, and not only in its origin and inspiration. Representing the most artistically developed form of this symbol, the double-disc and Z-rod displays a confidence on the part of the sculptor that reveals it to have been carved by Pictish hands. The absence of Pictish parallels for the other carvings is not problematic as they need not be contemporaneous with the double disc and Z-rod but could be Iron Age or modern, or a combination of both.[129] Like Dunadd, the rock outcrop on Trusty's Hill probably includes carvings that range widely in date, as the presence of modern graffiti attests.

Even if the double-disc and Z-rod symbol was Pictish in execution, it need not have been carved on a military expedition. The symbol has also been interpreted as commemorating a marital alliance between the ruling aristocracies of Pictland and either the North British kingdom of *Rheged* or, given the symbol's late date, the Angles of Northumbria.[130] However, this interpretation of the function of Pictish symbols, proposed by Dr Anthony Jackson,[131] has been rejected comprehensively.[132] Alternatively, the symbol may have had a religious symbolism, perhaps related to the ritual associations of hillforts and hilltops and possibly attracted by the presence of earlier carvings and their perceived significance. Trusty's Hill lies only 22 km (14 miles) across Wigtown Bay from the important ecclesiastical centre of Whithorn, which had links with Pictland and probably attracted Pictish pilgrims. Although there is nothing overtly Christian about any of the carvings on Trusty's Hill, the travels of Pictish pilgrims may explain the presence of a Pictish symbol so far outside Pictland. Although its interpretation remains unclear, the double-disc and Z-rod symbol on Trusty's Hill cannot be accepted as evidence of the capture of this hillfort by the Picts.

## Power Struggles of Dál Riata

Returning to *Dál Riata*, the military importance of forts is apparent from the internal power struggles of the early eighth century, in which the dominant royal dynasties of *Cenél nGabráin* and *Cenél Loairn* fought over the kingship. The internecine nature and proximity of this conflict, as well as the importance of its outcome to relations between the kingship of *Dál Riata* and the community of Iona, made it of particular interest to the annalists. The annalistic entries are more frequent and contain greater detail than those recording other wars and this provides unique insights into the nature of warfare in *Dál Riata* and, by extension, Pictland. Most notably, this warfare is characterised by attacks on forts rather than pitched battles. In a period of 33 years, only 3 land battles and 1 naval battle are recorded, in contrast to a range of activity involving forts, comprising the (re)construction of 3 forts, 3 burnings, 2 destructions and 1 siege. Uniquely, some of these attacks are specifically attributed to two kings of *Dál Riata*, Selbach mac Ferchair (699–723) and his son, Dúngal mac Selbaich (723–?726).

The importance of forts in the warfare associated with this power struggle is revealed in a series of annalistic entries. Dunollie, the principal stronghold of *Cenél Loairn*, was burned in 698[133] and presumably rebuilt because it was then destroyed by Selbach in 701.[134] *Ailén Daingen* was constructed in 703.[135] In 712, Selbach burned *Tairpert Boitter*, Tarbert in Kintyre, and besieged *Aberte*, Dunaverty, on the Mull of Kintyre.[136] In 714, Dunollie was (re)built by Selbach and *Ailén Daingen* was destroyed.[137] The construction and destruction of fortifications continued during the reign of Dúngal. *Ailén mac Craich* was built in 725[138] and *Tairpert Boitter* was burned again, this time by Dúngal, in 731.[139] Where they are identifiable, the forts concerned are of strategic importance, controlling not only territory and communication routes but also, of vital importance in *Dál Riata*, natural harbours and landfalls.[140]

If the warfare recorded in *Dál Riata* during the early eighth century was typical of that fought by the Picts and Scots, then military actions involving forts in other areas and periods are greatly under-represented in the annals. Of course, this warfare may have been different in nature. In contrast to the episodic warfare between hostile kingdoms that occasionally culminated in a large pitched battle, this internal warfare in *Dál Riata* may have been more attritional in nature and placed a greater importance on the capture and control of territory. Forts clearly played a central role in this. But, at the very least, it alerts us to the possibility that more, and possibly most, warfare fought by the Picts and Scots was focused on forts, their besieging, capture, plunder and destruction, than is immediately apparent from the sources.

## Viking Attacks

The ninth century saw the eclipse of Pictish power by the Scots and the shift of power eastwards into the traditional heartland of the Picts, where many formerly Pictish royal centres continued in use as the power centres of the kings of *Alba*. The advent of Viking raids must have ensured the continued importance of these forts throughout the ninth century. In probably 848, the

Danes laid waste to Pictland as far as Clunie and Dunkeld (both Perthshire).[141] These were probably fortified royal centres and may be identified with the hillfort on the King's Seat, Dunkeld, and the site now occupied by Clunie Castle, where the outer earthworks suggest an earlier fort.[142] The entry is ambiguous but suggests that Clunie and Dunkeld were either targeted by the raiders or withstood the attack and prevented the Danes from plundering more extensively. Other Viking raids in *Fortriu* presumably involved attacks on royal forts and, although none are recorded, this simply reflects the paucity and terseness of documentary sources during the ninth century. Coastal forts must have been most vulnerable and, consistent with this, King Domnall mac Causantín (Donald son of Constantine, 'Donald II') was killed by the Vikings at Dunottar in 900.[143]

The northern and western isles and coasts were particularly exposed to Viking raids and yet, with the exception of attacks on Iona,[144] these are unrecorded. Archaeological evidence from some promontory forts on the Moray coast may help to fill the gap. A late phase of fortification, possibly against the Vikings, was constructed at Green Castle, Portknockie. Burned structural timbers from a timber-laced rampart there yielded carbon-14 dates of 655±40 and 740±45 AD,[145] although these seem too early to link this refortification to the Viking threat. The defences of Burghead may also have been refurbished in the ninth century to counter this new threat, and this may be supported by a carbon-14 date of 865±40 AD.[146] The final destruction of Burghead, attested in archaeological evidence of intense burning, is commonly attributed to a Viking attack, with accumulations of wind-blown sand indicating that the fort was subsequently abandoned.[147] Burghead's name includes Norse *burg*, denoting a fortified place. But although this attests Norse linguistic influence and perhaps even a Viking presence in the area, the name may have been given to Burghead after the fortress was destroyed.

The small number of Viking attacks recorded on Scottish forts are overshadowed by the siege of Dumbarton Rock in 870. This episode reveals the changing character of warfare involving forts during the ninth century. In probably one of the largest military actions involving a fortress in northern Britain, the Dublin Vikings under Amlaíb and Imhar (Ívar) besieged Dumbarton Rock, royal fortress of the Strathclyde Britons, for four months, only capturing it when its defenders were forced to surrender because their water supply dried up.[148] This siege was unparalleled in its scale and duration. The attackers were clearly prepared to commit considerable resources to taking the fortress, presumably reflecting the extensive spoils they believed their efforts would yield. This is supported by accounts of the plundering of Dumbarton and enslavement of its occupants.[149]

## CHAPTER SEVEN

# Naval Warfare

The geography of Scotland north of the Forth–Clyde isthmus dictated that the sea was of great importance to the Picts and the Scots. Characterised by a largely mountainous and inaccessible interior, northern Scotland has a long coastline. Broad estuaries on its eastern seaboard and sea lochs on its western and northern seaboards penetrate deep inland, while extensive archipelagos lie off its northern and western coasts. Indeed, the territory of *Dál Riata* comprised only scattered islands and peninsulas. The sea formed the highways between these otherwise remote realms and was fundamental to the existence of *Dál Riata*, the arteries of the kingdom. The importance of sea travel in *Dál Riata* is confirmed by contemporary sources: fifty-five separate voyages and thirty-five voyages or naval expeditions are recorded or implied in Adomnán's *Life of Columba* and Scottish entries in the Irish annals respectively.[1] These sources, both written on Iona, reveal the tiny isle as the hub of an extensive maritime network.[2]

The maritime connections of *Dál Riata* and Pictland are most apparent in the context of trading links. Adomnán[3] records the presence of the master and sailors of a vessel from Gaul at the 'chief place of the district' (*caput regionis*), probably a royal centre, in *Dál Riata* and based his account of the sites of the Holy Land, *De Locis Sanctis*, on the testimony of a bishop from Merovingian Gaul who reached Iona after being blown off course and shipwrecked. These links are confirmed by evidence of exotic imports from the Continent and the Mediterranean, including pottery from vessels used to import foodstuffs, glass vessels and materials such as orpiment and porphyry.[4]

Naval warfare and coastal raiding among the Picts and the Scots have received less attention than the study of maritime trade. Perhaps the technology and organisation required seem incompatible with such peripheral peoples or with the stereotype of marauding barbarians. Yet that was not the case with the Vikings, whose seafaring achievements have tended to overshadow those of the peoples of early medieval Britain. The neighbouring peoples of the Picts and Scots possessed shipbuilding technology, naval power and traditions of naval warfare in the centuries before the Vikings.[5] The Anglo-Saxons were accomplished shipwrights and seamen,[6] bringing them from their Germanic homelands and into direct contact with the Picts. The Irish were also renowned for their navigational skills and exploits,[7] their achievements characterised by the seafaring saint, Brendan the Navigator.[8] Given the maritime traditions of these neighbouring peoples, it would be surprising if the Picts and Scots did not also possess comparable skills and technology.

Indeed, both the Picts and Scots were perceived as *gentibus transmarinis*, 'peoples from across the sea'.[9] This reflects an enduring southern perspective, first recorded during the first century,[10] of Scotland north of the Forth–Clyde isthmus as a separate island, the land seemingly divided by wide estuaries on either side. But this label did not rest merely on geographical misconceptions. The Picts and Scots were both perceived to be nautical peoples, as their origin myths emphasise. According to Bede,[11] 'Pictish seafarers' sailed from Scythia 'in a few longships', arriving first in Ireland before settling in northern Britain. Similarly, the *Senchus fer nAlban*[12] relates how the sons of Erc, the mythical founders of *Dál Riata*, 'went forth' with a 'ship expedition' from Ireland to found their new kingdom. Although these accounts are mythical, they presumably reflect the contemporary seafaring capabilities, traditions and reputations of the Picts and Scots.

This chapter considers all aspects of Pictish and Scottish naval warfare, from obligation and organisation, through naval battles and maritime raids, before concluding with a look at the types of vessels used. Although the evidence is limited, it provides glimpses of a remarkable and largely unrecognised record of Pictish and Scottish naval achievement.

## NAVAL OBLIGATION AND ORGANISATION

The importance of naval warfare to the Scots is emphasised by the existence of a formal system for assessing naval obligation and service in *Dál Riata*. This was done in exactly the same way as military obligation and service were assessed.[13] The *Senchus fer nAlban*[14] records that the unit of assessment in each of the three *cenél* of *Dál Riata* was the house (*tech*) and that every group of twenty houses was obliged to provide 'two seven-benchers' (*da shecht-sess*).[15] This obligation is directly related to the number of oarsmen required to crew a ship, which is why the *Senchus* specifies the size of the vessels concerned in this manner. With a minimum of 15 men crewing a 7-bencher, 14 oarsmen (2 to a bench) and 1 steersman, each group of 20 houses was required to provide at least 30 men for naval service. The frequency and duration of this naval service is not apparent but, like military service, it was presumably owed by free commoners who spent most of their time working the land. However, Adomnán's[16] frequent references to sailors (*nautae, navigantes, navigatores*) implies the existence of a professional group, as do the specialised navigational and seafaring skills that they possessed.

The basis of naval obligation among the Picts is not recorded, but may have been similar to that of the Scots. As late as 1304, each *davach* in the Aboyne area of Aberdeenshire was ordered to crew a galley of twenty oars, presumably with one man from each household.[17] This indicates that, as in *Dál Riata c.* 700, the unit of assessment was the house and obligation for naval service was calculated in groups of twenty houses. But it is unclear whether this represents a survival of Pictish naval obligation or of Scottish practices introduced sometime after the eclipse of Pictish power in the mid-ninth century.

The *Senchus* records that naval service was levied to crew a 'sea expedition' (*fecht mara*) and an 'expeditionary force for sea-voyaging' (*fecht immora for iomram*).[18] These terms appear to have been interchangeable and *fecht* reveals that this obligation involved warfare. This contrasts with the 'ship expedition' (*an longas do lodar*) of 150 men by which, according to tradition, the sons of Erc set out for *Dál Riata*. As with military obligation, the *Senchus* calculates naval obligation within each kin group of *Dál Riata*, indicating that this was the basis on which fleets were organised but attesting a centralised authority capable of raising a fleet from across *Dál Riata*. When adjusted to compensate for an internal error,[19] the total numbers of men levied from each *cenél* enables the size of those fleets to be calculated, given that each ship had a minimum crew of 15. *Cenél nGabráin* could raise 840 men, crewing 56 ships, *Cenél Loairn* could raise 630 men, crewing 42 ships, and *Cenél nOengusa* could raise 645 men, crewing 43 ships. This gives a total naval strength for *Dál Riata* of 141 ships, with crews totalling 2,115 men. But allowing for relief crews suggests an even higher level of naval obligation in *Dál Riata*.[20]

Despite the significance they must have had in naval organisation and warfare, only two references to a fleet (Latin, *clas[s]em*; Irish, *murcoblach*) of *Dál Riata* are recorded in the Irish annals, in 567 and 733.[21] No indication of the fleets' composition or strength is given on either occasion. More information is available concerning the size of Pictish fleets. One reference suggests the scale of Pictish naval obligation and organisation and the importance placed on naval warfare by the Picts. In 729, 'A hundred and fifty Pictish ships were wrecked upon *Ros Cuissine*',[22] presumably when they were driven onto a headland (*ros*) during a storm. Although it is unclear if this represents the entire fleet or just the vessels lost, this was a very sizeable force, of comparable size to the entire fleet of

*Dál Riata.* Assuming a minimum crew of 15 for each ship, as the *Senchus* records was the case in *Dál Riata*, this fleet would have required crews totalling at least 2,250 men. But the possible presence of relief crews on campaign suggests that the fleet's total strength may have been up to three times this.[23]

Regardless of the presence of relief crews, the existence of such extensive naval assets indicates that both the Picts and Scots possessed trained and experienced fleets and were organised for naval warfare on an impressive scale. While this might indicate the existence of professional sailors, a mid-tenth-century reference to a 'fleet of summer warriors' (*Classi[s] Somarlidiorum*)[24] suggests that crews were levied on a seasonal basis. Summer naval service would have avoided the key agricultural seasons of spring and autumn and would have had the added advantage of avoiding the more unsettled weather conditions, perhaps including those in which the Pictish fleet was wrecked on *Ros Cuissine.*

*Ros Cuissine* is Troup Head (Banffshire),[25] which is occupied by the Iron Age promontory fort of Cullykhan or Castle Point.[26] Although sherds of late Roman pottery and a carbon-14 date of 317±40 AD indicate that the fort was reoccupied around the fourth century, there is no evidence that it was refortified then and it is unclear if it was still in use when the fleet was destroyed. Nevertheless, some coastal promontory forts were probably associated with Pictish naval bases. The promontories provided shelter, forming natural harbours in their lee, and sometimes retained their significance to later seafarers. It is unlikely to be coincidental that two promontory forts on the Moray Firth, Burghead (*see* Plate 27) and the Green Castle at Portknockie, are adjacent to modern harbours.[27] This association was particularly significant in the case of Burghead, where the largest known Pictish fortress overlooks one of the most sheltered natural harbours on the Moray coast.[28] Indeed, the utility of the location is emphasised by the construction in the early nineteenth century of a harbour and associated planned village at Burghead, when the fortress suffered extensive damage.[29]

The promontory forts of the Moray coast were probably 'home ports' with their own warships.[30] Coastal promontory forts elsewhere in Pictland probably had a similar function to those along the Moray coast, although none have been dated firmly to the early medieval period. The mooring of Pictish naval vessels near promontory forts would have provided mutual defence, although it is unlikely that all these vessels were permanently engaged in naval duties. Forts occupying prominent cliff-top locations may have been able to direct fleets by beacons.[31] In another modern echo of Burghead's significance to the Picts, the seaward tip of the promontory was, until recently, occupied by a coastguard station.

The Beauly Firth and the sheltered upper reaches of the Moray Firth were also ideal natural harbours from which a Pictish fleet could control the Moray coast and conduct naval operations further afield. Indeed, the kings of the Northern Picts probably imposed their overlordship over Orkney, and possibly a more extensive northern coastal and insular territory, with a sizeable fleet based here. The most likely candidate is Inverness, where the multiple channels and islands that once formed the delta of the River Ness at its confluence with the Moray Firth created a natural port.[32] This is supported by the presence of a sub-king of Orkney who was held hostage in the fortified royal centre of King Bridei son of Maelchon at or near Inverness.[33]

The fleet wrecked on *Ros Cuissine* was probably levied around the Moray Firth and was presumably one of several Pictish fleets. Political organisation and geographical factors indicate that Pictish navies were probably either provincial in composition or that the Northern and Southern Picts had separate fleets. This may be supported by a reference to a fleet of *Fortriu* in 733.[34] Although a scribal error for the fleet of *Dál Riata*,[35] the annalist may have confused two fleets. As *Fortriu* was the dominant province of, and synonymous with, southern Pictland, it would almost certainly have had a fleet. This fleet was probably based in the Firth of Tay, perhaps also using the Firth of Forth and the Montrose Basin, from which it would have controlled the eastern seaboard of Pictland.

A similar situation existed in *Dál Riata*, where two historically recorded forts, at least one of them a royal fortress, occupy commanding positions overlooking important landfalls. Dunaverty dominates a gently shelving sandy beach on the Mull of Kintyre, the nearest landfall in *Dál Riata* to Ireland. Dunadd lies on the River Add (*see* Plate 5), near its confluence with Loch Crinan, which was described in 1792 as 'the best harbour upon a great tract of the western coast',[36] with anchorages on its northern and southern sides.[37] Dunollie occupies a headland on the north side of Oban Bay, a natural harbour and safe anchorage sheltered by the island of Kerrera.[38] Oban Bay was the nearest principal landfall to Iona, but was of wider strategic significance. Commanding the confluence of the Firth of Lorne, the Lynn of Lorne and the Sounds of Kerrera and Mull, Oban Bay was an ideal base from which to conduct naval operations around the coasts and isles of *Dál Riata* and further afield. *Tairpert Boitter* presumably controlled the narrow isthmus between East Loch Tarbert and West Loch Tarbert and the natural harbours at their heads.[39] Although no traces of a hillfort are detectable, *Tairpert Boitter* may have occupied the site now overlain by the medieval royal castle of Tarbert, Loch Fyne, on a rocky knoll above East Loch Tarbert harbour.[40] The association of another royal fort in *Dál Riata* with a harbour is suggested by the ability of King Dúngal to escape to Ireland in 734, despite having been wounded by the Picts, who then destroyed the unidentified fort of *Dún Leithfinn*.[41]

As with land armies, fleets were commanded by kings and nobles. In 568, Conall mac Comgaill, King of *Dál Riata*, led his fleet on a raiding expedition, accompanied by his ally, Colmán Bec mac Diarmait, high-king of the Meath-based Southern *Uí Néill* dynasty of *Clann Cholmáin*.[42] In 719, Selbach, King of *Dál Riata*, led *Cenél Loairn* in a naval battle in which 'a number of nobles [*comites*]' were killed.[43] Selbach's opponents belonged to the rival kindred of *Cenél nGabráin*, led by Dúnchad Bec, 'King of Kintyre'.[44] Less certainly, Eóganán mac Óengusa (Uuen son of Unuist) (?837–9), King of both *Dál Riata* and the Picts, was killed in a possible naval battle against a Viking fleet from Dublin.[45]

## NAVAL BATTLES AND MARITIME RAIDS

Coastal raids on Roman Britain, or at least their threat, almost certainly pre-date the earliest recorded appearance of the Picts and Scots. This is apparent from the flanking defences beyond the western ends of both the Antonine Wall and Hadrian's Wall. In the former case, the forts of Bishopton, Lurg Moor and Outerwards protect the south side of the Firth of Clyde, while the western end of Hadrian's Wall continues along the south side of the Solway Firth as far as Bowness-on-Solway. A chain of forts, fortlets and signal stations, as closely spaced as those along the wall itself, then stretched south along the Cumbrian coast for 39 km (24 miles) to Burrow Walls, Workington, and possibly as far as St Bees or even Ravenglass, 81 km (50 miles) south of Bowness.[46] The effort expended in constructing and manning these defences reflects the gravity with which the threat from across the Solway Firth and the Irish Sea was viewed. On the east coast, the siting of forts at Carriden, Cramond and Inveresk on the southern shore of the Firth of Forth, and at South Shields on the Tyne, attests a different response to a similar concern. Here, the probable role of Cramond and South Shields as naval bases suggests a greater emphasis on naval defence, involving interception at sea, rather than on static coastal fortifications. In conjunction, both coastal fortifications and naval units were intended to defend the porous coastal frontiers against northern raiders, who could outflank the linear frontier defences simply by crossing the adjacent estuaries. These defences reveal that the peoples of northern Britain posed a threat of attack from the sea during the mid-second century. That threat appears to have increased from the earliest recorded appearance of the Picts in the third century.

The Picts and Scots were raiding the coasts of Roman Britain by the 360s. This culminated in the 'Barbarian Conspiracy' of 367, when they joined the *Attacotti* and Saxons in invading Roman Britain, while the Franks and Saxons attacked the coasts and frontiers of Roman Gaul.[47] There is little evidence of destruction on Hadrian's Wall in 367, suggesting that the Picts and Scots did not penetrate the frontier defences but simply bypassed them by sailing down the east and west coasts of Britain. The raiders' objective was to locate estuaries that would carry them inland where they could attack areas that were both wealthier and more lightly defended, presumably including towns and villages located on rivers. The Romans responded to this threat with a greater emphasis on both coastal and urban defences, measures that were central to the Theodosian restoration after 367.

The maritime threat faced by Roman Britain is described memorably by Gildas:[48] 'there eagerly emerged from the coracles that had carried them across the sea-valleys the foul hordes of Scots and Picts'. This describes coastal navigation rather than seafaring and seaborne rather than naval operations; attacks *from* the sea rather than *at* sea. In response, the Romans 'put to flight across the sea the columns of their [Pictish and Scottish] rivals'.[49] A panegyric by Claudian,[50] composed in January 400, provides independent corroboration and a more precise date. Claudian gives expression to a thankful Britannia, implying that Britain was under seaborne attack from the *Scotti* and Saxons and faced an unspecified threat from the Picts: 'Then . . . Britannia spoke: "When neighbouring peoples would have killed me, Stilicho gave me forts – for the *Scotti* stirred against all Ireland and my sea foamed beneath the hostile oars. Stilicho took such care, I do not fear the Scottish javelin not tremble at the Pict, nor on all my coast search each doubtful wind for the approaching Saxon."'

In some areas, the Romans adopted a system of defence-in-depth against Pictish and Scottish seaborne attacks. Of particular interest is a chain of at least five late fourth-century Roman fortified signal stations stretching 62 km (39 miles) along the coasts of Co. Durham and north Yorkshire, at Huntcliff, Goldsborough, Ravenscar, Scarborough, Filey and probably Whitby.[51] These most likely belonged to a more extensive coastal defence system that stretched from Hartlepool or even Tynemouth to Flamborough Head and was supported by a series of inland forts, possibly including those at Malton, Cawthorn and Lease Rigg. That these defences were constructed against Pictish raiders is indicated by their north-eastern location and late date. This maritime frontier has been labelled the 'Pictish Shore',[52] paralleling the late Roman 'Saxon Shore' fortifications constructed around the coast of south-eastern Britain to defend the province from Anglo-Saxon attacks.[53] Gildas[54] describes how, shortly before they abandoned the province (in 410), the Romans 'placed towers overlooking the sea at intervals on the south coast, where they kept their ships: for they were afraid of the wild barbarian beasts attacking on that front too'. The latter comment implies that the northern coasts were also under attack.

The Roman signal stations of the 'Pictish Shore' were carefully sited to enable them to signal each other, along the coast, rather than inland. This indicates that their function was not just to give advance warning of seaborne raids but presumably also to take action against them. This they would have done by alerting and coordinating the interception of hostile craft, before they could land, by naval vessels operating from the Tyne, Tees and Humber estuaries. Ships of the *Classis Britannica* were intended to counter the maritime threat to Roman Britain, but were based mainly in the south-east to deter attacks from northern Germany and the Low Countries. In the late fourth century, Roman Britain's first line of defence against seaborne raids was units of scouting skiffs (*scaphae exploratoriae*), whose function was 'to intercept convoys of enemy shipping or by studious surveillance to detect their approach or intentions'.[55] Although the enemy is not identified, the name by which the Britons referred to these vessels provides a clue. This is given in variant texts as *picatos*, *pictas*, and *pictos*, which may be a pun on *Picti*,[56] suggesting that these boats were defending Roman Britain against coastal raids by the Picts. Alternatively, these vessels may have derived their name from their resemblance to Pictish currachs,[57] with which the Romans, therefore, must have been familiar. Or the name simply may indicate that these scouting vessels were painted, reflecting Vegetius' statement that their 'sails and rigging are dyed Venetian blue, which resembles the ocean waves; and even the wax with which the ships' sides are covered is also dyed'.[58]

The study of Pictish and Scottish naval warfare is also hindered by the terseness of annalistic entries. This is exacerbated by the annalists' tendency of referring to naval battles by the nearest landfall, hindering the distinction between land and sea battles unless there is a specific reference to the sea or fleets. This occurs rarely and only one sea battle (Latin, *bellum maritimum*; Irish, *cath maritimum*) is recorded explicitly. On 6 October 719, rival *cenéla* of *Dál Riata* clashed in the battle of *Ard Nesbi*, in which *Cenél nGabráin* defeated *Cenél Loairn*.[59] The importance, and therefore probably scale, of this battle is indicated by those leading the opposing fleets, Selbach, King of *Dál Riata* (of *Cenél Loairn*), and Dúnchad Bec, 'King of Kintyre' (of *Cenél nGabráin*), as well as the deaths there of several nobles. Although *Ard Nesbi* remains unidentified, this

22. *The Glamis Manse, Angus, cross-slab. While the men in the bottom left-hand scene engage in single combat with axes, the mythological associations of the axe are apparent from the centaur-like creature in the top right-hand scene.* (Crown Copyright: Royal Commission on the Ancient and Historical Monuments of Scotland.)

23. *The axe-wielding Rhynie man, as portrayed on a stone from Barflat, Rhynie (Rhynie 7).*
(Copyright: Tom and Sybil Gray Collection.)

24. *A Pictish warrior, as drawn by John White in 1588. Derived from a combination of Classical sources, contemporary accounts of the 'wild Irish' and White's own experiences of the native North Americans he encountered on his expedition to Virginia with Sir Walter Raleigh in 1585, this epitomises the perception of the Picts as naked and painted or tattooed barbarians.* (Copyright: The British Museum.)

25. *Three cloaked foot soldiers, each armed with a spear, on the reverse of the badly eroded cross-slab at Eassie, Angus (detail). To their right stands a 'triumph tree', with human heads impaled on the ends of its branches, and, beside it, a warrior with sword drawn holds what may be another head in his left hand.* (Crown Copyright: Royal Commission on the Ancient and Historical Monuments of Scotland.)

26. *The massive double-linked silver chain from Whitecleugh, Crawfordjohn, Lanarkshire. Although found outside Pictland, its terminal is decorated with two Pictish symbols (only one of which, a divided or notched rectangle, is visible here). The high gold content of such chains suggests that they were produced from recycled late Roman silver-gilt vessels.* (Copyright: Trustees of the National Museums of Scotland 2002.)

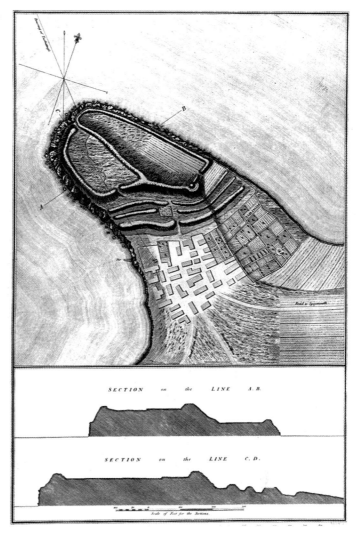

27. *Burghead promontory fort, Morayshire, as surveyed by General William Roy in 1747–55 and illustrated in his* The Military Antiquities of the Romans in North Britain *(1793). As well as its naturally defended position, Burghead's strategic significance is strengthened by the adjacent natural harbour in its lee.* (Crown Copyright: Royal Commission on the Ancient and Historical Monuments of Scotland.)

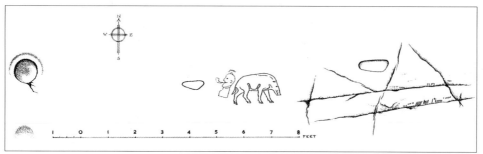

28. *A plan of the various carvings on a shelf of outcropping bedrock just outside the 'citadel' and below the summit at Dunadd. These comprise, from left to right, a stone-cut basin with surrounding ring, a lightly pecked-out impression of a human foot, the head and shoulders of a pipe-smoking figure with the legend 'KING FERGUS', a boar, the sunken impression of a human foot and two lines of ogam script, using natural fissures in the rock as base-lines.* (Crown copyright: Historic Scotland.)

29. *The boar carving at Dunadd. The deliberate damage to the boar's back and the top of its head is clearly visible as an extensively pitted area.* (Crown Copyright: Royal Commission on the Ancient and Historical Monuments of Scotland.)

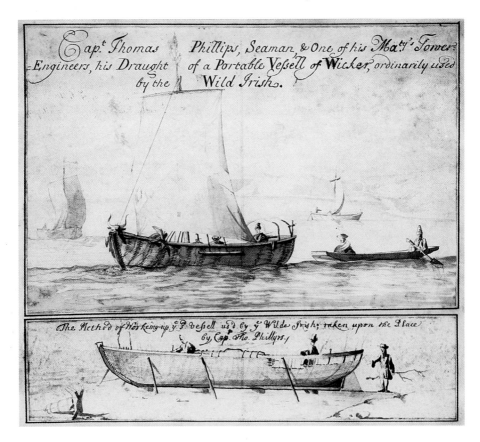

31. *The ship depicted in the lower scene on the reverse of the cross-slab known as St Orland's Stone, Cossins, Angus.* (Copyright: Tom and Sybil Gray Collection.)

Opposite, below: 30. *A currach, 'a portable Vessell of Wicker, ordinarily used by the Wild Irish', illustrated and described by Captain Thomas Phillips in the late seventeenth century. The boat-building techniques employed were essentially unchanged from those of the early medieval period.* (Pepys Library, Magdalene College, Cambridge, ms 2934, f. 41.)

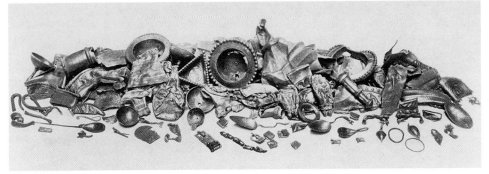

32. *Part of the massive hoard of late Roman silverware deposited on Traprain Law, East Lothian. Most of the silver vessels had been cut and folded for distribution and/or recycling by being melted down.* (Copyright: Trustees of the National Museums of Scotland 2002.)

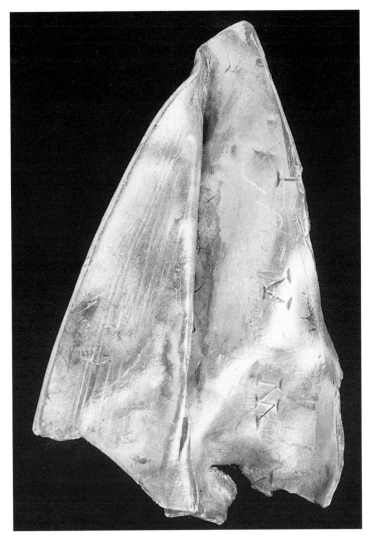

33. *The cut and crushed fragment of the bowl of a late Roman spoon from the Norrie's Law, Fife, hoard. The inscribed letters* IVMV, *probably an abbreviation of the original owner's name, are clearly visible.* (Copyright: Trustees of the National Museums of Scotland 2002.)

battle was fought offshore from a promontory (*ard*), possibly off Kintyre. The terseness of the annalistic entries means that nothing is known of the nature and size of the fleets involved, the tactics used, or the course of the battle. Despite the paucity of evidence, the battle of *Ard Nesbi* holds the notable distinction of being the earliest explicitly recorded naval battle fought in the British Isles.

But references to other naval battles may remain unidentified. A good candidate for a naval battle which is not explicitly recorded as such occurred almost a century earlier. This battle was fought on the same day in 637 as the battle of *Mag Rath* (Moira, Co. Down) and, like it, arose from the involvement of *Dál Riata* in Irish affairs, specifically a struggle between two dynasties of the Northern *Ui Néill*.[60] In the battle of *Sailtire*, *Cenél Conaill* defeated a combined force of *Dál Riata* and *Cenél nEógain*.[61] *Sáil-tíre*, 'Land's Heel', is traditionally identified as Kintyre[62] and its southern tip, the Mull of Kintyre, is the nearest point of mainland Scotland to Ireland. Clearly, a battle between Scottish and Irish forces required a naval component, at least for transporting troops, and the location of this engagement suggests that it was a naval battle fought off Kintyre.

Although no naval battles involving the Picts are recorded, Pictish naval capabilities were probably comparable with those of their neighbours. Indeed, it may be no coincidence that the references to Pictish and Scottish fleets noted above and the earliest recorded naval battle occur within fourteen years of each other. This may represent a period during which both the Picts and Scots were flexing their naval power, increasingly conscious of the strategic gains to be won by dominating the seas. The Viking attacks on *Dál Riata* and Pictland during the ninth century are another possible context for naval warfare, although there is no explicit evidence. A later epic records a battle between the men of *Dál Riata* and a Viking fleet of sixty-five ships.[63] Although this suggests a naval encounter, it is more likely identified with an unnamed battle, probably within *Fortriu*. A more reliable annalistic source records that the men of *Fortriu* (*firu Fortrenn*) were defeated by an army of Dublin Vikings in 839.[64]

This apparent confusion between land and sea battles is attributable to the movement of armies by sea. Given suitable currents and winds, it would often have been more effective for an army to sail down the coast than to travel overland. *The Gododdin*[65] refers to 'the vessel . . . of the warband from over the Firth [of Forth]', revealing that some Pictish warriors made the crossing from Fife to join the *Gododdin* on their ill-fated expedition, rather than take the circuitous overland route. Armies were not only transported by sea when fighting external enemies. The wreck of 150 Pictish ships on *Ros Cuissine* in 729 occurred during an internal war for the Pictish kingship, indicating that the fleet had been mustered for service within Pictish waters or to transport an army around the coast of Pictland. This was also the case in *Alba*, when a 'fleet of summer warriors was slain in Buchan'.[66] This may have occurred at or on the River *Collyne*, the Cullen Water, in 962,[67] although it is unclear whether this was a naval or land battle. Sea travel was both strategically and tactically advantageous, as it enabled the rapid projection of force across large distances and increased the element of surprise in an attack. It was not only quicker but, in the right weather conditions, was also less hazardous, as it reduced the risk of ambush.

The movement of armies by sea erodes the distinction between 'armies' and 'navies' in the conventional sense. Instead, as the *Senchus fer nAlban* reveals, fighting men were liable for service in both an 'expeditionary force of the hostings' and an 'expeditionary force for sea-voyaging'. Ships' crews, therefore, were sailors at sea and soldiers on land. The principal distinction here was not whether the expeditionary force fought on land or at sea, but how it travelled to the theatre of operations. In most cases, the objective of a sea expedition was to reach its destination, disembark and plunder the area, engaging the enemy only if they met opposition, before re-embarking and returning home with their spoils. This type of warfare is more familiar from Viking raiding, but the Picts and Scots mounted seaborne raids over wide distances from a much earlier date. The Picts and Scots presumably developed their capability, tactics and taste for coastal raiding from their experiences attacking later Roman Britain.

Seaborne attacks on the Hebrides, Orkney, Ireland and probably the Isle of Man are recorded. In 568, Conall mac Comgaill, King of *Dál Riata*, led an expedition to plunder the Inner Hebrides (*fecht i nIardoman*), specifically the islands of Islay and Seil.[68] The next King of *Dál Riata*, Aedán mac Gabráin, mounted several long-range maritime attacks. These began with one or two expeditions to Orkney (*fecht Orc*) in 580 and/or 581,[69] it being unclear whether the annals record separate events or duplicate the entry. Then, striking as far south as he had north, Aedán won probably two battles in *Manu* in 582 and 583, the different wording of the entries in the *Annals of Ulster* suggesting that these record separate events.[70] On linguistic grounds, this is likely to be the Isle of Man rather than *Manau*, the area around the head of the Firth of Forth.[71] Although it is unclear whether the battles of *Manu* were naval engagements or were fought on the island, they clearly attest the naval power of *Dál Riata*. Aedán was renowned for maritime warfare and the Welsh triads refer to his warband 'who went to sea for their lord'.[72] A skirmish was fought on

Skye in 701[73] and Orkney was again the target in 709, when the men of
*Dál Riata* defeated the men of Orkney in battle,[74] although once again it
is unclear whether this was fought on land or at sea.

Ireland was a much closer target than Orkney, but was probably
attacked less frequently because of the close political links between *Dál
Riata* and particularly the kingdoms of Ulster. Nevertheless, the
involvement of *Dál Riata* in battles in Ireland attests the importance of
moving armies by sea. Naval activity by *Dál Riata* against Ireland is also
recorded, with possibly three expeditions in 733 alone. That year,
Dúngal mac Selbaich, King of *Dál Riata*, attacked Tory Island, off the
north coast of Co. Donegal, where he forcibly removed the former
Pictish king, Bridei son of Unuist, from the sanctuary of the monastery
to which he had retired. Dúngal also invaded the island of *Cuirenrigi*,
possibly Inch in Lough Swilly, off the Inishowen peninsula (Co.
Donegal), although the annals differ on whether this occurred on the
same occasion or was a separate expedition.[75] In 733, the Scottish fleet
crossed to Ireland to support Flaithbertach, high-king of *Cenél Conaill*,
probably in their dispute with *Cenél nEógain* over the high-kingship of
the Northern *Uí Neill*. After first sailing to *Inis hOinae*, possibly
Inishowen, the Scots were then heavily defeated and many were drowned
in the River Bann,[76] although it is unclear if this battle was fought on or
beside the river.

Island monastic sites were vulnerable to seaborne raiding. Such raids
were not only conducted against neighbouring kingdoms but also
occurred within *Dál Riata*. Adomnán[77] relates how Ioan son of Conall
looted the monastery of St Colmán in Ardnamurchan three times, on the
last of those raids 'returning, laden with booty, to his ship'. Ioan and his
accomplices stowed their spoils on board, illustrating the use of ships in
rapidly transporting quantities of plunder over distances. But Columba
invoked divine intervention and the ship foundered in a squall between
Mull and Coll.

Fewer Pictish than Scottish seaborne attacks are recorded, reflecting
the poorly documented nature of the Picts. However, the impressive
range of these attacks, from Orkney to the Bristol Channel, attests Pictish
seafaring capabilities. Monasteries on the scattered islands of *Dál Riata*
were particularly vulnerable to seaborne raids, as later Viking attacks
confirm. But, in earlier centuries, these same monastic settlements in the
Inner Hebrides were attacked by the pagan Picts. The Picts raided
Comgall's monastery on Tiree in the mid-sixth century, taking their spoils
with them in their ships, and were probably responsible for killing the
abbot and community of Eigg.[78] No later attacks of this nature are
recorded, possibly suggesting that they declined or stopped when the

Northern Picts were converted to Christianity, a gradual process that began in the late sixth century.

The presence of a sub-king of Orkney, held hostage inside the fort of King Bridei son of Maelchon at or near Inverness in the late sixth century,[79] is of interest here. This probably represents the aftermath of a campaign in Orkney, presumably to subdue an uprising or impose the payment of tribute on a recalcitrant subject king. Orkney was the target again in 682, when the islands were laid waste by Bridei son of Bile.[80] As Bridei was King of the Southern Picts, this attack may reflect hostilities between the Northern Picts and the Southern Picts, which may also be attested in the sieges of *Dun Baitte* in 680 and Dunottar in 681.[81]

Perhaps explaining the hostility to the Picts, evident in *De excidio*, Gildas experienced Pictish naval power at first hand. Gildas was forced to flee in a small boat for the safety of Glastonbury when his retreat on the island of *Echin* – Flat Holm, in the Bristol Channel off the Glamorgan coast – was harried by 'pirates' (*piratae*) from Orkney.[82] Although the 'pirates' are not explicitly described as Picts, there can be little doubt from their origin on Orkney that they were. There was no meaningful distinction between Pictish and Scottish piracy and naval warfare, other than in the perception of the victim. Orkney's location, near the northern tip of the Pictish mainland, and topography, with many sheltered bays and gently shelving beaches, made it an ideal base from which to mount maritime raids down both the eastern and western coasts of Britain. But this also made Orkney both attractive and vulnerable to such attacks. Indeed, the recorded attacks on Orkney may have been punitive raids in retaliation for plundering by Orcadian raiders. Orkney was not only attacked by the Picts and Scots. Claudian's[83] claim that 'Orkney ran red with Saxon slaughter' suggests Saxon raiding after the *barbarica conspiratio* of 367 and the Saxons also attacked the islands in the mid-fifth century.[84] A late source claims that Edwin, King of Northumbria (616–33), brought Orkney under Anglian overlordship.[85] However, the islands do not appear in the original passage by Bede[86] on which this claim is based, and the reference to Orkney was presumably inserted at a later date to emphasise the extent of Northumbrian power.

Pictish and Scottish naval expeditions included long-range voyages in what can be treacherous seas and clearly required competent navigational and seafaring skills. Most of the Pictish and Scottish naval expeditions recorded were against Orkney or the Hebrides. But Pictish and Scottish naval forces were not confined to the seas off their coasts. The lands bordering the Irish Sea were within range of both the Picts and Scots, as recorded raids on north-east Ireland and the Isle of Man demonstrate. And Whithorn, in Northumbrian-controlled Galloway, is described in a later source as situated on 'the farthest shore of the Angles, and open to the raidings of the Scots and Picts'.[87] But the expedition from Orkney to the Bristol Channel provides a unique insight into Pictish maritime capability, confirming their ability to make round voyages of some 1,300 miles (2,100 km). Much of the English coast was therefore within range of Pictish naval operations. But, in contrast to earlier assaults on Roman Britain, there is no evidence of Pictish or Scottish coastal raiding on Anglo-Saxon England, although the discovery of some Anglo-Saxon artefacts on Pictish and Scottish sites indicates maritime links of some sort with at least eastern England.[88]

## WARSHIPS

What type or types of ship did the Picts and Scots use for naval warfare? Although limited and fragmentary, the combined evidence of literary references, sculptural depictions and archaeological discoveries provides insights into the form, construction and capabilities of Pictish and Scottish ships. While ships may have been invested with a religious symbolism in early Irish literature and sculpture,[89] the evidence cited here may be accepted at face value. References to the form and construction of ships is included in saints' lives as incidental information and the sculptural representations have no overtly religious associations. Even the ship portrayed on a Pictish cross-slab appears on the reverse, the side usually dominated by secular or mythological, rather than biblical, scenes.

Ships and sea travel in *Dál Riata* feature prominently in Adomnán's *Life of Columba*. Adomnán[90] refers to vessels by a wide range of Latin terms and words borrowed from Old Irish: ship (*longa navis, navigium, navis*), freight ship (*navis oneraria*), boat (*alno, barca, caupallus, cimba, cimbula, navicella, navicula*), skiff (*scafa*), currach (*curucus*, from Old Irish *currach*) and raft (*ratis*). Of these, *navis* is the most frequently used. These various terms, some related to size, others to construction or function, clearly refer to various types of vessel. But Adomnán uses them imprecisely, sometimes referring to the same vessel by more than one word, presumably to avoid repetition. As a result, it is difficult to distinguish sea-going vessels from those used for inland navigation and it is unclear if this is always a valid distinction. The Gaelic equivalents of several of these terms survive in placenames around the Argyll coast; for example, Port na Curaich is, according to tradition, the beach where Columba first landed on Iona.

There are fewer documentary references to Pictish ships, but no reason to believe that they differed significantly in form from those of the Scots. Indeed, Gildas[91] refers to both the Picts and Scots swarming from the currachs (*de curucis*) in which they had crossed the sea. Pictish vessels are referred to by the same terminology as Scottish ships: those wrecked in 729 are *long*,[92] the Picts reputedly sailed from Scythia in *longae navis*,[93] the leader of a Pictish warband arrived in Skye on a *navicula*[94] and the Picts conducted their naval raids in *barc*, boats or ships.[95] How these vessels were referred to in the Pictish language is unknown, but the fact that neighbouring peoples used standard terms indicates that Pictish vessels belonged to recognisable types.

'Warships' are poorly represented in the sources. The Latin for warship, *navis longa*, was borrowed into Old Irish as *long*, the standard word for a full-sized sailing ship. This suggests that ships were associated primarily with warfare when the word was first borrowed, presumably reflecting Irish raids on Roman Britain. But the word later lost this specific meaning. Adomnán,[96] in his only explicit reference to an all-wooden ship, refers to a *longa navis* only once, preferring *navis*. This may reflect an economy of expression, rather than any distinction in function. Moreover, the *longa navis* concerned is unlikely to have been a warship because its 'dressed timbers of pine and oak' were transported by monks from Iona. A reference to an alder boat (*alno*)[97] reveals that other woods were also used, if timbers of adequate size were available. Although its name implies an all-wood construction, the vessel concerned was on the River Ness, suggesting that this was a smaller craft for inland navigation.

The use of dressed timbers of pine and oak for the construction of one ship and the presence of a bilge-sump or bailing-well (*sentina*) in another[98] indicates that these were substantial, sea-going vessels. Although used by monks on these occasions, similar types of ship may also have been used in naval warfare. As the methods of construction and materials available for building warships were identical to those used for other types of ship, warships probably varied little from other sea-going vessels. In order to cope with conditions on the open sea, such ships were probably distinguished by their larger size and sturdier construction. Impressionistic images of such ships, previously thought to be Viking but now reassessed as Pictish,[99] occur as graffito sketches scratched on slate and sandstone from Jarlshof (Shetland).[100] Sketches of a prow and a stern clearly depict plank-built ships, the timbers represented by multiple lines on the ships' hulls. Although now badly eroded, this feature also occurs on the ship depicted on the reverse of the cross-slab known as St Orland's Stone, Cossans (Angus)[101] (*see* Plate 31). The prominence of these lines suggests that these ships were clinker-built, with overlapping planks, rather than carvel-built, with flush planks laid edge-to-edge. The gaps between the planks were presumably caulked with pitch to make the hull watertight.

That the ships portrayed in the Jarlshof sketches and on St Orland's Stone were sea-going vessels is apparent from their high, curving prows and sterns, enabling them to withstand heavier seas. The ship carved on a wall of Jonathan's Cave, East Wemyss (Fife), also has a prominent curving prow and upturned stern. This image was pecked using a very similar technique to the Pictish symbols in the Wemyss caves and is probably also Pictish,[102] although some doubts persist.[103] Adomnán[104] refers to the prows (*prorae*) of Scottish and Irish ships and a Pictish *navicula*. Animal-headed prows, possibly of totemic or symbolic significance or intended to strike fear into the enemy, occur on two Pictish logboats.[105] This suggests that the high prows and sterns of larger, sea-going vessels, which would have provided more scope for such treatment, may also have been decorated. The steering oar or rudder was attached to the stern. A broad rudder was mounted on the stern of a ship depicted in a graffito from Jarlshof, while another sketch depicts a vessel with rudder raised, ready for landing. In both cases it is unclear what side of the ship the rudder was on. But the rudder of the ship portrayed on St Orland's Stone is mounted on the port side, rather than the conventional starboard or 'steerboard'.

Other types of vessel were also used for sea-going navigation and, presumably, for naval warfare by the Picts and Scots. A Pictish war leader sailed on a *navicula*,[106] although not into battle, at least on the occasion recorded. Gildas[107] states that the Picts and Scots raided Britain *de curucis*, which he says were black. This is usually translated as 'coracles', round, curved-bottomed vessels for one person, propelled by paddling, and used on inland waters in Scotland, Ireland and Wales into the twentieth century.[108] The discovery that an early Bronze Age burial at Barns Farm, Dalgetty (Fife), had been placed in a coracle[109] demonstrates that such vessels existed in prehistoric Scotland. The sole surviving coracle from Scotland, used to guide floating logs on the River Spey, had a heavy, hoop-like basket-work frame of withies.[110] But the vessels referred to by Gildas were probably currachs. Of similar construction to the coracle, but larger in size, the currach or curragh was a wooden- or wicker-framed vessel, covered with pitched animal hides, giving them their black appearance.

The construction of a currach is described in *The Voyage of St Brendan*:[111] 'Brendan and his companions made a currach, using iron tools. The ribs and frame were of wood . . . and the covering was tanned ox-hide stretched over oak bark. They greased all the seams on the outer surface of the skin with fat and stored away spare skins inside the currach, together with forty days' supplies, fat for waterproofing the skins, tools and utensils.' An enduring shipbuilding technique, the currach was used in western Ireland into the twentieth century, although latterly with a covering of tarred canvas[112] (*see* Plate 30).

Easily constructed, the currach was probably the most extensively used type of vessel among the Picts and Scots. Of deceptively strong construction, the currach could carry a crew of several people, as well as livestock and goods, as the reference to a cargo ship and their use in raiding demonstrates. Hide-covered boats had the added advantage of being light; Adomnán[113] mentions a man sitting under a ship (*navi*), which was presumably upturned. That they were portable would have been particularly important in *Dál Riata*, where the deeply indented coastline meant that the ability to carry or haul ships overland, even over short distances, could reduce significantly the length of a journey. In addition, this added mobility could provide an added element of surprise in warfare, enabling attacks to be mounted from directions and in locations that their enemies did not anticipate. However, the capacity of the currach was limited and Adomnán[114] twice describes timbers for a ship and a church being towed behind currachs and skiffs, rather than transported on board.

Currachs were widely used for sea-going navigation throughout their long history. In addition to Brendan's navigational feats, Adomnán[115] describes how Cormac, a monk of Iona, sailed a ship (*navis*) with a prow (*prora*), stern (*puppis*) and covering of hide (*pellicium tectum*) north for fourteen days and nights, 'beyond the range of human exploration' and, on other occasions, 'over the limitless ocean' to Orkney. The sea-going capability of the currach is demonstrated by reconstructions using traditional materials and techniques, notably by Tim Severin.[116] In 1997, a reconstruction of a six-oared currach sailed from Ireland to Iona with a crew of eight to celebrate the 1,400th anniversary of St Columba's death.

Currachs were propelled by both oars and sails. Gildas[117] records that the Scots and Picts 'came relying on their oars as wings, on the arms of their oarsmen, and on the winds swelling their sails'. And *The Voyage of St Brendan*[118] describes how 'a mast, a sail, and various pieces of equipment for steering were fitted into the vessel'. This mast was erected amidships. In contrast, a graffito from Jarlshof shows the mast forward of midships, with eight oars fore and sixteen oars aft. This would have enabled the collapsible mast to be unstemmed and stowed in rough or calm seas, giving increased stability and reduced wind resistance. This may explain the absence of a mast on the ships depicted on St Orland's Stone and in Jonathan's Cave. Adomnán[119] demonstrates a keen awareness of different winds and their significance. He also refers frequently to sails (*velis*), sailing and rigging (*rudentes*), including raising the sail yards (*antemnae*) in the form of a cross, hoisting the sails, sailing with full sails and sails making the ropes taut.[120] A striped, square-rigged sail and outer rigging lines are shown on the sketches from Jarlshof. The rigging, used for supporting the mast and operating the sails, was probably attached to the prow and stern.

But sea travel could not always rely on the availability of suitable winds. Adomnán[121] describes how twelve currachs were becalmed at the mouth of the River Shiel (Argyll/Invernesshire) on their way to Iona: 'in still weather the sailors were sweeping the sea with their oars'. However, the oarsmen could not proceed against a headwind and had to seek shelter until the wind changed. The verb 'to row' (*remigare*) is also used of longer sea voyages, including from Britain to Derry and from Ireland to Iona.[122] And when a ship encountered a sea monster between Iona and Tiree, the rowers (*remiges*) quickly lowered the sail and made good their escape,[123] obviously having greater confidence in their own propulsion than that of the winds. Oars and sail complemented each other but could also be used together. Cormac's ship was travelling 'with full sails' when the blades of its oars (*palmulas*) were damaged by sea creatures.[124]

The need for ships to provide their own propulsion must have been an important factor in determining their size and complement. With their greater requirement for speed and manoeuvrability, warships in particular may have been crewed by more oarsmen than other vessels. The importance of oarsmen is apparent from the *Senchus fer nAlban*. Its unit of two seven-benchers refers to seven oars on either side of a ship which, with a steersman on the rudder, gives a nominal crew of fifteen for each vessel. But one must be cautious when attempting to calculate the size of a crew from the number of oars. Anglo-Saxon and Viking ships, as well as the medieval Scottish *birlinn* or West Highland galley, carried up to three crewmen to each oar on long voyages and in wartime, space permitting.[125] This not only provided a relief crew or crews, enabling speed to be maintained over long distances, but also ensured the availability of a larger and fitter fighting force when the enemy was reached. Although the issue of relief crews further complicates the calculation of crew sizes, this suggests that the complement of a seven-bencher in wartime could be as many as 45: three crews of 14 ($7 \times 2$) oarsmen, two steersmen and a captain.[126] This suggests that the burden of military obligation in *Dál Riata* was even higher than suspected previously.[127]

There are other indications that both the Picts and Scots had such large ships. In 737, in the only record of the size of a ship's crew, Fáilbe,

Abbot of Applecross (Ross and Cromarty), drowned at sea with his 22 sailors, presumably the crew of a single ship.[128] That an abbot's ship had a crew of 22 suggests that a warship would have had a larger crew, perhaps with one or two relief crews. A graffito from Jarlshof depicts a ship with 24 oars held aloft as the ship prepares to land. The absence of perspective in the sketch makes it unclear whether the oars on only one or both sides of the vessel are shown. But, assuming that all oars are shown, this ship would have required a minimum of 24 oarsmen, with a relief crew, 2 helmsmen and a captain perhaps giving a total complement of 51 in wartime.

The other Pictish ships depicted in sculpture are smaller in size. The ship on St Orland's Stone has only five people in it, although this may reflect artistic convention and actually represent a larger vessel. One of the ship's occupants is distinguished by his larger size and location in the bow, facing the ship's crew, suggesting that he commands the vessel. Two oars are depicted on the ship's starboard side, indicating that it would have had four in all. Two smaller characters sit opposite and facing both oarsmen, an arrangement which, if repeated on the port side, would give the ship a minimum crew of nine. This arrangement is most unusual and it perhaps portrays the presence of relief oarsmen, their (then) less active role indicated by their smaller size. The ship on the walls of Jonathan's Cave has five oars and a rudder, although the only crew member shown is the helmsman. The odd number of oars suggests that only those on one side of the ship are shown, giving a minimum crew of eleven.

Remarkably, one form of vessel from this period survives in water-logged conditions. Of 154 logboats recorded in Scotland, only 8 have been subjected to radiocarbon dating. Of these, 4 belong to the early medieval period, 2 of which are from Pictland: Errol 2, from the Habbiebank, a sandbank in the inner estuary of the Tay (Perthshire), is dated to 485±40 AD, and Loch of Kinnordy (Angus), is dated to 735±40 AD.[129] This is a high proportion of the total and, although little can be inferred with confidence from such a small sample, it suggests that logboats were widely used by the Picts. Logboats have also been found in *Dál Riata*, although none have been dated. However, two logboats discovered in Loch Glashan (Mid Argyll)[130] may have been associated with the early medieval crannog there.

Logboats would have been suitable for calmer inland and sheltered waters, although the findspot of the Errol 2 logboat attests their use in estuaries. Whether of wood or hide-covered, even sea-going boats, with their shallow draught and oared propulsion, were ideally suited for inland navigation and the tidal waters encountered in estuaries. The Errol 2 and Loch of Kinnordy logboats are both constructed from hollowed-out single trunks of oak, a simple technology but one that could produce impressive and substantial boats. The Errol 2 boat was 8.9 m long and up to 1.3 m in beam on discovery, although both boats have since suffered from shrinkage and splitting or warping as they dried out. The Loch of Kinnordy logboat is of exceptional craftsmanship, with its sides and bottom measuring between only 20 mm and 40 mm thick.[131] Both logboats have distinctive prows, carved in the form of animal heads, possibly boars.[132]

Despite the insights into naval obligation and organisation provided by the *Senchus*, several issues remain unresolved. Fundamentally, it is unclear whether the seven-bencher was the standard warship in *Dál Riata* when the *Senchus* was recorded, or if it belongs to an earlier period and had become the unit of naval obligation by the seventh century. It is also uncertain what type of vessel the seven-bencher was. The reassessment of its maximum crew size suggests that it was not a currach, but a larger ship, probably of wooden construction. And, although it records the obligation for crewing seven-benchers, the *Senchus* does not define responsibility for their construction and maintenance. This omission either reflects the narrow terms of reference of the *Senchus* or perhaps indicates that seven-benchers were provided by the king or lord.

Although the evidence of Pictish and Scottish ships is fragmentary, it is still consistent with the status of the Picts and Scots as naval powers. Logboats confirm that early medieval vessels can survive and other forms of Pictish or Scottish craft may await discovery, preserved in the silts of a loch bed or an estuary foreshore.

## CHAPTER EIGHT

# The Spoils of War

The spoils of war played a pivotal role in the heroic ideals surrounding early medieval warfare, reflecting the importance of prowess in battle and of generosity to the warband. Seizing booty therefore provided one of the strongest motives for the warfare and raiding of the Picts and Scots. The prizes concerned were not only material but also, and equally important in an heroic society, comprised the glory, in the form of honour and reputation, to be gained in warfare. In some cases, these spoils may have been the primary motivation for military action, while they may simply have been a by-product in others. For example, a royal fortress may have been a legitimate military target, either in its own right or as part of a wider strategy. But it may also have had a symbolic significance as a result of its association with kings and its status as a centre of royal power and their associated rituals, as was probably the case at Dunadd.[1] In addition, royal fortresses probably contained portable wealth in the form of agricultural produce, livestock, precious raw materials, finished products and potential slaves. The spoils of war are of direct importance to the nature of Pictish and Scottish warfare and the study of its wider economic and social significance.

One factor links several of the motives apparent in Pictish and Scottish warfare. The power of early medieval kings was largely dependent on their ability to levy, mobilise and reward their supporters, particularly the nobles who raised the army and led it into battle. This they did through the conquest of new lands and/or by seizing booty, which were then redistributed among the king's followers. These activities were essential to the maintenance of royal power and the survival of the kingship and resulted in an almost continuous quest for new territories and sources of wealth. Raiding, whether by land or sea, provided an attractive solution to the military and logistical problems posed by territorial expansion, requiring a smaller force, involving greater speed, mobility and therefore maximising the benefits of surprise, as well as minimising the risk of casualties by not seeking involvement in pitched battles. This is not symptomatic of the 'barbarian' or primitive status of the Picts and Scots. Plunder was an important source of income for many kingdoms in the early medieval West, for example, the Carolingian empire.[2]

## MATERIAL SPOILS: ROMAN METALWORK

The Picts and Scots were attracted by the material wealth of later Roman and post-Roman Britain. Roman Britain had been a source of precious metalwork since at least the late second century. Faced with a revolt just as the emperor Severus was about to campaign in Parthia in 197, Virius Lupus, the governor of Roman Britain, was forced to buy peace from the *Caledonii* and *Maeatae* 'for a great sum'.[3] These official payments were probably the origin of several hoards of Roman coins belonging to this period that have been found in east central and north-east Scotland, including two hoards recently discovered at Birnie (Morayshire).[4] Such payments may have brought temporary respite from native attacks, but they also provided an incentive for future raids on Roman Britain, either to plunder the riches that the province demonstrably possessed or to force Rome into buying peace again. Native aggression was rewarded either way. No wonder the *Caledonii* and *Maeatae* were described as being 'very fond of plundering'.[5]

Later Roman Britain, with its portable wealth concentrated in cities, towns and villas, must have been viewed as a source of rich and relatively easy pickings by adventurous Picts and Scots. But identifying the proceeds of raiding on Roman Britain in the archaeological record is difficult. Although Roman artefacts are sometimes found on non-Roman sites in Scotland,[6] their volume is comparatively small and their quality poor. Moreover, this material was derived predominantly from the Roman military presence during the late first and second centuries. The more impressive Roman artefacts found in Scotland, such as a fourth-century gold crossbow brooch with niello (a black silver oxide paste) inlay from the Moray Firth area,[7] tend to be later in date and occur as stray or casual finds rather than on archaeological sites. These could have reached their findspots by various mechanisms, including exchange, trade, diplomatic gift, bribery or plunder. In contrast, the severed gilt-bronze lower leg from a statue discovered at Milsington (Roxburghshire)[8] represents plunder from a Roman fortress. However, there is no evidence to link this with either the Picts or Scots and it may pre-date the earliest recorded appearance of both peoples.

One of the most spectacular discoveries of late Roman material in Scotland is the Traprain 'treasure', a huge hoard of Roman silverware discovered within the hillfort on Traprain Law (East Lothian) in 1919[9] (*see* Plate 32). This comprised the fragmentary remains of richly decorated late Roman silver plate: bowls, dishes, flagons, plates and spoons. Cut up and folded into parcels for distribution and/or in preparation for the melting pot, this hack-silver had instead been deposited as a hoard in the early fifth century. Various excavations on Traprain have also yielded substantial quantities of Roman coins and jewellery as well as native artefacts.[10] It is widely claimed that the Roman silverware from Traprain represents a diplomatic gift or bribe to ensure peaceful relations with the *Votadini*, the local population group, or payment for the services of their mercenaries, and that the *Votadini* was therefore a Roman client state.[11] But it seems more likely that the silver plate represents plunder, as cut plate also occurs in two fifth-century hoards of Roman coins and silver ingots discovered in Ireland, at Balline (Co. Limerick) and Ballinrees (Co. Londonderry),[12] where the existence of a client relationship with Rome is most unlikely.

Regardless of the mechanisms by which it reached Traprain Law, this hoard vividly illustrates the riches that could be plundered from Roman Britain and attests the circulation of substantial quantities of late Roman silverware in northern Britain. Traprain lies south of the Forth, outside the territory occupied by the historical Picts, and there is nothing to link the Traprain hoard with the Picts. Nevertheless, the Picts also had access to Roman silverware, as the presence of hack-silver in the Norrie's Law hoard demonstrates. The proportion of even the surviving contents of the Norrie's Law hoard comprising Roman hack-silver is debatable. Dr Lloyd Laing states that it was 'mainly composed of Roman hack silver and objects made from it', while Dr James Graham-Campbell believes that 'on the basis of the surviving material the proven Roman element is small'.[13] More fundamentally, only around 750 g of the hoard's contents, from an estimated total weight of 12.5 kg of silver artefacts discovered, survived in the mid-nineteenth century.[14] The overall proportions of late Roman and Pictish artefacts within the hoard therefore remain unknown. Most of the surviving contents of the hoard, around 100 out of a total of 119 items, comprise 'small pieces of amorphous scrap' silver,[15] not definitively identifiable to specific artefacts.

The 'armour', 'helmet' and 'shield' reportedly found at Norrie's Law may have been misidentified fragments of late Roman tableware, particularly a silver picture plate, which may explain the equestrian figure on the 'shield'.[16] However, several features exhibited by the large silver plaque or roundel are inconsistent with this interpretation. Its surviving fragments are too thin and flat to have been cut from a late Roman dish or plate, while the former presence of two smaller discs riveted to the roundel is also anomalous.[17] The Norrie's Law hoard is difficult to interpret from the few surviving fragments and the terse nineteenth-century accounts of its discovery. But the possibility that the hoard included a Roman shield, helmet and scale armour suggests that these may also have originated as plunder, taken either during a raid on later Roman Britain or after defeating a Roman army in battle. Intriguingly, the Norrie's Law hoard may comprise the deposited contents of a pagan shrine where Roman armour was offered to a Pictish deity in gratitude for the Picts' victory or a successful raid.[18] This, however, is dependent on the acceptance of an early, probably fifth-century, date for the hoard.

Despite the uncertainty surrounding the interpretation of much of its contents, the Norrie's Law hoard contains items that may be identified as pieces of late Roman silverware. These fragments include one from the rim of a cup and two from vessels with folded rims,[19] possibly belonging to cups similar to those found in the Traprain Law hoard. Perhaps associated with these, a silver roundel, 80 mm in diameter and with a central boss and cordoned rim, may be the base of a cup, again with parallels from Traprain Law.[20] A fragment of a bar or ring with punched-dot ornament is interpreted as either part of a late Roman ingot or a Hiberno–Viking arm-ring.[21] But of undeniably late Roman origin is the cut and folded bowl of a silver spoon[22] (*see* Plate 33). This is inscribed in Latin majuscules with the letters IVMV, probably an abbreviation of its owner's name and paralleled by ownership inscriptions on spoons from late Roman Britain. The date of deposition of the Norrie's Law hoard remains controversial, with dates proposed ranging from the early fifth to the second half of the seventh centuries.[23] If deposition occurred towards the end of this range, the cut plate may have been in circulation for some time. This would reveal that the Norrie's Law hoard, and possibly others, represent only the final phase in long and possibly complex sequences of activity.

One of the most striking aspects of the archaeological record of later Roman Britain is its huge hoards of precious metalwork, variously comprising silverware, gold and silver coins and jewellery. The most impressive are those from Hoxne and Mildenhall (both Suffolk), Thetford (Norfolk) and Water Newton (Huntingdonshire).[24] Although their contents are similar to those of the Traprain treasure, their condition is not. The complete vessels of the East Anglian hoards contrast with the hack-silver from Traprain. The intact condition of their contents suggests that these hoards were intended to be retrieved and they are widely believed to have been buried for safekeeping. But claims that they were hidden from raiding Picts and Scots[25] seem unlikely. The hoards concerned are concentrated in south-eastern Britain, where Anglo-Saxon raiders presumably posed a greater threat. And although the deposition of these hoards reflects the unsettled situation at the end of Roman Britain, they may have been buried to hide them not from marauding barbarians but from Romano-British officials who were requisitioning precious metalwork to fund the defence and government of the increasingly beleaguered province.[26]

Roman silver plate may have been cut up for two main reasons. It assists the distribution of spoils in easily quantifiable amounts among large numbers of people. That this is why the Traprain silverware was dismembered is suggested by the presence of a piece of lead wrapped in one packet of silver. This was probably intended to mislead someone about the weight of silver they were receiving. Hack-silver was also an intermediate stage in the recycling of precious metals, facilitating their melting down, as the crucibles used were small. Although this fate did not befall the Traprain hoard it may have been intended for recycling at some point before it was buried, probably as a votive deposit.[27] But most Roman metalwork that fell into the hands of the Picts and North Britons was probably melted down and reused to produce their own styles of jewellery. This is implied by the high gold content (4.24 per cent) of the silver used in the manufacture of at least one 'Pictish' chain, from Hordwheel (Berwickshire), suggesting that Roman silver-gilt plate was being recycled to make native decorative metalwork.[28]

These massive, double-linked chains, the heaviest of which weighs 2.9 kg (92.5 oz troy), were probably worn around the neck as symbols of social status and may date to the sixth century. 'Pictish' chains pose problems of interpretation, particularly as only three of them have been discovered within the area of historical Pictland, in contrast to the nine found in southern Scotland,[29] including one from Traprain Law.[30] Nevertheless, one chain found outside Pictland, at Whitecleugh, near Crawfordjohn (Lanarkshire) (see Plate 26), has a terminal decorated with a pair of Pictish symbols.[31] These include a double disc and Z-rod with close parallels in Pictish sculpture and metalwork in Fife, where similar examples occur in the Wemyss Caves and on the plaques from the Norrie's Law hoard. The predominantly southern distribution of the 'Pictish' chains is usually explained by their loss to southern raiders or invaders, specifically during the Northumbrian occupation of Southern Pictland in the mid-seventh century.[32] But this fails to explain why no chains have been found inside Northumbria itself. Instead of all the chains being Pictish, their distribution suggests that at least some were associated with the North British kingdom of *Gododdin*.[33]

Finds of Roman metalwork and the quantities and composition of native silverwork discovered in Scotland point to the effectiveness of raids on later Roman Britain by the Picts and North Britons. The principal objective of their raiding was portable wealth, rather than any ambitions of invasion, conquest and settlement. As a result, the temporary nature of these incursions diminished their impact on Roman Britain and probably facilitated the rapid recovery of imperial authority after the 'Barbarian Conspiracy' of 367.

## DEVASTATIO: RAVAGING ENEMY TERRITORY

Pictish and Scottish raiding continued after the departure of the Romans, this time directed against the newly emerged British kingdoms to the south. However, there is little evidence of these attacks, archaeological or documentary. According to Gildas,[34] 'year after year they [the Picts and Scots] had greedily taken heaps of plunder overseas with none to resist them', although this later reduced so that 'the Picts . . . occasionally carried out devastating raids of plunder'. It was presumably during one of their greater incursions that the Picts were defeated in the 'Alleluia victory' of 429.[35]

Although the archaeological record provides some evidence of raiding during the Roman period, it yields few clues about Pictish and Scottish raiding during the early medieval period. Anglo-Saxon artefacts found in Pictland include a silver mount from a ninth-century blast-horn found at Burghead[36] and two probably ninth-century strap-ends from the Brough of Birsay (Orkney) and Hurly Hawkin (Angus).[37] Finds are surprisingly scarce. Most Anglo-Saxon coin finds on Scotland are from the Hebrides and date to the tenth and eleventh centuries,[38] presumably reflecting Viking contacts with Anglo-Saxon England. Nevertheless, a coin of Alfred, deposited after 875, was found at Burghead.[39] The outstanding Anglo-Saxon artefact from *Dál Riata* is a seventh-century gold and garnet setting from a very high-quality item of jewellery, found at Dunadd.[40] But the volume of material concerned is small and, although the artefacts may have been plundered from Anglo-Saxon England, other interpretations are possible. These artefacts may have reached Pictland by various means, including trade or as gifts. The discovery of an ogam-inscribed knife handle made from red deer antler, found at Weeting (Norfolk),[41] probably dating to the eighth century, indicates coastal contacts with Anglo-Saxon England, but its exact significance is unclear. But while documentary sources provide no evidence of Pictish or Scottish raids on England, there are terse references to Anglo-Saxon seaborne attacks on Pictland.[42]

Material wealth was a trait of early medieval kingship. The epithet of Mynyddog Mwynfawr, 'the Wealthy', the supposed North British king mentioned in *The Gododdin*, boasts of his royal riches, while the fortress of Bridei son of Maelchon, King of the Northern Picts, boasted a royal treasury (*thesauris regis*).[43] Although the only item in it recorded by Adomnán was a magic stone, Bridei's treasury may also have held the spoils of battle, as well as tribute collected from those under his overlordship. A treasury was probably required to manage and store securely the wealth flowing through the king's hands.

Plundered goods, the proceeds of raiding or warfare, probably featured prominently among the wealth of Pictish and Scottish kings. Wealth was more important as a means of financing largesse to the king's supporters, rather than in its own right. This is reflected in another royal epithet, that of Rhydderch Hael, Rhydderch 'the generous', King of the Strathclyde Britons (*fl. c.* 580, d. *c.* 615?).[44] Plunder would have been divided among the victors according to custom, perhaps in a similar manner to Welsh practice. There, a lord was liable for distributing two-thirds of the spoils among his followers, retaining one-third for himself, according to the tenth-century *Laws of Hywel Dda*.[45] Referring to the redistribution of Irish Christians taken as slaves in a fifth-century raid by the Strathclyde Britons, St Patrick criticises 'they who allot poor baptised women as prizes'.[46] Raiding was of great socio-political importance because the redistribution of war booty was used to reward loyalty and military service and was therefore central to the maintenance of royal and aristocratic power. Not surprisingly, the acquisition of portable wealth was one of the principal motives of early medieval warfare, frequently as part of a wider military objective, such as the siege of a royal fortress.[47] But some expeditions, by land or sea, may have been conducted with the express intention of plundering. Indeed, the importance of raiding as a source of booty and its social context is revealed by references to the raids mounted by members of the royal kin group of *Cenél nGabráin* against ecclesiastical and lay targets alike.[48]

As with other forms of warfare, Scottish kings also led plundering expeditions. In 565, Conall mac Comgaill, King of *Dál Riata*, led a fleet into Seil and Islay, where it 'took from them many spoils',[49] in the earliest recorded example of *Cenél nGabráin* raiding islands belonging to another royal kindred of *Dál Riata*. Aedán mac Gabráin (574–?608) led a plundering expedition into Strathclyde,[50] its status as one of the 'Three Unrestrained Ravagings of the Island of Britain' attesting its scale and/or the volume of plunder seized. And *The Prophecy of Berchán*[51] refers to plundering by three kings of *Alba*, boasting that 'there will be no noble court not plundered' by Domnall mac Causantín (889?–900) and that 'forays will be excessive under his reign'. *The Prophecy of Berchán* also describes Dubh mac Máel Choluim (Duff son of Malcolm) (962–6) and Cuilén mac Iduilb (Cullen son of Idulf) (966–71) as 'Two kings . . . the pair plundering equally'.

Contemporary sources use typically laconic and formulaic terminology to record such raids. The most prominent among these is *devastatio*, the 'laying waste' or 'ravaging' of an area. Several incidents of *devastatio*, both perpetrated by and inflicted on the Picts and Scots are recorded. Although they contain few details, these sources provide some insights into the nature of this activity. *Devastatio* was usually the privilege of a victorious army and either accompanied an invasion or followed a victory in battle. *Devastationes* involved more than just harrying, but were both more violent and destructive in character. Widespread plundering was almost certainly an integral part of this process, accompanied by the destruction of anything that could not be removed either forcibly or conveniently, probably including forts, churches, dwellings and crops. Indiscriminate slaughter and hostage-taking probably completed the picture. But *devastatio* did not involve the lasting conquest or occupation of a kingdom and contrasts with Unuist's *percutio*, 'striking, beating, killing', of *Dál Riata* in 741,[52] which initiated a decade of Pictish overlordship.

The violence integral to *devastationes* transcends the terseness of the sources. Ecgfrith, King of Northumbria, 'devastated their [the Picts'] kingdoms with cruel and savage ferocity' (*regna atroci ac feroci sevicia devastaret*) in 685 before he and his army were annihilated in the battle of Dunnichen.[53] Similarly, Unuist son of Uurguist (820–34), King of the Picts, and his army 'most cruelly laid waste' (*crudelissima vastacione*) to the (possibly) Strathclyde Britons.[54] Unuist's earlier namesake 'laid waste [*vastavit*] the territory of *Dál Riata*' in 736[55] after defeating the Scots in battle at *Cnoc Cairpri*.[56] Ailpín, father of King Cináed mac Ailpín, is recorded as having 'entirely destroyed and devastated [*destruxit et devastavit*]' Galloway.[57] The probable outcome of a *devastatio* conducted after a success on the battlefield is recorded in one source. After the Northumbrian army defeated the Picts in the Plain of *Manau* in 672, 'the king's companies came back laden with spoil', including slaves or hostages.[58] But *devastatio* could also be inflicted by a defeated army in their retreat through hostile territory. Domnall Brecc 'without cause wasted [*vastante*] the province of Domnall grandson of Ainmuire', probably *Cenél Conaill* territory in north-western Ireland, after the Scots' defeat in the battle of *Mag Rath* in Ulster in 637.[59] Other terms are used occasionally instead of *devastatio*, as when the *Dál Riata* 'ravaged, plundered, destroyed' (*populati sunt*) the Ulster kingdoms of the *Cruithin* and the *Ulaid* in 691.[60]

Maritime expeditions also conducted *devastationes*. The Anglo-Saxons 'laid waste' (*vastaverunt*) the Orkney Isles in the mid-fifth century[61] and Orkney was again 'laid waste' (*devastatio*) in 682, this time by the Pictish King Bridei son of Bile.[62] The destructive nature of the latter attack is emphasised by a parallel entry recording that Bridei 'destroyed' (*deletae sunt*) Orkney.[63] Of all seaborne raiders, the Vikings are notable for the frequency of their attacks and for the extent of the areas they laid waste.

The Danes ravaged Pictland as far as Clunie and Dunkeld during the reign of Cináed mac Ailpín (843–58), while Viking armies 'laid waste and plundered' *Fortriu* in 864 and, possibly in a reference to the same campaign, ravaged 'Pictland' in 866.[64] Plundering and ravaging, as the latter example suggests, probably went hand-in-hand in early medieval (and, indeed, later) warfare, with the aggressors plundering what could be taken and destroying what could not. The Vikings also laid waste (*vastaverunt*) to 'Pictland' during the reign of Domnall mac Causantín (889?–900) and plundered (*predaverunt*) Dunkeld and all *Alba* in 903.[65]

More detailed references to plundering appear in saints' lives but do not concern the aftermath of battles. Churches, monasteries and their associated settlements were attractive targets. They housed rich metalwork in the form of eucharistic vessels and reliquaries and provided a ready supply of slaves. Poorly defended and often isolated, they were also vulnerable to raiding. Pictish fleets operated as far south as the Bristol Channel in search of plunder. In their raid on Gildas' monastic retreat on the island of Flat Holm, off the Glamorgan coast, Pictish raiders seized Gildas' servants, 'along with [unspecified] spoils and all the furniture of their dwelling'.[66] Hebridean monasteries posed a closer target and were particularly exposed to attacks from the western seaboard of Pictland. Raids on Eigg and Tiree,[67] two of the most important Scottish monasteries after Iona, are recorded. St Comgall's monastery on Tiree was plundered in the mid-sixth century, when 'many heathen robbers of the Picts invaded the village [where Comgall's monastery stood], to carry off everything that was there, both human beings and cattle . . . the spoilers took to their ships St Comgall's brethren with all their substance'.[68]

Destruction by fire was probably an indispensable element of *devastatio* and may explain the firing of several forts.[69] After being stripped of any valuables, or if any opposition was encountered, forts, churches or settlements were fired, sometimes together with their occupants. The plundering and/or burning of churches and monasteries was commonplace in early medieval Ireland[70] and is also recorded in *Dál Riata*. Donnán, Abbot of Eigg, and his community, recorded as numbering between 52 and 150 monks, were burned alive on Eigg in 617,[71] probably after they had sought refuge in the church. The perpetrators of the attack are unidentified in contemporary sources and are simply referred to as 'sea-raiders'.[72] This at least suggests a motive. That the attack was accompanied by the looting of the monastery on Eigg is supported by the title of a lost Irish tale, 'The Plundering of Donnán of Eigg' (*Argain Donnán Ego*).[73] Pictish raiders were probably responsible for this attack, which may be paralleled by that on Comgall's monastery on Tiree in the mid-sixth century. This identification is supported by geography. Eigg lay off the western coast of Pictland but near the frontier with *Dál Riata*, in what was probably a contested border zone, vulnerable to raiding. Local tradition also identifies the culprits as the Picts and maintains that the monastery was fired on the orders of a Pictish queen, in reprisal for the monastic community grazing their livestock on her land.[74] The practice of firing buildings after plundering their contents may also explain the burning of *Mag Luinge*, a monastery on Tiree, in 673.[75]

Scottish churches were not only plundered by hostile and presumably pagan Picts but, on occasion, were also targeted systematically by members of the royal dynasties of *Dál Riata*. Adomnán[76] describes the sons of Conall mac Domnaill, who were members of the royal dynasty of *Cenél nGabráin* (*de regio Gabrani*), as 'persecutors of churches'. Ioan son of Conall sacked (*devastaverat*) the 'house' (i.e. church or monastery) of St Colmán in Ardnamurchan on three occasions, 'carrying off all that he found there' and returning 'laden with booty' (*preda*) on his third plundering (*depredationem*).[77] As a royal activity, raiding was not only confined to warfare against hostile peoples. Although the background to these incidents is unknown, it is probably significant that Ioan's raids were directed at an ecclesiastical foundation in the territory of a rival kindred of *Dál Riata*, *Cenél Loairn*.

At least one king of *Dál Riata* also attacked a monastery, although primarily for political motives rather than plunder. In 733, Dúngal mac Selbaich profaned the sanctuary of the monastery on Tory Island, off the coast of Co. Donegal, to capture Bridei son of Unuist, the exiled Pictish king.[78] With the extension of Scottish power over Pictland from *c.* 843, the focus of their raids switched to their wealthy southern neighbour, Northumbria, and its ecclesiastical centres. During his reign, Cináed mac Ailpín seized the important Northumbrian monastery of Old Melrose,[79] while the Scots 'laid waste [*vastaverunt*] the land of St Cuthbert and plundered [*spoliaverunt*] the monastery of Lindisfarne' in 883X96.[80] Such raids, or their threat, could also have been used to impose tribute on a neighbouring people and it is probably no coincidence that *The Prophecy of Berchán* refers to Cináed, 'whose name will be the tribute-taker'.[81] Although the opportunity to take plunder or exact tribute would have been seized eagerly on these occasions, there was probably an additional, strategic, motive behind these raids, that of extending the southern influence and territory of *Alba*.

Small secular settlements, particularly those in border areas, were also vulnerable to raiding. Adomnán[82] relates Columba's vision that 'the district bordering upon the shores of the lake of Crogreth . . . is now being plundered [*populantur*] by barbarian marauders [*vastatores*]', presumably pagan Picts. Although a man's family had escaped to a hill, all the cattle were driven away and all the household furniture seized. This reveals the types of booty taken in raids on non-royal settlements, although its occupants must have been reasonably well off to have possessed cattle and furniture. The hill concerned is A'Cruach, near Loch Rannoch (Argyll).[83] Its proximity to the border between *Dál Riata* and Pictland suggests a low-intensity border warfare between Picts and Scots of the type that characterised the later Anglo-Scottish Border.

Cattle raiding probably featured prominently in this border warfare, as it did in early medieval Ireland and on the Anglo-Scottish border during the high Middle Ages. Indeed, in the first recorded incident of Borders cattle reiving, in 950 Máel Coluim mac Domnaill (Malcolm son of Donald, 'Malcolm I'), King of *Alba*, led the 'Raid of the White Ridges' (*predam Albi Do[r]sorum*) into Northumbria as far as the River Tees, seizing 'many herds of cattle'.[84] After precious metalwork, cattle were probably the most sought-after form of plunder and tribute because of their value as an indicator of status, a medium for exchange and the added attraction that this type of plunder transported itself.[85] Plundered cattle could also be transported by ship, as the Picts did after their raid on St Comgall's monastery on Tiree.[86] So prominent was the 'desperate incursion' of the cattle raid in Highland society that it survived into the eighteenth century in the Western Isles as one of 'the ancient and modern customs of the inhabitants'.[87]

## HUMAN SPOILS: SLAVES AND HOSTAGES

Another important prize of raiding and warfare by the Picts and Scots was people. Captives seized in the aftermath of a battle or in raiding normally had two uses, as slaves or hostages. The distinction was primarily one of status.

In a slave-owning society, raiding and warfare provided a plentiful supply of slaves and this was the fate of ordinary soldiers and commoners who were captured. Although there is no evidence of this among the Scots, the Picts are recorded as both slaves and slavers. The spoils taken by the Northumbrian army that defeated the Picts in the Plain of *Manau* in 672 included slaves or hostages. Indeed, the phrase 'chains returned upon their [the Picts'] necks'[88] suggests that the Northumbrians went equipped specifically for this purpose. Conversely, Northumbrian survivors of the battle of Dunnichen were enslaved.[89] No slave shackles have been found in *Dál Riata* or Pictland, although examples are known from Iron Age Britain and early medieval Ireland.[90]

Defeated armies were not the only source of slaves. Slave-taking was one of the major motives behind raiding. Máel Coluim mac Domnaill seized not only cattle but also 'a multitude of people' in his raid on Northumbria in 950.[91] Ecclesiastical foundations were particularly easy targets for slavers. The Orkney 'pirates' who raided Gildas' island retreat seized his servants, carrying them off into exile[92] and, presumably, slavery. And the monks of St Comgall who were seized from their monastery on Tiree by Pictish raiders[93] were probably enslaved. The martyrdom of Donnán and his community on Eigg in 617 may represent the outcome of an unsuccessful slaving expedition, their church fired after they sought refuge inside it in an attempt to escape capture.

Slave raiding and trading knew no borders but was truly international in nature. An Irish slave woman was kept by the druid of Bridei son of Maelchon, King of the Northern Picts, when Columba visited in the late sixth century.[94] This may attest Pictish raiding on Ireland, but slaves may also have reached Pictland indirectly, as a result of slave trading. Indeed, the Picts were acquiring Irish slaves as early as the fifth century. St Patrick[95] criticises 'the man who delivers Christians into the hands of *Scotti* and Picts' and writes of 'sons and daughters [of the Irish Church] who . . . have been carried far off and transported to distant lands . . . and there freeborn men have been sold, Christians reduced to slavery . . . as slaves of the . . . Picts'. Other Christians were killed and unspecified plunder taken during the same raid.[96] Most of Patrick's criticism was directed not at the Picts, but at the king whose soldiers had seized these recently baptised converts to Christianity in a raid on Ireland. The identity of this king, Coroticus, is still debated[97] but he is described in a later source as King of Dumbarton (*regem Aloo*, i.e. *Ail*).[98] The Strathclyde Britons were raiding Ireland and trading some of the slaves they captured there with the Picts. Slaving was still international in character during the ninth century. *The Prophecy of Berchán*[99] states that Giric mac Dúngail (878–89?), King of *Alba*, 'will have slaves with him in his house: English, Vikings and Britons'.

Unlike commoners, noble or royal captives were unlikely to be traded as slaves. Their status made them useful bargaining chips in extracting political concessions and/or ransoms, the nature of which depended on the political context and the identities of the hostage and hostage-taker. An Irish tale purporting to explain how Fiachna mac Baetán became 'King of Scotland' indicates that hostages were given when an army was no longer able to continue the fight: 'the King of Scotland, he escaped from the battle, and as he had not a sufficient number to do battle again, he gave hostages to the King of Ireland'.[100] In particular, the holding of royal hostages symbolised the subject status of a kingdom and could ensure its compliance and payment of tribute. This explains the presence of the subject King (*regulus*) of Orkney whom Columba met at the court of Bridei.[101] This indicates that the sub-king of Orkney had recently rebelled against, or been brought under, the overlordship of the King of the Northern Picts, to whom he presumably owed tribute. Other cases of royal hostages may be recorded. Dúngal, King of *Dál Riata*, and his brother Feradach were captured 'and bound in chains' when the Picts invaded *Dál Riata* in 736.[102] This was presumably done to remove possible sources of future opposition and may also have assisted with the imposition of Pictish overlordship on, and the extraction of tribute from, *Dál Riata*.

Hostages were used by the Vikings to exact tribute on a larger scale than before. Like slave raiding and trading, this was a truly international enterprise. In 866, 'The Vikings laid waste and plundered *Fortriu*, and they took many hostages with them as pledges for tribute; for a long time afterwards they continued to pay them tribute.'[103] The hostages seized on that raid, or the 200 ship-loads of captured Angles, Britons and Picts or 'Albans' seized by the same Dublin Vikings in 870–1, were still generating income in 874–5, when a Viking king was slain attempting to collect tribute.[104] Nevertheless, hostages were probably held to extract specific benefits on a short-term basis, in contrast to slavery, which was probably a permanent state. The taking of hostages may not always have yielded the desired outcome. Although recorded only in John of Fordun's fourteenth-century chronicle,[105] Alpín, allegedly King of *Dál Riata*, reportedly fought the Picts in battle in 834 but was 'defeated, taken, and all ransom being refused, beheaded'. But the fate of most prisoners, whose lowly status brought few or no benefits, was presumably slavery or death. Indeed, some prisoners appear to have been executed without any attempt to extract tribute.[106]

## THE QUEST FOR GLORY

Personal reputation was of great importance in heroic society, which was intensely status conscious. Warfare played a fundamental role in this process. Requiring great bravery, physical strength and stamina, as well as tactical and strategic skills, warfare provided an important means of maintaining and enhancing social standing. This was just as important as the more tangible spoils of war and it must have provided a strong motivating factor to participate and acquire glory in warfare. Kings were war leaders first and foremost and, as they relied upon the support of their nobles, their reputation in battle was central to their rule. Several Pictish and Scottish kings fought battles early in their reigns. This may reflect challenges to their kingship before they had the opportunity to consolidate their power. Alternatively, it may parallel the 'royal prey' (*crech ríg*) in early medieval Ireland, in which a newly installed king and his warband mounted a cattle raid on a neighbouring kingdom.[107] As in Ireland, newly inaugurated Pictish and Scottish kings may have sought to mark the start of their kingship and demonstrate their bravery and martial prowess with a successful battle or raid against a traditional enemy. An additional motive was that a successful expedition would yield plunder which could then be redistributed among the king's followers, thereby ensuring that the new king received the support of his nobles and officials. The inaugural raid or battle cemented a king's relationship – military, social and economic – with his people. Kings also patronised court poets to sing their praises in an oral literary tradition that survived in Highland Scotland, Ireland and Wales throughout the medieval period and, in some cases, beyond.[108]

The themes of personal bravery and honour are prominent in early medieval literature and find their greatest expression in epic or heroic poetry, the supreme example of which is the North British *The Gododdin*. *The Gododdin* portrays warfare as an élite activity in which the warrior's honour and reputation were more important than victory or even survival. Indeed, *The Gododdin*'s celebration of an army that was all but wiped out gives the impression that the result was only of secondary importance. The army of the *Gododdin* went in search of glory and they found it in death. No Pictish or Scottish heroic poetry survives, although the close similarities between the cultures of the Picts, Scots and North Britons means that it almost certainly existed. Indeed, their shared heroic values are reflected by the inclusion in *The Gododdin* of several verses celebrating Pictish warriors who fought with the *Gododdin*:[109]

> When he attacked the realm's frontier, his fame was exquisite.
> The gold-torqued man used to deserve his wine.
> The splendid man used to present a sheer, bright array.
> The noble hero used to lead a hundred men,
> A foreign horseman of most refined nature,
> Cian's only young son, from beyond *Bannawg*.

This emphasis on personal bravery is reflected in the identification of military events with a specific individual, invariably a king. Thus, the battle of Dunnichen is described as the 'battle of Ecgfrith'[110] and the 'conquest' of the Picts by the Scots is personally attributed to Cináed mac Ailpín. Like their North British counterparts, Pictish and Scottish kings were probably the subject of eulogies praising their warlike qualities and achievements in battle. All that survives of these are the heroic epithets used to describe some kings of *Dál Riata* and *Alba* in later sources. *Duan Albanach*,[111] an eleventh-century verse history based on an earlier regnal list, refers to 'Aedán of the many dissensions' (Aedán mac Gabráin), 'the valiant hero Causantín' (Causantín mac Fergusa) (789–820) and 'Causantín, brave was his contests' (Causantín mac Cináeda, 'Constantine I') (862–76). Another source states of Domnall mac Ailpín (Donald son of Alpin, 'Donald I') (858–62) that 'in war he was a vigorous soldier'. *The Prophecy of Berchán* praises the prowess in battle of the kings of *Alba*, including their plundering and hostage-taking,[112] by allegedly foretelling their victories. For example, it states of Causantín mac Cináeda that 'The countenance through whom three battles will be won over Vikings of pure colour; a fourth battle, *Cathluaire*, [will be won] over the king of Britons of green mantles'.[113] Referring to Domnall mac Causantín, it predicts that 'the kingship of the king will be forceful, after casting his enemies into nothingness'.[114] And it prophesies of Idulb mac Causantín (Indulf, son of Constantine) (954–62), 'Woe to Britons and Saxons during his time, during the reign of the champion of fine weapons.'[115] But the strongest praise is reserved for Cinaed mac Ailpín in verses that reflect the mythologisation of the assimilation of the Picts by the Scots as a specific event involving the conquest of the Picts by the Scots:[116]

A youth from the clan of his son will take the kingship of Scotland by force of his strength. . . . He is the first king from the men of Ireland in Scotland who will take kingship in the east; it will be after strength of spear and sword, after sudden death, after sudden slaughter.

Only two Pictish kings are celebrated in surviving fragments of praise poems. But, perhaps significantly, these are two of the most successful Pictish warrior kings. Unuist son of Uurguist is celebrated in a quatrain that a Middle Irish tract on versecraft attributes to a legendary chief poet of the King of *Alba*:[117]

Good the day when Unuist took *Alba*,
hilly *Alba*, with its strong chiefs;
He brought battle to towns, with boards,
with feet and hands and with broad shields.

Uniquely, a short poem celebrating Bridei son of Bile's victory over a Northumbrian army at Dunnichen in 685 also survives:[118]

Today Bridei gives battle
over his grandfather's land,

unless it is the command
of God's Son that it be restored.

Today Oswiu's son [Ecgfrith] was slain
in battle against iron swords,
even though he did penance,
it was a penance too late.

Today Oswiu's son was slain,
who used to have dark drinks:
Christ has heard our prayer
That Bridei would save Breo.

This provides a unique perspective on the battle and its celebration, demonstrating the existence of a literary tradition concerning the battle of Dunnichen.

Although no Pictish or Scottish heroic epics survive, the value placed on the possession of martial prowess and the honour and glory that it brought are still evident among the Picts and Scots. Pictish sculpture hints at a heroic genre that no longer survives in literary form. Old Testament heroes, particularly David and Samson, are prominent in Pictish Christian iconography.[119] These striking images, for example, of David rending the jaws of a lion, attest a society that values acts of individual bravery and physical strength. The same themes of personal valour are also represented in secular scenes in Pictish sculpture. These include portrayals of single combat, such as the duelling swordsmen on the Shandwick cross-slab and the axe-wielding warriors on the Glamis Manse cross-slab,[120] as well as the many hunting scenes, in which ferocious beasts are confronted, and of warriors striking aggressive poses with their weapons poised in the 'ready' position (*see* Plates 9, 22 and 23).

Despite the absence of documentary evidence, the existence of a specifically Pictish heroic tradition is supported by the existence of a small number of battle scenes that probably illustrate heroic poems and in front of which these epics were perhaps recited. Poorly preserved examples occur on the Eassie cross-slab (*see* Plate 25), with its cloaked foot soldiers, 'triumph tree' and decapitation scene,[121] and on the Dunkeld 2 cross-slab (the 'Apostles' Stone),[122] where the status of the scene depicting mounted and foot soldiers as a battle is confirmed by the adjacent pile of bodies. But by far the best preserved and most impressive sculptural representation of warfare is the remarkable battle scene that occupies most of the reverse of the cross-slab in Aberlemno churchyard[123] (*see* Plate 8). Carved in low relief with incised detail, this panel depicts two opposing forces, almost certainly representing the Picts and Northumbrians at Dunnichen, which lies only 10 km south of Aberlemno. The figures on the left-hand side of the scene are recognisably Pictish in appearance, as characters with similar clothing, hairstyles and weapons are portrayed on many Pictish stones. The figures on the right-hand side are helmeted, distinguishing them from Pictish warriors, who are always shown bare-headed.[124] The helmets depicted, with their prominent nasal and cheek/neck guards, are identifiably Anglo-Saxon in style. Indeed, the best surviving example, the Coppergate helmet from York,[125] was found within Northumbrian territory.

The dating of the Aberlemno churchyard cross-slab is controversial, with dates proposed ranging from 685, the year of the battle, to the mid-ninth century.[126] Its dating is complicated by the possibility that the obverse, decorated with a cross and interlaced design, is of a later date than the battle scene.[127] This may explain why the cross-slab is usually dated on artistic grounds up to a century later than the battle.[128] The Coppergate helmet dates to c. 750–75, within a century of the battle of Dunnichen, although the swords portrayed in the battle scene appear to be later.[129] The earliest dates proposed enable the Aberlemno churchyard cross-slab to be interpreted as a monument to this great Pictish victory. More probably, the cross-slab was erected within the lifetime of someone who had fought at Dunnichen, perhaps in his youth, and may have marked the grave of a veteran of the battle. The later dates do not preclude the identification of the Aberlemno battle scene with the battle of Dunnichen. Indeed, this gives the battle scene an added significance as evidence of the transmission over time of presumably oral heroic traditions concerning the battle and the Picts' victory over the Northumbrians.

The arrangement of the Aberlemno battle scene in four separate episodes in three tiers or registers suggests that it was intended to be read as a narrative. But it is unclear whether these scenes represent the entire encounter or comprise 'edited highlights', depicting crucial episodes during the battle. Nevertheless, the scene is widely believed to depict real people and actual events. With the exception of a small concluding scene inserted in the lower right-hand corner, the sequence may be read from bottom to top. Mounted warriors, their spears held underarm (Picts) or overarm (Northumbrians) ready to thrust and throw respectively, attack each other in the bottom row. This probably represents the battle's opening cavalry charges, in which the combatants would have used their spears as the armies approached and locked in combat.[130] A ranked formation of Pictish infantrymen then confronts an attacking Northumbrian cavalryman in the middle row. This depicts the next and main stage of the battle, in which foot soldiers, comprising the body of the army, either advance behind a successful cavalry charge or are left exposed to the enemy's cavalry after their own are killed or repulsed. But the latter was not the case here because the top row depicts the rout of a Northumbrian cavalryman, his discarded sword and shield behind him and with a Pictish horseman, sword drawn, in hot pursuit. The single Northumbrian warrior depicted in each row of the scene may be interpreted as either symbolising Ecgfrith's entire army or portraying a notable individual within it, presumably Ecgfrith himself. The fleeing cavalryman may therefore symbolise the routing of the Northumbrian army. The final, death, scene is considered below.[131]

## CHAPTER NINE

# *The Battle-dead*

The only outcomes for a defeated army were flight, enslavement or death. This stark reality is revealed by Bede's[1] account of the fate of the Northumbrian army defeated by the Picts in the battle of Dunnichen in 685: 'many of the English were either slain by the sword or enslaved or escaped by flight from Pictish territory'. Death is an inevitable consequence of warfare and must have been the fate of many Picts and Scots at war. Indeed, so normal and accepted was death in warfare that Columba prophesied that a man would die 'neither in battle, nor in the sea',[2] emphasising the unusual character of this fatality and revealing that these were the commonest forms of death. The human carnage inflicted in battles fought by the Picts and Scots is occasionally recorded in documentary sources and, more rarely, sculpture. These records reveal something about not only the character and human costs of combat but also Pictish and Scottish attitudes towards warfare.

## CASUALTIES

Where they exist at all, casualty records for battles fought by the Picts and Scots are characteristically terse. Annalistic entries sometimes append to the record of a battle the names of a couple of men killed in it. A typical entry of this type records: 'The battle of *Srath Ethairt* [was won] by Talorcan son of Eanfrith, King of the Picts, in which Dúnchad mac Conaing and Congal mac Ronain were slain.'[3] The small number of named individuals recorded in this way indicates that these were not the only casualties incurred, but were evidently considered important enough to merit an obituary or death record. This is confirmed by several entries recording the killing in battle of kings, other members of the royal kin group, particularly the brothers and sons of kings, and occasionally nobles and royal officials.[4] Indeed, the killing of royal or noble combatants sometimes appears to the annalists to have outweighed the significance of the battle in which they fell, occasionally resulting in the recording of the deaths but with no reference to the battle itself. This is the case with one record of the deaths of Bran and Domangart, sons of Aedán mac Gabráin, who were killed in a battle in *Círcenn* in 596.[5]

148

Despite the terseness of the annals, the deaths of several kings in battle are recorded. Of the kings of *Dál Riata*, Connad Cerr was killed in the battle of *Fid Eóin* in Ireland in 629[6] and Domnall Brecc fell in the battle of Strathcarron against the Strathclyde Britons in 642.[7] The violent deaths of four other kings of *Dál Riata* may also have occurred in battle.[8] The killings of fewer Pictish kings in battle are recorded, reflecting the more limited sources concerning the Picts. Nevertheless, Bridei son of Maelchon was killed in the battle of *Asreth* in 584.[9] Kings appear to have faced a higher risk in the wars against the Vikings. Eóganán mac Óengusa, King of both *Dál Riata* and Pictland,[10] and Áed mac Boanta, King of *Dál Riata*, were killed in a battle against the Vikings in 839.[11] And two kings of *Alba*, Causantín mac Cináeda and Causantín mac Áeda, met similar fates in 877 and 937 respectively.[12]

The death in battle of provincial kings is also recorded. Talorcan, the Pictish king killed by the Britons at *Catoic* in 750,[13] was possibly King of Atholl. Áed, 'King of Pictland', who was killed in battle by the Vikings, probably in *Fortriu*, in 904[14] may have been a provincial ruler within *Alba*. Alternatively, this may be a misplaced reference to Áed mac Cináeda, King of *Alba*, who was killed in 878, during a period that saw many Viking attacks, although his obituary records that he was killed by his own people.[15] The recorded deaths of some kings in the same year as battles is also suggestive of their being killed on the battlefield. For example, the Scots were routed by the Picts in 558 or 560,[16] the earlier date coinciding with the death of Gabráin, King of *Dál Riata*. One of the commonest means of death for Pictish and Scottish kings must have been in battle.

So great was this occupational hazard that early medieval kings were almost expected to die in battle, as contemporary sources imply. Columba prophesied that a king of the Strathclyde Britons would die a peaceful death.[17] And when the men of *Alba* under Causantín mac Áeda defeated the Vikings on Tyneside (possibly the Haddington Tyne) in 918, 'neither king nor *mormaer* was lost'.[18] Both events were so unusual that they merited recording. The risks must have been even greater in internal battles for possession of the kingship, where the conflict was usually resolved by the deaths of all but one of the contenders.

Casualty figures for battles fought by the Picts and Scots are exceptionally rare. This may be because most casualties were common foot soldiers, who were of little concern to contemporary chroniclers, in contrast to those individuals of high status whose deaths were sometimes recorded. Alternatively, the terse information may reflect the relatively light casualties sustained. Early medieval warfare was fought by lightly armed and highly mobile troops, giving the losing side the option of fleeing the field, sometimes even before battle was joined, as in the 'Alleluia victory' of 429.[19] Moreover, the relatively small size of armies[20] would have limited the capacity for sustaining numerically, though not proportionately, high casualties. More probably, the chaos of battle and its aftermath gave the losing side little or no opportunity to count their dead even if they wanted to. In keeping with this, the only recorded casualty figure for a Scottish or Pictish army is for a victorious side. Columba reportedly prophesied that the Scots lost 303 men in battle against the *Miathi* in 574X97.[21] Adomnán would have had no cause to exaggerate the casualties incurred by his own side and the precision of his figure suggests that the victorious Scots conducted a body count on this occasion. If the victors lost 303 men in this battle one can only imagine the losses sustained by the defeated *Miathi* but they were probably at least two or three times as many. But the number of Scottish dead cannot be taken at face value. Although one out, the body count of 303 may represent about 300 plus the two sons of King Aedán mac Gabráin, Artuir and Echoid Find, who are specifically recorded as having been killed in the battle. However, 303 also suggests the influence of literary convention.[22]

The only other casualty figures belong to a later period and possibly a different, more intense, form of warfare, the ninth- and tenth-century wars against the Vikings. In addition to the loss of kings of both *Dál Riata* and Pictland, 'others almost innumerable were slain' in battle, probably in *Fortriu*, in 839.[23] In a Viking attack on Dunkeld and all *Alba* in 904, 'Áed, "king of Pictland", fell [in battle] against the two grandsons of Ívar, and against Catol, along with five hundred men'.[24] Although ambiguous, this suggests that 500 men in Áed's army were killed. The recorded death of 'several thousand' Vikings in battle against the Scots at the unlocated *Brunanburh* in 937[25] indicates, if accurate, another scale of warfare altogether. But this entry also highlights that most armies habitually exaggerate the number of casualties they inflict, and sometimes suffer, in order to emphasise the completeness of their victory and their heroism in overcoming daunting odds. This makes meaningful assessment of contemporary casualty figures difficult in any period but the paucity of evidence means that this problem is barely encountered in the study of Pictish and Scottish warfare.

Although figures are rarely recorded, many battles fought by the Picts and/or Scots involved heavy casualties. For example, despite having 'a large and strong army', Aedán mac Gabráin 'lost almost his entire army' in the battle of *Degsastán* in 603.[26] 'Host upon host' of Picts were killed by King Ecgfrith's Northumbrian army in the Plain of *Manau* in 672.[27] And when the men of *Fortriu* were defeated in an unnamed battle by the Vikings in 839, in addition to three named fatalities, 'others almost innumerable were slain'.[28] The Irish annals use various formulae to record heavy casualties sustained in battle, including Latin *caedes* and *strages*, 'slaughter, massacre'. The slaughter of Pictish or Scottish armies is recorded on three occasions: the Scots, probably by the Britons, in the Vale of Leven or Loch Lomond in 704,[29] the Picts by the Northumbrians in the Plain of *Manau* in 711,[30] and the Picts by the Britons at *Catoic* in 750.[31] Emphasising the losses involved, other battles resulted in 'great slaughter' (*caedes magna*, *strages magna*): the Scots by *Cenél nEógain* in Inishowen or in the River Bann in 733,[32] the 'Picts' by the Danes in 875[33] and the Vikings by the men of *Fortriu* in 904.[34] And 'countless Saxons [*recte*, Angles] were slaughtered' by the army of Unuist son of Uurguist (820–34) in a battle on the River Tyne, according to the St Andrews foundation legend.[35]

The wounded remain conspicuous by their absence from records of battles involving the Picts and/or Scots. Indeed, there is only a single reference to a combatant being wounded, apparently during the siege of a fortress rather than in battle: '*Dún Leithfinn* is destroyed after the wounding of Dúngal; and he fled to Ireland.'[36] Dúngal's survival and escape indicate that he was only lightly wounded, while his status as King of *Dál Riata* probably ensured that he received medical attention. Common soldiers are unlikely to have been so fortunate, particularly if they belonged to the losing side. The prospect of a ransom may have saved the wounded of high status, but there was no incentive for assisting ordinary soldiers, who were probably finished off as the victors plundered the battlefield.[37] Those who were not killed in this way probably died from loss of blood, shock, hypothermia or exposure. Clean wounds could be dressed and simple fractures splinted but, even on the winning side, the more seriously wounded would have stood little chance of survival and may have been left to die a slow and excruciating death on the battlefield. Penetrating wounds to the abdomen, chest or head would have had a high risk of becoming infected and were probably nearly always fatal. The absence of references to the wounded suggests that very few of them survived. But one must be wary here of the modern tendency to underestimate both the effectiveness of 'primitive' medicine and the remarkable resilience of the human body, which can sometimes withstand and recover from the most appalling injuries.

In early medieval warfare, more combatants were probably killed not in the battle itself, but in the rout that frequently followed it.[38] In its headlong flight from the battlefield, a routed and panic-stricken army lost the ability and perhaps also the will to defend itself and was therefore vulnerable to further losses. Topography could pose a greater threat than the enemy in a rout. Many battles were fought at or near rivers or lochs, reflecting their strategic significance as boundary markers and/or natural routes of access. Such locations frequently resulted in large numbers of warriors drowning, particularly if one side was routed. When the combined army of Picts and Saxons was routed by the Britons in the 'Alleluia victory' of 429, 'many in their hasty flight were drowned in a river which they tried to cross'.[39] And, in a battle in the Plain of *Manau* in 672, so many Picts were killed that their dead 'filled two rivers with the slain and his [Ecgfrith, King of Northumbria's] men crossed dry-shod over the corpses to slay the fugitives'.[40] Not only was a 'great slaughter' inflicted on the Scots in *Inis hOinae* in 733, in which 'a countless host was destroyed', but also 'a countless number of them were drowned in the River Bann, after their defeat',[41] presumably in an attempt to escape the carnage. The drowning of 'many Picts' in *Land Abae*,[42] possibly Lundaff, now Kinloch (Perthshire),[43] in 676 may reflect the aftermath of an otherwise unrecorded Pictish defeat. If so, the number of casualties sustained during the rout were presumably greater than those in the battle itself, which may be why the battle is not even recorded. A parallel for this exists in the rout of the Scots in an otherwise unrecorded battle.[44]

Survivors of battle were usually enslaved or taken hostage,[45] but some prisoners were executed. In the clearest evidence for the killing of a captive king in the aftermath of a battle, Artgal, King of the Strathclyde Britons, was captured in the battle of *Cathluaire* in 872 and killed on the order of Causantín mac Cináeda, the victorious King of *Alba*.[46] The treatment of prisoners may have changed during the wars with the Vikings, possibly reflecting the greater ferocity of this warfare and the Vikings' lack of awareness of, or respect for, traditional conventions of war. This may have been reciprocated by the Scots. In a battle fought between the men of *Fortriu* and the Vikings *c.* 918, 'many of the Vikings were killed after their defeat',[47] suggesting their summary execution. This indicates a new savagery in warfare, perhaps motivated by revenge for previous atrocities.

Various motives may have led to the killing of prisoners. In 733, Dúngal mac Selbaich, King of *Dál Riata*, seized Bridei, son of the Pictish king Unuist son of Uurguist, from the monastery on Tory Island, off the Irish coast.[48] Bridei's death is recorded in 736, the same year as Unuist's invasion of *Dál Riata*.[49] Although not stated, the implication is that Bridei was deliberately killed by Dúngal, and that this prompted Unuist's invasion or was either in revenge for the Pictish attack or to prevent his liberation. In the context of internal or domestic warfare, some prisoners were probably killed because of the continued threat that they posed by providing a potential focus of opposition. The 730s also saw the capture and drowning by Unuist of two members of the Pictish royal kin group, including a king of Atholl.[50] But their capture is not recorded as occurring in battle and these events probably reflect Unuist's attempts to eliminate remaining opponents from the struggle for the Pictish kingship of 724–9. Nevertheless, drowning may have been the traditional means of executing royal prisoners, possibly with ritual undertones.[51]

Another form of death with possibly ritual features is recorded in the Irish annals by the Latin *iugulatio*, literally 'the cutting of the throat (of)', but used more generally to denote a violent death.[52] The killings of five kings of *Dál Riata* are recorded as *iugulationes*: Domangart (673), Domnall (696), Eochaid (697), Fiannamail (700) and Ainfcellach (719).[53] Although the circumstances of the first four *iugulationes* are unrecorded, these kings were probably killed in dynastic disputes. But killings on the battlefield could also be described as *iugulationes*, as with those of the sons of Aedán mac Gabráin in a battle in *Círcenn* in 596,[54] two sons of Nechtan son of Dar Garta in a conflict among *Cenél Comgaill* in 710[55] and of Ainfcellach in a battle against his brother Selbach at *Finnglen* in 719,[56] probably Finglen on the Braes of Lorn near Loch Avich (Argyll).[57] But in no case is the cause of death recorded and the nature and significance of these *iugulationes* remain unclear.

## THE FATE OF THE BATTLE-DEAD

The aftermath of a battle must have presented an eerie and gruesome sight, the battlefield littered with the detritus of war, the battered and broken bodies of the dead and dying, their horses and weapons. The fate of those Picts and Scots killed in battle remains obscure and is illuminated by neither archaeological nor documentary evidence. However, the means by which the dead were disposed probably varied according to their number, social status and a range of military and topographic factors, including the number of survivors, the threat of further attack, the location of the battlefield and the nature of the terrain. The victors are more likely than the vanquished to have had the opportunity to retrieve the bodies of their slain warriors for burial and, depending on the number of corpses involved, this is most likely to have occurred in mass graves on the battlefield itself. The grave pits required for the disposal of the dead probably offer one of the best prospects for identifying the location of a battle, through aerial reconnaissance or geophysical survey. Moreover, any surviving skeletal remains within such graves may provide evidence not just about how the dead were killed, but also about the weapons used, the battle itself and therefore the nature of early medieval warfare in general. This approach is well established in the study of both medieval and prehistoric warfare, as with the analysis of a mass grave from the battle of Towton in 1461.[58] The application of such established archaeological techniques to the study of early medieval warfare is now required but is, of course, dependent on the discovery of relevant material for analysis.

References to the retrieval and burial or disposal of Irish, Northumbrian and North British warriors killed in battle[59] suggests that the human skeletal remains of victims of early medieval warfare may await discovery and analysis. But there is no indication of how common this was and no evidence of it among the Picts and Scots. Instead of being buried, the corpses of many, perhaps most, warriors, particularly those on the losing side, are more likely to have been left where they fell. Any human remains left exposed to the elements would have decayed and/or have been consumed or scattered by animals or birds, leaving little or no archaeological evidence. The battle-dead are frequently described as providing carrion for animals and birds in Anglo-Saxon and North British heroic poetry.[60] For example, an interpolated verse in *The Gododdin*[61] celebrates the fate of a king of *Dál Riata* who was killed in battle against the Strathclyde Britons in Strathcarron in 642: 'the head of Domnall Brecc, ravens gnawed it'. This same theme also occurs among the Picts and Scots. Referring to his success in reducing his enemies to carrion, *The Prophecy of Berchán*[62] describes Cináed mac Ailpín as 'a man who will feed scald-crows, will conquer in battle'. Mirroring this motif in Pictish sculpture, and in an obvious metaphor of death in combat, the Aberlemno battle scene depicts a crow or raven picking at a corpse (*see* Plate 8). Without mass graves, early medieval battlefields may be more difficult to locate by archaeological means.

The Aberlemno battle scene graphically depicts the outcome of the battle of Dunnichen and the fate of those on the losing side. The narrative sequence ends with a prostrate warrior, his shield lying beside him and a spear projecting from his helmeted head (*see* Plate 8). The warrior's helmet is of Anglian style, while his split-sided hauberk reveals him to be a cavalryman such as those depicted earlier in the sequence. This scene may either symbolise the carnage of the Northumbrian army as a whole or depict the gory fate of a senior Northumbrian casualty. Pictish sculpture frequently uses size to convey status. As the dead warrior is larger than any of the other figures depicted in this scene, it presumably represents Ecgfrith, King of Northumbria. Ecgfrith's body is reputed to have been treated with respect and conveyed to Iona, where it was interred alongside the kings of *Dál Riata* and saints of Iona.[63] However, this misunderstanding arises from the poem celebrating the Pictish victory,[64] which states literally that Ecgfrith 'does penance, it is in Iona', a metaphor for his penance being too late or in vain. This does not mean that Ecgfrith's body was buried on Iona but simply reflects later Scottish and Irish traditions of Iona as a royal burial place.[65] In reality, Ecgfrith's body is unlikely to have been treated so reverently and it is surely no coincidence that his body is depicted providing carrion for the crows.

The artefactual detritus of war may have attracted more interest in the aftermath of a battle than the disposal of the dead. The victors probably retrieved whatever spoils they could. After the Pictish and Saxon army routed in the 'Alleluia victory' of 429 'threw away their weapons in headlong flight', 'the scattered spoils were collected' by the victorious Britons.[66] Stripping the dead of anything of value, including jewellery, weapons, armour and clothing would have been routine practice after a battle. Even broken weapons could be repaired or their raw materials recycled.

## THE CULT OF THE SEVERED HEAD

As well as being robbed, the dead may also have been mutilated and body parts, particularly heads, removed by the victors. Indeed, the verse about the death of Domnall Brecc has been interpreted as evidence that his severed head was taken by the victorious North Britons as a war trophy.[67] Among the pagan Celts, head-hunting belonged to a complex system of military practices, social values and religious beliefs centred around the cult of the head.[68] The head was perceived as the seat of the soul and was also the war trophy *par excellence*, incontrovertible evidence of an enemy's death and identity. Moreover, for peoples, pagan or Christian, whose funerary rituals ensured the translation of the soul of the dead to the afterlife this would have been the ultimate indignity inflicted on the defeated. The taking and display of heads is recorded by several Classical historians and confirmed by the presence of severed skulls or headless skeletons on several Iron Age sites. This practice is most strikingly attested in the pre-Roman Iron Age of southern Gaul. There, human skulls, at least some belonging to the victims of warfare, were displayed in niches in the porticos of temples in the hillforts of Entremont, Nages and Roquepertuse.[69] There is also evidence of this practice in later Iron Age Scotland in the form of a skull fragment, drilled with holes for suspending it, found in a broch at Hillhead (Caithness).[70] Human heads were the ultimate gift to the gods, made in expectation of receiving favours in return.

Although head-hunting and the cult of the head are widely associated with pagan Celtic religion, aspects survived among Christianised societies. Irish annals record the decapitation of enemies into the medieval period, while the taking and display of human heads feature prominently in early medieval Irish and Welsh epic literature. This practice continued into the modern era. The heads of executed traitors were displayed on London Bridge as late as 1746, when Lord Lovat met this fate for supporting the 1745 Jacobite Rebellion.

Was the taking and display of human heads also practised by the Picts and Scots? There is no evidence for this within *Dál Riata*, although Adomnán's[71] references to the decapitation of three Irish kings in two separate incidents attests an awareness of the practice. The only documentary evidence for it by the Picts is in later sources, although the frequency of this theme suggests that it has a historical basis. Before the battle of Dunnichen in 685, Bishop Wilfrid is said to have had a vision of Ecgfrith's decapitation.[72] Beheading was also the recorded fate of King Aethelstan after the Anglo-Saxons were defeated by the Picts under Unuist son of Uurguist (820–34) in a battle near the River Tyne. According to the St Andrews foundation legend,[73] Unuist then had Aethelstan's head fixed to a stake on an island in the Firth of Forth. After being captured in a battle in 834, Alpín, allegedly King of *Dál Riata*, was reportedly beheaded by the Picts when the Scots refused to pay a ransom, according to John of Fordun.[74] And Donnán, Abbot of Eigg, was beheaded by raiders in 617 along with his monks.[75] The perpetrators may also have been Picts.[76]

Archaeological evidence of decapitation among the Picts, in the form of cut-marks on several human vertebrae found in the Sculptor's Cave at Covesea (Nairnshire),[77] initially appears to be convincing proof of the taking of human heads. But, despite the presence of Pictish symbols carved on the cave walls,[78] it is unclear whether these human remains date to the early medieval period and there is no evidence that these beheadings were associated with warfare. Instead, decapitation may have been a feature of pagan Pictish mortuary rituals, paralleling practices in Roman Britain and Anglo-Saxon England.[79] Nevertheless, this confirms the existence of beliefs associated with the human head within the area of historic Pictland and, against this background, it seems plausible that a cult of the severed head was practised by the Picts.

Pictish sculpture provides better evidence for both the taking and display of human heads. Although now badly eroded and picturesquely misinterpreted as 'a pot with a tree or flower growing in it',[80] the reverse of the Eassie Priory (Angus) cross-slab actually depicts a branch or tree with nine severed human heads impaled on its branches (*see* Plate 25). Beside it stands a warrior with his sword drawn in the 'ready' position and holding a severed head in his outstretched left hand. This scene probably depicts the aftermath of a battle, with the severed heads of the vanquished displayed as war trophies, while the adjacent warrior has just severed another head to add to the tree. Although it is unclear if decapitation was the means of killing or the heads concerned were removed from those killed in battle, there may have been a sacrificial element to the taking of heads, which were then offered to the gods or ancestors. The branch or tree is set in a square base, indicating that it is not *in situ* but, as it requires support, is movable. This may be a portable war trophy, shrine or standard that was moved between the battlefield and royal hall. As a symbol of martial prowess and victory, its function was presumably to boost the morale of the Pictish army and encourage acts of heroism before warriors went into battle, as well as to insult, intimidate and demoralise their enemies. The dead have not only been mutilated but also have suffered the further indignity of having their decapitated heads displayed. Such grisly spectacles were not confined to early medieval warfare; Goya's *Great Deeds! Against the Dead!* (1810–12) portrays the same practice in the Peninsular War.

The scene on the Eassie Priory cross-slab is paralleled in early medieval Irish literature. In *Táin Bó Cuailnge*,[81] the Ulster hero Cúchulainn decapitates four opponents and mounts their heads on the points of a forked branch or tree, deliberately prepared and erected for that purpose. With macabre sarcasm, *Cath Maige Rátha* (*The Battle of Magh Ráth*)[82] possibly refers to the decapitated heads mounted on a *bile buada*, 'tree of triumph, victory, virtue': 'in which tree the inferior people and debilitated of the men of Ireland were seated, looking on at the battle'.

The Eassie Priory stone depicts a Pictish 'triumph tree', presumably referring to the aftermath of a specific battle, as the adjacent depiction of cloaked foot soldiers supports. Reflecting their symbolic significance, 'triumph trees' themselves may have been the focus of warfare, paralleling the attacks made on sacred trees in early medieval Ireland.[83] One battle is of particular interest in this context. In 728, competitors for the Pictish kingship fought a battle at *Monid Craebe/Monidhcrobh*,[84] the 'hill of the tree', Moncreiffe Hill. The tree concerned must have been at least a conspicuous landmark, but Irish parallels suggest that it was also sacred to a Pictish kingdom.[85] This tree may have been associated with the fort on Moncreiffe Hill[86] and/or a royal inauguration site, for which there are also Irish parallels.[87] The battle of *Monid Craebe/Monidhcrobh* was therefore fought at a place that would have had great symbolic significance in a war for the Pictish kingship. But whether the tree concerned was a 'triumph tree', used to display the severed heads of enemies, is unclear.

Other sculptural scenes also depict decapitated warriors. Sueno's Stone depicts two piles of severed heads, one lying beside a line of seven headless corpses (*see* Plate 7). The battle scene on the Dunkeld 2 cross-slab (the 'Apostles' Stone')[88] includes four prostrate figures, at least one of whom has been decapitated, his severed head lying at his feet. Six decapitated heads are also claimed to be portrayed lower down the stone[89] but these probably belonged to figures that are now scarcely visible as a result of erosion. The reverse of the same stone does depict a group of ten apparently decapitated heads, although this may be the sculptor's way of representing a crowd.[90] The bird-headed creatures on the Papil cross-slab stone hold a severed human head between their beaks.[91] Combining the physical characteristics of carrion birds and men, these creatures may represent gods of war or death and symbolise the aftermath of battle. These are a graphic confirmation of the enduring role of decapitation in Pictish and Scottish warfare.

## ATTITUDES TO WARFARE

Contemporary attitudes towards early medieval warfare are expressed most explicitly in references to the battle-dead. In the absence of a surviving Pictish or Scottish heroic tradition, there is no equivalent of *The Gododdin* to articulate heroic ideals and glorify the battle-dead. However, ecclesiastical sources convey the attitudes of the Church to, and its involvement in, warfare, providing some unique insights into the moral dimension of warfare.

Ecclesiastical sources vary considerably in the sentiments they express. Adomnán[92] refers to Aedán mac Gabráin's 'unhappy victory' (*infelix . . . victoria*) over the *Miathi* in 574X97, in which 303 men of Aedán's army, including two of his sons, were killed. The annals occasionally express opinions on the human costs of warfare. These range from an individual loss, such as the 'untimely death' of a Pict, Finnguine son of Deile Roith, in battle against the Northumbrians in the Plain of *Manau* in 711[93] to the 'great, lamentable and horrible battle . . . cruelly fought' between the Scots and Vikings at *Brunanburh* in 937.[94] Internal warfare caused particular anguish to the annalists, who refer to a 'woeful battle' fought among the Picts at *Caislén Credi/Castellum Credi* in 728.[95] But the wider point that the annalists were presumably making is that battles for the kingship could, and should, have been avoidable within a well-regulated system of royal succession, in which the Church played a central role.

In contrast, the Northumbrian monk Eddius Stephanus[96] makes no attempt to disguise his contempt for the Picts, likening them to swarms of ants and describing them as 'bestial peoples with savage minds', even though – or, more probably, because – the Picts were simply trying to liberate themselves from Northumbrian domination. Eddius[97] claims that King Ecgfrith of Northumbria was 'merciful to his enemies', yet relishes his account of the slaughter Ecgfrith inflicted on the Picts in the Plain of *Manau* in 672[98] as 'marvellous to relate'. Eddius'[99] partisan attitude is evident from his lamenting the battle of Dunnichen as 'a woeful disaster' in which Ecgfrith 'and the flower of his army had been mown down'. Bede, on the other hand, records disapprovingly that Ecgfrith laid waste the territories of the Picts with 'brutal and ferocious cruelty'.[100] At best, Eddius expresses the Church's ambivalent attitude: warfare was acceptable, even desirable, depending on which side won or lost. These views strongly reflect the close relationship that existed between the Church and the competing kingships of early medieval northern Britain.

Iona sources display a different ambivalence, frequently employing militaristic imagery in references to senior clerics and religious activities. For example, Adomnán[101] regularly refers to monks as 'soldiers of Christ' (sing. *Christi miles*, pl. *christianae militiae*) and Columba as 'an island soldier' (*insulanus miles*), while another abbot of Iona is commemorated as 'Faílbe, the warrior of Iona'.[102] However, before his arrival on Iona, Columba's involvement in warfare may have been more active than these metaphors suggest. The preface to the hymn *Altus Prosator*[103] records that Columba wrote it 'to beg forgiveness on the score of the battle of *Cúl Dreimne* which he had won against Diarmait mac Cerbaill; and of the other battles that had been fought because of him'. Irish sources attribute a more direct involvement to Columba, identifying 'the three battles that he had fought in Ireland'.[104] Columba's participation in these battles may be supported by a reference to his sailing from Ireland with twelve 'fellow-soldiers' (*commilitones*).[105]

The close relationship that existed between kingships and the Church[106] would have ensured ecclesiastical support for military ventures. This was certainly in the Church's interest. Much of the Church's wealth, in both land and valuables, came as gifts from the king and, in turn, originated in the proceeds of plunder or conquest. But the involvement of the Church in warfare was not simply restricted to the receipt of some of the proceeds. Senior clerics such as Columba were often members of royal or aristocratic kin groups and would therefore have had a close interest in the outcome of wars and battles involving their kinfolk. These close links ensured the active participation of the Church in the psychological preparation for war, not just at the muster but also on the battlefield. The early medieval Church was neither neutral nor pacifist.

Armies fought with divine blessing and victory was believed to be ordained by God. Ecgfrith's victory over the Picts in the Plain of *Manau* in 672 was attributed to divine intervention: 'for he conquered with few soldiers, not with arms; but by the virtue of God'.[107] These beliefs also feature prominently in the cults of several saints, notably Columba. In particular, divinely conferred powers to foresee or determine the course of battles were attributed to some saints. This was a particular attribute of Columba:[108] 'And in the terrible crashings of battles, by virtue of prayer he obtained from God that some kings were conquered, and other rulers were conquerors. This special favour was bestowed by God . . . on him, not only while he continued in this present life, but also after his departure from the flesh.' Adomnán[109] relates three incidents illustrating different aspects of these supernatural faculties. Columba led his monks in prayer before the Scots went into battle against the *Miathi*, while his vision of the battle of *Móin Daire Lothair* in Ulster 'gave a complete account . . . not only of the fighting of the battle, but also of those kings to whom the Lord granted victory over their enemies'. In a third episode, a vision of Columba appeared in the Northumbrian camp and gave encouragement to King Oswald on the night before his decisive battle with the British King Cadwallon near Hexham in 633. This suggests that the Angles of Northumbria also believed in these powers of Columba.

Such beliefs were held widely in the early medieval West[110] and are recorded among the other peoples of northern Britain. Other saints are also associated with similar powers. In the only account linking such an incident to the Picts, Unuist son of Uurguist (Óengus son of Fergus, 'Óengus II') (820–34) and his army were inspired by a vision of St Andrew to defeat the Anglo-Saxons in the Plain of *Merc*, according to the twelfth-century foundation myth of St Andrews.[111] St Cuthbert, whose cult was prominent in Northumbria, performs a similar role. In 'a miracle of God and St Cuthbert, much to be observed and magnified', 'Christ's soldier Cuthbert' appeared to King Guthred (883–*c*. 895) in a vision, encouraging him to attack a numerically superior Scottish army in the battle of Mundingdene and assuring him that the Scots 'are already in God's sight dead'.[112]

Anything associated with Columba was believed to confer miraculously protective powers in battle. An account of two battles, the latter fought in 918, provides an unusually detailed insight into this, and of the religious beliefs surrounding warfare, perhaps accentuated by the fact that the Scots were fighting pagans:[113]

> The men of *Fortriu* and the Vikings fought a battle. The men of *Alba* fought this battle steadfastly, moreover, because Columba was assisting them, for they had prayed fervently to him, since he was their apostle, and it was through him that they received faith. For on another occasion, when King Ívarr was a young lad and he came to plunder *Alba* with three large troops, the men of *Alba*, lay and

clergy alike, fasted and prayed to God and Columba until morning, and beseeched the Lord, and gave profuse alms of food and clothing to the churches and to the poor, and received the Body of the Lord from the hands of their priests, and promised to do every good thing as their clergy would best urge them, and that their battle-standard in the van of every battle would be the Crozier of Columba – and it is on that account that it is called the *Cathbuaid* ['Battle Triumph'] from then onwards; and the name is fitting, for they have often won victory in battle with it, as they did at that time, relying on Columba. They acted the same way on this occasion. Then this battle was fought hard and fiercely; the men of *Alba* won victory and triumph.

The *Cathbuaid* was not the only relic of Columba to be carried into battle and, unlike the Crozier, two of these relics survive. Similar powers were attributed to the *Cathach*, or 'Battler', a sixth- or early seventh-century psalter traditionally attributed to Columba.[114] The properties of the *Cathach* are described in a late *Life of Columba*,[115] completed in 1532, concerning Columba's participation in the battle of *Cúl Dreimne* in Ireland in 561: 'If it is borne three times sunwise around the army of *Cenél Conaill* when they go into battle, they will come back triumphant. And it is in the breast of a *comharba* [i.e. a successor of Columba as abbot, in this case probably of Derry], or a cleric without mortal sin on him . . . that it is proper for the *Cathach* to be when going around that army.'

These explicit accounts and the names of the relics concerned attest the perceived significance of carrying relics of Columba into battle. So powerful were these beliefs that they survived in Scotland into the Middle Ages. The *Breccbennach* of St Columba was carried by the Abbot of Arbroath at the battle of Bannockburn in 1314, where it was presumably used to bless the Scottish army.[116] This is usually identified as the Monymusk reliquary, a house-shaped shrine for holding relics.[117] In all these cases, kings were deploying saints' relics on the battlefield in an attempt to invoke the victory-conferring powers associated with the saints concerned and harness spiritual powers alongside their military strength. These beliefs explain the presence of Christian dedicatory inscriptions on the St Ninian's Isle chape and the Coppergate helmet.[118] The motive behind such inscriptions was presumably to commend the owner to the protection of God.[119]

Events on the battlefield were interpreted as manifestations of divine will and, just as victory in battle could be bestowed by God, so could defeat. Another common theme in early medieval literature is that of military disaster as a punishment for sins. In particular, the destruction of the Picts by Cináed mac Ailpín was attributed to divine punishment for the wickedness of their liturgy and (ecclesiastical) laws.[120] This was believed to be the case even when the transgression was not apparent. In c. 915, Causantín mac Áeda led a joint Scottish–Northumbrian army with the intention of recovering for the ousted King Ealdred his Northumbrian kingdom, only to be defeated by the Vikings at Corbridge 'through what sin I know not'.[121] The best documented example of a defeat being interpreted as divine punishment concerns the battle of Dunnichen in 685. Bede[122] attributes Ecgfrith's death and the slaughter of most of the Northumbrian army at Dunnichen to divine retribution for Ecgfrith's expedition against the Irish, 'an inoffensive people who had always been most friendly to the English', in 684, during which churches and monasteries were destroyed and prisoners seized. In response to the curses of the Irish for vengeance, Ecgfrith's punishment was that he rejected the advice of those who tried to persuade him not to embark on his fateful campaign against the Picts, thus resulting in defeat, disaster and death.

The Church had a central role in providing moral and spiritual support to kings and their armies. But the Church also attempted to moderate the effects of warfare. The prime example of this is the *Lex Innocentium*, 'Law of the Innocents', promulgated by Adomnán at the Synod of Birr, in Co. Offaly, Ireland, in 697, and later known as *Cáin Adamnáin*, 'Adomnán's Law'.[123] Although of questionable effectiveness, this was intended to protect women, children and clerics from violence in either peace or war. The *Lex Innocentium* was not only of interest in Ireland, as the surviving list of guarantors, both ecclesiastics and laymen, attests. Among the royal signatories to the *Lex Innocentium* are Bridei son of Derilei, King of the Picts ('Bruide mac Derilei *ri Cruithintuathi*'), and Eochaid mac Domangairt, King of *Dál Riata* ('Euchu ua Domnall *ri*'),[124] although there is no reason to believe that they attended the synod in person. *Dál Riata* and Pictland were clearly in step not only with ecclesiastical laws protecting non-combatants, but also the wider moral framework that prompted such initiatives in the first place.

But while the Church was active in moves to protect non-combatants, it benefited from warfare. Much of the Church's lands and wealth were donated by kings after being obtained through conquest and/or in battle. The Church therefore had a vested interest in the success of their side in battle and this underpins the enthusiasm for warfare of ecclesiastical commentators such as Eddius Stephanus, as long as their side was victorious. Warfare was predominantly a secular activity but the Church clearly played an active role, providing divine legitimation for the kings who raised and led armies and divine sanction for the victory of those armies in battle, thereby boosting the morale of the army.

Early medieval warfare is sometimes claimed to have been 'ritual' in character,[125] although it is unclear how 'ritual warfare' is defined or identified. However, there is no evidence that any wars of the Picts and Scots were 'ritual' in nature. Where the circumstances are recorded or may be inferred, battles were motivated by a desire to control resources, usually territory and/or power. While military objectives were undeniably secular, many aspects of early medieval warfare incorporated elements of ritual. For example, the cumulative effect of the codes of conduct and honour that surrounded the warband, the taking and display of severed heads and the involvement of clerics and the Church, probably give warfare a prominent and powerful ritual dimension. But even this ritual quality made warfare no less 'real' for the combatants and others affected by the scourge of war.

# *Notes*

An expanded version of these notes can be found in the Bibliography.


## INTRODUCTION

1. E.g. Macdougall (ed.) 1991; Simpson, G.G. (ed.) 1992; McCorry 1997; Caldwell 1998; Reese 1999; Royle (ed.) 1999.
2. Cessford 1996a: 32. The only general discussions are Alcock 1993a: 12–21; Laing and Laing 1993: 59–64; Foster 1996: 101–7.
3. Foster 1997: 12–13.
4. E.g. Hawkes, S. (ed.) 1989; Griffith 1995; Underwood 1999; Siddorn 2000.
5. E.g. Forsyth, K. 2000a: 23–6.
6. P. 8.


## CHAPTER ONE

1. Ammianus, XX, 1, 1; ed. Rolfe 1982, vol. 2: 3.
2. St Patrick, *Epistola*, 15; trans. Hood 1978: 58.
3. Gildas, *De excidio*, 14, 19.1; trans. Winterbottom 1978: 21, 23.
4. Eddius, VSW, 19; trans. after Colgrave 1927: 41.
5. Bede, HE, I.12.
6. Wainwright (ed.) 1955.
7. Henderson, I. 1967; Ritchie, G. and Ritchie, A. 1981: 159–82; Friell and Watson (eds) 1984; Smyth 1984: 36–83; Small (ed.) 1987; Ritchie, A. 1989; Laing and Laing 1993; Sutherland 1994; Cummins 1995; Nicoll (ed.) 1995; Foster 1996; 1997; Henry (ed.) 1997; Dunbavin 1998; Carver 1999.
8. Bede, HE, I.1.
9. Jackson, K.H. 1955; Forsyth, K. 1995a; 1997a; Cummins 2001.
10. On whom see Rivet (ed.) 1966; Ritchie, G. and Ritchie, A. 1981: 89–120; Hingley 1992; 1998; MacKie 1995; Armit 1997.
11. Pan. Lat. Vet., VIII, 11, 4; trans. Mynors 1994: 126.
12. Ammianus, XXVI, 4, 5; trans. Rolfe 1982, vol. 2: 587, 589.
13. Ammianus, XXVII, 8, 5; trans. after Rolfe 1982, vol. 3: 53.
14. Bede, HE, I.1.
15. Jackson, K.H. 1959.

16.  Adomnán, VSC, II.46.
17.  Bede, HE, III.4, V.9.
18.  Adomnán, VSC, II.42.
19.  Henderson, I. 1971: 39; 1975: 96; Ritchie, A. 1985.
20.  Broun 2000.
21.  AT s.a. 739.6; AU s.a. 738.7.
22.  Broun 1998a; 2000: 32–5, 37–40.
23.  Bannerman 1974: 73–5, 118–32.
24.  Thomas, C. 1972.
25.  Nieke and Duncan 1988.
26.  Campbell, E. 1999: 11–15; 2001.
27.  Bannerman 1974: 118–32.
28.  Bannerman 1974: 108–15; Dumville 2000b.
29.  Pp. 104–7.
30.  Ed. and trans. Bannerman 1974: 46, 49.
31.  Sharpe 2000.
32.  Broun 1998b.
33.  Hudson 1991.
34.  Anderson, M.O. 1982; Broun 1994a; 1994b; 1997; 1998c; Cowan and McDonald (eds) 2000; Herbert 2000; Clancy and Crawford 2001; Woolf, A. 2001; Driscoll 2002.
35.  Bannerman 1974.
36.  Smyth 1984: 84–140; Herbert 1988; 1999; Bourke (ed.) 1997; Lacey 1997; Broun and Clancy (eds) 1999.
37.  Bannerman 1974; Nieke and Duncan 1988; Laing and Laing 1993; Foster 1996; Campbell, E. 1999; Sharpe 2000.
38.  Henderson, I. 1994a: 44–8; Broun 1995.
39.  Hughes 1980.
40.  Anderson, M.O. 1973: 77–102.
41.  Forsyth, K. 2000a.
42.  Cameron, A. 1970.
43.  Miller 1974; Clarkson 1994.
44.  Hughes 1972: 117–19; Smyth 1972: 33–41; Bannerman 1974: 9–26; Herbert 1988: 21–3.
45.  AClon s.a. 563; AFM s.a. 554; AT s.a. 560.2; AU s.a. 557.2, 559.2 (repeated entry); CS s.a. 560.3.
46.  Hughes 1972: 109–10; Dumville 1985: 84.
47.  Bannerman 1974; Ó Corráin 1980.
48.  Pp. 15–18, 112–13.
49.  Cowan 1981; Hudson 1998; Dumville 2000a.
50.  Hawkes and Mills (eds) 1999.
51.  Eds Lapidge and Dumville 1984.

52.   Pp. 122, 138.

53.   Whittington and Soulsby 1968; Whittington 1974; Nicolaisen 1976: 149–72; 1995; 1996; Fraser, I.A. 1987.

54.   Pp. 23, 89, 92–3.

55.   Forsyth, K. 2000a: 29–30; Koch 2000.

56.   Close-Brooks 1987a; 1987b.

57.   Ralston 1980; 1987a.

58.   Triscott 1980; 1981.

59.   Alcock 1981a: 159–61, 168–73; 1981b; Alcock and Alcock 1988; 1993: 242–76; Alcock et al. 1990.

60.   Lane and Campbell 2000.

61.   Dickson and Brough 1989; Alcock et al. 1990: 202, 217–18.

62.   Pp. 100–5, 108–10.

63.   Alcock 1981a: 168–71; Alcock et al. 1990: 201–2; p. 101.

64.   Among extensive literature, for guides see RCAHMS 1994a; 1999; Mack 1997; 1998a. For analysis and interpretation see Thomas, A.C. 1964; Jackson, A. 1984; Laing and Laing 1985a; Driscoll 1986; Samson 1992; Forsyth 1997b; Mack 1998b; Cummins 1999.

## CHAPTER TWO

1.   Pp. 26–30.

2.   Gerriets 1983; Kelly 1988: 26–33; Charles-Edwards 1993: 337–63; Ó Cróinín 1995: 141–3.

3.   Anderson, M.O. 1973: 135–6, 158–63; Bannerman 1974: 27–156; Alcock 1987a: 216–19; Sharpe 2000: 51, 53–61.

4.   Bannerman 1974: 28–39; Sharpe 2000: 53–5.

5.   Pp. 112–13.

6.   Pp. 37–8.

7.   Jackson, K.H. 1959.

8.   Bannerman 1974: 132–41.

9.   Trans. Anderson, A.O. 1922, vol. 1: 83.

10.   Trans. after Bannerman 1974: 48.

11.   Trans. Bannerman 1974: 48–9; p. 30.

12.   On which see Nieke 1983.

13.   Bannerman 1974: 147; Anderson, M.O. 1973: 158–60; Sharpe 2000: 56–9.

14.   Pp. 112–13.

15.   Trans. Mac Neill 1923: 275, 300–1.

16.   TYP, 29; ed. and trans. Bromwich 1978; 57, 264.

17.   P. 127.

18.   Alcock 1987a: 216–19.

19.   Evans 1997a: 31.

20. Bede, HE, IV.22.
21. Alcock 1993a: 45.
22. Chaps 3, 6 and 7.
23. On which see Hollister 1962: 40–1, 47; Powicke 1962: 1–25; Brooks 1971; Hart 1971; Abels 1988: 100–15.
24. Watson, W.J. 1926: 407–14; Whittington and Soulsby 1968; Whittington 1974; Nicolaisen 1976: 151–8; 1995: 11–13; 1996: 6–17.
25. Sharpe 2000: 49.
26. Forsyth, K. (ed.) forthcoming.
27. Jackson, K. 1972; Broun forthcoming.
28. Trans. Jackson, K. 1972: 33.
29. Pp. 40–1.
30. Trans. Jackson, K. 1972: 34, 35, 88–90.
31. Duncan, A.A.M. 1975: 389.
32. Thomas, F.W.L. 1886: 200–9; Skene 1890, vol. 3: 223; Watson, W.J. 1926: 235–6; MacKerral 1944: 50–2; Jackson, K. 1972: 116–17; Barrow 1973: 267–74, 276–7, 367–8; Bannerman 1974: 141; Duncan, A.A.M. 1975: 317–21.
33. Bede, HE, IV.22; see also Alcock 1993a: 45.
34. Pennant 1998 [1774]: 316.
35. Forsyth, W.M.A. 1900: 339.
36. Barrow 1973: 273; 1981a: 15; Duncan, A.A.M. 1975: 318.
37. Barrow 1973: 59–60.
38. Easson 1986; Broun 1995: 5.
39. Evans 1997a: 30–1.
40. 37; trans. Mac Neill 1923: 303.
41. Chaps 3, 5 and 7.
42. Duncan, A.A.M. 1975: 378–82.
43. Broun 2000.
44. Alcock 1997: 7.
45. Thomas, A.C. 1964: 66; Mack 1997: 1.
46. Alcock 1997.
47. Eddius Stephanus, VSW, 19; trans. Webb 1983: 126.
48. Watson, W.J. 1926: 103, 128; Nicolaisen 1976: 42, 44.
49. Pp. 112–13.
50. *The Gododdin*, B$^1$.11 = A.78; trans. Koch 1997: 27.
51. P. 31.
52. P. 21.
53. P. 99.
54. Pp. 99, 105.
55. Barrow 1981b.
56. Driscoll 1998: 152–4; Aitchison 2000: 77–106.

57.  AT s.a. 729.4.

58.  AT s.a. 719.4; AU s.a. 718.6.

59.  AT s.a. 719.5; AU s.a. 718.7.

60.  AU s.a. 641.1.

## CHAPTER THREE

1.  Enright 1996; Evans 1997a.

2.  Zosimus, IV, 35, 5.

3.  *The Gododdin*, B$^2$.24 = B$^1$.3 = A.48; trans. Koch 1997: 3.

4.  *The Gododdin*, B$^1$.13; trans. Koch 1997: 41.

5.  *The Gododdin*, B$^2$.29 = A.68, B$^2$.32 = A.70, B$^1$.4, A.2, A.24, A.44; trans. Koch 1997: 11, 13, 31, 55, 81, 97.

6.  *The Gododdin*, B$^2$.32 = A.70, A.5, A.18, A.24; trans. Koch 1997: 13, 57, 73, 81 and pp. 180, 194.

7.  *The Gododdin*, B$^2$.26, A.10; trans. Koch 1997: 7, 61.

8.  Woolf, R. 1976; Frank 1991.

9.  Chadwick, H.M. 1912; Chadwick and Chadwick 1932; Evans 1997b.

10. As Jackson, K.H. (1969: 18) suggests.

11. TYP, 29; ed. and trans. Bromwich 1978; 57, 264; see also Bannerman 1974: 83, n. 4.

12. Adomnán, VSC, II.23; eds and trans Anderson and Anderson 1991: 126–7.

13. *The Gododdin*, B$^2$.27, B$^1$.13, A.9, A.22; trans. Koch 1997: 9, 41, 61, 77.

14. Jackson, K.H. 1969: 78–9, 99, 103, 108, 130; Koch 1997: 167, 184; see also Clarkson 1992; Cruickshank 1993; Cessford 1994a.

15. *The Gododdin*, A.9; trans. Koch 1997: 61.

16. AClon s.a. 627; AT s.a. 629.1; CS s.a. 629.1; see also Anderson, A.O. 1922, vol. 1: 152–4; Anderson, M.O. 1973: 150–1; Bannerman 1974: 98–9, 106.

17. Bede, HE, III.1; see also ASC s.a. 617.

18. Byrne 1973: 72–4, 114–18, 124–8.

19. P. 16.

20. AU s.a. 726.3.

21. Anderson, A.O. 1922, vol. 1: 223, n. 1.

22. Jackson 1963: 319; Anderson, M.O. 1973: 182, n. 239.

23. Hudson 1994a: 20.

24. AFM s.a. 835. Hudson (1994a: 41–2) claims that this entry is a late fabrication, but provides no supporting evidence.

25. Pp. 130–42.

26. AFM s.a. 728; see also AClon s.a. 730; AT s.a. 733.4; on the locations see Anderson, A.O. 1922, vol. 1: 229, n. 3.

27. Bannerman 1974: 100; on the battle see AFM s.a. 617; AI s.a. 615; AT s.a. 622.1; AU s.a. 621.1; CS s.a. 622.1; Anderson, A.O. 1922, vol. 1: 145–6.

28. Anderson, A.O. 1922, vol. 1: 226, n. 1; Watson, W.J. 1926: 50, 401; Anderson, M.O. 1973: 178; Hudson 1994a: 27.
29. AU s.a. 728.2.
30. AU s.a. 838.9, 903.4.
31. Ed. Anderson, M.O. 1973: 259.
32. *The Prophecy of Berchán*, 120; ed. and trans. Hudson 1996: 41, 83.
33. *Senchus fer nAlban*, trans. Bannerman 1974: 48–9.
34. Adomnán, VSC, I.8; eds and trans Anderson and Anderson 1991: 32, 33.
35. ASC s.a. 603.
36. *The Gododdin*, B$^1$.11 = A.78; trans. Koch 1997: 27.
37. AU s.a. 735.2.
38. P. 18.
39. P. 17.
40. Adomnán, VSC, I.8; trans Anderson and Anderson 1991: 33.
41. Anderson, A.O. 1922, vol. 1: 96–7, n. 5; Watson, W.J. 1926: 58–9; Wainwright 1955: 23–4, 40, 51.
42. AClon s.a. 603; ASC s.a. 603; AT s.a. 600.2; AU s.a. 599.1, Bede, HE, I.34.
43. But see Blair 1954: 157–8, n. 2.
44. Pp. 37–8.
45. *The Gododdin*, B$^2$.38, B$^1$.8, B$^1$.9, B$^1$.20 = A.60, A.8, A.10, A.18, A.21, A.59; trans. Koch 1997: 23, 35, 37, 49, 59, 61, 73, 77, 109; see also Jackson, K.H. 1969: 4, 13–18, 25–6; Evans 1997a: 30, n. 11.
46. See also Evans 1997a: 31, n. 15.
47. CS s.a. 904.6.
48. *The Gododdin*, B$^2$.26, A.10; trans. Koch 1997: 7, 61.
49. Eddius Stephanus, VSW, 19; trans. Colgrave 1927: 41.
50. Bede, HE, I.34.
51. Symeon of Durham, HSC; ed. Arnold 1882, vol. 1: 213–14; trans. Anderson, A.O. 1908: 63.
52. Adomnán, VSC, I.33; eds and trans Anderson and Anderson 1991: 62–3.
53. Adomnán, VSC, II.23; eds and trans Anderson and Anderson 1991: 32–3, 126–7.
54. Fridegoda, *Life of Saint Wilfrid*; ed. Raine 1879: 127; trans. Anderson, A.O. 1908: 36–7, n. 4.
55. Anderson, A.O. 1922, vol. 1: 60, n. 5.
56. P. 41.
57. Hudson 1994b; pp. 159–62.
58. Regnal lists A and B; trans. Anderson, A.O. 1922, vol. 1: cxix; ed. Anderson, M.O. 1973: 90, 246, 262.
59. *Duan Albanach*; trans. Jackson, K.H. 1957: 131.
60. Kelly 1988: 19.
61. *Críth Gablach*, trans. Mac Neill 1923: 304.

62. *Vita Sancti Lasriani*, 12; ed. Heist 1965: 343; see also Anderson, M.O. 1973: 149; Bannerman 1974: 87.
63. ASC s.a. 710; AT s.a. 711.3; AU s.a. 710.3.
64. AClon s.a. 710; AT s.a. 713.5, 713.8; AU s.a. 712.4, 712.7.
65. AT s.a. 750.3; AU s.a. 749.4; *Brut y Tywysogyon* s.a. 750; *Brut y Saesson* s.a. 750 (both trans. Anderson, A.O. 1922, vol. 1: 239, n. 4); ACamb s.a. 750; AClon s.a. 746.
66. Skene 1886, vol. 1: 295; Anderson, A.O. 1922, vol. 1: 239, n. 4.
67. AU s.a. 749.11.
68. AU s.a. 760.4.
69. *Cogadh Gaedhel re Gallaibh*, trans. after Anderson, A.O. 1922, vol. 1: 351–2, n. 7.
70. AT s.a. 560.2; see also AFM s.a. 554; AU s.a. 559.2; CS s.a. 560.
71. AU s.a. 653.5; see also AT s.a. 654.4; CS s.a. 651.
72. Pp. 143–5.
73. Adomnán, VSC, I.8; eds and trans Anderson and Anderson 1991: 32, 33.
74. AU s.a. 735.2; p. 90.
75. AU s.a. 728.2.
76. Anderson, A.O. 1922, vol. 1: 163–4, n. 3; but see Jackson 1959: 37; Bannerman 1974: 102, n. 6.
77. AT s.a. 638.1; CS s.a. 637.1.
78. P. 149.
79. Wainwright 1948; Marsden 1994a; Alcock 1996a; Cruickshank 1999; Fraser, J.E. 2002.
80. Henderson, I. 1967: 47–50; Anderson, M.O. 1973: 145–9; forthcoming; Bannerman 1974: 80–90.
81. AT s.a. 576.1; AU s.a. 575.1, 575.3.
82. AU s.a. 579.2, 580.3, 581.1, 582.3. On the location see Anderson, A.O. 1922, vol. 1: 89–90, n. 3.
83. On which see Anderson, A.O. 1922, vol. 1: 96, n. 2, 118–19, nn. 4, 5; Henderson, I. 1967: 49; Anderson, M.O. 1973: 36–7; Bannerman 1974: 84–5; Broun 2000: 40–1.
84. AU s.a. 589.2.
85. Adomnán, VSC, I.8–9; trans Anderson and Anderson 1991: 31, 33.
86. AU s.a. 595.3; AT s.a. 596.2 attributes the loss of all four sons to this battle.
87. Adomnán, VSC, I.9; eds and trans Anderson and Anderson 1991: 33.
88. P. 35.
89. Henderson, I. 1967: 60–6, 86–8; Anderson, M.O. 1973: 177–8, 182–7; forthcoming; Smyth 1984: 73–5.
90. AU s.a. 728.2.
91. Bede, HE, V.23.
92. AU s.a. 730.6, 733.6, 733.7, 735.1, 740.6, 740.10.

93. CB s.a. 740.
94. Symeon, *Historia Regum Anglorum* s.a. 744, trans. Anderson, A.O. 1908: 56.
95. ACamb s.a. 750; AClon s.a. 746; AT s.a. 750.3; AU s.a. 749.4; see also Anderson, A.O. 1922, vol. 1: 239, n. 4.
96. Pp. 35–6.
97. Adomnán, VSC, I.8–9; AClon s.a. 590; AT s.a. 596.2; AU s.a. 595.3.
98. AT s.a. 629.1; AU s.a. 628.3.
99. AU s.a. 735.1.
100. Pp. 38, 105.
101. AClon s.a. 728; AFM s.a. 725; AT s.a. 731.4; AU s.a. 730.6; see also Anderson, A.O. 1922, vol. 1: 228, n. 1; Anderson, M.O. 1973: 183, n. 244.
102. *The Gododdin*, B$^1$.13; trans. Koch 1997: 41.
103. *Chronicle of Huntingdon*, trans. Anderson, A.O. 1922, vol. 1: 270.
104. On which see Hudson 1991.
105. Pp. 75–6.
106. Aitchison 1999: 17–19.
107. Jackson, K. 1972: 108; Duncan, A.A.M. 1975: 110; Clancy and Crawford 2001: 41.
108. Hamp 1986.
109. AFM s.a. 916; AU s.a. 917.4; FAI, 429 (for ?918).
110. AT s.a. 976.7.
111. AU s.a. 1014.2.
112. Jackson, K. 1972: 102–10.
113. Jackson, K. 1972: 110–14; Barrow 1973: 66–7.
114. AFM s.a. 565; see also AU s.a. 567; ABL s.a. 583; AI s.a. 568; pp. 120, 136.
115. Ed. Skene 1867: 139.
116. AT s.a. 719.5; AU s.a. 718.7.
117. AU s.a. 735.1.
118. AU s.a. 728.2.
119. Adomnán, VSC, I.33; eds and trans Anderson and Anderson 1991: 62–3; on which see Dumville 1978.
120. Adomnán VSC, I.35; trans Anderson and Anderson 1991: 65.
121. Duncan, A.A.M. 1975: 110–11.
122. Pp. 130–42.
123. Pp. 104–5.

## CHAPTER FOUR

1. Green, C. 1963; Bruce-Mitford 1978; Carver 1998.
2. Härke 1989; 1992a; 1992b; Dickinson and Härke 1992: 63–70; Geake 1997: 67–76; Lucy 2000: 1, 3–4, 74, 87–8, 149, 166–7.
3. Henderson, J. 1989; Härke 1990; Lucy 1997; Shepherd 1999; Stoodley 1999.

4. Davidson 1962; Wilson, D.M. 1966; Swanton 1973; 1974; Bone 1989; Dickinson and Härke 1992; Underwood 1999; Stephenson 2002.

5. Temple 1976: figs 155, 159–60, 163, 192, 195, 200–3, 263, 270, 275, 307–8, 310; Swanton 1980; Carver 1986.

6. Cassius Dio, *History*, 76.12.4.

7. Claudian, second poem on *Stilicho's Consulship* (XXII), 254–5; ed. and trans. Miller 1974: 143, n. 12.

8. Gildas, *De excidio*, 19.2; trans. Winterbottom 1978: 23; see also Bede, HE, I.12.

9. Gildas, *De excidio*, 17.2; trans. Winterbottom 1978: 22.

10. Christian 1905; Craw 1930; Lane and Campbell.

11. Alcock and Alcock 1988: 121–4.

12. Young 1891: 445.

13. Young 1893: 91; Abercromby 1907: 203.

14. Ritchie, J.N.G. 1969: 37, 39.

15. Anderson, J. 1881: 122; Laing and Laing 1985b: 281.

16. Laing and Laing 1985b.

17. Ritchie, J.N.G. 1969; Gilbert, J.M. 1978; Macaulay 1996; Ritchie, A. 1989: 24–5; Cruickshank 1994a; 1999: 27–9; 2000.

18. Laing 2000a: 86–99; 2001: 241, 243.

19. Pp. 86–8.

20. Southwick 1981; Jackson, A. 1984: 165–73; 1993; Sellar 1993; Cummins 1995: 138–44.

21. Alcock 1998: 533–4; Laing 2000a: 83–4.

22. Petersen 1919.

23. Grieg 1940: 158–9.

24. But see Laing 2000a: 89.

25. Laing 2000a: 89, 92, fig. 7.

26. Christison 1905: 318; Lane and Campbell 2000: 162.

27. Lane and Campbell 2000: 162.

28. Craw 1930: 116, 118, figs 5, 36; Breeze et al. 1976: 84; Lane and Campbell 2000: 162.

29. Grieg 1940: 13 and fig. 2.

30. Owen and Welander 1995: 759–61, 767–8.

31. Henderson, I. 1998a: 159, n. 25.

32. Lane and Campbell 2000: 149–71, 201–12, 218–20.

33. Adomnán, VSC, II.29; trans. Scott, B.G. 1991: 183.

34. Allen and Anderson 1993, vol. 1: 67, 70; Mack 1997: 20, 27; Cessford 1998; Cummins 1999: 128–30.

35. Thomas, A.C. 1964: 52–3, no. 17, 86; Laing and Laing 1985a: 269; 1993: 109–10; Cruickshank 1990: 4; Sutherland 1994: 111; 1997: 16; Foster 1996: 72, fig. 46.e; Mack 1997: 20; Carver 1999: 20.

36. Cessford 1998.
37. Allen and Anderson 1993, vol. 2: 477–9, fig. 508; RCAHMS 1994a: 6; 1999: 23, no. 72; pp. 107–8.
38. Feachem 1950: 207; Thomas, A.C. 1961: 68–9; 1964: 53, no. 18; Cessford 1994b: 84–5; Cummins 1995: 78; 1999: 80; Mack 1997: 28, 137; Sutherland 1997: 16; Laing 2000b.
39. Radford 1953: 237; Laing and Laing 1985a: 266–7.
40. Ritchie, J. 1916: 279–85; Thomas, A.C. 1964: 94; Close-Brooks 1981a: 331; Laing and Laing 1985a: 267; Mack 1997: 86.
41. Allen and Anderson 1993, vol. 2: 71–2, 210–11, figs 69, 227B; Burt 1994: 21; Henderson, I. 1998a: 158–9.
42. Thier and Mont 1996.
43. Laing 2000a: 84–9.
44. Allen and Anderson 1993, vol. 2: 80, 210–11, 224, 227, figs 72A, 81, 227B, 235B, 240B; Laing 200a: 84–5, figs 1 and 2h.
45. Davidson 1962: 62–4; Wilson, D.M. 1966: pls II–VIII; Shadrake and Shadrake 1997: 76–81.
46. Laing 2000a: 87–93; 2001: 241, 243.
47. O'Dell et al. 1959; Wilson, D.M. 1970; Small et al. 1973; Close-Brooks 1981b; Youngs (ed.) 1989: 108–12.
48. Wilson, D.M. 1973: 58–60, no. 11, 118–21; Laing 1993a: 104, no. 232.
49. Bone 1989: 66–7, figs 5.4–5; Henderson, I. 1998a: 158–9.
50. Callander 1933: 33–4; Laing 1993a: 105, no. 238; Laing and Laing 1985b: 282; 1993: 61.
51. Laing 1975: 48–9; Webster and Backhouse 1991: 223, no. 177.
52. Buist 1839; Chalmers, P. 1848: 15; Way 1849; Anderson, J. 1881: 34–42, 51, 68, 185; 1884: 238–47; RCAHMS 1933: 185–6, no. 378; Stevenson 1976: 248–50; Graham-Campbell 1992; 1993; Allen and Anderson 1993, vol. 1: lxxxiii–lxxxv, vol. 2: 368–9; Laing 1993a: 36, 76–9, 98–100, nos 120–2, 211–18; 1994; Laing and Laing 1993: 112–16.
53. Buist 1839: 3; see also Leighton 1840: 134; Stuart 1867: 78; Laing 1994: 11–12.
54. Buist 1839: 3.
55. Way 1849: 243.
56. Buist 1839: pl. 1, no. 9.
57. Rynne 1983.
58. Smith, A.N. 1998.
59. Henderson, I., 1998a: 159.
60. Driscoll 1988a: 178–87; 1988b.
61. Allen and Anderson 1993, vol. 2: 224, 298–9, figs 235B, 312B.
62. Wilson, D.M. 1973: 64–7, nos 15–16, 121–2; Youngs (ed.) 1989: 110, nos 102–3; Webster and Backhouse 1991: 223–4, nos 178a and b; Laing 1993a: 103–5, nos 236–7.

63. Youngs (ed.) 1989: 110; Brown, J. 1993.

64. Okasha 1996: 29.

65. Jackson, K.H. 1960; 1973.

66. Davidson 1962: 77–82, 96–103; Okasha 1992a; Underwood 1999: 54, 56.

67. Okasha 1992b.

68. Wilson, D.M. 1973: 60–4, nos 12–14; Youngs (ed.) 1989: 109–10, nos 99–101; Laing 1993a: 104, 233–5.

69. O'Dell et al. 1959: 260–1; Wilson, D.M. 1973: 122–3; Close-Brooks 1981b; Laing 1993a: 104; Haywood 2001: 93.

70. Laing 1975: 66; Close-Brooks 1981b.

71. McRoberts 1963: 306–13; 1965: 236–45; Richardson 1993: 33.

72. Adomnán, VSC, II.39; trans Anderson and Anderson 1991: 157.

73. Adomnán, VSC, II.24, 25.

74. Adomnán, VSC, I.47; trans Anderson and Anderson 1991: 85.

75. Adomnán, VSC, II.24; trans Anderson and Anderson 1991: 129.

76. Adomnán, VSC, II.24, 25; trans Anderson and Anderson 1991: 129, 131.

77. Pp. 79–80.

78. Curle, C.L. 1982: 91–2, 97–8; Ritchie, A. 1989: 52–4; Burt 1991: 6; RCAHMS 1994a: 19; 1999: 36, no. 166; Mack 1997: 132.

79. Curle, C.L. 1982; Ritchie, A. 1983; 1989: 52–5; Morris, C.D. 1995.

80. P. 75.

81. Christison 1905: 318–19, figs 55–8; Craw 1930: 117–18, fig. 5, no. 37; Duncan, H.B. 1982: figs 10–11.

82. Alcock and Alcock 1988: 141, fiche 2: D12, no. 18, fig. 16, no. 18.

83. Young 1891: 445.

84. Young 1893: 91; Abercromby 1907: 203.

85. Curle, C.L. 1982: 44, illus. 27.

86. Alcock 1984: 24.

87. Campbell, E. 1998.

88. Ross, J.J. 1854: 297; Close-Brooks 1981a: 334; Allen and Anderson 1993, vol. 2: 42, fig. 39.

89. Swanton 1973: 8–9; Harrison 1993a: 51; see also Swanton 1974; Underwood 1999: 43.

90. Duncan, H.B. 1982, 7–8; Lane and Campbell 2000: 162.

91. Alcock and Alcock 1988: 141.

92. Cassius Dio, *History*, 76.12.3; trans. Carey 1970, vol. 9: 265.

93. On which see Frere 1978: 199–203; Reed 1978; Salway 1981: 227–30.

94. MacGregor, M. 1976, vol. 2, nos 177–9, 182–4; Raftery n.d. [1981]; 1983: 119–24, figs 120–2; 1984: 112–15; 1998; Laing and Laing 1987: 214.

95. MacGregor, M. 1976, vol. 1: 85–6.

96. Heald 2001; Lynn 2001: 6.

97. Thomas, A.C. 1964: 51, no. 15, 52, fig. 4; Kermack 1997: 10; Mack 1997: 6; Sutherland 1997: 12; see also Peterson 1996: 90, 118, 127.

98. Diack 1944; Jackson, A. 1984: 128–9; Gilbert, I. 1995: 107–8, 150; Cummins 1999: 8–9, 25; Joss 2000.

99. Allen and Anderson 1993, vol. 1: xxxiii–xxxiv.

100. RCAHMS 1933: 57, no. 117; 1994a: 7; 1999: 18, no. 39.3, 25, no. 81; Shepherd and Shepherd 1980: 217–19; Mack 1997: 42–3, 88.

101. Mack 1997: 10; although not noted by Alcock 1996b.

102. Barclay and Halliday 1983; Atkinson and Henry 1998: 3.

103. Mack 1997: 10, 42.

104. Leighton 1840: 135.

105. Buist 1839: pl. 1, no. 8.

106. Graham-Campbell 1992: 249; 1993: 115; Laing 1994: 31–2.

107. Laing 1994: 20–1, no. 21.

108. Laing 1994: 20, nos 22–3.

109. Way 1849: 256, no. 11; Ritchie, A. 1989: 54; Laing and Laing 1990: 134; 1993: 113; Laing 1994: 34; Graham-Campbell 1992: 250; Cessford 1996b: 31; Foster 1996: 103.

110. P. 58.

111. Pp. 84–8.

112. Ritchie, J.N.G. 1969: 39; Laing and Laing 1985b: 281; 1993: 62; Carver 1999: 55.

113. Ritchie, J.N.G. 1969: 35; Phillips, E.J. 1975: 178; Keppie 1998: 62–4, 77, pl. 3, no. 5; Ritchie, W.F. and Ritchie, J.N.G. 1985: 40–1.

114. Raftery 1983: 107, no. 279.

115. Ritchie, J. 1916: 279–85; Ritchie, J.N.G. 1969: 33, 37; Thomas, A.C. 1964: 94; Mack 1997: 86.

116. P. 75.

117. Pp. 61–2.

118. Allen and Anderson 1993, vol. 2: 289–90, fig. 306B.

119. Sutherland 1994: 197.

120. P. 60.

121. Allen and Anderson 1993, vol. 2: 71–2, 80, 214–15, 219, figs 69, 72A, 228B, 231A; Burt 1994: 21.

122. E.g. Nicolle 1984: pl. D3, 36.

123. Henderson, I. 1998a: 160; 1998b: 26.

124. Stevenson 1956a: 93–6; RCAHMS 1975: 110–11; Allen and Anderson 1993, vol. 2: 377–9, fig. 393; Laing 1995; Fisher 2001: 120.

125. Nicolle 1984: 36; Stead 1993: 26; Henderson, I. 1998a: 160; Carver 1999: 55.

126. Stead 1993: 10–20, 23–6; 1998: 14–23, 114–23; Parfitt 1995: 64–72.

127. Laing 1995: 4.

128. Ritchie, J.N.G. 1969: 37–8; Allen and Anderson 1993, vol. 2: 219, 227, figs 231A, 240A; Atkinson 1993: 10; Burt 1993; Ritchie, A. 1994: 8–10.

129. Allen and Anderson 1993, vol. 2: 81, figs 72A, 81; Burt 1994: 22–3.

130. Ritchie, J.N.G. 1969: 39.

131. Dickinson and Härke 1992: 43–50; Watson, J. 1994; Underwood 1999: 78–81; Stephenson 2002.

132. Allen and Anderson 1993, vol. 2: 224, 260, figs 235B, 269B.

133. Dickinson and Härke 1992: 43–4.

134. Allen and Anderson 1993, vol. 2: 249, 263, figs 260B, 273B.

135. Allen and Anderson 1993, vol. 2: 306, fig. 321.

136. Mack 1997: 2.

137. Dickinson and Härke 1992: 4–24, 31–5; Underwood 1999: 81–5; Stephenson 2002.

138. Allen and Anderson 1993, vol. 2: 138, 248–9, 321, 323, figs 139A, 260B, 334D.

139. P. 87.

140. Contrary to Carver 1999: front cover illustration.

141. Allen and Anderson 1993, vol. 2: 305–6, 315, figs 321, 329.

142. Laing and Laing 1985b: 281.

143. P. 79.

144. Bruce-Mitford 1978: 55–66; Dickinson and Härke 1992: 27–30; Underwood 1999: 86, 88; Stephenson 2002: 50–2.

145. Anderson, J. 1881: 34–42, 51, 68, 185; 1884: 238–47; Stevenson 1976: 249; Graham-Campbell 1992: 253–6; 1993; Allen and Anderson 1993, vol. 1: lxxxiii–lxxxvi, vol. 2: 280–1, 368–9; Laing 1993a: 98–9, nos 210–12, 103, 105, no. 239; 1994: 13, nos 2–3, 30–2.

146. MacGregor, M. 1976, vol. 2, no. 349; Graham-Campbell 1992: 252; Laing 1994: 13, no. 1, 23–4.

147. *The Gododdin*, B².34, A.11, A.36, A.88; trans. Koch 1997: 17, 63, 93, 129.

148. Trans. Clancy 1998: 180.

149. Sheridan 1992; 1996.

150. Manley 1985.

151. Underwood 1999: 23, 26–35, 146.

152. Allen and Anderson 1993, vol. 2: 71–2, 115–16, 235–6, 331, figs 69, 120, 250B, 344; Burt 1994: 21; RCAHMS 1994a: 15; 1999: 22–3, no. 63.1, 28, no. 114, 33, no. 141; Mack 1997: 69, 108, 119; Ritchie, J.N.G. 1997: 120–1.

153. Curle, A.O. 1935: 310, figs 48.6, 49.6; Laing 1997: 131, no. 11; Ritchie, A. 1997a: 42–3, fig. 3.

154. Gilbert, J.M. 1978; Macaulay 1996.

155. Wise 1979: 38.

156. Anderson, J. 1881: 123.

157. Thomas, A.C. 1964: 52, no. 16; Peterson 1996: 78, 105, 127; Kermack 1997: 10; Mack 1997: 2.

158. Allen and Anderson 1993, vol. 2: 96–7, figs 99, 99A.

159. Allen and Anderson 1993, vol. 1: 63; Sutherland 1994: 118; Cruickshank 1995: 25–7; Brodie 1996: 22; Peterson 1996: 108.

160. Thomas, A.C. 1964: 62, no. 46.

161. Pp. 142–7.

162. Simpson, W.D. 1930: 59; MacGregor 1978: 318–19; Credland 1980: 16; Samson 1983: 474–5, no. 96.

163. Munro 1882: 217, fig. 216; MacGregor, A. 1976: 317–20; Credland 1980: 12.

164. Craw 1930: 117–18, fig. 5, nos 38–40 (where they are described as 'spearheads'); Duncan, H.B. 1982: 7; Alcock and Alcock 1988: 141, fiche 2: D12–13; Campbell, E. 1999: 56–7; Lane and Campbell 2000: 160–2.

165. Duncan, H.B. 1982: fig. 11.

166. Petersen 1919: 36–47; Harrison 1993b: 50; Underwood 1999: 72–5; Siddorn 2000: 19, 55.

167. Laing and Laing 1985b: 282; Foster 1996: 103.

168. Allen and Anderson 1993, vol. 2: 221–3, fig. 234A; Atkinson 1993: 9; Burt 1993; RCAHMS 1994a: 21; 1999: 21, no. 55.2; Mack 1997: 65.

169. Shepherd and Shepherd 1980; RCAHMS 1994a: 10; 1999: 19, no. 39.7; Alcock 1998: 532–3.

170. Allen and Anderson 1993, vol. 2: 48–50, 221–3, figs 48B, 234A; RCAHMS 1994a: 18; 1999: 28–9, no. 115; Mack 1997: 108.

171. Adomnán, VSC, II.20; eds and trans Anderson and Anderson 1991: 122–3.

172. Giraldus Cambrensis, *Topographia Hiberniae*, III.100.

173. Allen and Anderson 1993, vol. 2: 215, 297–8, fig. 228B, 311C; Burt 1993; Trench-Jellicoe 1997: 165–6, fig. 4.

174. Allen and Anderson 1993, vol. 2: 13–14, 221, 306–7, figs 9, 233A, 321, 322A.

175. Laing 1993b: 29–31.

176. Robertson, N.M. 1992; RCAHMS 1994a: 20; 1999: 42, no. 199; Turner, V. 1994.

177. Laing and Laing 1985b: 282; 1993: 61.

178. Laing 2000a: 93.

179. Wilson, D.M. 1968: 144; 1976: 255–7.

180. Young 1891: 445; 1893: 91.

181. Alcock and Alcock 1988: 141, illus. 8, no. 26, fiche 2: D13–14; Alcock 1993a: 31, fig. 13.2, 35.

182. Pp. 67–8.

183. Duncan, H.B. 1982: 4–6; Lane and Campbell 2000: 162–3.

184. Adomnán, VSC, I.47; trans Anderson and Anderson 1991: 85.

185. Henderson, I. 1998a: 161–5.
186. Okasha 1992a.
187. Henderson, I. 1994b: 80–1; 1998a: 155, 164.
188. Meyer 1912, vol. 2: 39; Anderson, A.O. 1922, vol. 1: 148.
189. AFM s.a. 620; AI s.a. 618; AT s.a. 624.5; CS s.a. 625.1.
190. Ritchie, A. 1972; 1989: 50; 1997a: 41; 1998a; 1998b; forthcoming; Carver 1999: 33–5.
191. Laing and Laing 1993: 62, 79.
192. Ritchie, A. 1972: 299.
193. Clarke 1998; Ritchie, A. 1998a; 1998b.
194. Herodian, III.14.8; trans. Whittaker 1969, vol. 1: 358.
195. Curle, J. 1932: 321; Burgess 1955; Piggott 1955: 38, 40.
196. Underwood 1999: 91–4.
197. *The Gododdin,* B².26, A.18, A.33, A.59, A.71; trans. Koch 1997: 7, 73, 89, 109, 113; see also Jackson, K.H. 1969: 14, 32.
198. Adomnán, VSC, II.24; eds and trans Anderson and Anderson 1991: 128–9.
199. Buist 1839: 3; see also Leighton 1840: 135; Stuart 1867, vol. 2: 78; Graham-Campbell 1992: 251; Laing 1994: 12.
200. Laing 1994: 35; on which see Robinson 1975: 153–61.
201. Pp. 132–3.
202. Alcock 1971: 360.
203. P. 69.
204. Siddorn 2000: 60–1.
205. Bruce-Mitford and Luscombe 1974; Bruce-Mitford 1978: 138–231; Tweddle 1992; for general accounts see Shadrake and Shadrake 1997: 68–75; Underwood 1999: 94–9.
206. Nicolle 1984: pl. d; Faulkner 2000: 162, fig. 70.
207. Buist 1839: 3; Leighton 1840: 135.
208. Graham-Campbell 1992: 249; Cruickshank 1994b: 9–11.
209. Laing 1994: 22, no. 33, 34–5.
210. de Paor 1963.
211. Laing 1975: 33; Laing and Laing 1985b: 280; Webster and Backhouse 1991: 174–5.
212. Stevenson 1955: 114; Smyth 1984: 76; Laing and Laing 1985b: 279, illus. 1b–c, 280.
213. Tweddle 1992.
214. Alcock 1984: 25; Laing and Laing 1985b: 280.
215. Cruickshank 1994b: 8–9; 1995.
216. Allen and Anderson 1993, vol. 2: 247–9, fig. 260B.
217. Laing and Laing 1985b: 280; 1993: 62.
218. Henderson, I. 1999: 175.

219. Cameron, A.D. 1969; Allen and Anderson 1993, vol. 2: 95–6, 517, figs 97, 566; Mack 1997: 145.
220. Jolly 1882: 341; Shepherd and Shepherd 1980: 216; RCAHMS 1999: 26, no. 90.
221. Laing and Laing 1985b: 280; 1993: 62.
222. Nicolle 1995: 192–5.
223. Allen and Anderson 1993, vol. 2: 11–12, 14, 221, 306–7, figs 6, 9, 233A, 321, 322A; Atkinson 1993: 9; Burt 1993; Laing 1993b: 29–31; RCAHMS 1994a: 21; 1999: 21, no. 55.2, 41, no. 194; Mack 1997: 56–7, 137.
224. Allen and Anderson 1993, vol. 2: 96–7, figs 99, 99A; RCAHMS 1994a: 14.
225. Laing and Laing 1985b: 280; 1993: 62; Mack 1997: 26, 106; Cummins 1999: 205; RCAHMS 1999: 26, no. 97.2.
226. P. 63.
227. Cessford 1994c.

# CHAPTER FIVE

1. Chadwick, N.K. 1958; Pyatt et al. 1991; 1995: 70–2; van der Veen et al. 1993.
2. Caesar, Julius, *De bello Gallico*, V.14; trans. after Handford 1951: 136, fn.
3. For contrasting interpretations see Chadwick, N.K. 1958: 156–7; Pyatt et al. 1995: 72.
4. Herodian, III.14.7–8; trans. Whittaker 1969, vol. 1: 358–9.
5. Pan. Lat. Vet., VIII, 11, 4; trans. Mynors 1994: 126.
6. Gildas, *De excidio*, 19; trans. Winterbottom 1978: 23.
7. Bede, HE, I.20; trans. Sherley-Price 1990: 70.
8. P. 89.
9. Claudian, *De consulatu Stilichonis*, II (XXII), 247; *de bello Gothico*, (XXVI) 419–20; trans. Platnauer 1922, vol. 2: 21, 157.
10. Jordanes, Trans. Chadwick, N.K. 1958: 153.
11. Isidore of Seville, *Etymologiae*, 19.23.7; trans. Ritchie, A. 1994: 5.
12. Trans. Gray 1998: 24.
13. Sutherland 1994: 78; Gray 1998.
14. Diack 1944: 28; Thomas, A.C. 1964: 88, 93; 1984: 181–3; Henderson, I. 1994a: 45; Sutherland 1994: 78, 83.
15. *Book of Kells*, e.g. ff. 130r, 200r.
16. Ritchie, A. 1994: 8–11; Gray 1998: 29.
17. Ritchie, A. 1994: 10.
18. Meyer 1915.
19. The secondary literature is extensive: Rhys 1904: 311–12; Watson, W.J. 1926: 66; Diack 1944: 24–7; Jackson, K.H. 1955: 160; Chadwick, N.K. 1958; Thomas, A.C. 1964: 88–93; 1984: 177, 181–3; Henderson, I. 1967: 33;

Nicolaisen 1976: 150; 1996: 4; Anderson, M.O. 1973: 125, 128; 1987: 7; Smyth 1984: 77; Ritchie, A. 1989: 5; 1994: 4–6; Sutherland 1994: 78; 1997: 8; Gray 1998; Carver 1999: 7; MacQuarrie, C.W. 1999.

20. Claudian, *The Third Consulship of Honorius* (VI), 54; ed. and trans. Platnauer 1922, vol. 1: 274–5.

21. Trans. Skene 1867: 33.

22. E.g. Ritchie, A. 1989: 5; 1994: 5.

23. Gray 1998: 28.

24. Piggott 1989: 63; Moser 1998: 68–84; Fleming 2000: 70–8.

25. Camille 1998: 284–97.

26. Glob 1969; Brothwell 1986; Stead et al. (eds) 1986; Turner and Scaife (eds) 1995; van der Sanden 1996; Green, M. 2001.

27. Taylor, G.W. 1986.

28. Pyatt et al. 1991; 1995.

29. Turner, R.C. 1995a: 109, 117–19; 1995b: 218–19.

30. Barclay and Halliday 1983; RCAHMS 1994a: 7; 1999: 23, no. 68; Mack 1997: 42–3; Atkinson and Henry 1998: 3.

31. P. 56.

32. P. 52.

33. Pp. 61–2.

34. Henderson, I. 1998b: 23, 25, 26.

35. Allen and Anderson 1993, vol. 2: 247–9, 260, fig. 260B, 269B.

36. Marwick 1924: 295–7; O'Meadhra 1993: 426–7, fig. 27.1; Ritchie, A. 1994: 13–14, fig. 9; Laing 1997: 132, fig. 7, 135, no. 24.

37. Stevenson 1981: 289; O'Meadhra 1993: 427–8, fig. 27.2; Ritchie, A. 1994: 13.

38. Allen and Anderson 1993, vol. 2: 258–60, 300, figs 269B, 313B; Ritchie, A. 1997b: 19.

39. Allen and Anderson 1993, vol. 2: 245–7, 321, figs 259B, 334D; PAS 1997; Henderson, I. 1999: 172.

40. Alcock and Alcock 1993: 240; Henderson, I. 1999: 172.

41. Cruickshank 1995: 24.

42. Forsyth 1995b.

43. Pp. 64–5.

44. Shepherd and Shepherd 1980; RCAHMS 1994a: 10, 18; 1999: 28–9, no. 115, 19, no. 39.7; Alcock 1998: 532–3; Allen and Anderson 1993, vol. 2: 48–50, fig. 48B.

45. Mack 1997: 88.

46. Allen and Anderson 1993, vol. 2: 219, fig. 231A; Burt 1993.

47. Carus-Wilson 1952: 360–3; Frere 1978: 317.

48. FAI, 429 (for ?909); pp. 160–1.

49. Adomnán, VSC, I.1; trans Anderson and Anderson 1991: 15.

50. Allen and Anderson 1993, vol. 2: 284–5, fig. 302; RCAHMS 1994b: 96, fig. C; 1999: 39, no. 183; PAS 1997.

51. PAS 1997.

52. On the horns depicted in Pictish sculpture see Purser 1992: 33.

53. Ritchie, A. 1989: 34; PAS 1997; Carver 1999: 56.

54. Allen and Anderson 1993, vol. 2: 62, 215, figs 59, 228B.

55. Graham-Campbell 1973.

56. Glover 1952; Brown, R.A. 1973: 34–42; Laing and Laing 1985b: 284; Davis 1989; Higham 1991; Alcock 1993a: 12–13; Cessford 1993; Harrison 1993a: 12; Hooper 1993; Jones, N.A. 1993; Rowland 1995.

57. Jackson, K.H. 1969: 28–30, 84–6; Alcock 1971: 334–5; 1987a: 300.

58. *The Gododdin*, B¹.13; trans. Koch 1997: 41, 184.

59. Beck 1992: 37–9, 117–48, 158–9, 162–4; Hughson 1993; 1997; 1999.

60. Pp. 145–7.

61. Ritchie, A. 1989: 24–5; Cruickshank 1994a; 1999: 27–9; 2000.

62. Jackson, K.H. 1969: 31, 149.

63. Pp. 40–1, 148–9.

64. AU s.a. 917.4.

65. Ritchie, A. 1997b: 18.

66. Allen and Anderson 1993, vol. 2: 295–6, fig. 309B.

67. Allen and Anderson 1993, vol. 2: 224, 249, 295–6, figs 235B, 260B, 309B.

68. Eddius, VSW, 19; trans. Webb 1983: 126.

69. Pp. 62–4.

70. Pp. 86–8.

71. Pp. 35–6.

72. Stead 1965; Harbison 1971; Greene 1972.

73. Piggott 1983: 195–238; 1992.

74. Tacitus, *Agricola*, 35–6.

75. Cassius Dio, 76.12.3; trans. Cary 1970, vol. 9: 263.

76. Cessford 2001: 32–4.

77. Livens 1976; MacGregor, M. 1976, vol. 1: 47–8, 71; Laing and Laing 1987.

78. Carter and Hunter 2001; 2002.

79. Adomnán, VSC, I.38, II.43; eds and trans Anderson and Anderson 1991: 70–1, 170–1.

80. Aitchison 1994: 162; Ritchie, J.N.G. 1997: 127.

81. Harbison 1971; Greene 1972.

82. Adomnán, VSC, II.28, III.23; eds and trans Anderson and Anderson 1991: 134–5, 216–7.

83. Adomnán, VSC, I.7; eds and trans Anderson and Anderson 1991: 30–1; AT s.a. 557.1; CS s.a. 558.

84. Trans. Clancy 1998: 102.

85. *The Gododdin*, B².37 = A.74; trans. Koch 1997: 21; see also Koch 1987.

86. Thomas, A.C. 1964: 53–4, 57; Sutherland 1994: 13; Kermack 1997: 12; 1998: 8–9; Mack 1997: 17; Cessford 2001: 27–31.

87. Allen and Anderson 1993, vol. 2: 127–8, fig. 132; Mack 1998a: 40.

88. Green, M. 1991.

89. Chalmers 1848: 9; see also Ritchie, A. 1995: 9, n. 1; Ritchie, J.N.G. 1997: 122.

90. Laing and Laing 1985b: 277–8; Allen and Anderson 1993, vol. 2: 331, fig. 344; Ritchie, A. 1997a: 8; Ritchie, J.N.G. 1997.

91. 2 Kings 2.

92. Anderson, J. 1881: 158; Laing and Laing 1985b: 278; Hudson 1994a: 9; Ritchie, J.N.G. 1997: 127; Ritchie, A. and Ritchie, G. 1998: 13.

93. Allen and Anderson 1993, vol. 2: 315, fig. 329A and B, 315; RCAHMS 1994b: 96, fig. B; 1999: 39, no. 183; PAS 1997.

94. Allen and Anderson 1993, vol. 2: 321, 323, figs. 334C, 334D; PAS 1997; Henderson, I. 1999: 172.

95. Alcock 1993a: 13.

96. Pp. 53–62.

97. Harrison 1993a: 30; 1993b: 12–13; Underwood 1999: 46, 89–91, 127, 129, 131–5, 146, 148; Siddorn 2000: 53–8.

98. P. 59.

99. *The Gododdin*, B².34; trans. Koch 1997: 17; see also Jackson 1969: 32–3.

100. Pp. 53–5.

101. Pp. 86–8.

102. On the battle see Wainwright 1948; Marsden 1994a; Alcock 1996a; Fraser, J.E. 2002; Cruickshank 1999.

103. Eddius, VSW, 19; trans. Webb 1983: 126.

104. AT s.a. 638.1; AU s.a. 637.1; CS s.a. 637.1.

105. AClon s.a. 728; AFM s.a. 725; AT s.a. 731.4; AU s.a. 730.6; see also Anderson, A.O. 1922, vol. 1: 228, n. 1; Anderson, M.O. 1973: 183, n. 244.

106. AT s.a. 560.2; see also AClon s.a. 563; AFM s.a. 554; AU s.a. 557.2, 559.2 (repeated entry); CS s.a. 560.3; on which see Anderson, M.O. 1973: 138.

107. Adomnán, VSC, I.8; trans Anderson and Anderson 1991: 33.

108. Bede, HE, I.34; trans. Sherley-Price 1990: 97.

109. Adomnán, VSC, I.9; trans Anderson and Anderson 1991: 33.

110. AClon s.a. 725; AT s.a. 728.4, 728.5, AU s.a. 727.4; on the locations see Reeves 1857: 383; Skene 1886, vol. 1: 280; Anderson, A.O. 1922, vol. 1: 224, n. 1; Watson, W.J. 1926: 400–1; Anderson, M.O. 1973: 177; Hudson 1994a: 24; Aitchison 2000: 77.

111. Bede, HE, I.20; trans. Sherley-Price 1990: 69–70.

112. P. 55.

113. AU s.a. 735.2.

114. Pp. 151–2.

## CHAPTER SIX

1. Feachem 1966; MacKie 1976; Ritchie, G. and Ritchie, A. 1981: 89–94; Cunliffe 1991: 328–9.
2. Feachem 1966: 60; Hogg 1979.
3. Alcock 1989: 328; 1993a: 19; see also Ralston 1996: 145.
4. Lane 1984; Campbell and Lane 1993.
5. Small 1972; Small and Cottam 1972; Stevenson 1972; Alcock 1984: 23.
6. Close-Brooks 1987a; 1987b.
7. Alcock 1981a: 153–4.
8. AT s.a. 714.2; AU s.a. 680.5, 682.3, 685.1, 693.4, 697.3, 700.8, 711.5, 713.2, 733.6, 735.1; Regnal Lists D, F, I; ed. Anderson, M.O. 1973: 267, 274, 283.
9. AU s.a. 679.5, 691.6, 733.7.
10. Reeves 1857: 378; Skene 1886, vol. 1: 263.
11. AT s.a. 728.5; AU s.a. 727.4.
12. Adomnán, VSC, II.33, 35.
13. Flanagan 1981.
14. AU s.a. 640.5, 702.6; Regnal List D; ed. Anderson, M.O. 1973: 267.
15. SC; ed. Anderson, M.O. 1973: 251; ed. Hudson 1998: 149.
16. Alcock 1981a: 157, 161, 177.
17. Alcock 1981a; 1981b; Alcock and Alcock 1988; 1990; 1993: 242–82; Alcock et al. 1990.
18. Alcock et al. 1990; Alcock and Alcock 1992.
19. Feachem 1955; Alcock 1984: 19–27; Foster 1998: 10–16.
20. Shepherd and Ralston 1979: 20–6; Shepherd 1983: 329–31; Ralston 1980; 1987a.
21. RCAHMS 1971: 64–77; 1975: 64–75; 1980: 72–90; 1982: 30–1; 1984: 72–101; 1988: 143–69.
22. Nieke 1990; Harding 1997.
23. Alcock 1981a: 172–3; Alcock and Alcock 1988; RCAHMS 1988: 149–59, no. 248; Lane and Campbell 2000.
24. Alcock 1984: 19.
25. Alcock 1981a: 166–71; Alcock et al. 1990; Lane and Campbell 2000.
26. Triscott 1980; 1981.
27. Aitchison 1999: 166–79.
28. Stevenson 1949; Feachem 1955: 71–82.
29. Alcock et al. 1990: 206–14.
30. Alcock et al. 1990: 210; Foster 1996: 44–6.
31. Feachem 1955: 79–80; 1966: 82, 84; 1977: 145; Wainwright 1955: 24, 30.
32. Pp. 114–16.
33. Alcock and Alcock 1990: 119–20.
34. Foster 1998: 11.

35. Ralston 1980; 1987a.
36. Macdonald, J. 1862; Mitchell and Drummond 1874: 647–51, 660–70; Young 1891; 1893.
37. Small 1969; Hogg 1975: 146–8; Edwards and Ralston 1980; Alcock 1984: 21; Shepherd 1993: 78–9.
38. Ralston 1987a: 17.
39. Abercromby et al. 1902: 230–4; RCAHMS 1994b: 52–3, 55, 57, 73, 74, 91, 92.
40. AT s.a. 725.2; AU s.a. 702.4, 724.2. On the interpretation of *ailén* see Anderson, A.O. 1922, vol. 1: 221, n. 6.
41. Munro 1882; Morrison 1985.
42. Scott and Scott 1960; Scott, J.G. 1961; RCAHMS 1988: 205–8, no. 354.
43. Trans. Anderson, A.O. 1922, vol. 1: 122.
44. Lamb 1980.
45. Carter et al. 1995: 443–4.
46. Hingley 1992: 19; Carter et al. 1995: 476–7.
47. See Ralston 1995 on hillfort defences in general.
48. Alcock 1981a: 168; Alcock et al. 1990: 200–4.
49. Small 1969: 64.
50. Caesar, Julius, *De bello Gallico*, VII.23; on which see Ralston 1995: 64–6.
51. MacKie 1976; Ralston 1987b; 1995: 66–7; Gentles 1993.
52. Sanderson et al. 1988: table 3.
53. Young 1891; Cotton 1954: 56–7, 63, 93–4; Ralston 1987a: 16; Alcock et al. 1990: 202.
54. Abercromby et al. 1902: 230–4; RCAHMS 1994b: 55, 57, 92.
55. Close-Brooks 1987a; 1987b: 27, 29; Alcock et al. 1990: 203.
56. Compare Aitchison 1994: 311; Eaton 2000.
57. Regnal List D; ed. Anderson, M.O. 1973: 267; trans. Anderson, A.O. 1922: vol. 1: 517–18.
58. Crawford, O.G.S. 1949: 59–61; Alcock 1981a: 177; Foster 1998: 16.
59. Adomnán, VSC, II.33–5; eds and trans Anderson and Anderson 1991: 142–7.
60. AT s.a. 686.1; AU s.a. 685.1; FAI, 96 (for 685).
61. Simpson, N. 1992.
62. Watson, W.J. 1926: 239; Wainwright 1948: 94–5; 1955: 30; Cruickshank 1999: 31.
63. Reeves 1857: 383; Watson, W.J. 1926: 400–1; Anderson, M.O. 1973: 177; Hudson 1994a: 24.
64. Feachem 1955: 79–80; 1966: 82, 84; 1977: 145; Wainwright 1955: 24, 30.
65. Anderson, M.O. 1973: 177–8.
66. Reeves 1857: 383; Skene 1886, vol. 1: 280; Anderson, A.O. 1922, vol. 1: 224, n. 1; Hudson 1994a: 24; Aitchison 2000: 77.

67. HE, III.16; trans. Colgrave 1994: 135.
68. AT s.a. 643.4; AU s.a. 642.4.
69. AU s.a. 685.1, 697.3, 711.2, 730.4.
70. AT s.a. 736.1; AU s.a. 735.1; pp. 000.
71. Skene 1867: cxxxi; 1886, vol. 1: 290; Anderson, A.O. 1922, vol. 1: 233, n. 1; Lane and Campbell 2000: 38.
72. SC; trans. Skene 1867: 8; trans. Anderson, A.O. 1922, vol. 1: 288; trans. Hudson 1998: 153.
73. Watson, W.J. 1926: 164; Hudson 1994a: 43–4.
74. Innes 2001; Simpson, C. 2001.
75. Anderson, M.O. 1955: 169; 1973: 250; Hudson 1998: 153, n. 7.
76. SC; trans. Anderson, A.O. 1922, vol. 1: 288; ed. Anderson, M.O. 1973: 250; trans. Hudson 1998: 152.
77. AU s.a. 779.1. On the fort see Alcock 1978; 1981a: 157, 159; Alcock and Alcock 1990.
78. Small 1969: 66; Shepherd 1993: 79; but see Edwards and Ralston 1980: 208; p. 110.
79. AU s.a. 682.3; Alcock 1981a: 168, 170; Alcock et al. 1990: 201–2.
80. AU s.a. 700.8.
81. AU s.a. 733.6; 733.7.
82. AU s.a. 640.5, 679.5, 680.5, 682.3, 691.6, 693.4, 702.6, 711.5.
83. AU s.a. 741.10; Anderson, A.O. 1922, vol. 1: 237, n. 8.
84. Anderson, A.O. 1922, vol. 1: 201, n. 4.
85. FAI, 388 (for 870).
86. Symeon of Durham, *Historia Regum Anglorum*; trans. after Anderson, A.O. 1908: 57.
87. AU s.a. 869.6; FAI, 388 (for 870).
88. Alcock 1978: 109; Alcock et al. 1992: 292, nos 26–7.
89. Pp. 130–42.
90. TYP, 54; trans. Bromwich 1978: 147; also trans. Anderson, A.O. 1922, vol. 1: 74, n. 1.
91. AU s.a. 869.6.
92. FAI, 388 (for 870).
93. AU s.a. 870.2; see also AClon s.a. 864; CS s.a. 871.
94. *Book of Leinster*, 190; eds Best and O'Brien 1965: 836; on which see Mac Cana 1980: 47, 100–1; MacQuarrie, A. 1993: 8, n. 2.
95. Bradbury 1992: 296–334.
96. Gravett 1990: rear cover; Bradbury 1992: rear cover.
97. Skene 1886, vol. 1: 263.
98. Skene 1886, Chaps 3 and 8.
99. AU s.a. 685.1
100. Watson, W.J. 1926: 508.

101. AU s.a. 682.3.
102. Henderson, I. 1967: 55.
103. AU s.a. 733.7.
104. AU s.a. 733.6.
105. AT s.a. 736.1; AU s.a. 735.1.
106. AU s.a. 735.1.
107. Pp. 141–2.
108. Campbell, M. 1976; RCAHMS 1988: 157–9; Laing 1997: 140, no. 2; Lane and Campbell 2000: 18–23.
109. Christison 1905: 298; Curle, C.L. 1940: 67; Curle and Henry 1943: 261, n.; Childe 1941: 291; Radford 1953: 238–9; Wainwright 1959: 275; Thomas, A.C. 1964: 40; Jackson, K. 1965: 302; Padel 1972: 89–91; Campbell, M. 1976; Anderson, M.O. 1973: 185–6; RCAHMS 1988: 158; 1992: 526–7, no. 281; Mack 1997: 136.
110. RCAHMS 1992: 526.
111. Gordon 1966: 217.
112. Allen and Anderson 1993, vol. 2: 97–8, 103–5, figs 100, 108; RCAHMS 1994a: 15; Mack 1997: 31, 111.
113. Jackson, K. 1965; RCAHMS 1988: 158.
114. Hicks 1993: 47–8.
115. Padel 1972: 89–92; Lane 1984: 47, 49; Laing and Laing 1993: 96; Forsyth, K. 1995a; 1996: 230–41; 2000b; Laing 1997: 140, no. 2; Campbell, E. 1999: 21; Lane and Campbell 2000: 22–3.
116. Thomas, F.W.L. 1879; Hamilton 1968: 151–6.
117. Lane 1984: 49; Laing and Laing 1993: 97; Campbell, E. 1999: 21; Lane and Campbell 2000: 247–9.
118. Morris, R.W.B. 1977: 75.
119. Jackson, K. 1965: 302; Alcock 1981a: 167; Ritchie, G. and Ritchie, A. 1981: 154; Lane 1984: 46; Laing and Laing 1993: 95; Mack 1997: 136.
120. Lane and Campbell 2000: 22.
121. P. 48.
122. Allen and Anderson 1993, vol. 2: 477–9, fig. 508; RCAHMS 1914: 14–16, nos. 13–14; 1994a: 6; 1999: 23, no. 72; Feachem 1950: 207; Radford 1953; Mack 1997: 28, 137; Laing 2000b.
123. Radford 1953; Thomas, A.C. 1961: 68–9; 1964: 86; 1981: 289, fig. 55; Laing 1975: 33; Laing and Laing 1985a: 266–7; Stell 1986: 121; Mac Lean 1992: 64–6; Hicks 1993: 47; Oram 1993: 14; Cessford 1994b; Cummins 1995: 76, 78; 1999: 75–6, 80–1; Mack 1997: 137; Sutherland 1997: 16.
124. Henderson, I. 1958: 50, n.; Mack 1997: 137; Laing 2000b.
125. Thomas, A.C. 1961.
126. Wainwright 1955: 43–4.
127. Jackson, A. 1984: table 2A:20.

128. Oram 1993: 15.
129. Cessford 1994b: 85–6; Laing 2000b: 11.
130. Cessford 1994b: 83; Laing 2000b: 11.
131. Jackson, A. 1984.
132. Driscoll 1986.
133. AU s.a. 697.3.
134. AU s.a. 700.8.
135. AT s.a. 703.4; AU s.a. 702.4.
136. AU s.a. 711.5; on the sites see RCAHMS 1971: 157–9, no. 309; Alcock 1981a: 157.
137. AT s.a. 714.2, 714.3; AU s.a. 713.2, 713.3.
138. AT s.a. 725.2; AU s.a. 724.2.
139. AU s.a. 730.4.
140. Pp. 114–16.
141. SC; ed. Anderson, M.O. 1973: 250; trans. Skene 1867: 8; trans. Anderson, A.O. 1922, vol. 1: 288; trans. Hudson 1998: 153.
142. Feachem 1966: 73–5; Alcock 1981a: 161; 1987b: 82; Alcock et al. 1990: 208–9; RCAHMS 1994b: 74, 89–91, 105, fig. A.
143. SC; trans. Anderson, A.O. 1922, vol. 1: 395–6; ed. Anderson, M.O. 1973: 251; trans. Hudson 1998: 155.
144. AI s.a. 795; AU s.a. 801.9, 805.8, 824.17.
145. AD 655±40 and 740±45; Edwards and Ralston 1980: 209; Alcock 1984: 22.
146. Edwards and Ralston 1980: 206, 208.
147. Small 1969: 67; Ritchie, A. 1989: 15; Shepherd 1993: 79; Foster 1998: 11.
148. AU s.a. 869.6; FAI, 388 (for 870).
149. P. 103.

## Chapter Seven

1. Bannerman 1974: 149–51.
2. O'Loughlin 1997.
3. Adomnán, VSC, I.28; on which see Thomas, C. 1990.
4. Alcock et al. 1990: 214–16; Alcock 1993a: 37–40; Lane 1994; Campbell, E. 1996a; 1996b; Wooding 1996; Lane and Campbell 2000: 98–102, 196, 241–3.
5. McGrail (ed.) 1990.
6. Hooper 1992; Gifford and Gifford 1999; Haywood 1999.
7. Marcus 1951; 1954a; 1954b; 1980: 3–32.
8. *Navigatio Sancti Brendani*; trans. Webb 1983: 209–45.
9. Gildas, *De excidio*, 14; ed. Winterbottom 1978: 93.
10. Tacitus, *Agricola*, 23.
11. Bede, HE, I.1.

12.    *Senchus fer nAlban*, ed. and trans. Bannerman 1974: 43, 49.
13.    Pp. 15–18.
14.    *Senchus fer nAlban*, ed. and trans. Bannerman 1974: 46–9.
15.    Bannerman 1974: 140, 152–4.
16.    Adomnán, VSC, I.4, 12, 18, 19, 28, II.12, 34, 39, 42, 45.
17.    Ed. Bain 1888, vol. 2: 435, no. 1633; Bannerman 1974: 141.
18.    Ed. and trans. Bannerman 1974: 46–9.
19.    Pp. 16–17.
20.    P. 127.
21.    AFM s.a. 565; AT s.a. 733.4.
22.    AT s.a. 729.2; Anderson, A.O. 1922, vol. 1: 226.
23.    P. 127.
24.    Ed. and trans. Hudson 1998: 151, 159.
25.    Anderson, A.O. 1922, vol. 1: 226, n. 2; Watson, W.J. 1926: 63.
26.    Greig 1970; 1971; 1972; Alcock 1984: 23; Ralston 1987a: 17; Foster 1998: 11.
27.    Graham 1979: 352–3, 357–8; Alcock 1984: 25.
28.    Small 1969: 61.
29.    P. 145.
30.    Ritchie, A. 1985: 203; Ralston 1987a: 22; Shepherd 1993: 79; Foster 1998: 11.
31.    Ritchie, A. 1997a: 41.
32.    Compare Graham and Gordon 1988: 269–74; Henderson, I. 1975: 96–7.
33.    Adomnán, VSC, II.42.
34.    FAI s.a. 733; Anderson, A.O. 1922, vol. 1: 230, n.
35.    AFM s.a. 728; AT s.a. 733.4.
36.    *Statistical Account*, vol. 8: 252, fn.
37.    Graham and Gordon 1988: 335–6.
38.    RCAHMS 1975: 194; Alcock 1981a: 157, 172; Graham and Gordon 1988: 334.
39.    On which see Graham and Gordon 1988: 339–40.
40.    Alcock 1981a: 177.
41.    AU s.a. 733.7; p. 105.
42.    AFM s.a. 565.
43.    AT s.a. 719.5; AU s.a. 718.7.
44.    AU s.a. 720.1; AT s.a. 721.1.
45.    P. 119.
46.    Breeze 1982: 83–4; Breeze and Dobson 1987: 43–5; Woolliscroft 2001: 88–102; Jones and Mattingly 2002: 109–16.
47.    Frere 1978: 390–7; Salway 1981: 375–84.
48.    Gildas, *De excidio*, 19.1–2; trans. Winterbottom 1978: 23.
49.    Gildas, *De excidio*, 17.3; trans. Winterbottom 1978: 22.

50. Claudian, *On Stilicho's Consulship*, XXII, 247–55; trans. after Miller 1974: 143, n. 12.

51. Haverfield 1912; Ramm 1978: 125–9; Frere 1978: 395–6; Welsby 1982: 116–18; Wilson, P.R. 1991; Ottaway 1996; 2001; Bell 1999.

52. Mann 1977: 14.

53. Johnson 1976; Johnston (ed.) 1977; Maxfield (ed.) 1989; Cotterill 1993; Pearson 2002.

54. Gildas, *De excidio*, 18.3; trans. Winterbottom 1978: 23.

55. Vegetius, *Epitoma Rei Militaris*, IV.37; trans. Milner 1996: 144.

56. Chadwick, N.K. 1958: 164–6; Johnstone 1980: 153.

57. Richmond 1955: 62.

58. Vegetius, *Epitoma Rei Militaris*, IV.37; trans. after Milner 1996: 144.

59. AT s.a. 719.5; AU s.a. 718.7.

60. Anderson, A.O. 1922, vol. 1: 162–3; Byrne 1973: 112–14; Anderson, M.O. 1973: 152; Bannerman 1974: 101–2, 106.

61. AClon s.a. 627; AT s.a. 637.2; AU s.a. 636.1; CS s.a. 636.2; on which see Byrne 1973: 113.

62. Pennant 1998 [1774]: 184; Craigie 1897: 452; Anderson, A.O. 1922, vol. 1: 162, n. 2; Watson, W.J. 1926: 92; but see Bannerman 1974: 102, n. 5.

63. Anderson, A.O. 1922, trans. *Cogadh Gaedhal re Gaillaibh*; vol. 1: 277.

64. AU s.a. 838.9.

65. *The Gododdin*, B².24 = B¹.3 = A.48; trans. Koch 1997: 3.

66. Trans. Hudson 1998: 159.

67. Hudson 1998: 159, n. 58.

68. ABL s.a. 583; AFM s.a. 565; AU s.a. 566.2, 567. AI s.a. 568 misinterprets this as the battle of '*Ard-Tommain*', a scribal error.

69. AU s.a. 579.2, 580.3.

70. AClon s.a. 504; AI s.a. 583; AT s.a. 505.2 (misplaced), 581.1, 582.2; AU s.a. 503.2 (misplaced), 581.1, 582.3; Bannerman 1974: 83.

71. Anderson, A.O. 1922, vol. 1: 89–90, n. 3; Bannerman 1974: 83–4.

72. TYP, 29; trans. Bromwich 1978: 57, but see p. 59, n. b.

73. AU s.a. 700.7.

74. AU s.a. 708.4.

75. AT s.a. 733.1; AU s.a. 732.1; on the location see Anderson, A.O. 1922, vol. 1: 229, n. 1.

76. AClon s.a. 730; AFM s.a. 728; AT s.a. 733.4; on the location see Anderson, A.O. 1922, vol. 1: 229, n. 3.

77. Adomnán, VSC, II.22; trans Anderson and Anderson 1991: 125.

78. Pp. 138–9.

79. Adomnán, VSC, II.42.

80. AT s.a. 682.5; AU s.a. 681.4; p. 137.

81. P. 102.

82. *Life of Gildas*; trans. Williams 1901: 408–9.
83. Claudian, *The Fourth Consulship of Honorius* (VIII), l. 31–2; trans. Miller 1974: 142, n. 6.
84. Claudian, *Historia Brittonum*, 38; ed. Morris 1980: 29.
85. William of Malmesbury, *Gesta Regum Anglorum*, trans. Anderson, A.O. 1908: 12, n. 4.
86. Bede, HE, II.9.
87. William of Malmesbury, *Gesta Pontificum*; trans. Anderson, A.O. 1908: 53, n. 3.
88. P. 135.
89. Wooding 2001a; 2001b.
90. Adomnán, VSC, I.1, 4, 5, 6, 12, 18, 19, 22, 28, 30, 33, 34, 36, 41, 47, II.3, 12, 14, 22, 27, 34, 38, 39, 42, 45, III.23.
91. Gildas, *De excidio*, 19.1; ed. and trans. Winterbottom 1978: 23, 94.
92. AT s.a. 729.2.
93. Bede, HE, I.1.
94. Adomnán, VSC, I.33.
95. Gildas, *Lebor Bretnach*; ed. and trans. Skene 1867: 42.
96. Adomnán, VSC, II.45; trans after Anderson and Anderson 1991: 175.
97. Adomnán, VSC, II.27.
98. Adomnán, VSC, II.12.
99. Ritchie, A. 1989: 5, 50; O'Meadhra 1993: 425, 427; but see Laing 1997: 131.
100. Curle 1935: 308–10, fig. 46; Hamilton 1956: 114–15, 121, 134, pl. XXI, nos 1–2; Johnstone 1980: 153; O'Meadhra 1993: 427–31, 436, fig. 27.2; Ritchie, A. 1989: 50; 1997a: 42; Laing 1997: 128, 131, nos 5–6.
101. Allen and Anderson 1993, vol. 2: 216–18, fig. 230B.
102. Johnstone 1980: 152–3; Ritchie and Stevenson 1993: 204, 207, fig. 25.6. On the caves and their carvings see also Patrick 1905–6; MacKie and Glaister 1981; Rankin 1989; Allen and Anderson 1993, vol. 2: 370–3, figs 388–90.
103. Lethbridge 1952: 124; le Bon 1992; Laing 1997: 140, no. 3.
104. Adomnán, VSC, I.5, 18, 33, 36.
105. P. 129.
106. Adomnán, VSC, I.33.
107. Gildas, *De excidio*, 19.1–2; trans. Winterbottom 1978: 23.
108. Hornell 1938a.
109. Watkins 1980.
110. Fenton 1972.
111. *Navigatio Sancti Brendani*, 4; trans. after Webb 1983: 214.
112. Hornell 1937; 1938a; 1938b; Marcus 1953; 1980: 3–15; MacCullagh 1992.
113. Adomnán, VSC, I.47.
114. Adomnán, VSC, II.45.

115. Adomnán, VSC, II.42; trans Anderson and Anderson 1991: 169.
116. Severin 1978.
117. Gildas, *De excidio*, 16; trans. Winterbottom 1978: 21.
118. 4; trans. Webb 1983: 214.
119. Adomnán, VSC, I.1, 4, 18, II.12, 15, 22, 34, 42, 45, III.23.
120. Adomnán, VSC, I.1, 18, II.34, 39, 42, 45; trans Anderson and Anderson 1991: 13, 43, 145, 161, 167, 169, 175, 177.
121. Adomnán, VSC, II.45; trans Anderson and Anderson 1991: 175.
122. Adomnán, VSC, I.2, III.23, *kapitulationes*, I.20.
123. Adomnán, VSC, I.19.
124. Adomnán, VSC, II.42; trans Anderson and Anderson 1991: 169.
125. Grant 1961: 253; Green, C. 1963: 103–13; MacGrail 1980: 49; Alcock 1987a: 218–19; Rixson 1998: 71–2.
126. Alcock 1987a: 219.
127. P. 17.
128. AU s.a. 736.2.
129. Mowat 1996: 28–30, 65–8, 129.
130. Mowat 1996: 58–60.
131. Mowat 1996: 66.
132. Mowat 1996: 30, 65–6.

## CHAPTER EIGHT

1. P. 106.
2. Reuter 1985.
3. Cassius Dio, *History*, 75.5.4; trans. Carey 1982: 217.
4. Hunter 2000; 2001; 2002a: 25–7; 2002b.
5. Cassius Dio, *History*, 76.12.2; trans. Cary 1982: 263.
6. Curle, J. 1932; Robertson, A.S. 1970.
7. Curle, J. 1932: 336–8, 392, no. 77A; Robertson, A.S. 1970: 223; Kent and Painter 1977, 28, no. 21; Henig 1995: 168; Johns 1996: 167, 198.
8. Macdonald, G. 1926: 7–9; Curle, J. 1932: 324–5, 365, no. 21; Robertson, A.S. 1970: 222.
9. Curle, A.O. 1923; Kent and Painter 1977: 123–4.
10. Burley 1956; Sekulla 1983.
11. E.g. Alcock 1971: 254.
12. Bateson 1973: 42–3, 63–4, 73–4.
13. Laing 1994: 11; Graham-Campbell 1992: 251.
14. Buist 1839; Stevenson 1976: 248; Graham-Campbell 1992: 246.
15. Laing 1994: 13, 20–2, nos 21–40.
16. Curle, J. 1932: 385; Graham-Campbell 1992: 250; 1993: 115.
17. Stevenson 1976: 249; Graham-Campbell 1992: 247; Laing 1994: 34.

18.  Laing 1994: 35.
19.  Laing 1994: 22, nos 32, 37–8.
20.  Laing 1994: 20, nos 23, 32.
21.  Laing 1994: 20, nos 24, 32; Graham-Campbell 1992: 248.
22.  Stevenson 1956b: 229; Graham-Campbell 1992: 246–7; Laing 1994: 20, nos 25, 34.
23.  Laing 1994: 34–5; Graham-Campbell 1992: 248, 252–6.
24.  Kent and Painter 1977: 29–39; Painter 1977a; 1977b; Johns and Potter 1983; Bland and Johns 1993; de la Bédoyère 1999: 153–63.
25.  Cummins 1995: 66.
26.  de la Bédoyère 1999: 158.
27.  Hill 1987.
28.  Dunglas and Smith 1881: 69–70; Stevenson 1956b: 229; Henderson, I. 1967: 212; Laing and Laing 1993: 11, 13, 142.
29.  Breeze, A. 1998.
30.  Edwards 1939.
31.  Henderson, I. 1979.
32.  Stevenson 1955: 101; Henderson, I. 1967: 212; 1979: 22; Laing 1975: 59; Laing and Laing 1993: 115–16.
33.  Cessford 1994d.
34.  Gildas, *De excidio*, 17.3, 21.1–2; trans. Winterbottom 1978: 22, 24.
35.  Bede, HE, I.20; Chaps 5 and 6.
36.  Graham-Campbell 1973.
37.  Curle, C.L. 1982, fig. 39, no. 432; Taylor, D.B. 1983: 229; Thomas, G. 2001: 45.
38.  Stevenson 1966: vi.
39.  Stevenson 1966: xviii.
40.  Lane and Campbell 2000: 150–1; Cowell 2000.
41.  Laing and Laing 1993: 21, fig. 12.
42.  P. 122.
43.  Adomnán, VSC, II.33.
44.  On whom see Macquarrie 1993: 7–8.
45.  *Laws of Hywel Dda*, ed. Richards 1954: 112.
46.  St Patrick, *Epistola*, 19; trans. Hood 1978: 58.
47.  Pp. 98, 103.
48.  Adomnán, VSC, II.22, 24.
49.  AFM s.a. 565.
50.  TYP, 54; trans. Bromwich 1978: 147; p. 103.
51.  *The Prophecy of Berchán*, 132, 144, 164; trans. Hudson 1996: 85, 86, 88.
52.  AU s.a. 740.10.
53.  Bede, *Life of Cuthbert*, 27; ed. and trans. Colgrave 1940: 242–3.
54.  St Andrews foundation myth; ed. Anderson, M.O. 1973: 259.

55.  AT s.a. 736.1; AU s.a. 735.1.

56.  P. 105.

57.  King lists F, I, D, K; ed. Anderson, M.O. 1973: 265, 271, 282, 286; trans. Skene 1867: 149, 172, 288; trans. Anderson, A.O. 1922, vol. 1: 270.

58.  Fridegoda, *Life of Saint Wilfrid*; trans. Anderson, A.O. 1908: 37, fn.

59.  Cumméne, quoted in Adomnán, VSC, III.5; trans Anderson and Anderson 1991: 191.

60.  AU s.a. 690.3.

61.  *Historia Brittonum*, 38; ed. and trans. Morris 1980: 29, 69.

62.  AT s.a. 682.5.

63.  AU s.a. 681.4.

64.  SC; trans. Hudson 1998: 153–4; FAI s.a. 864.

65.  SC; ed. and trans. Hudson 1998: 150, 155.

66.  *Life of Gildas*; trans. Williams 1901: 401; p. 122.

67.  Macdonald, A. 1974: 57–64; RCAHMS 1928: 220, no. 668.

68.  *Life of St Comgall of Bangor*; trans. Anderson, A.O. 1922, vol. 1: 53–4.

69.  Pp. 100–2.

70.  Lucas 1967.

71.  AI s.a. 619; AT s.a. 617.1; AU s.a. 616.1; CS s.a. 617; Anderson, A.O. 1922, vol. 1: 142–4; see also Watson, W.J. 1926: 63; Marsden 1995: 189–92.

72.  *Martyrology of Gorman*, 17 April; trans. Anderson, A.O. 1922, vol. 1: 143, n. 1.

73.  *Book of Leinster*, 190; eds Best and O'Brien 1965: 836.

74.  Marsden 1995: 191.

75.  AU s.a. 672.1.

76.  Adomnán, VSC, II.22; eds and trans Anderson and Anderson 1991: 125, 129.

77.  Adomnán, VSC, II.22; eds and trans Anderson and Anderson 1991: 124–5.

78.  AT s.a. 733.1; AU s.a. 732.1.

79.  SC; trans. Hudson 1998: 153.

80.  Symeon of Durham, HSC; ed. Arnold 1882, vol.1: 214; trans. after Anderson, A.O. 1908: 62.

81.  121; trans. Hudson 1996: 84.

82.  Adomnán, VSC, I.46; eds and trans Anderson and Anderson 1991: 82, 83, 85.

83.  Watson, W.J. 1926: 78.

84.  SC; ed. and trans. Hudson 1998: 150–1, 158.

85.  Lucas 1989: 125–99; Alcock 1993a: 46.

86.  *Life of St Comgall of Bangor*, trans. Anderson, A.O. 1922, vol. 1: 53–4.

87.  Martin 1716: 101–2.

88.  Fridegoda, *Life of Saint Wilfrid*; trans. Anderson, A.O. 1908: 37, fn.

89.  Bede, HE, IV.26.

90. Thompson 1993; but see Scott, B.G. 1978.
91. SC; trans. Hudson 1998: 158.
92. *Life of Gildas*; trans. Williams 1901: 401; pp. 122, 138.
93. P. 138.
94. Adomnán, VSC, II.33.
95. *Epistola*, 12, 15; trans. Hood 1978: 57, 58; on which see Dumville 1993: 117–31.
96. St Patrick, *Epistola*, 3, 4, 13.
97. Dumville 1993: 107–15.
98. Muirchú, preface; trans. Hood 1978: 83.
99. *The Prophecy of Birchán*, 138; trans. Hudson 1996: 84.
100. *How Fiachna mac Baedáin Obtained the Kingdom of Scotland*; trans. Marstrander 1911: 119.
101. Adomnán, VSC, II.42.
102. AT s.a. 736.1; AU s.a. 735.1.
103. FAI s.a. 866; see also AU s.a. 865.1, AClon s.a. 864; Anderson, A.O. 1922, vol. 1: 292.
104. AU s.a. 869.6, 870.2; FAI, 393 (for 871); SC; trans. Hudson 1998: 154; Anderson, A.O. 1922, vol. 1: 352.
105. Fordun, *Chronica Gentis Scotorum*, IV.2; trans. Skene 1872: 135.
106. P. 152.
107. Ó Riain 1973; Lucas 1989: 146–8.
108. Macinnes 1968; Thomson 1968; Carney 1973; Williams 1974.
109. *The Gododdin*, B$^1$.13; trans. Koch 1997: 41; see also B$^2$.27, A.9, A.22; trans. Koch 1997: 9, 61, 77.
110. Adomnán, VSC, II.46.
111. Trans. Jackson 1957: 129, 131, 133.
112. *Prose and Verse Chronicle* s.a. 859, trans. Skene 1867: 177–8; trans. Anderson, A.O. 1922, vol. 1: 291.
113. *The Prophecy of Berchán*, 128; trans. Hudson 1996: 84.
114. *The Prophecy of Berchán*, 154; trans. Hudson 1996: 87.
115. *The Prophecy of Berchán*, 161; trans. Hudson 1996: 88.
116. *The Prophecy of Berchán*, 121–2; trans. Hudson 1996: 84.
117. Trans. after Clancy 1998: 144; see also Forsyth, K. 2000a: 28.
118. Trans. Clancy 1998: 115.
119. Henderson, I. 1986; Alcock 1995; Carrington 1997; Hawkes, J. 1997.
120. Allen and Anderson 1993, vol. 2: 71–2, 221–3, figs 69, 234A.
121. Pp. 156–7.
122. RCAHMS 1994b: 96, fig. B; 1999: 39, no. 183; PAS 1997: Dunkeld.
123. Allen and Anderson 1993, vol. 2: 210–11, fig. 227B; Alcock 1993b: 233–5; Cruickshank 1994a; 1999: 28–9; 2000.
124. P. 69.

125. Tweddle 1992; Underwood 1999: 102–3.
126. Laing 2001: 241.
127. Cruickshank 1994a: 41; Laing 2001: 241.
128. On the dating of the cross-slab see also: Henderson, I. 1967: 132; 1993; Ritchie, A. 1992: 33; Alcock 1993b: 234; Laing and Laing 1993: 130–1.
129. P. 49.
130. Pp. 79–80.
131. P. 154.

## CHAPTER NINE

1. Bede, HE, IV.26; trans. Colgrave 1994: 222.
2. Adomnán, VSC, I.47; trans after Anderson and Anderson 1991: 85.
3. AT s.a. 654.4; AU s.a. 653.5; CS s.a. 651.4.
4. Pp. 39–41.
5. AU s.a. 595.3.
6. AClon s.a. 627; AT s.a. 629.1, 629.6; AU s.a. 628.1; CS s.a. 629.1; Anderson, A.O. 1922, vol. 1: 152–4; Anderson, M.O. 1973: 150–1.
7. AClon s.a. 681; AT s.a. 642.2, 685.3; AU s.a. 641.1, 685.2; CS s.a. 642, 682 (all the entries in the 680s are misplaced).
8. P. 153.
9. AT s.a. 752.3 (a misplaced entry).
10. Anderson, M.O. 1973: 193–4.
11. AU s.a. 838.9.
12. Regnal lists D, F, G, I; ed. Anderson, M.O. 1973: 267, 274, 283; *The Prophecy of Berchán*, 128; trans. Hudson 1996: 84; ASC s.a. 937; AU s.a. 936.6; SC; trans. Hudson 1998: 157.
13. AU s.a. 749.4.
14. CS s.a. 904.6.
15. AU s.a. 877.2.
16. AClon s.a. 563; AT s.a. 560.2; AU s.a. 557.2, 559.2 (repeated entry); CS s.a. 560.3.
17. Adomnán, VSC, I.15.
18. AU s.a. 917.4; see also AFM s.a. 916.
19. P. 89.
20. Pp. 32–3.
21. Adomnán, VSC, I.8; trans Anderson and Anderson 1991: 33; Chaps 3 and 6.
22. Pp. 32–3.
23. AU s.a. 838.9.
24. CS s.a. 904.6.

25.   AU s.a. 936.6.
26.   Bede, HE, I.34; trans. Sherley-Price 1990: 97.
27.   Eddius, VSW, 19; trans. Webb 1983: 126.
28.   AU s.a. 838.9.
29.   AT s.a. 704.2; AU s.a. 703.1; CS s.a. 700.1.
30.   AT s.a. 711.3; AU s.a. 710.3.
31.   AT s.a. 750.3.
32.   AFM s.a. 728; AT s.a. 733.4.
33.   AU s.a. 874.3.
34.   AU s.a. 903.4.
35.   Ed. Skene 1867: 184.
36.   AU s.a. 733.7.
37.   P. 155.
38.   Pp. 88–90.
39.   Bede, HE, I.21; trans. Sherley-Price 1990: 70.
40.   Eddius, VSW, 19; trans. Webb 1983: 126.
41.   AFM s.a. 728; AT s.a. 733.4.
42.   AU s.a. 675.3.
43.   Skene 1867: 471.
44.   AT s.a. 560.2; p. 89.
45.   P. 140.
46.   AU s.a. 871.5; CS s.a. 872.3; Hudson 1994a: 53.
47.   FAI, 429 (for ?918).
48.   AT s.a. 733.1; AU s.a. 732.1.
49.   AClon s.a. 733; AT s.a. 736.1; AU s.a. 735.1.
50.   AT s.a. 734.4, 739.6; AU s.a. 733.5, 733.6; on the victim's kingship see AT
      s.a. 739.6; AU s.a. 738.7.
51.   Aitchison 1998: 113–16.
52.   Aitchison 1998: 111–13.
53.   AU s.a. 672.2; 695.1, 696.4, 699.4, 718.6; AT s.a. 696.1, 719.4.
54.   AT s.a. 596.2; AU s.a. 595.3.
55.   AU s.a. 709.4.
56.   AT s.a. 719.4; AU s.a. 718.6.
57.   Skene 1886, vol. 1: 284; Anderson, A.O. 1922, vol. 1: 218, n. 6.
58.   Fiorato et al. (eds) 2000.
59.   Adomnán, VSC, I.8; Bede, HE, IV.22; *The Gododdin*, A.15, B².34.
60.   Jackson, K.H. 1969: 41; Harrison 1993a: 48; Evans 1997a: 128–9.
61.   *The Gododdin*, B¹.1 = A.78; trans. after Jackson 1969: 99, 147; on which see
      Gruffydd 1996.
62.   *The Prophecy of Berchán*, 121; trans. Hudson 1996: 84.
63.   Marren 1993: 26; Marsden 1994b.
64.   Pp. 144–5.

65. On which see Marsden 1994b.
66. Bede, HE, I.20; trans. Sherley-Price 1990: 70.
67. Hudson 1994a: 14.
68. Reinard 1913; Lambrechts 1954; Ross 1958; 1967: 61–126; 1986: 50–2; Burl 1981: 210–33; Whimster 1981, vol. 1: 185–8; Ross and Feachem 1984; Ó hÓgáin 1999: 49–54; Green, M. 1992: 114–18; 2001: 93–110.
69. Benoît 1955a; 1955b; 1975; 1981.
70. Green, M. 2001: 104–5.
71. Adomnán, VSC, I.12, 39.
72. Eadmer, *Life of Bishop Wilfrid*, 43; trans. Raine 1879, vol. 1: 206.
73. Ed. Skene 1867: 184.
74. Ed. Skene 1867: 184.
75. *Martyrology of Donegal*, 17 April, trans. Anderson, A.O. 1922, vol. 1: 144, fn.
76. Pp. 138–9.
77. Benton 1931: 207.
78. Allen and Anderson 1993, vol. 2: 129–31; RCAHMS 1999: 35, no. 154.
79. Harman et al. 1981; Whimster 1981, vol. 1: 188, 211, no. 19.1, 217, no. 31, 281, no. 37; O'Brien 1999: 7, 54–5.
80. Allen and Anderson 1993, vol. 2: 218–19, fig. 231B; see also Burt 1993; RCAHMS 1999: 21, no. 54.
81. Trans. Kinsella 1970: 73.
82. Trans. O'Donovan 1842: 235; see also Lucas 1963: 19.
83. Lucas 1963: 25–6.
84. AClon s.a. 725; AT s.a. 728.4, 728.5; AU s.a. 727.4.
85. Watson, W.J. 1926: 401.
86. P. 99.
87. Lucas 1963: 20, 25–6.
88. RCAHMS 1994b: 96, fig. B; 1999: 39, no. 183; PAS 1997.
89. PAS 1997.
90. PAS 1997.
91. Allen and Anderson 1993, vol. 2: 13–14, fig. 9; Laing 1993b: 30–1.
92. Adomnán, VSC, I.8; trans Anderson and Anderson 1991: 33.
93. AU s.a. 710.3.
94. AU s.a. 936.6.
95. AT s.a. 728.5; AU s.a. 727.4.
96. Eddius Stephanus, VSW, 19.
97. Eddius Stephanus, VSW, 19; trans. Colgrave 1927: 41; trans. Webb 1983: 126.
98. Pp. 150–1, 152.
99. Eddius Stephanus, VSW, 19; trans. Colgrave 1927: 43.
100. Eddius Stephanus, *Life of Cuthbert*, 27; trans. Webb 1983: 77.
101. Adomnán, VSC, second preface (twice), I.2, 20, 32, 36, 40, 43, 49, II.4, 10, 27, 31, 42, III.7, 23 (twice).

102. *Martyrology of Óengus*, trans. Anderson, A.O. 1922, vol. 1: 185, n. 2.

103. Trans. Anderson, A.O. 1922, vol. 1: 97.

104. *Lebar Brecc; Liber Hymnorum*, trans. Anderson, A.O. 1922, vol. 1: 98, fn.

105. Adomnán, VSC, III.4 (recte III.3).

106. Hudson 1994b.

107. Fridegoda, *Life of Saint Wilfrid*; trans. Anderson, A.O. 1908: 36–7, n. 4.

108. Adomnán, VSC, I.1; trans Anderson and Anderson 1991: 15.

109. Adomnán, VSC, I.1, 7, 8; trans Anderson and Anderson 1991: 31.

110. Airlie 1994: 37–40.

111. Ed. Anderson, M.O. 1973: 259.

112. Symeon, HSC; trans. Anderson, A.O. 1908: 62–3.

113. FAI, 429 (for ?909).

114. Ed. Lawlor 1917; on which see Esposito 1920; Alexander 1978: 28–9, no. 4; Ó Floinn 1995: 150–4; Herity and Breen 2003.

115. Mánus Ó Dónaill, *Betha Colaim Chille*, 182–5; trans. Clancy 1999: 26.

116. Clancy 1999: 25.

117. Anderson, J. 1910: 260–5; Eeles 1934; Stevenson 1983: 473–4; Spearman and Youngs 1989; Ó Floinn 1995: 144–9; but see Caldwell 2001.

118. Pp. 51–2.

119. Okasha 1992b: 1015.

120. SC; trans. Hudson 1998: 152; on which see Anderson, M.O. 1973: 197.

121. Symeon, *Historia de Sancto Cuthberto*; trans. Anderson, A.O. 1908: 64.

122. Bede, HE, IV.26; trans. Sherley-Price 1990: 254.

123. Trans. Márkus 1997; trans. Ní Donnchadha 2001; see also Ní Donnchadha 1996; O'Loughlin (ed.) 2001.

124. Ní Donnchadha 1982: 212, 214.

125. E.g. Halsall 1989.

# Bibliography

PRIMARY SOURCES

ABL: 'Annals from the *Book of Leinster*': ed. and trans. W. Stokes, *The Tripartite Life of St Patrick, with Other Documents Relating to that Saint*, 2 vols, Rolls Series 89, London, HMSO, 1887: vol. 2, pp. 512–29

ACamb: *Annales Cambriae*: ed. J.W. Ab Ithel, *Annales Cambriae*, Rolls Series 20, London, Longman, Green, Longman and Roberts, 1860; ed. and trans. E. Phillimore, '*Annales Cambriae*', *Y Cymmrodor* 9 (1888): 141–83

AClon: *Annals of Clonmacnoise*: ed. D. Murphy, *The Annals of Clonmacnoise, being Annals of Ireland from the Earliest Period to AD 1408*, Dublin, University Press for the Royal Society of Antiquaries of Ireland, 1896; repr. Felinfach, Dyfed, Llanerch, 1993

Adomnán, *Cáin Adomnáin*: trans. G. Márkus, *Adomnán's 'Law of the Innocents'*, Glasgow, Blackfriars Books, 1997; trans. M. Ní Dhonnchadha, in O'Loughlin (ed.), 2001

——, *De Locis Sanctis*: ed. and trans. D. Meehan, *Adomnán's De Locis Sanctis*, Scriptores Latini Hiberniae 3, Dublin, Dublin Institute for Advanced Studies, 1983

——, *Lex Innocentium*: see Adomnán, *Cáin Adomnáin*

——, VSC: *Vita Sancti Columbae*: eds and trans A.O. Anderson and M.O. Anderson, *Adomnán's Life of Columba*, rev. edn, Oxford Medieval Texts Series, Oxford, Clarendon Press, 1991; first published Edinburgh, Oliver & Boyd, 1961

AFM: *Annals of the Four Masters*: ed. and trans. J. O'Donovan, *Annala Rioghachta Eireann: Annals of the Kingdom of Ireland by the Four Masters, from the Earliest Period to the Year 1616*, 2nd edn, 7 vols, Dublin, Hodges and Smith, 1856

AI: *Annals of Inisfallen*: ed. and trans. S. Mac Airt, *The Annals of Inisfallen (MS Rawlinson B.503)*, Dublin, Dublin Institute for Advanced Studies, 1951

Ammianus Marcellinus, *Rerum gestarum libri*: ed. and trans. J.C. Rolfe, *Ammianus Marcellinus*, 3 vols, Loeb Classical Library, London, William Heinemann, rev. edn, 1982; first published 1935–9

ASC: *Anglo-Saxon Chronicle*: gen. eds D. Dumville and S. Keynes, *The Anglo-Saxon Chronicle: a Collaborative Edition*, 17 vols, Cambridge, Brewer, 1983–95; trans. M. Swanton, *The Anglo-Saxon Chronicle*, London, J.M. Dent, 1996

AT: *Annals of Tigernach*: ed. and trans. W. Stokes, '*The Annals of Tigernach*', *Revue*

*Celtique* **16** (1895): 374–419; **17** (1896): 6–33, 119–263, 337–420; **18** (1897): 9–59, 150–97, 267–303; repr. as *The Annals of Tigernach*, 2 vols, Felinfach, Dyfed, Llanerch, 1993

AU: *Annals of Ulster*: eds and trans S. Mac Airt and G. Mac Niocaill, *The Annals of Ulster (to AD 1131)*, Dublin, Dublin Institute for Advanced Studies, 1983

Bede, HE: *Historia Ecclesiastica Gentis Anglorum*: eds and trans B. Colgrave and R.A.B. Mynors, *Bede's Ecclesiastical History of the English People*, Oxford, Clarendon Press, 1969; trans. L. Sherley-Price, rev. R.E. Latham, *Bede: Ecclesiastical History of the English People*, rev. edn, Harmondsworth, Penguin, 1990; trans. B. Colgrave, in McClure and Collins (eds), 1994: pp. 1–295

Bede, *Life of Cuthbert*: ed. and trans. B. Colgrave, *Two Lives of Saint Cuthbert: A Life by an Anonymous Monk of Lindisfarne and Bede's Prose Life*, Cambridge, Cambridge UP, 1940: pp. 141–307; repr. 1985; trans J.F. Webb, 'Bede: Life of Cuthbert', in Farmer (ed.), 1983: pp. 39–102

*Book of Kells*: facsimile edn, with commentary, 2 vols, Luzern, Faksimile-verlag, 1990

*Book of Leinster*: eds R.I. Best and M.A. O'Brien, *The Book of Leinster, formerly Lebar na Núachongbála*, vol. 4, Dublin, Dublin Institute for Advanced Studies, 1965

Caesar, Julius, *de Bello Gallico*: ed. and trans. H.J. Edwards, *Caesar: the Gallic War*, Loeb Classical Library no. 72, Cambridge, Mass., Harvard UP, 1986

Cassius Dio: ed. and trans. E. Cary, *Dio's Roman History*, 9 vols, Loeb Classical Library, London, William Heinemann, 1970–82; first published 1914–27

*Cath Maige Rátha*: ed. and trans. J. O'Donovan, *The Banquet of Dun na n-Gedh, and the Battle of Magh Rath: an Ancient Historical Tale*, Dublin, Irish Archaeological Society, 1842: pp. 89–321

CB: trans. B. Colgrave, 'Continuations', in McClure and Collins (eds), 1994: pp. 296–8

Claudian, *Panegyrics*: ed. and trans. M. Platnauer, *Claudian*, 2 vols, Loeb Classical Library, London, William Heinemann, 1922

*Críth Gablach*: trans. Mac Neill, 1923: pp. 281–306

CS: ed. and trans. W.M. Hennessy, *Chronicum Scotorum: a Chronicle of Irish Affairs, from the Earliest Times to AD 1135*, Rolls Series 46, London, Longmans, Green, Reader and Dyer, 1866

*Duan Albanach*: ed. and trans. K. Jackson, 'The Duan Albanach', *Scottish Historical Review* **36** (1957): 125–37

Eadmer, *Life of Bishop Wilfrid*: ed. J. Raine, *Vita Wilfridi Episcopi*, in *The Historians of the Church of York*, 3 vols, Rolls Series 71, London, Longman & Co., 1879–94: vol. 1, pp. 161–226

Eddius Stephanus, VSW: *Vita Sancti Wilfrithi*: ed. and trans. B. Colgrave, *The Life of Bishop Wilfrid by Eddius Stephanus*, Cambridge, Cambridge UP, 1927; repr. 1985; trans J.F. Webb, 'Eddius Stephanus: Life of Bishop Wilfrid', in Farmer (ed.), 1983: pp. 103–82

FAI: *Fragmentary Annals of Ireland*: ed. and trans. J.N. Radner, *Fragmentary Annals of Ireland*, Dublin, Dublin Institute for Advanced Studies, 1978

# Bibliography

Fordun, John of, *Chronica Gentis Scotorum*: trans. F.J.H. Skene, *John of Fordun's Chronicle of the Scottish Nation*, Edinburgh, Historians of Scotland, 1872; repr. 2 vols, Felinfach, Dyfed, Llanerch, 1993

Fridegoda, *Life of Saint Wilfrid*: ed. J. Raine, *Vita S. Wilfridi*, in *Historians of the Church of York*, 3 vols, Rolls Series 71, London, Longman & Co., 1879–94: vol. 1, pp. 105–59

Gildas, *De excidio et conquestu Britanniae*: ed. and trans. M. Winterbottom, *Gildas: the Ruin of Britain and other Works*, History from the Sources, Arthurian Period Sources 7, London, Phillimore, 1978

Giraldus Cambrensis, *Topographia Hiberniae*: trans. J.J. O'Meara, *Giraldus Cambrensis (Gerald of Wales): The History and Topography of Ireland (Topographia Hiberniae)*, rev. edn, Dublin, Dollmen Press, 1982

*The Gododdin*: ed. and trans. K.H. Jackson, *The Gododdin: the Oldest Scottish Poem*, Edinburgh, Edinburgh UP, 1969; ed. and trans. J.T. Koch, *The Gododdin of Aneirin: Text and Context from Dark-Age North Britain*, Cardiff, University of Wales Press, 1997

Herodian: ed. and trans. C.R. Whittaker, *Herodian*, 2 vols, London, Heinemann, 1969–70

*Historia Brittonum*: ed. and trans. J. Morris, *Nennius: British History and the Welsh Annals*, History from the Sources, Arthurian Period Sources 8, London, Phillimore, 1980: pp. 50–84

*How Fiachna mac Baedáin Obtained the Kingdom of Scotland*: ed. and trans. C. Marstrander, *Ériu* 5 (1911): 112–19

*Laws of Hywel Dda*: ed. and trans. M. Richards, *The Laws of Hywel Dda*, Cambridge, Cambridge UP, 1954

*Life of Gildas*: ed. and trans. H. Williams, 'Vita II: "Vita Gildae", Written by Caradoc of Llancarvan (or Nancarvan)', *Gildas*, Part II (=*Cymmrodorion Record Series*, no. 3), London, David Nutt for the Honourable Society of Cymmrodorion, 1901: pp. 390–413

Muirchú: ed. and trans. A.B.E. Hood, *Saint Patrick: His Writings and Muichu's Life*, History from the Sources, Arthurian Period Sources 9, London, Phillimore, 1978: pp. 61–98

*Navigatio Sancti Brendani*: trans. J.F. Webb, 'The Voyage of St Brendan', in Farmer (ed.), 1983: pp. 209–45

*Pan. Lat. Vet.*: *Panegyrici Latini Veteres*: ed. and trans. R.A.B. Mynors, *In Praise of Later Roman Emperors: the Panegyrici Latini*, Berkeley, Ca., University of California Press, 1994

*The Prophecy of Berchán*: ed. and trans. B.T. Hudson, *The Prophecy of Berchán: Irish and Scottish High-Kings of the Early Middle Ages*, Westport, Conn., Greenwood Press, 1996

St Patrick, *Epistola*: ed. and trans. A.B.E. Hood, *Saint Patrick: His Writings and Muichu's Life*, History from the Sources, Arthurian Period Sources 9, London, Phillimore, 1978: pp. 35–8, 55–9

SC: *Scottish Chronicle*: ed. and trans. B.T. Hudson, '"The Scottish Chronicle"', *Scottish Historical Review* 77 (1998): 129–61

# Bibliography

*Senchus fer nAlban*: ed. and trans. J. Bannerman, *Studies in the History of Dalriada*, Edinburgh, Scottish Academic Press: pp. 41–9

Symeon of Durham, HSC: ed. T. Arnold, '*Historia de Sancto Cuthberto*', *Symeonis Monachi Opera Omnia*, Rolls Series 75, 2 vols, 1882, 1885: vol. 1, pp. 196–214

Tacitus, *Agricola*: ed. and trans. M. Hutton, revised R.M. Ogilvie, in *Tacitus*, vol. 1, rev. edn, Loeb Classical Library no. 35, Cambridge, Mass., Harvard UP, 1970: pp. 3–115

*Táin Bo Cuailnge (The Cattle Raid of Cooley)*: trans. T. Kinsella, *The Táin*, Oxford, Oxford UP, 1970

TYP: ed. and trans. R. Bromwich, *Trioedd Ynys Prydein: the Welsh Triads*, Cardiff, University of Wales Press, 2nd edn, 1978; first published 1961

*Uraicecht Becc*: trans. Mac Neill, 1923: pp. 272–81

Vegetius, *Epitoma Rei Militaris*: trans. N.P. Milner, *Vegetius: Epitome of Military Science*, Translated Texts for Historians 16, Liverpool, Liverpool UP, 2nd rev. edn 1996; first published 1993

*Vita Sancti Lasriani*: ed. W.W. Heist, *Vita Sanctorum Hiberniae ex codice olim Salmanticensi nunc Bruxellensi*, Subsidia Hagiographica 28, Brussels, Société des Bollandistes, 1965: pp. 340–3

Zosimus, *Historia Nova*: trans. R.T. Ridley, *Zosimus, Historia Nova*, Canberra, Australian Association for Byzantine Studies, 1982

## SECONDARY SOURCES

Abels, R.P. 1988. *Lordship and Military Obligation in Anglo-Saxon England*, Berkeley, Ca., University of California Press

Abercromby, J. 1907. 'The Relative Chronology of some Cinerary Urn Types of Great Britain and Ireland', *Proc. Soc. Antiq. Scotland* **41** (1906–7): 185–274

Abercromby, J., Ross, T. and Anderson, J. 1902. 'Account of the Excavation of the Roman Station at Inchtuthil, Perthshire, Undertaken by the Society of Antiquaries in 1901', *Proc. Soc. Antiq. Scotland* **36** (1901–2): 182–242

Airlie, S. 1994. 'The View from Maastricht', in Crawford (ed.), 1994: pp. 33–46

Aitchison, N.B. 1994. *Armagh and the Royal Centres in Early Medieval Ireland: Monuments, Cosmology and the Past*, Woodbridge, Cruithne Press/Boydell & Brewer

—— 1998. 'Regicide in Early Medieval Ireland', in G. Halsall (ed.), *Violence and Society in the Early Medieval West*, Woodbridge, Boydell Press: pp. 108–25

—— 1999. *Macbeth: Man and Myth*, Stroud, Sutton

—— 2000. *Scotland's Stone of Destiny: Myth, History and Nationhood*, Stroud, Tempus

Alcock, L. 1971. *Arthur's Britain: History and Archaeology, AD 367–634*, Harmondsworth, Penguin

—— 1978. 'A Multi-Disciplinary Chronology for Alt Clut, Castle Rock, Dumbarton', *Proc. Soc. Antiq. Scotland* **107** (1975–6): 103–13

—— 1981a. 'Early Historic Fortifications in Scotland', in G. Guilbert (ed.), *Hillfort Studies: Essays for A.H.A. Hogg*, Leicester, Leicester UP: pp. 150–80

—— 1981b. 'Early Historic Fortifications of Scotland', *Current Archaeology* **79**: 230–6

—— 1984. 'A Survey of Pictish Settlement Archaeology', in Friell and Watson (eds), 1984: pp. 7–41

—— 1987a. *Economy, Society and Warfare among the Britons and Saxons*, Cardiff, University of Wales Press

—— 1987b. 'Pictish Studies: Present and Future', in Small (ed.), 1987: pp. 80–92

—— 1989. 'An Heroic Age: War and Society in Northern Britain, AD 450–850. Rhind Lectures, 1988–89: a Synopsis', *Proc. Soc. Antiq. Scotland* **118** (1988): 327–34

—— 1993a. *The Neighbours of the Picts: Angles, Britons & Scots at War and at Home*, Groam House Lecture Series, n.p. [Rosemarkie], Groam House Museum Trust

—— 1993b. 'Image and Icon in Pictish Sculpture', in Spearman and Higgitt (eds), 1993: pp. 230–6

—— 1995. 'What is David Doing to a Lion?', *Pictish Arts Soc. J.* **7** (spring 1995): 1–2

—— 1996a. 'The Site of the "Battle of Dunnichen"', *Scottish Historical Review* **75**: 130–42

—— 1996b. '*Ur*-Symbols in the Pictograph-System of the Picts', *Pictish Arts Soc. J.* **9** (spring 1996): 2–5

—— 1997. 'How many Picts were there?', *Pictish Arts Soc. J.* **11** (summer 1997): 6–8

—— 1998. 'From Realism to Caricature: Reflections on Insular Depictions of Animals and People', *Proc. Soc. Antiq. Scotland* **128**: 515–36

Alcock, L. and Alcock, E.A. 1988. 'Reconnaissance Excavations on Early Historic Fortifications and other Royal Sites in Scotland, 1974–84. 2, Excavations at Dunollie Castle, Oban, Argyll, 1978', *Proc. Soc. Antiq. Scotland* **117** (1987): 119–47

—— 1990. 'Reconnaissance Excavations on Early Historic Fortifications and other Royal Sites in Scotland, 1974–84. 4, Excavations at Alt Clut, Clyde Rock, Strathclyde, 1974–5', *Proc. Soc. Antiq. Scotland* **120**: 95–149

—— 1993. 'Reconnaissance Excavations on Early Historic Fortifications and other Royal Sites in Scotland, 1974–84; 5: A, Excavations & other Fieldwork at Forteviot, Perthshire, 1981; B, Excavations at Urquhart Castle, Inverness-shire, 1983; C, Excavations at Dunnottar, Kincardineshire, 1984', *Proc. Soc. Antiq. Scotland* **122** (1992): 215–87

Alcock, L., Alcock, E.A. and Driscoll, S.T. 1990. 'Reconnaissance Excavations on Early Historic Fortifications and other Royal Sites in Scotland, 1974–84: 3, Excavations at Dundurn, Strathearn, Perthshire, 1976–77', *Proc. Soc. Antiq. Scotland* **119** (1989): 189–226

Alcock, L., Alcock, E.A., Bateson, J.D. and Webster, P.V. 1992. 'Excavations at Alt Clut, 1974–5: Catalogue of Coins, Metal Objects and Romano-British Pottery', *Proc. Soc. Antiq. Scotland* **122**: 289–93

Alexander, J.J.G. 1978. *Insular Manuscripts, 6th to the 9th Century*, A Survey of Manuscripts Illuminated in the British Isles, vol. 1, London, Harvey Miller

Allen, J. Romilly and Anderson, J. 1993. *The Early Christian Monuments of Scotland*, reprinted, with an introduction by I. Henderson, Balgavies, Angus, Pinkfoot Press; first published 1903, Edinburgh, Society of Antiquaries of Scotland

Anderson, A.O. 1908. *Scottish Annals from English Chroniclers, AD 500 to 1286*, London, David Nutt; repr. 1991, Stamford, Paul Watkins

—— (ed. and trans.) 1922. *Early Sources of Scottish History, AD 500 to 1286*, 2 vols, Edinburgh, Oliver and Boyd; repr. 1990, Stamford, Paul Watkins

Anderson, A.O. and Anderson, M.O. (eds and trans) 1961. *Adomnán's Life of Columba*, Edinburgh, Oliver & Boyd

Anderson, J. 1881. *Scotland in Early Christian Times*, Rhind Lectures in Archaeology for 1880, Edinburgh, David Douglas

—— 1884. 'Notice of the Gold Ornaments Found at Lower Largo, and of the Silver Ornaments, &c, Found at Norrie's Law, Near Largo, Recently Presented to the Museum by Robert Dundas, Esq of Arniston', *Proc. Soc. Antiq. Scotland* **18** (1883–4): 233–47

—— 1910. 'The Architecturally Shaped Shrines and other Reliquaries of the Early Celtic Church in Scotland and Ireland', *Proc. Soc. Antiq. Scotland* **44** (1909–10): 259–81

Anderson, M.O. 1955. Review of J.H. Cockburn, *The Celtic Church in Dunblane*, *Scottish Historical Review* **34**: 168–71

—— 1973. *Kings and Kingship in Early Scotland*, Edinburgh, Scottish Academic Press; 2nd edn, 1980

—— 1982. 'Dalriada and the Creation of the Kingdom of the Scots', in D. Whitelock, R. McKitterick and D. Dumville (eds), *Ireland in Early Medieval Europe: Studies in Memory of Kathleen Hughes*, Cambridge, Cambridge UP: pp. 106–32

—— 1987. 'Picts – the Name and People', in Small (ed.), 1987: pp. 7–14

—— forthcoming. Entries on Pictish kings, *New Dictionary of National Biography*, Oxford, Oxford UP

Armit, I. 1997. *Celtic Scotland*, London, B.T. Batsford/Historic Scotland

Atkinson, N. 1993. *Pictish Stones of Angus*, Forfar, Angus Libraries and Museums

Atkinson, N. and Henry, D. 1998. *A Sense of Place: Picts and the Early Church in East Angus and the Mearns*, Pictish Arts Society Field Trip Guide, Balgavies, Pinkfoot Press

Bain, J. (ed.) 1881–8. *Calendar of Documents Relating to Scotland, Preserved in Her Majesty's Public Record Office, London*, 4 vols, Edinburgh, HM General Register House

Bannerman, J. 1974. *Studies in the History of Dalriada*, Edinburgh, Scottish Academic Press

Barclay, G.J. and Halliday, S.P. 1983 'A Rock-Carving from Westerton, Angus District', *Proc. Soc. Antiq. Scotland* **112** (1982): 561–3

Barrow, G.W.S. 1966. 'The Anglo-Scottish Border', *Northern History* **1**: 21–42; rev. version of *The Border: Inaugural Lecture Delivered at King's College, Newcastle-upon-Tyne*, Durham, 1962

—— 1973. *The Kingdom of the Scots: Government, Church and Society from the Eleventh to the Fourteenth Century*, London, Edward Arnold

—— 1981a. *Kingship and Unity: Scotland 1000–1306*, The New History of Scotland 2, London, Edward Arnold

—— 1981b. 'Popular Courts in Early Medieval Scotland: Some Suggested placename Evidence', *Scottish Studies* **25**: 1–24; repr. in G.W.S. Barrow, *Scotland and its Neighbours in the Middle Ages*, London, Hambledon Press, 1992: pp. 217–46

Bateson, J.D. 1973. 'Roman Material from Ireland: a Re-Consideration', *Proceedings of the Royal Irish Academy* **73** (sec. C): 21–97

Beck, R. 1992. *Scotland's Native Horse: Its History, Breeding and Survival*, Wigtown, GC Book Publishers

Bell, T.W. 1999. 'A Roman Signal Station at Whitby', *Archaeological Journal* **155** (1998): 303–22

Benoît, F. 1955a. *L'art primitif Méditerranéen de la Vallée du Rhône*, Aix-en-Provence, Éditions Ophrys

—— 1955b. 'Le sanctuaire aux "esprits" d'Entremont', *Cahiers de préhistoire et d'archéologie* **4**: 38–69

—— 1975. 'The Celtic Oppidum of Entremont, Provence', in R. Bruce-Mitford (ed.), *Recent Archaeological Excavations in Europe*, London, Routledge & Kegan Paul: pp. 226–59

——1981. *Entremont*, Paris

Benton, S. 1931. 'The Excavation of the Sculptor's Cave, Covesea, Morayshire', *Proc. Soc. Antiq. Scotland* **65** (1930–1): 177–216

Blair, P.H. 1954. 'The Bernicians and their Northern Frontier', in N.K. Chadwick (ed.), *Studies in Early British History*, Cambridge, Cambridge UP: pp. 137–72

Bland, R. and Johns, C. 1993. *The Hoxne Treasure: an Illustrated Introduction*, London, British Museum Press for the Trustees of the British Museum

Bone, P. 1989. 'The Development of Anglo-Saxon Swords from the Fifth to the Eleventh Century', in Hawkes (ed.), 1989: pp. 63–70

Bourke, C. (ed.) 1995. *From the Isles of the North: Early Medieval Art in Ireland and Britain*, Proceedings of the Third International Conference on Insular Art, Belfast, HMSO

—— (ed.) 1997. *Studies in the Cult of St Columba*, Dublin, Four Courts Press

Bradbury, J. 1992. *The Medieval Siege*, Woodbridge, Boydell Press

Breeze, A. 1998. 'Pictish Chains and Welsh Forgeries', *Proc. Soc. Antiq. Scotland* **128**: 481–4

Breeze, D.J. 1982. *The Northern Frontiers of Roman Britain*, London, B.T. Batsford

Breeze, D.J., Close-Brooks, J. and Ritchie, J.N.G. 1976. '"Soldiers" Burials at Camelon, Stirlingshire, 1922 and 1975', *Britannia* **7**: 73–95

Breeze, D.J. and Dobson, B. 1987. *Hadrian's Wall*, Harmondsworth, Penguin

Brodie, J. 1996. 'Ancient Pictorial Carvings on Stones in Scotland – Some Observations on their Meaning', *Pictish Arts Soc. J.* **9** (spring 1996): 21–8

Brooks, N. 1971. 'The Development of Military Obligations in Eighth- and Ninth-Century England', in P. Clemoes and K. Hughes (eds), *England Before the Conquest: Studies in Primary Sources Presented to Dorothy Whitelock*, Cambridge, Cambridge UP: pp. 69–84

Brothwell, D. 1986. *The Bog Man and the Archaeology of People*, London, British Museum Publications

Broun, D. 1994a. 'The Origin of Scottish Identity', in C. Bjørn, A. Grant and K.J. Stringer (eds), *Nations, Nationalism and Patriotism in the European Past*, Copenhagen, Academic Press: pp. 35–55

—— 1994b. 'The Origin of Scottish Identity in its European Context', in Crawford (ed), 1994: pp. 21–31

—— 1995. 'The Picts in Documentary History', in Nicoll (ed.), 1995: pp. 3–5

—— 1997. 'Dunkeld and the Origin of Scottish Identity', *Innes Review* **48**: 112–24; repr. in Broun and Clancy (eds), 1999: pp. 95–111

—— 1998a. '*Fortriu/Fortrenn*: an Editorial Confession', *Innes Review* **49**: 93–4

—— 1998b. 'Pictish Kings, 761–839: Integration with *Dál Riata* or Separate Development?', in Foster (ed.), 1998: pp. 71–83

—— 1998c. 'Defining Scotland and the Scots Before the Wars of Independence', in D. Broun, R.J. Finlay and M. Lynch (eds), *Image and Identity: the Making and Re-Making of Scotland Through the Ages*, Edinburgh, John Donald: pp. 4–17

—— 2000. 'The Seven Kingdoms in De situ Albanie: a Record of Pictish Political Geography or Imaginary Map of Ancient *Alba*?', in Cowan and McDonald (eds), 2000: pp. 24–42

Broun, D. forthcoming. 'Lordship over Land in the Property Records in the Book of Deer', in K. Forsyth (ed.), forthcoming

Broun, D. and Clancy, T.O. (eds) 1999. *Spes Scotorum: Hope of Scots. Saint Columba, Iona and Scotland*, Edinburgh, T&T Clark

Brown, J. 1993. 'St Ninian's Isle Silver Hoard: the Inscriptions', in J. Bately, M.P. Brown and J. Roberts (eds), *A Palaeographer's View: the Selected Writings of Julian Brown*, London, Harvey Miller: pp. 245–51; first published in O'Dell et al., 1959: pp. 250–5

Brown, R.A. 1973. *Origins of English Feudalism*, London, Allen and Unwin

Bruce-Mitford, R. and Luscombe, M.R. 1974. 'The Benty Grange Helmet', in R. Bruce-Mitford (ed.), *Aspects of Anglo-Saxon Archaeology: Sutton Hoo and other Discoveries*, London, Gollancz: pp. 223–42

Bruce-Mitford, R. 1978. *The Sutton Hoo Ship Burial*, Vol. 2: *Arms, Armour and Regalia*, London, British Museum Publications for the Trustees of the British Museum

Buist, G. 1839. *Report on the Silver Fragments in the Possession of General Durham, Largo, Commonly Called the Silver Armour of Norrie's Law*, Cupar, Fifeshire Literary and Antiquarian Society

Burgess, E.M. 1955. 'Technical Note on the Fragment of Iron Mail from Carlingwark Loch', in Piggott, 1955: p. 50

Burl, A. 1981. *Rites of the Gods*, London, J.M. Dent & Sons

Burley, E. 1956. 'A Survey and Catalogue of the Metalwork from Traprain Law', *Proc. Soc. Antiq. Scotland* **89** (1955–6): 118–226

Burt, J.R.F. 1991. 'An Illustrated Catalogue of the Pictish Stones of Orkney', *Pictish Arts Society Newsletter* **9** (winter 1991): 1–8

Burt, J.[R.F.] 1993. *Pictish Arts Society Field Trip Guide,* Pictish Arts Society Field Guide 1, Edinburgh, Pictish Arts Society

Burt, J.R.F. 1994. *In and Around Easter Ross,* Pictish Arts Society Field Guide 2, Edinburgh, Pictish Arts Society

——, Bowman, E.O. and Robertson, N.M.R. (eds) 1994. *Stones, Symbols and Stories: Aspects of Pictish Studies,* Proceedings from the Conferences of the Pictish Arts Society, 1992, Edinburgh, Pictish Arts Society

Byrne, F.J. 1973. *Irish Kings and High-Kings,* London, B.T. Batsford

Caldwell, D.H. 1998. *Scotland's Wars and Warriors: Winning Against the Odds,* Discovering Historic Scotland, Edinburgh, Stationery Office

—— 2001. 'The Monymusk Reliquary: the *Breccbennach* of St Columba?', *Proc. Soc. Antiq. Scotland* 131: 267–82

Callander, J.G. 1933. 'A Collection of Prehistoric Relics from the Stevenston Sands, Ayrshire, and Other Objects in the National Museum', *Proc. Soc. Antiq. Scotland* **67** (1932–3): 26–34

Cameron, A. 1970. *Claudian: Poetry and Propaganda at the Court of Honorius,* Oxford, Clarendon Press

Cameron, A.D. 1969. 'Pictish Symbol Stone at West Balblair, Beauly, Inverness-shire', *Proc. Soc. Antiq. Scotland* **101** (1968–9): 288–9

Camille, M. 1998. *Mirror in Parchment: the Luttrell Psalter and the Making of Medieval England,* London, Reaktion Books

Campbell, E. 1996a. 'Trade in the Dark Age West: a Peripheral Activity?', in Crawford (ed.): pp. 79–91

—— 1996b. 'The Archaeological Evidence for External Contacts: Imports, Trade and Economy in Celtic Britain, AD 400–800', in K.R. Dark (ed.), *External Contacts and the Economy of Late Roman and Post-Roman Britain,* Woodbridge, Boydell: pp. 83–96

—— 1998. 'Spearhead', in Sharples, 1998: p. 159

—— 1999. *Saints and Sea-Kings: the First Kingdom of the Scots,* Edinburgh, Canongate with Historic Scotland

—— 2001. 'Were the Scots Irish?', *Antiquity* **288**: 285–92

Campbell, E. and Lane, A. 1993. 'Celtic and Germanic Interaction in Dalriada: the 7th-Century Metalworking Site at Dunadd', in Spearman and Higgitt (eds), 1993: pp. 52–63

Campbell, M. 1976. 'Rock-Carvings at Dunadd', *Kist* **12**: 1–7

Caplan, J. (ed.) 2000. *Written on the Body: the Tattoo in European and American History,* London, Reaktion Books

Carney, J. 1973. 'Society and the Bardic Poet', *Studies: an Irish Quarterly Review* **62**: 233–50

Carrington, A.J. 1997. 'David Imagery and the Chase Motif in Pictish Sculpture', *Studia Celtica* **30** (1996): 147–58

Carter, S. and Hunter, F. 2001. 'The Newbridge Cart Burial', *Scottish Archaeological News* **36** (summer 2001): 1–2

—— 2002. 'The Newbridge Chariot', *Current Archaeology* **178**: 413–15

Carter, S.P., McCullagh, R.P.J. and MacSween, A. 1995. 'The Iron Age in Shetland: Excavations at Five Sites Threatened by Coastal Erosion', *Proc. Soc. Antiq. Scotland* **125**: 429–82

Carus-Wilson, E. 1952. 'The Woollen Industry', in M. Postan and E.E. Rich (eds), *The Cambridge Economic History of Europe*, vol. 2: *Trade and Industry in the Middle Ages*, Cambridge, Cambridge UP: pp. 360–3

Carver, M.O.H. 1986. 'Contemporary Artefacts Illustrated in Late Saxon Manuscripts', *Archaeologia* **108**: 117–45

Carver, M.[O.H.] 1998. *Sutton Hoo: Burial Ground of Kings*, London, British Museum Press

—— 1999. *Surviving in Symbols: a Visit to the Pictish Nation*, Edinburgh, Canongate with Historic Scotland

Cessford, C. 1993. 'Cavalry in Early Bernicia: a Reply', *Northern History* **29**: 185–7

—— 1994a. 'Saxons, Irish and Picts in *Y Gododdin*', *Pictish Arts Soc. J.* **5** (spring 1994): 24–6

—— 1994b. 'Pictish Raiders at Trusty's Hill?', *Transactions of the Dumfriesshire and Galloway Natural History and Antiquarian Society* **69**: 81–8

—— 1994c. 'Pictish Helmets', *Pictish Arts Soc. J.* **6** (autumn 1994): 33–4

—— 1994d. 'Early Historic Chains of Power', *Pictish Arts Soc. J.* **6** (autumn 1994): 19–26

—— 1996a. Review of Foster 1996, *Pictish Arts Soc. J.* **10** (winter 1996): 32–3

—— 1996b. 'Pictish Silver and the Gododdin Poem', *Pictish Arts Soc. J.* **9** (spring 1996): 30–1

—— 1998. 'Tongs and "Tuning Forks"', *Pictish Arts Soc. J.* **13** (winter 1998): 4–6

—— 2001. 'Pictish Wheeled Vehicles', *Pictish Arts Soc. J.* **15** (2000): 27–41

Chadwick, H.M. 1912. *The Heroic Age*, Cambridge, Cambridge UP

Chadwick, H.M. and Chadwick, N.K. 1932. *The Growth of Literature*, vol. 1: *The Ancient Literatures of Europe*, Cambridge, Cambridge UP

Chadwick, N.K. 1958. 'The Name Pict', *Scottish Gaelic Studies* **8**: 146–76

Chalmers, G. 1848. *Caledonia: or, a Historical and Topographical Account of North Britain from the Most Ancient to the Present Times*, 2nd edn, 3 vols, London, T. Cadell; first published 1807–24

Chalmers, P. 1848. *The Ancient Sculptured Monuments of the County of Angus*, Edinburgh, Bannatyne Club

Chapman, J.C. and Mytum, H.C. (eds) 1983. *Settlement in North Britain 1000 BC–AD 1000: Papers Presented to George Jobey, Newcastle-upon-Tyne, December 1982*, BAR British Series 118, Oxford, BAR

Charles-Edwards, T.M. 1993. *Early Irish and Welsh Kinship*, Oxford, Clarendon Press

Childe, V.G. 1941. 'Rock Engravings in Scotland', *Antiquity* **15**: 290–1

Christison, D. 1905. 'Report on the Society's Excavations of Forts on the Poltalloch Estate, Argyll, in 1904–5', *Proc. Soc. Antiq. Scotland* **39** (1904–5): 259–322

Clancy, T.O. (ed.) 1998. *The Triumph Tree: Scotland's Earliest Poetry, 550–1350*, Edinburgh, Canongate

—— 1999. 'Columba, Adomnán and the Cult of Saints in Scotland', in Broun and Clancy (eds), 1999: pp. 3–33

Clancy, T.O. and Crawford, B.E. 2001. 'The Formation of the Scottish Kingdom', in R.A. Houston and W.W.J. Knox (eds), *The New Penguin History of Scotland: From the Earliest Times to the Present Day*, London: Allen Lane/Penguin Press: pp. 28–95

Clarke, A. 1998. 'Small Rounded Pebbles', in Sharples, 1998: pp. 178, 180

Clarkson, T.J. 1992. 'The Gododdin and the Picts', *Pictish Arts Soc. J.* **2** (winter 1992): 2–4

—— 1994. 'Stilicho, Claudian and the Picts', *Pictish Arts Soc. J.* **6** (autumn 1994): 27–30

Close-Brooks, J. 1981a. 'Excavations in the Dairy Park, Dunrobin, Sutherland, 1977', *Proc. Soc. Antiq. Scotland* **110** (1978–80): 328–45

—— 1981b. *St Ninian's Isle Treasure*, Edinburgh, HMSO (unpaginated)

—— 1987a. 'Excavations at Clatchard Craig, Fife', *Proc. Soc. Antiq. Scotland* **116** (1986): 117–84

—— 1987b. 'Clatchard Craig, a Pictish Hillfort in Fife', in Small (ed.), 1987: pp. 27–30

Cotterill, J. 1993. 'Saxon Raiding and the Role of the Late Roman Coastal Forts of Britain', *Britannia* **24**: 227–39

Cotton, M.A. 1954. 'British Camps with Timber-Laced Ramparts', *Archaeological Journal* **111**: 26–105

Cowan, E.J. 1981. 'The Scottish Chronicle in the Poppleton Manuscript', *Innes Review* **32**: 3–21

Cowan, E.J. and McDonald, R.A. (eds) 2000. *Alba: Celtic Scotland in the Medieval Era*, East Linton, Tuckwell Press

Cowell, M.R. 2000. 'Report on the Examination of a Gold and Garnet Stud from Dunadd, Argyll', in Lane and Campbell, 2000: pp. 273–4

Craigie, W.A. 1897. 'Gaelic Words and Names in the Icelandic Sagas', *Zeitschrift für celtische Philologie* **1**: 439–54

Craw, J.H. 1930. 'Excavations at Dunadd and at Other Sites on the Poltalloch Estates, Argyll', *Proc. Soc. Antiq. Scotland* **64** (1929–30): 111–46

Crawford, B.E. (ed.) 1994. *Scotland in Dark Age Europe*, St John's House Papers no. 5, St Andrews, Committee for Dark Age Studies, University of St Andrews

—— 1996. *Scotland in Dark Age Britain*, St John's House Papers no. 6, Aberdeen, Scottish Cultural Press

Crawford, O.G.S. 1949. *The Topography of Roman Scotland North of the Antonine Wall*, Cambridge, Cambridge UP

Credland, A.G. 1980. 'Crossbow Remains', *Journal of the Society of Archer-Antiquaries* **23**: 12–19

Cruickshank, G.[D.R.] 1990. *Picts: A New Book by Anna Ritchie. An Appraisal by Graeme Cruickshank*, Pictish Arts Society Occasional Paper 1, Edinburgh, Pictish Arts Society

—— 1993. 'More on the Gododdin and the Picts', *Pictish Arts Soc. J.* **3** (spring 1993): 27–8

—— 1994a. 'Explaining the Aberlemno Battle-Scene', in Burt et al. (eds), 1994: pp. 39–43

Cruickshank, G.D.R. 1994b. 'Did the Picts Wear Helmets?', *Pictish Arts Soc. J.* **5** (spring 1994): 8–11

Cruickshank, G.[D.R.] 1995. 'Of Pictish Helmets and other Objects', *Pictish Arts Soc. J.* **7** (spring 1995): 22–8; corrigenda, *Pictish Arts Soc. J.* **9** (spring 1996): 41

—— 1999. *Battle of Dunnichen*, Balgavies, Angus, Pinkfoot Press; first published 1985 as *Nechtansmere 1300: a Commemoration*, Forfar, Forfar and District Historical Society

Cruickshank, G.D.R. 2000. 'The Battle of Dunnichen and the Aberlemno Battle-Scene', in Cowan and McDonald (eds), 2000: pp. 69–87

Cummins, W.A. 1995. *The Age of the Picts*, Stroud, Sutton

—— 1999. *The Picts and their Symbols*, Stroud, Sutton

—— 2001. *The Lost Language of the Picts*, Balgavies, Angus, Pinkfoot Press

Cunliffe, B. 1991. *Iron Age Communities in Britain: An Account of England, Scotland and Wales from the Seventh Century BC until the Roman Conquest*, 3rd edn, London, Routledge; first published 1974

Curle, A.O. 1923. *The Treasure of Traprain: a Scottish Hoard of Roman Silver Plate*, Glasgow, Maclehose

—— 1935. 'An Account of the Excavation of a Dwelling of the Viking Period at "Jarlshof", Sumburgh, Shetland, Carried out on behalf of H.M. Office of Works', *Proc. Soc. Antiq. Scotland* **69** (1934–5): 265–324

Curle, C.L. 1940. 'The Chronology of the Early Christian Monuments of Scotland', *Proc. Soc. Antiq. Scotland* **74** (1939–40): 60–116

—— 1982. *Pictish and Norse Finds from the Brough of Birsay, 1934–74*, Society of Antiquaries of Scotland Monograph Series 1, Edinburgh, Society of Antiquaries of Scotland

Curle, C.L. and Henry, F. 1943. 'Early Christian Art in Scotland', *Gazette des Beaux-Arts* **24**: 257–72

Curle, J. 1932. 'An Inventory of Objects of Roman and Provincial Roman Origin Found on Sites in Scotland not Definitely Associated with Roman Constructions', *Proc. Soc. Antiq. Scotland* **66** (1931–2): 277–400

Davidson, H.R.E. 1962. *The Sword in Anglo-Saxon England: its Archaeology and Literature*, Oxford, Clarendon Press; new edn 1994, Woodbridge, Boydell Press

Davis, R.H.C. 1989. 'Did the Anglo-Saxons have Warhorses?', in Hawkes (ed.), 1989: pp. 141–4

de la Bédoyère, G. 1999. *The Golden Age of Roman Britain*, Stroud, Tempus de Paor, L. 1963. 'Some Vine Scrolls and Other Patterns in Embossed Metal from Dumfriesshire', *Proc. Soc. Antiq. Scotland* **94** (1960–1): 184–95

Diack, F.C. 1944. *The Inscriptions of Pictland: an Essay on the Sculptured and Inscribed Stones of the North-East and North of Scotland, with Other Writings and Collections,* Aberdeen, Third Spalding Club

Dickinson, T. and Härke, H. 1992. *Early Anglo-Saxons Shields* (=*Archaeologia* **110**), London, Society of Antiquaries of London

Dickson, J.H. and Brough, D.W. 1989. 'Biological Studies of a Pictish Midden', *Dissertationes Botanicae* **135**: 155–66

Driscoll, S.T. 1986. 'Symbol Stones and Pictish Ethnography', Review of A. Jackson, *Symbol Stones of Scotland, Scottish Archaeological Review* **4**.1: 59–64

—— 1988a. 'The Relationship between History and Archaeology: Artefacts, Documents and Power', in Driscoll and Nieke (eds), 1988: pp. 162–87

—— 1988b. 'Power and Authority in Early Historic Scotland: Pictish Stones and other Documents', in J. Gledhill, B. Bender and M. Larsen (eds), *State and Society: the Emergence and Development of Social Hierarchy and Political Centralisation,* London, Unwin Hyman: pp. 215–36

—— 1998. 'Picts and Prehistory: Cultural Resource Management in Early Medieval Scotland', *World Archaeology* **30**: 142–58

—— 2002. *Alba: the Gaelic Kingdom of Scotland, AD 800–1124,* Edinburgh, Birlinn/Historic Scotland

Dumville, D.[N.] 1978. '"Primarius cohortis" in Adomnán's Life of Columba', *Scottish Gaelic Studies* **13**: 130–1

——1985. 'On Editing and Translating Medieval Irish Chronicles: the *Annals of Ulster*', *Cambridge Medieval Celtic Studies* **10**: 67–86

Dumville, D.N. 1993. *Saint Patrick, AD 493–1993,* Studies in Celtic History 13, Woodbridge, Boydell Press

Dumville, D.[N.] 2000a. 'The Chronicle of the Kings of Alba', in Taylor (ed.), 2000: pp. 73–86

Dumville, D.N. 2000b. '*Cethri Prímchenéla Dáil Riata*', *Scottish Gaelic Studies* **20**: 170–91

Dunbavin, P. 1998. *Picts and Ancient Britons: an Exploration of Pictish Origins,* Nottingham, Third Millennium Publications

Duncan, A.A.M. 1975. *Scotland: The Making of the Kingdom,* The Edinburgh History of Scotland, vol. 1, Edinburgh, Oliver & Boyd

Duncan, H.B. 1982. *Aspects of the Early Historic Period in South-West Scotland,* unpublished M.Phil. thesis, University of Glasgow

Dunglas, Lord and Smith, J.A. 1881. 'Notice of the Discovery of a Massive Silver Chain of Plain Double Rings or Links at Hordwell, Berwickshire, with Notes on Similar Chains Found in Scotland', *Proc. Soc. Antiq. Scotland* **15** (1880–1): 64–70

Easson, A. 1986. *Systems of Land Assessment in Scotland Before 1400,* unpublished Ph.D. thesis, University of Edinburgh

Eaton, T. 2000. *Plundering the Past: Roman Stonework in Medieval Britain,* Stroud, Tempus

Edwards, A.J.H. 1939. 'A Massive Double-linked Silver Chain', *Proc. Soc. Antiq. Scotland* 73 (1938–9): 326–7

Edwards, K.J. and Ralston, I. 1980. 'New Dating and Environmental Evidence from Burghead Fort, Moray', *Proc. Soc. Antiq. Scotland* **109** (1977–8): 202–10

Eeles, F.C. 1934. 'The Monymusk Reliquary or Brecbennoch of St Columba', *Proc. Soc. Antiq. Scotland* **68** (1933–4): 433–8

Enright, M.J. 1996. *Lady with a Mead Cup: Ritual, Prophecy and Lordship in the European Warband from La Tène to the Viking Age*, Blackrock, Co. Dublin, Four Courts Press

Esposito, M. 1920. 'The Cathach of St Columba', *County Louth Archaeological Journal* **4** (1916–20): 80–3

Evans, S.S. 1997a. *The Lords of Battle: Image and Reality of the Comitatus in Dark-Age Britain*, Woodbridge, Boydell Press

—— 1997b. *The Heroic Poetry of Dark-Age Britain: an Introduction to its Dating, Composition, and Use as a Historical Source*, Lanham, Maryland, UP of America

Farmer, D.H. (ed.) 1983. *The Age of Bede*, Harmondsworth, Penguin

Faulkner, N. 2000. *The Decline and Fall of Roman Britain*, Stroud, Tempus

Feachem, R.W. 1950. 'A New Pictish Symbol-Stone in the Lowlands', *Proc. Soc. Antiq. Scotland* **84** (1949–50): 206–8

—— 1955. 'Fortifications', in Wainwright (ed.), 1955: pp. 66–86

—— 1966. 'The HillForts of Northern Britain', in Rivet (ed.), 1966: pp. 59–87

—— 1977. *Guide to Prehistoric Scotland*, London, B.T. Batsford

Fenton, A. 1972. 'The Currach in Scotland, with a Note on the Floating of Timber', *Scottish Studies* **16**: 61–81

Fiorato, V., Boylston, A. and Knusel, C. (eds) 2000. *Blood Red Roses: The Archaeology of a Mass Grave from the Battle of Towton, AD 1461*, Oxford, Oxbow Books

Fisher, I. 2001. *Early Medieval Sculpture in the West Highlands and Islands*, Monograph Series 1, Edinburgh, RCAHMS/Society of Antiquaries of Scotland

Flanagan, D. 1981. 'Common Elements in Irish Placenames: *dun, rath, lios*', *Bulletin of the Ulster Placename Society* **3**: 16–29

Fleming, J. 2000. 'The Renaissance Tattoo', in Caplan (ed.), 2000: pp. 61–82

Forsyth, K. 1995a. 'Language in Pictland, Spoken and Written', in Burt (ed.), 1995: pp. 7–10

—— 1995b. 'The Inscriptions on the Dupplin Cross', in Bourke (ed.), 1995: pp. 237–44

—— 1996. *The Ogham Inscriptions of Scotland: an Edited Corpus*, unpublished Ph.D. thesis, Harvard University

—— 1997a. *Language in Pictland: the Case Against 'Non-Indo-European Pictish'*, Studia Hameliana 2, Utrecht, de Keltische Draak

—— 1997b. 'Some Thoughts on Pictish Symbols as a Formal Writing System', in Henry (ed.), 1997: pp. 85–98

—— 2000a. 'Evidence of a Lost Pictish Source in the *Historia Regum Anglorum* of Symeon of Durham', in Taylor (ed.), 2000: pp. 19–34

—— 2000b. 'Appendix 1: The Ogham Inscription at Dunadd', in Lane and Campbell, 2000: pp. 264–72

—— (ed.) forthcoming. *Studies in the Book of Deer: 'This Splendid Little Book'*, Dublin, Four Courts Press

Forsyth, W.M.A. 1900. *In the Shadow of Cairngorm: Chronicles of the United Parishes of Abernethy and Kincardine*, Inverness, Northern Counties Publishing Co.

Foster, S.M. 1996. *Picts, Gaels and Scots: Early Historic Scotland*, London, B.T. Batsford/ Historic Scotland

—— 1997. 'The Picts: Quite the Darkest of the Peoples of Dark Age Britain?', in Henry (ed.), 1997: pp. 5–17

—— 1998. 'Before Alba: Pictish and Dál Riata Power Centres from the Fifth to Late Ninth Centuries AD', in S. Foster, A. Macinnes and R. MacInnes (eds), *Scottish Power Centres: from the Early Middle Ages to the Twentieth Century*, Glasgow, Cruithne Press: pp. 1–31

—— (ed.) 1998. *The St Andrews Sarcophagus: a Pictish Masterpiece and its International Connections*, Dublin, Four Courts Press

Frank, R. 1991. 'The Ideal of Men Dying with their Lord in *The Battle of Maldon*: Anachronism or *Nouvelle Vague*?', in I. Wood and N. Lund (eds), *People and Places in Northern Europe, 500–1600: Essays in Honour of Peter Hayes Sawyer*, Woodbridge, Boydell, pp. 95–106

Fraser, I.A. 1987. 'Pictish Placenames: Some Topographic Evidence', in Small (ed.), 1987: pp. 68–72

Fraser, J.E. 2002. *The Battle of Dunnichen, 685*, Stroud, Tempus

Freeman, P.W.M. and Pollard, A. (eds) 2001. *Fields of Conflict: Progress and Prospect in Battlefield Archaeology*, BAR International Series 958, Oxford, Archaeopress

Frere, S. 1978. *Britannia: A History of Roman Britain*, 3rd edn, London, Routledge & Kegan Paul; first published 1967

Friell, J.G.P. and Watson, W.G. (eds) 1984. *Pictish Studies: Settlement, Burial and Art in Dark Age Northern Britain*, BAR British Series 125, Oxford, BAR

Geake, H. 1997. *The Use of Grave-Goods in Conversion-Period England, c. 600–c. 850*, BAR British Series 261, Oxford, John and Erica Hedges/Archaeopress

Gentles, D. 1993. 'Vitrified Forts', *Current Archaeology* 133: 18–20

Gerriets, M. 1983. 'Economy and Society: Clientship According to the Irish Laws', *Cambridge Medieval Celtic Studies* 6 (winter 1983): 43–62

Gifford, E. and Gifford, J. 1999. 'The Art of Anglo-Saxon Shipbuilding', in Hawkes and Mills (eds), 1999: pp. 73–86

Gilbert, I. 1995. *The Symbolism of the Pictish Stones in Scotland: a Study of Origins*, Dorchester, Speedwell Books

Gilbert, J.M. 1978. 'Crossbows on Pictish Stones', *Proc. Soc. Antiq. Scotland* 107 (1975–6): 316–17

Glob, P.V. 1969. *The Bog People*, London, Faber & Faber

Glover, R. 1952. 'English Warfare in 1066', *English Historical Review* 67: 1–18

Gordon, C.A. 1966. 'The Pictish Animals Observed', *Proc. Soc. Antiq. Scotland* 98 (1964–6): 215–24

Graham, A. 1979. 'Old Harbours and Landing-Places on the East Coast of Scotland', *Proc. Soc. Antiq. Scotland* **108** (1976–7): 332–65

Graham, A. and Gordon, J. 1988. 'Old Harbours in Northern and Western Scotland', *Proc. Soc. Antiq. Scotland* **117** (1987): 265–352

Graham-Campbell, J. 1973. 'The 9th-Century Anglo-Saxon Horn-Mount from Burghead, Morayshire, Scotland', *Medieval Archaeology* **17**: 43–51

—— 1992. 'Norrie's Law, Fife: on the Nature and Dating of the Silver Hoard', *Proc. Soc. Antiq. Scotland* **121** (1991): 241–59

—— 1993. 'The Norrie's Law Hoard and the Dating of Pictish Art', in Spearman and Higgitt (eds), 1993: pp. 115–17

Grant, I.F. 1961. *Highland Folk Ways*, London, Routledge & Kegan Paul

Gravett, C. 1990. *Medieval Siege Warfare*, Oxford, Osprey

Gray, K.A. 1998. 'Tattoo Redux: Picti, Pechts and the Motherland', *Pictish Arts Soc. J.* **12** (spring 1998): 24–39

Green, C. 1963. *Sutton Hoo: the Excavation of a Royal Ship-Burial*, London, Merlin Press; 2nd, rev. edn, 1986

Green, M.[J.] 1991. *The Sun-Gods of Ancient Europe*, London, B.T. Batsford

Green, M.J. 1992. *Dictionary of Celtic Myth and Legend*, London, Thames & Hudson

—— (ed.) 1995. *The Celtic World*, London, Routledge

Green, M.[J.] 2001. *Dying for the Gods: Human Sacrifice in Iron Age and Roman Europe*, Stroud, Tempus

Greene, D. 1972. 'The Chariot as Described in Irish Literature', in C. Thomas (ed.), *The Iron Age in the Irish Sea Province*, CBA Research Report 9, London, Council for British Archaeology

Greig, J.C. 1970. 'Excavations at Castle Point, Troup', *Aberdeen University Review* **143**: 274–83

Greig, [J.]C. 1971. 'Excavations at Cullykhan, Castle Point, Troup, Banffshire', *Scottish Archaeological Forum* **3**: 15–21

—— 1972. 'Cullykhan', *Current Archaeology* **32** (May 1972): 227–31

Grieg, S. 1940. *Viking Antiquities in Scotland* = H. Shetelig (ed.), *Viking Antiquities in Great Britain and Ireland*, Part 2, Oslo, H. Aschehoug & Co.

Griffith, P. 1995. *The Viking Art of War*, London, Greenhill Books

Gruffydd, G. 1996. 'The Strathcarron Interpolation (*Canu Aneirin*, lines 966–71)', *Scottish Gaelic Studies* **17**: 172–8

Halsall, G. 1989. 'Anthropology and the Study of Pre-Conquest Warfare and Society: the Ritual War in Anglo-Saxon England', in Hawkes (ed.), 1989: pp. 155–77

Hamilton, J.R.C. 1956. *Excavations at Jarlshof, Shetland*, Ministry of Public Building and Works Archaeological Reports 1, Edinburgh, Her Majesty's Stationery Office

—— 1968. *Excavations at Clickhimin, Shetland*, Ministry of Public Building and Works Archaeological Reports 6, Edinburgh, Her Majesty's Stationery Office

Hamp, E.P. 1986. 'Scottish Gaelic *Mormair*', *Scottish Gaelic Studies* **14**: 138–41

Harbison, P. 1971. 'The Old Irish "Chariot"', *Antiquity* **45**: 171–7

Harding, D.W. 1997. 'Forts, Duns, Brochs and Crannogs: Iron Age Settlements in Argyll', in J.N.G. Ritchie (ed.), *The Archaeology of Argyll*, Edinburgh, Edinburgh UP: pp. 118–40

Härke, H. 1989. 'Early Saxon Weapon Burials: Frequencies, Distributions and Weapon Combinations', in Hawkes (ed.), 1989: pp. 49–61

—— 1990. '"Warrior Graves"? The Background of the Anglo-Saxon Weapon Burial Rite', *Past and Present* **126**: 22–43

—— 1992a. 'Changing Symbols in a Changing Society: the Anglo-Saxon Weapon Burial Rite in the Seventh Century', in Carver (ed.), 1992: pp. 149–65

—— 1992b. *Angelsächsische Waffengräber des 5–7 Jahrhunderts*, Beihefte der Zeitschrift für die Archäologie des Mittelalters, Cologne and Bonn, Rheinland-Verlag

Harman, M., Molleson, T.I. and Price, J.L. 1981. 'Burials, Bodies and Beheadings in Romano-British and Anglo-Saxon Cemeteries', *Bulletin of the British Museum: Natural History (Geology)* **35.3**: 145–88

Harrison, M. 1993a. *Anglo-Saxon Thegn, 449–1066 AD*, Warrior Series 5, London, Osprey Military

—— 1993b. *Viking Hersir, 793–1066 AD*, Warrior Series 3, London, Osprey Military

Hart, C.R. 1971. 'The Tribal Hidage', *Transactions of the Royal Historical Society* (fifth series) **21**: 133–58

Haverfield, F.J. 1912. 'Notes on the Roman Coast Defences of Britain, Especially in Yorkshire', *Journal of Roman Studies* **2**: 201–13

Hawkes, J. 1997. 'Old Testament Heroes: Iconographies of Insular Sculpture', in Henry (ed.), 1997: pp. 149–58

Hawkes, J. and Mills, S. (eds) 1999. *Northumbria's Golden Age*, Stroud, Sutton

Hawkes, S.C. (ed.) 1989. *Weapons and Warfare in Anglo-Saxon England*, Oxford University Committee for Archaeology Monograph 21, Oxford, Oxbow Books

Haywood, J. 1999. *Dark Age Naval Power: a Reassessment of Frankish and Anglo-Saxon Seafaring Activity*, Hockwold-cum-Wilton, Norfolk, Anglo-Saxon Books; first published 1991, London, Routledge

—— 2001. *The Historical Atlas of the Celtic World*, London, Thames & Hudson

Heald, A. 2001. 'Knobbed Spearbutts of the British and Irish Iron Age: New Examples and New Thoughts', unpublished lecture given at the Archaeological Research in Progress conference, Edinburgh, 26 May 2001

Henderson, I. 1958. 'The Origin Centre of the Pictish Symbol Stones', *Proc. Soc. Antiq. Scotland* **91** (1957–8): 44–60

—— 1967. *The Picts*, London, Thames & Hudson

—— 1971. 'North Pictland', in E. Meldrum (ed.), *The Dark Ages in the Highlands: Ancient Peoples, Local History, Archaeology*, Inverness, Inverness Field Club: pp. 37–52

——1975. 'Inverness, a Pictish Capital', in L. Maclean (ed.), *The Hub of the Highlands: the Book of Inverness and District*, Inverness, Inverness Field Club/Paul

Harris: pp. 91–108; reprinted 1990, Edinburgh, Inverness Field Club/James Thin, Mercat Press

—— 1979. 'The Silver Chain from Whitecleugh, Shieldholm, Crawfordjohn, Lanarkshire', *Transactions of the Dumfriesshire and Galloway Natural History and Antiquarian Society* **54**: 20–8

—— 1986. 'The "David Cycle" in Pictish Art', in J. Higgitt (ed.), *Early Medieval Sculpture in Britain and Ireland*, BAR British Series 152, Oxford, BAR: pp. 87–123

—— 1993. Untitled letter, *Pictish Arts Soc. J.* **3** (spring 1993): 48

—— 1994a. 'The Picts: Written Records and Pictorial Images', in Burt et al. (eds), 1994: pp. 44–66

—— 1994b. 'The Insular and Continental Context of the St Andrews Sarcophagus', in Crawford (ed.), 1994: pp. 71–102

—— 1998a. '*Primus inter pares*: the St Andrews Sarcophagus and Pictish Sculpture', in Foster (ed.), 1998: pp. 97–167

—— 1998b. 'Descriptive Catalogue of the Surviving Parts of the Monument', in Foster (ed.), 1998: pp. 19–35

—— 1999. 'The Dupplin Cross: a Preliminary Consideration of its Art-Historical Context', in Hawkes and Mills (eds), 1999: pp. 161–77

Henderson, J. 1989. 'Pagan Saxon Cemeteries: a Study of the Problem of Sexing by Grave Goods and Bones', in C.A. Roberts, F. Lee and J. Bintliff (eds), *Burial Archaeology: Current Research, Methods and Developments*, BAR British Series 211, Oxford, BAR: pp. 77–83

Henig, M. 1995. *The Art of Roman Britain*, London, B.T. Batsford

Henry, D. (ed.) 1997. *The Worm, the Germ, and the Thorn: Pictish and Related Studies Presented to Isabel Henderson*, Balgavies, Angus, Pinkfoot Press

Herbert, M. 1988. *Iona, Kells and Derry: the History and Hagiography of the Monastic Familia of Columba*, Oxford, Clarendon Press

——1999. 'The Legacy of Columba', in T.M. Devine and J.F. McMillan (eds), *Celebrating Columba: Irish–Scottish Connections 597–1997*, Edinburgh, John Donald: pp. 1–14

—— 2000. '*Rí Éirenn, Rí Alban*: Kingship and Identity in the Ninth and Tenth Centuries', in Taylor (ed.), 2000: pp. 62–72

Herity, M. and Breen, A. 2003. *The Cathach of Colum Cílle: an Introduction*, Dublin, Royal Irish Academy

Hicks, C. 1993. *Animals in Early Medieval Art*, Edinburgh, Edinburgh UP

Higham, N.[J.] 1991. 'Cavalry in Early Bernicia?', *Northern History* **27**: 236–41

Hill, P. 1987. 'Traprain Law: the Votadini and the Romans', *Scottish Archaeological Review* **4.2**: 85–91

Hingley, R. 1992. 'Society in Scotland from 700 BC to AD 200', *Proc. Soc. Antiq. Scotland* **122**: 7–53

—— 1998. *Settlement and Sacrifice: the Later Prehistoric People of Scotland*, Edinburgh, Canongate Books/Historic Scotland

Hogg, A.H.A. 1975. *HillForts of Britain*, London, Hart-Davies, MacGibbon

—— 1979. *British HillForts: an Index*, Occasional Paper of the HillFort Study Group 1, BAR British Series 62, Oxford, BAR

Hollister, C.W. 1962. *Anglo-Saxon Military Institutions on the Eve of the Norman Conquest*, Oxford, Clarendon Press

Hooper, N. 1992. 'Some Observations on the Navy in Late Anglo-Saxon England', in M. Strickland (ed.), *Anglo-Norman Warfare: Studies in Late Anglo-Saxon and Anglo-Norman Military Organization and Warfare*, Woodbridge, Boydell Press: pp. 17–27

—— 1993. 'The Aberlemno Stone and Cavalry in Anglo-Saxon England', *Northern History* **29**: 188–96

Hornell, J. 1937. 'The Curraghs of Ireland', *Mariner's Mirror* **23**: 74–83, 148–75

—— 1938a. *British Coracles and Irish Curraghs*, London, Bernard Quaritch

—— 1938b. 'The Curraghs of Ireland', *Mariner's Mirror* **24**: 5–23

Hudson, B.T. 1991. 'The Conquest of the Picts in Early Scottish Literature', *Scotia: Interdisciplinary Journal of Scottish Studies* **15**: 13–25

—— 1994a. *Kings of Celtic Scotland*, Westport, Conn., Greenwood

—— 1994b. 'Kings and Church in Early Scotland', *Scottish Historical Review* **73**: 145–70

—— 1998. '"The Scottish Chronicle"', *Scottish Historical Review* **77**: 129–61

Hughes, K. 1972. *Early Christian Ireland: an Introduction to the Sources*, London, Methuen

—— 1980. 'Where are the Writings of Early Scotland?', in D. Dumville (ed.), *Celtic Britain in the Early Middle Ages*, Studies in Celtic History 2, Woodbridge, Boydell Press: pp. 1–21

Hughson, I.[I.] 1993. 'Pictish Horse Carvings', *Glasgow Archaeological Journal* **17** (1991–2): 53–61

—— 1997. 'Horses in the Early Historic Period: the Evidence of the Pictish Sculptured Stones', in S. Davies and N.A. Jones (eds), *The Horse in Celtic Culture: Medieval Welsh Perspectives*, Cardiff, University of Wales Press: pp. 23–42

Hughson, I.I. 1999. 'Pictish Horses and Pictish Society', in R. Black, W. Gillies and R. Ó Maolalaigh (eds), *Celtic Connections: Proceedings of the 10th International Congress of Celtic Studies*, vol. 1: *Language, Literature, History, Culture*, East Linton, Tuckwell Press: pp. 211–21

Hunter, F. 2000. 'Birnie (Birnie Parish): Iron Age Settlement; Roman Coin Hoard and Brooches; Medieval Smiddy', *Discovery and Excavation in Scotland 1999*: 63

—— 2001. 'Birnie (Birnie Parish): Roman Coin Hoard; Iron Age Settlement; Medieval Settlement', *Discovery and Excavation in Scotland* (new series) **1** (2000): 58–9

—— 2002a. 'Native Power and Roman Politics: An Iron Age Settlement & Roman Coin Hoards at Birnie, Moray', *History Scotland* **2.4** (July/August 2002): 22–8

—— 2002b. 'Birnie: Buying a Peace on the Northern Frontier', *Current Archaeology* **181**: 12–16

Innes, J. 2001. 'Saint's Fort Found after 1,400 Years', *The Scotsman*, 27 June 2001

Jackson, A. 1984. *The Symbol Stones of Scotland: an Anthropological Resolution to the Problem of the Picts*, Stromness, Orkney Press

—— 1993. 'Further Thoughts on Sueno's Stone', in Sellar (ed.), 1993: pp. 91–5

Jackson, K.H. 1955. 'The Pictish Language', in Wainwright (ed.), 1955: pp. 129–66

—— 1959. 'Edinburgh and the Anglian Occupation of Lothian', in P. Clemoes (ed.), *The Anglo-Saxons: Studies in Some Aspects of their History and Culture*, London, Bowes & Bowes: pp. 35–42

Jackson, K.[H.] 1960. 'The St Ninian's Isle Inscription: a Re-Appraisal', *Antiquity* **34**: 38–42

——1963. Review of A.O. Anderson and M.O. Anderson (eds and trans), *Adomnán's Life of Columba*, *English Historical Review* **78**: 317–20

——1965. 'The Ogam Inscription at Dunadd', *Antiquity* **39**: 300–2

Jackson, K.H. 1969. *The Gododdin: the Oldest Scottish Poem*, Edinburgh, Edinburgh UP

Jackson, K.[H.] 1972. *The Gaelic Notes in the Book of Deer*, Cambridge, Cambridge UP

Jackson, K.II. 1973. 'Appendix A. The Inscriptions', in Small et al. (eds), 1973: pp. 167–73

Johns, C. 1996. *The Jewellery of Roman Britain: Celtic and Classical Traditions*, London, University College London Press

Johns, C. and Potter, T. 1983. *The Thetford Treasure*, London, British Museum

Johnson, S. 1976. *The Roman Forts of the Saxon Shore*, London, Elek

Johnston, D.E. (ed.) 1977. *The Saxon Shore*, CBA Research Report 18, London, Council for British Archaeology

Johnstone, P. 1980. *The Sea-Craft of Prehistory*, London, Routledge & Kegan Paul

Jolly, W. 1882. 'On Cup-Marked Stones in the Neighbourhood of Inverness; with an Appendix of Cup-Marked Stones in the Western Isles', *Proc. Soc. Antiq. Scotland* **16** (1881–2): 300–401

Jones, B. and Mattingly, D. 2002. *An Atlas of Roman Britain*, Oxford, Oxbow; first published 1990, London, Blackwell

Jones, N.A. 1993. 'The Horses of the Gododdin', *Pictish Arts Soc. J.* **4** (autumn 1993): 1–13

Joss, J.P. 2000. 'The Sacred Tree', *Pictish Arts Soc. J.* **14** (1999): 35–7

Keeley, L.H. 1996. *War Before Civilization: the Myth of the Peaceful Savage*, Oxford, Oxford UP

Kelly, F. 1988. *A Guide to Early Irish Law*, Early Irish Law Series 3, Dublin, Dublin Institute for Advanced Studies

Kent, J.P.C. and Painter, K.S. (eds) 1977. *Wealth of the Roman World: Gold and Silver AD 300–700*, London, British Museum Publications for the Trustees

Keppie. L.J.F. 1998. *Roman Inscribed Sculptured Stones in the Hunterian Museum, University of Glasgow*, Britannia Monograph Series 13, London, Society for the Promotion of Roman Studies

Kermack, S. [O.] 1997. 'An Attempt on the Meaning of the Pictish Symbols – Part I', *Pictish Arts Soc. J.* **11** (summer 1997): 9–18

Kermack, S.O. 1998. 'An Attempt on the Meaning of the Pictish Symbols – Part II', *Pictish Arts Soc. J.* **12** (spring 1998): 2–13

# Bibliography

Koch, J.T. 1987. '"Llawr en assed", "The Laureate Hero in the War-Chariot" (CA 932): Some Recollections of the Iron Age in the Gododdin', *Études Celtiques* **24**: 253–78

—— 1997. *The Gododdin of Aneirin: Text and Context from Dark-Age North Britain*, Cardiff, University of Wales Press

—— 2000. '*Ovania* and /wu/, /wo-/ < Celtic /wo-/, /we-/ (,/wi/) in Pictish', appendix to Forsyth, 2000: pp. 33–4

Lacey, B. 1997. *Colum Cille and the Columban Tradition*, Dublin, Four Courts Press

Laing, L. 1975. *The Archaeology of Late Celtic Britain and Ireland, c. 400–1200 AD*, London, Methuen

—— 1993a. *A Catalogue of Celtic Ornamental Metalwork in the British Isles, c. AD 400–1200*, Nottingham Monographs in Archaeology 5, BAR British Series 229, Oxford, Tempus Reparatum

—— 1993b. 'The Papil, Shetland, Stones and their Significance', *Pictish Arts Soc. J.* **4** (autumn 1993): 28–36

—— 1994. 'The Hoard of Pictish Silver from Norrie's Law, Fife', *Studia Celtica* **28**: 11–38

—— 1995. 'The Date and Significance of the Ardchattan Stone', *Pictish Arts Soc. J.* **8** (autumn 1995): 2–7

—— 1997. 'Alternative Celtic Art – Early Medieval Non-Pictish Sketches on Stone in Britain', *Studia Celtica* **30** (1996): 127–46

—— 2000a. 'The Chronology and Context of Pictish Relief Sculpture', *Medieval Archaeology* **44**: 81–114

—— 2000b. 'The Pictish Symbols at Trusty's Hill, Anwoth, Kirkcudbrightshire', *Pictish Arts Soc. J.* **14** (1999): 10–12

—— 2001. 'The Date of the Aberlemno Churchyard Stone', in Redknap et al. (eds), 2001: pp. 241–51

Laing, L. and Laing, J. 1985a. 'The Date and Origin of the Pictish Symbols', *Proc. Soc. Antiq. Scotland* **114** (1984): 261–76

—— 1985b. 'Archaeological Notes on Some Scottish Early Christian Sculptures', *Proc. Soc. Antiq. Scotland* **114** (1984): 277–87

—— 1987. 'Scottish and Irish Metalwork and the "*Conspiratio Barbarica*"', *Proc. Soc. Antiq. Scotland* **116** (1986): 211–22

—— 1990. *Celtic Britain and Ireland, AD 200–800: The Myth of the Dark Ages*, Dublin, Irish Academic Press

—— 1993. *The Picts and the Scots*, Stroud, Alan Sutton

Lamb, R. 1980. *Iron Age Promontory Forts in the Northern Isles*, BAR British Series 79, Oxford, BAR

Lambrechts, P. 1954. *L'Exaltation de la tête dans la pensée et dans l'art des Celtes*, Dissertationes archaeologicae gandenses 2, Brugge

Lane, A. 1984. 'Some Pictish Problems at Dunadd', in Friell and Watson (eds), 1984: pp. 43–62

—— 1994. 'Trade, Gifts and Cultural Exchange in Dark-Age Western Scotland', in Crawford (ed.), 1994: pp. 103–15

Lane, A. and Campbell, E. 2000. *Dunadd: an Early Dalriadic Capital*, Cardiff Studies in Archaeology, Oxford, Oxbow Books

Lapidge, M. and Dumville, D. (eds) 1984. *Gildas: New Approaches*, Woodbridge, Boydell Press

Lawlor, H.J. (ed.) 1917. 'The Cathach of St Columba', *Proceedings of the Royal Irish Academy* **33C** (1916–17): 241–443

le Bon, E. 1992. 'The Jonathan's Cave Boat Carving: a Question of Authenticity?', *International Journal of Nautical Archaeology* **21.4**: 337–42

Leighton, J.M. 1840. *History of the County of Fife, from the Earliest Period to the Present Time*, 3 vols, Glasgow, Swan

Lethbridge, T.C. 1952. *Boats and Boatmen*, London, Thames & Hudson

Livens, R.G. 1976. 'A Don Terret from Anglesey with a Discussion of the Type', in G.C. Boon and J.M. Lewis (eds), *Welsh Antiquity: Essays Mainly on Prehistoric Topics Presented to H.N. Savory upon his Retirement as Keeper of Archaeology*, Cardiff, National Museum of Wales: pp. 149–62

Lucas, A.T. 1963. 'The Sacred Trees of Ireland', *Journal of the Cork Historical and Archaeological Society* **68**: 16–54

—— 1967. 'The Plundering and Burning of Churches in Ireland, 7th to 16th Century', in E. Rynne (ed.), *North Munster Studies: Essays in Commemoration of Monsignor Michael Moloney*, Limerick, Limerick Field Club: pp. 172–229

—— 1989. *Cattle in Ancient Ireland*, Kilkenny, Boethius Press

Lucy, S.J. 1997. 'Housewives, Warriors and Slaves? Sex and Gender in Anglo-Saxon Burials', in J. Moore and E. Scott (eds), *Invisible People and Processes: Writing Gender and Childhood into European Archaeology*, London, Leicester UP: pp. 150–68

Lucy, S.[J.] 2000. *The Anglo-Saxon Way of Death*, Stroud, Sutton

Lynn, D. 2001. 'Archaeological Research in Progress 2001', *Scottish Archaeological News* **36** (summer 2001): 6–7

Macaulay, J.S. 1996. 'A Review of the Pictish Crossbow', *Pictish Arts Soc. J.* **10** (winter 1996): 2–6

Mac Cana, P. 1980. *The Learned Tales of Medieval Ireland*, Dublin, Dublin Institute for Advanced Studies

McClure, J. and Collins, R. (eds) 1994. *Bede: The Ecclesiastical History of the English People, The Greater Chronicle, Bede's Letter to Egbert*, Oxford, Oxford UP

McCorry, H. 1997. *The Thistle at War*, Edinburgh, National Museums of Scotland

Mac Cullagh, R. 1992. *The Irish Currach Folk*, Dublin, Wolfhound

Macdonald, A. 1974. 'Two Major Early Monasteries of Dalriata: Lismore and Eigg', *Scottish Archaeological Forum* **5** (1973): 47–70

Macdonald, G. 1926. 'Note on Some Fragments of Imperial Statues and of a Statuette of Victory', *Journal of Roman Studies* **16**: 1–16

Macdonald, J. 1862. 'Historical Notices of "the Broch" or Burghead, in Moray, with an Account of its Antiquities', *Proc. Soc. Antiq. Scotland* **4** (1860–2): 321–69

Macdougall, N. (ed.) 1991. *Scotland and War, AD 79–1918*, Edinburgh, John Donald

McGrail, S. 1980. 'Ships, Shipwrights and Seamen', in Graham-Campbell, 1980: pp. 36–63

—— (ed.) 1990. *Maritime Celts, Frisians and Saxons*, CBA Research Report 71, London, Council for British Archaeology

MacGregor, A. 1978. 'Two Antler Crossbow Nuts and Some Notes on the Early Development of the Crossbow', *Proc. Soc. Antiq. Scotland* **107** (1975–6): 317–21

MacGregor, M. 1976. *Early Celtic Art in North Britain: a Study of Decorative Metalwork from the Third Century BC to the Third Century AD*, 2 vols, Leicester, Leicester UP

Macinnes, J. 1968. 'The Oral Tradition in Scottish Gaelic Poetry', *Scottish Studies* **12**: 29–43

Mack, A. 1997. *Field Guide to the Pictish Symbol Stones*, Balgavies, Angus, Pinkfoot Press

—— 1998a. '*Field Guide* update', *Pictish Arts Soc. J.* **12**: 40–2

—— 1998b. *The Association of Pictish Symbol Stones with Ecclesiastical, Burial and 'Memorial' Areas*, Balgavies, Angus, Pinkfoot Press

MacKerral, A. 1944. 'Ancient Denominations of Agricultural Land in Scotland: a Summary of Recorded Opinions, with Some Notes, Observations, and Reflections', *Proc. Soc. Antiq. Scotland* **78** (1943–4): 39–80

MacKie, E.W. 1976. 'The Vitrified Forts of Scotland', in D.W. Harding (ed.), *Hillforts: Later Prehistoric Earthworks in Britain and Ireland*, London, Academic Press: pp. 205–35

—— 1995. 'The Early Celts in Scotland', in Green (ed.), 1995: pp. 654–70

MacKie, E.W. and Glaister, J.M. 1981. *The Wemyss Caves, Fife: an Interim Report on New Investigations in 1980*, Glasgow, Hunterian Museum, University of Glasgow

Mac Lean, D. 1992. 'The Date of the Ruthwell Cross', in B. Cassidy (ed.), *The Ruthwell Cross: Papers from the Colloquium Sponsored by the Index of Christian Art, Princeton University, 8 December 1989*, Princeton, N.J., Index of Christian Art, Department of Art and Archaeology, Princeton University: pp. 49–70

Mac Neill, E. 1923. 'Ancient Irish Law: the Law of Status or Franchise', *Proceedings of the Royal Irish Academy* **36** (section C): 265–316

Macquarrie, A. 1993. 'The Kings of Strathclyde, *c.* 400–1018', in A. Grant and K.J. Stringer (eds), *Medieval Scotland: Crown, Lordship and Community*, Edinburgh, Edinburgh UP: pp. 1–19

MacQuarrie, C.W. 1999. 'Insular Celtic Tattooing: History, Myth and Metaphor', *Études Celtiques* **33** (1997): 159–89; abridged as 'Insular Celtic Tattooing: History, Myth and Metaphor', in Caplan (ed.), 2000: pp. 32–45

McRoberts, D. 1963. 'The Eccesiastical Significance of the St Ninian's Isle Treasure', *Proc. Soc. Antiq. Scotland* **94** (1960–1): 301–14

—— 1965. 'The Eccesiastical Character of the St Ninian's Isle Treasure', in A. Small (ed.), *The Fourth Viking Congress*, Edinburgh, Oliver & Boyd for the University of Aberdeen: pp. 224–46

Manley, J. 1985. 'The Archer and the Army in the Late Saxon Period', *Anglo-Saxon Studies in Archaeology and History* **4**: 223–35

Mann, J.C. 1977. '*Duces* and *Comites* in the Fourth Century', in Johnston (ed.), 1977: pp. 11–15

Marcus, G.J. 1951. 'Irish Pioneers in Ocean Navigation of the Middle Ages', *Irish Ecclesiastical Record* **76**: 353–63, 469–79

—— 1953. 'The Scotic Currach', *Scottish Gaelic Studies* **7**: 105–14

—— 1954a. 'Factors in Early Celtic Navigation', *Études Celtiques* **6** (1953–4): 312–27

—— 1954b. 'Further Light on Early Irish Navigation', *Irish Ecclesiastical Record* **81**: 93–100.

—— 1980. *The Conquest of the North Atlantic*, Woodbridge, Boydell Press

Marren, P. 1993. *Grampian Battlefields: the Historic Battles of North East Scotland from AD 84 to 1745*, Edinburgh, Mercat Press; first published 1990, Aberdeen, Aberdeen UP

Marsden, J. 1994a. 'Fight at the Pool of Herons: Pictish Victory, AD 685', *Military Illustrated* **71** (April 1994): 29–31

—— 1994b. *The Tomb of the Kings: an Iona Book of the Dead*, Felinfach, Dyfed, Llanerch

—— 1995. *Sea-Road of the Saints: Celtic Holy Men in the Hebrides*, Edinburgh, Floris Books

Martin, M. 1703. *A Description of the Western Islands of Scotland*, London, A. Bell

Marwick, H. 1924. 'Two Sculptured Stones Recently Found in Orkney', *Proc. Soc. Antiq. Scotland* **58** (1923–4): 295–9

Maxfield, V.A. (ed.) 1989. *The Saxon Shore: a Handbook*, Exeter Studies in History 25, Exeter, University of Exeter

Meyer, K. 1912–17. *Zur Keltischen Wortkunde*, Sitzungsberichte der Königlichen preussischen Akademie der Wissenschaften, philologisch-historischen Klasse, 7 vols

—— 1915. 'Tatowierung bei den Iren', *Zeitschrift für celtische Philologie* **10**: 400–1

Miller, M. 1974. 'Stilicho's Pictish War', *Britannia* **6** (1975): 141–5

Mitchell, A. and Drummond, J. 1874. 'Vacation Notes in Cromar, Burghead and Strathspey. Including Notice of One of the Supposed Burial-Places of St Columba', *Proc. Soc. Antiq. Scotland* **10** (1872–4): 603–89

Morris, C.D. 1995. 'Birsay: an Orcadian Centre of Political and Ecclesiastical Power: a Retrospective View on Work in the 1970s and 1980s', *Studia Celtica* **29**: 1–28

Morris, R.W.B. 1977. *The Prehistoric Rock Art of Argyll*, Poole, Dolphin Press

Morrison, I. 1985. *Landscape with Lake Dwellings*, Edinburgh, Edinburgh UP

Moser, S. 1998. *Ancestral Images: the Iconography of Human Origins*, Stroud, Sutton

Mowat, R.J.C. 1996. *The Logboats of Scotland*, Oxbow Monograph 68, Oxford, Oxbow Books

Munro, R. 1882. *Ancient Scottish Lake Dwellings or Crannogs*, Edinburgh, David Douglas

Nicolaisen, W.F.H. 1976. *Scottish Placenames: their Study and Significance*, London, B.T. Batsford

—— 1995. 'Pictish Place Names', in Nicoll (ed.), 1995: pp. 11–13

—— 1996. *The Picts and their Place Names*, Groam House Lecture Series, Rosemarkie, Groam House Museum Trust

Nicoll, E.H. (ed.) 1995. *A Pictish Panorama: the Story of the Picts and a Pictish Bibliography*, Balgavies, Angus, Pinkfoot Press

Nicolle, D. 1984. *Arthur and the Anglo-Saxon Wars*, Men-at-Arms Series 154, Oxford, Osprey

—— 1995. *Medieval Warfare Source Book: Warfare in Western Christendom*, London, Arms and Armour Press

Ní Dhonnchadha, M. 1982. 'The Guarantor List of *Cáin Adomnáin*, 697', *Peritia* 1: 178–215

—— 1996. 'The *Lex Innocentium*: Adomnán's Law for Women, Clerics and Children, 697 AD', in M. O'Dowd and S. Wichert (eds), *Chattel, Servant or Citizen: Women's Status in Church, State and Society*, Belfast, Institute of Irish Studies, Queen's University of Belfast: pp. 58–69

Nieke, M. 1983. 'Settlement Patterns in the First Millennium AD: a Case Study of the Island of Islay', in Chapman and Mytum (eds), 1983: pp. 299–325

—— 1990. 'Fortifications in Argyll: Retrospect and Future Prospect', in I. Armit (ed.), *Beyond the Brochs: Changing Perspectives in the Later Iron Age in Atlantic Scotland*, Edinburgh, Edinburgh UP: pp. 131–42

Nieke, M.R. and Duncan, H.B. 1988. 'Dalriata: the Establishment and Maintenance of an Early Historic Kingdom in Northern Britain', in Driscoll and Nieke (eds), 1988: pp. 6–21

O'Brien, E. 1999. *Post-Roman Britain to Anglo-Saxon England: Burial Practices Reviewed*, BAR British Series 289, Oxford, John and Erica Hodges/Archaeopress

Ó Corráin, D. 1980. Review of Bannerman 1974, *Celtica* 13: 168–82

Ó Cróinín, D. 1995. *Early Medieval Ireland, 400–1200*, London, Longman

O'Dell, A.C., Stevenson, R.B.K., Brown, T.J., Plenderleith, H.J. and Bruce-Mitford, R.L.S. 1959. 'The St Ninian's Isle Silver Hoard', *Antiquity* 33: 241–68

Ó Floinn, R. 1995. '*Insignia Columbae* I', in Bourke (ed.), 1995: pp. 136–61

Ó hÓgáin, D. 1999. *The Sacred Isle: Belief and Religion in Pre-Christian Ireland*, Woodbridge, Suffolk and Wilton, Cork, Boydell Press/Collins Press

Okasha, E. 1992a. 'Anglo-Saxon Inscribed Sheaths from Aachen, Dublin and Trondheim', *Medieval Archaeology* 36: 59–66

—— 1992b. 'The Inscriptions: Transliteration, Translation and Epigraphy', in Tweddle, 1992: pp. 1012–15

—— 1996. 'The Early Christian Carved and Inscribed stones of South-West Britain', in Crawford (ed.), 1996: pp. 21–35

O'Loughlin, T. 1997. 'Living in the Ocean', in Bourke (ed.), 1997: pp. 11–23

—— (ed.) 2001. *Adomnán at Birr, AD 697: Essays in Commemoration of the Law of the Innocents*, Dublin, Four Courts Press

O'Meadhra, U. 1993. 'Viking-Age Sketches and Motif-Pieces from the Northern Earldoms', in C.E. Batey et al. (eds), 1993: pp. 423–40

Oram, R.D. 1993. 'The Mythical Pict and the Monastic Pedant: the Origins of the Legend of the Galloway Picts', *Pictish Arts Soc. J.* 4 (autumn 1993): 14–27

# Bibliography

Ó Riain, P. 1973. 'The "Crech Ríg" or "Royal Prey"', *Éigse: Journal of Irish Studies* **15**: 23–30

Ottaway, P. 1996. *Romans on the Yorkshire Coast*, York, York Archaeological Trust/English Heritage

—— 2001. 'Excavations on the Site of the Roman Signal Station at Carr Naze, Filey, 1993–94', *Archaeological Journal* **157** (2000): 79–199

Owen, O. and Welander, R. 1995. 'A Traveller's End? – An Associated Group of Early Historic Artefacts from Carronbridge, Dumfries and Galloway', *Proc. Soc. Antiq. Scotland* **125**: 753–70

Padel, O.J. 1972. *Inscriptions of Pictland*, unpublished M.Litt. thesis, University of Edinburgh

Painter, K.S. 1977a. *The Mildenhall Treasure: Roman Silver from East Anglia*, London, British Museum

—— 1977b. *The Water Newton Early Christian Silver*, London, British Museum

Parfitt, K. 1995. *Iron Age Burials from Mill Hill, Deal*, London, British Museum

PAS 1997. *Pictish Arts Society Field Trip 1997: Abernethy and North of Fife*, Field Guide 4, Edinburgh, Pictish Arts Society [unpaginated]

Patrick, J. 1905–6. 'The Sculptured Caves of East Wemyss', *The Reliquary and Illustrated Archaeologist* **11** (1905): 73–84, 249–63; **12** (1906): 37–47

Pearson, A. 2002. *The Roman Shore Forts: Coastal Defences of Southern Britain*, Stroud, Tempus

Pennant, T. 1998 [1774, 1776]. *A Tour in Scotland and Voyage to the Hebrides, 1772*, ed. A. Simmons, introduction by C.W.J. Withers, Edinburgh, Birlinn; first published in two parts, Chester, John Monk

Petersen, J. 1919. *De Norske Vikingesverd: En Typologisk-Kronologisk Studie over Vikingetidens Vaaben*, Oslo, Kristiana

Peterson, E. 1996. *The Message of Scotland's Symbol Stones*, Ruthven, PCD Ruthven Books

Phillips, E.J. 1975. 'The Roman Distance Slab from Bridgeness', *Proc. Soc. Antiq. Scotland* **105** (1972–4): 176–82

Piggott, S. 1955. 'Three Metal-Work Hoards of the Roman Period from Southern Scotland', *Proc. Soc. Antiq. Scotland* **87** (1952–3): 1–50

—— 1983. *The Earliest Wheeled Transport: from the Atlantic Coast to the Caspian Sea*, London, Thames & Hudson

—— 1989. *Ancient Britons and the Antiquarian Tradition*, London, Thames & Hudson

—— 1992. *Wagon, Chariot and Carriage: Symbol and Status in the History of Transport*, London, Thames & Hudson

Pollard, T. and Oliver, N. 2002. *Two Men in a Trench: Battlefield Archaeology – the Key to Unlocking the Past*, London, Michael Joseph

Powicke, M. 1962. *Military Obligation in Medieval England: a Study in Liberty and Duty*, Oxford, Oxford UP

Purser, J. 1992. *Scotland's Music: a History of the Traditional and Classical Music of Scotland from Earliest Times to the Present Day*, Edinburgh, Mainstream/BBC Scotland

Pyatt, F.B., Beaumont, E.H., Lacy, D., Magilton, J.R. and Buckland, P.C. 1991. '*Non Isatis sed Vitrum* or the Colour of Lindow Man', *Oxford Journal of Archaeology* **10.1**: 61–73

Pyatt, F.B., Beaumont, E.H., Buckland, P.C., Lacy, D., Magilton, J.R. and Storey, D.M. 1995. 'Mobilisation of Elements from the Bog Bodies Lindow II and III, and some Observations on Body Painting', in Turner and Scaife (eds), 1995: pp. 62–73

Radford, C.A.R. 1953. 'The Pictish Symbols at Trusty's Hill, Kirkcudbrightshire', *Antiquity* **27**: 237–9

Raftery, B. 1983. *A Catalogue of Irish Iron Age Antiquities*, 2 vols, Marburg, Veröffentlichung des Vorgeschichtlichen Seminars Marburg

—— 1984. *La Tène in Ireland: Problems of Origins and Chronology*, Marburg, Veröffentlichung des Vorgeschichtlichen Seminars Marburg

—— 1998. 'Knobbed Spearbutts Revisited', in M. Ryan (ed.), *Irish Antiquities: Essays in Memory of Joseph Raftery*, Bray, Wordwell: pp. 97–110

—— n.d. [1981] 'Knobbed Spearbutts of the Irish Iron Age', in B.G. Scott (ed.), *Studies in Early Ireland: Essays in Honour of M.V. Duignan*, n.p. [Belfast], n.p. [Association of Young Irish Archaeologists]: pp. 75–92

Ralston, I. 1980. 'The Green Castle and the Promontory Forts of North-East Scotland', in L.M. Thoms (ed.), *Settlements in Scotland 1000 BC–AD 1000* (= *Scottish Archaeological Forum* **10** (1978)), Edinburgh, Edinburgh UP: pp. 27–40

—— 1987a. 'Portknockie: Promontory Forts and Pictish Settlement in the North-East', in Small (ed.), 1987: pp. 15–26

—— 1987b. 'The Yorkshire Television Vitrified Wall Experiment at East Tullos, City of Aberdeen District', *Proc. Soc. Antiq. Scotland* **116** (1986): 17–40

—— 1995. 'Fortifications and Defence', in Green (ed.), 1995: pp. 59–81

—— 1996. 'Recent Work on the Iron Age Settlement Record in Scotland', in T.C. Champion and J.R. Collis (eds), *The Iron Age in Britain and Ireland: Recent Trends*, Sheffield, J.R. Collis Publications: pp. 133–53

Ramm, H. 1978. *The Parisi*, London, Duckworth

Rankin, F. 1989. *Guide to the Wemyss Caves*, East Wemyss, Save the Wemyss Ancient Caves Society

Redknap, M., Edwards, N., Youngs, S., Lane, A., and Knight, J. (eds) 2001. *Pattern and Purpose in Insular Art: Proceedings of the Fourth International Conference on Insular Art Held at the National Museum & Gallery, Cardiff, 3–6 September 1998*, Oxford, Oxbow

Reed, N. 1978. 'The Scottish Campaigns of Septimius Severus', *Proc. Soc. Antiq. Scotland* **107** (1975–6): 92–102

Reese, P. 1999. *The Scottish Commander: Scotland's Greatest Military Leaders from Wallace to World War II*, Edinburgh, Canongate

Reeves, W. 1857. *Vita Sancti Columbae, Auctore Adamnano, Monasterii Hiensis Abbate. The Life of Columba, Founder of Hy; Written by Adamnan, Ninth Abbot of that Monastery*, Dublin, Irish Archaeological Society/Bannatyne Club no. 103

Reinard, A. 1913. 'Les Têtes Coupées et les Trophées en Gaule', *Revue Celtique* **34**: 38–60, 253–86

Reuter, T. 1985. 'Plunder and Tribute in the Carolingian Empire', *Transactions of the Royal Historical Society* (fifth series) **35**: 75–94

Rhys, J. 1904. *Celtic Britain*, London: Society for Promoting Christian Knowledge; reprinted Twickenham, Senate, 1996

Richardson, H. 1993. 'Remarks on the Liturgical Fan, Flabellum or Rhipidion', in Spearman and Higgitt (eds), 1993: pp. 27–34

Richmond, I.A. 1955. *Roman Britain*, Pelican History of England 1, Harmondsworth, Penguin

Ritchie, A. 1972. 'Painted Pebbles in Early Scotland', *Proc. Soc. Antiq. Scotland* **104** (1971–2): 297–301

—— 1983. 'Birsay Around AD 800', *Orkney Heritage* **2**: 46–66

—— 1985. 'Orkney in the Pictish Kingdom', in C. Renfrew (ed.), *The Prehistory of Orkney: BC 4000–1000 AD*, Edinburgh, Edinburgh UP: pp. 183–204

—— 1989. *Picts: an Introduction to the Life of the Picts and the Carved Stones in the Care of the Secretary of State for Scotland*, Edinburgh, HMSO

—— 1992. Review of G. Cruickshank, *The Battle of Dunnichen, Pictish Arts Soc. J.* **2** (autumn 1992): 31–4

—— 1994. *Perceptions of the Picts: from Eumenius to John Buchan*, Groam House Lecture Series, Rosemarkie, Groam House Museum Trust

—— 1995. 'Meigle and Lay Patronage in Tayside in the 9th and 10th Centuries AD', *Tayside and Fife Archaeological Journal* **1**: 1–10

—— 1997a. 'The Picts in Shetland', in Henry (ed.), 1997: pp. 35–46

—— 1997b. *Meigle Museum: Pictish Carved Stones*, Edinburgh, Historic Scotland

—— 1998a. 'Painted Pebbles', in Sharples, 1998: pp. 176–8

—— 1998b. 'Appendix 2: Painted Pebbles', in Sharples, 1998: pp. 218–19

—— forthcoming. 'Two Painted Pebbles from Shetland', *Proc. Soc. Antiq. Scotland*

Ritchie, A. and Ritchie, G. 1998. *Scotland: an Oxford Archaeological Guide*, Oxford, Oxford UP

Ritchie, J. 1916. 'Description of Sculptured Symbol Stone at Rayne . . . Aberdeenshire', *Proc. Soc. Antiq. Scotland* **50** (1915–16): 279–87

Ritchie, J.N.G. 1969. 'Shields in North Britain in the Iron Age', *Scottish Archaeological Forum* **1**: 31–40

—— 1997. 'Recording Early Christian Monuments in Scotland', in Henry (ed.), 1997: pp. 119–28

Ritchie, G. [J.N.] and Ritchie, A. 1981. *Scotland: Archaeology and Early History*, Ancient Peoples and Places 99, London, Thames & Hudson

Ritchie, J.N.G. and Stevenson, J.N. 1993. 'Pictish Cave Art at East Wemyss, Fife', in Spearman and Higgitt (eds), 1993: pp. 203–8

Ritchie, W.F. and Ritchie, J.N.G. 1985. *Celtic Warriors*, Aylesbury, Shire Publications

Rivet, A.L.F. (ed.) 1966. *The Iron Age in Northern Britain*, Edinburgh, Edinburgh UP

Rixson, D. 1998. *The West Highland Galley*, Edinburgh, Birlinn

Robertson, A.S. 1970. 'Roman Finds from Non-Roman Sites in Scotland: More Roman "Drift" in Caledonia', *Britannia* 1: 198–226

Robertson, N.M. 1992. 'The Dog-Headed Man of Shetland', *Pictish Arts Soc. J.* **2** (autumn 1992): 27–8

Robinson, H.R. 1975. *The Armour of Imperial Rome*, London, Arms & Armour Press

Ross, A. 1958. 'The Human Head in Insular Pagan Celtic Religion', *Proc. Soc. Antiq. Scotland* **91** (1957–8): 10–43

—— 1967. *Pagan Celtic Britain: Studies in Iconography and Tradition*, London, Routledge and Kegan Paul

—— 1986. *The Pagan Celts*, London, B.T. Batsford; first published as *Everyday Life of the Pagan Celts*, 1970

Ross, A. and Feachem, R. 1984. 'Heads Baleful and Benign', in Miket and Burgess (eds), 1983: pp. 338–52

Ross, J.J. 1854. 'Notices of Two Ancient Graves Recently Opened in the Vicinity of Dunrobin Castle, Sutherlandshire', *Proc. Soc. Antiq. Scotland* **1** (1851–5): 297–9

Rowland, J. 1995. 'Warfare and Horses in the *Gododdin* and the Problem of Catraeth', *Cambrian Medieval Celtic Studies* **30** (winter 1995): 13–40

Royal Commission on the Ancient and Historical Monuments of Scotland 1914. *Fifth Report and Inventory of Monuments and Constructions in Galloway*, vol. 2: *County of the Stewartry of Kirkcudbright*, Edinburgh, HMSO

—— 1928. *Ninth Report with Inventory of Monuments and Constructions in the Outer Hebrides, Skye and the Small Isles*, Edinburgh, HMSO

—— 1933. *Eleventh Report with Inventory of Monuments and Constructions in the Counties of Fife, Kinross, and Clackmannan*, Edinburgh, HMSO

—— 1971. *Argyll: an Inventory of the Ancient Monuments*, vol. 1, *Kintyre*, n.p. [Edinburgh], RCAHMS

—— 1975. *Argyll: an Inventory of the Ancient Monuments*, vol. 2, *Lorne*, n.p. [Edinburgh], RCAHMS

—— 1980. *Argyll: an Inventory of the Monuments*, vol. 3, *Mull, Tiree, Coll and Northern Argyll*, n.p. [Edinburgh], RCAHMS

—— 1982. *Argyll: an Inventory of the Monuments*, vol. 4, *Iona*, n.p. [Edinburgh], RCAHMS

—— 1984. *Argyll: an Inventory of the Monuments*, vol. 5, *Islay, Jura, Colonsay & Oronsay*, n.p. [Edinburgh], RCAHMS

—— 1988. *Argyll: an Inventory of the Monuments*, vol. 6, *Mid Argyll and Cowal: Prehistoric & Early Historic Monuments*, Edinburgh, RCAHMS

—— 1992. *Argyll: an Inventory of the Monuments*, vol. 7, *Mid Argyll and Cowal: Medieval & Later Monuments*, Edinburgh, RCAHMS

—— 1994a. *Pictish Symbol Stones: a Handlist, 1994*, Edinburgh, RCAHMS

—— 1994b. *South-East Perth: an Archaeological Landscape*, Edinburgh, RCAHMS

—— 1999. *Pictish Symbol Stones: an Illustrated Gazetteer*, Edinburgh, RCAHMS

Royle, T. (ed.) 1999. *Scottish War Stories*, Edinburgh, Polygon

Rynne, E. 1983. 'Some Early Iron Age Sword-Hilts from Ireland and Scotland', in A. O'Connor and D.V. Clarke (eds), *From the Stone Age to the 'Forty-Five': Studies Presented to R.B.K. Stevenson*, Edinburgh, John Donald: pp. 188–97

Salway, P. 1981. *Roman Britain*, The Oxford History of England, vol. 1A, Oxford, Clarendon Press

Samson, R. 1983. 'Finds from Urquhart Castle in the National Museum, Edinburgh', *Proc. Soc. Antiq. Scotland* **112** (1982): 465–76

—— 1992. 'The Reinterpretation of the Pictish Symbols', *Journal of the British Archaeological Association* **145**: 29–65

Sanderson, D.C.W., Placido, F. and Tate, J.O. 1988. 'Scottish Vitrified Forts: TL Results from Six Study Sites', *Nuclear Tracks and Radiation Measurement* **14**: 307–16

Scott, B.G. 'Iron "Slave-collars" from Lagore Crannog, Co. Meath', *Proceedings of the Royal Irish Academy* 78 (Sec. C): 213–30

—— 1991. *Early Irish Iron Working*, n.p. [Belfast], Ulster Museum

Scott, J.G. 1961. 'The Excavation of a Crannog at Loch Glashan, Mid-Argyll', *Archaeological Newsletter* **7.1**: 20–1

Scott, J.G. and Scott, M. 1960. 'Loch Glashan Crannog, Argyll', *Discovery and Excavation in Scotland, 1960*, pp. 8–9

Sekulla, M.F. 1983. 'The Roman Coins from Traprain Law', *Proc. Soc. Antiq. Scotland* **112** (1982): 285–94

Sellar, W.D.H. 1993. 'Sueno's Stone and its Interpreters', in Sellar (ed.), 1993: pp. 97–116

—— (ed.) 1993. *Moray: Province and People*, Edinburgh, Scottish Society for Northern Studies

Severin, T. 1978. *The Brendan Voyage*, London, Hutchinson

Shadrake, D. and Shadrake, S. 1997. *Barbarian Warriors: Saxons, Vikings, Normans*, Brassey's History of Uniforms Series, London, Brassey

Sharpe, R. 2000. 'The Thriving of Dalriada', in Taylor (ed.), 2000: pp. 47–61

Sharples, N. 1998. *Scalloway: a Broch, Late Iron Age Settlement and Medieval Cemetery in Shetland*, Cardiff Studies in Archaeology/Oxbow Monograph 82, Oxford, Oxbow Books

Shepherd, D.J. 1999. 'Archaeology amd the Social Meaning of Bearing Weapons in Anglo-Saxon Society Before the Christian Conversion', in J. Carman and A. Harding (eds), *Ancient Warfare: Archaeological Perspectives*, Stroud, Sutton: pp. 219–48

Shepherd, I.A.G. 1983. 'Pictish Settlement Problems in North-East Scotland', in Chapman and Mytum (eds), 1983: pp. 327–56

—— 1993. 'The Picts in Moray', in Sellar (ed.), 1993: pp. 75–90

Shepherd, I.A.G. and Ralston, I.B.M. 1979. *Early Grampian: A Guide to the Archaeology*, Aberdeen, Department of Physical Planning, Grampian Regional Council

Shepherd, I.A.G. and Shepherd, A.N. 1980. 'An Incised Pictish Figure and a New Symbol Stone from Barflat, Rhynie, Gordon District', *Proc. Soc. Antiq. Scotland* **109** (1977–8): 211–22

Sheridan, A. 1992. 'Two Scottish Firsts – the Rotten Bottom Longbow', *PAST* (Newsletter of the Prehistoric Society) **14**: 6

—— 1996. 'The Oldest Bow . . . and Other Objects', *Current Archaeology* **149**: 188–90

Siddorn, J.K. 2000. *Viking Weapons & Warfare*, Stroud, Tempus

Simpson, C. 2001. 'Bird's Eye View Reveals Clues to Dunblane's Legendary Fort', *The Herald* (Glasgow), 27 June 2001

Simpson, G.G. (ed.) 1992. *The Scottish Soldier Abroad, 1247–1967*, University of Aberdeen Mackie Monograph 2, Edinburgh, John Donald

Simpson, N. 1992. 'Focus on Dunnichen', *Pictish Arts Soc. J.* **1** (spring 1992): 2–5

Simpson, W.D. 1930. 'Urquhart Castle', *Transactions of the Gaelic Society of Inverness* **35** (1929–30): 51–82

Skene, W.F. (ed.) 1867. *Chronicles of the Picts, Chronicles of the Scots, and other Early Memorials of Scottish History*, Edinburgh, HM General Register House

—— 1886–90. *Celtic Scotland: a History of Ancient Alban*, 3 vols, Edinburgh, David Douglas; 2nd edn, first published 1876–80

Small, A. 1969. 'Burghead', *Scottish Archaeological Forum* **1**: 61–8

—— 1972. 'Craig Phadraig Vitrified Fort', *Discovery and Excavation in Scotland 1972*, Edinburgh, Scottish Regional Group, Council for British Archaeology: p. 23

—— (ed.) 1987. *The Picts: a New Look at Old Problems*, Dundee, n.p.

Small, A. and Cottam, M.B. 1972. *Craig Phadrig: Interim Report on 1971 Excavation*, Department of Geography Occasional Papers 1, Dundee, University of Dundee

Small, A., Thomas, A.C. and Wilson, D.M. 1973. *St Ninian's Isle and its Treasure*, 2 vols, Aberdeen University Studies Series 152, London, Oxford UP for the University of Aberdeen

Smith, A.N. 1998. 'Sword Components', in Sharples, 1998: pp. 158–9

Smyth, A.P. 1972. 'The Earliest Irish Annals: the First Contemporary Entries, and the Earliest Centres of Recording', *Proceedings of the Royal Irish Academy* **72** (sec. C): 1–48

—— 1984. *Warlords and Holymen: Scotland AD 80–1000*, The New History of Scotland 1, London, E.A. Arnold; repr. Edinburgh, Edinburgh UP, 1989

Southwick, L. 1981. *The So-Called Sueno's Stone at Forres*, Elgin, Moray District Library

Spearman, R.M. and Higgitt, J. (eds) 1993. *The Age of Migrating Ideas: Early Medieval Art in Northern Britain and Ireland*, Edinburgh and Stroud, National Museums of Scotland/Alan Sutton

Spearman, R.M. and Youngs, S. 1989. 'House-Shaped Shrine, the "Monymusk" Reliquary', in Youngs (ed.), 1989: pp. 134–5, 163

*Statistical Account* 1793. 'Parish of Kilmartin', ed. M. Gray, *The Statistical Account of Scotland, 1791–1799*, vol. 8, *Argyll (Mainland)*, Wakefield, EP Publishing, 1983: pp. 249–68; first published 1791–2, ed. J. Sinclair, *The Statistical Account of Scotland*, vol. 8: 90–109

Stead, I.M. 1965. 'The Celtic Chariot', *Antiquity* **39**: 259–65

—— 1993. 'Many More Iron Age Shields from Britain', *Antiquaries Journal* **71** (1991): 1–35

—— 1998. *The Salisbury Hoard*, Stroud, Tempus

Stead, I.M., Bourke, J.B. and Brothwell, D. (eds) 1986. *Lindow Man: the Body in the Bog*, London, British Museum Publications for the Trustees of the British Museum

Stell, G. 1986. *Exploring Scotland's Heritage: Dumfries and Galloway*, Edinburgh, HMSO

Stephenson, I.P. 2002. *The Anglo-Saxon Shield*, Stroud, Tempus

Stevenson, R.B.K. 1949. 'The Nuclear Fort of Dalmahoy, and Other Dark Age Capitals', *Proc. Soc. Antiq. Scotland* **83** (1948–9): 186–97

—— 1955. 'Pictish Art', in Wainwright (ed.), 1955: pp. 97–128

—— 1956a. 'The Chronology and Relationships of Some Irish and Scottish Crosses', *Journal of the Royal Society of Antiquaries of Ireland* **86**: 84–96

—— 1956b. 'Pictish Chain, Roman Silver and Bauxite Beads', *Proc. Soc. Antiq. Scotland* **88** (1954–6): 228–30

—— 1966. *Sylloge of Coins of the British Isles, 6: National Museum of Antiquities of Scotland, Edinburgh. Part 1, Anglo-Saxon Coins (with Associated Foreign Coins)*, London, British Academy

—— 1972. 'Note on a Mould from Craig Phadrig', in Small and Cottam, 1972: pp. 49–51

—— 1976. 'The Earlier Metalwork of Pictland', in J.V.S. Megaw (ed.), *To Illustrate the Monuments: Essays on Archaeology Presented to Stuart Piggott*, London, Thames & Hudson: pp. 245–51

—— 1981. 'Christian Sculpture in Norse Shetland', *Frodskaparrit* **28–9**: 283–92

—— 1983. 'Further Notes on the Hunsterston and "Tara" Brooches, Monymusk Reliquary and Blackness Bracelet', *Proc. Soc. Antiq. Scotland* **113**: 469–77

Stoodley, N. 1999. *The Spindle and the Spear: a Critical Enquiry into the Construction and Meaning of Gender in the Early Anglo-Saxon Burial Rite*, BAR 288, Oxford, Archaeopress

Stuart, J. 1867. *Sculptured Stones of Scotland*, vol. 2, Edinburgh, Spalding Club

Sutherland, E. 1994. *In Search of the Picts: a Dark Age Nation*, London, Constable

—— 1997. *A Guide to the Pictish Stones*, Edinburgh, Birlinn

Swanton, M.J. 1973. *The Spearheads of the Anglo-Saxon Settlements*, n.p. [London], Royal Archaeological Institute

—— 1974. *A Corpus of Pagan Anglo-Saxon Spear-Types*, BAR 7, Oxford, BAR

—— 1980. 'The Manuscript Illustration of a Helmet of Benty Grange Type', *Journal of the Arms & Armour Society* **10.1**: 1–5

Taylor, D.B. 1983. 'Excavation of a Promontory Fort, Broch and Souterrain at Hurly Hawkin, Angus', *Proc. Soc. Antiq. Scotland* **112** (1982): 215–54

Taylor, G.W. 1986. 'Tests for Dyes', in Stead et al. (eds), 1986: p. 41

Taylor, S. (ed.) 2000. *Kings, Clerics and Chronicles in Scotland, 500–1297: Essays in Honour of Marjorie Ogilvie Anderson on the Occasion of her Ninetieth Birthday*, Dublin, Four Courts Press

Temple, E. 1976. *Anglo-Saxon Manuscripts, 900–1066*, A Survey of Manuscripts Illuminated in the British Isles, vol. 2, London, Harvey Miller

# Bibliography

Thier, K. and Mont, E.G. 1996. 'A Note on Meigle 2', *Pictish Arts Soc. J.* **9** (spring 1996): 32

Thomas, A.C. 1961. 'Excavations at Trusty's Hill, Anwoth, 1960', *Transactions of the Dumfriesshire and Galloway Natural History and Antiquarian Society* **38**: 58–70

—— 1964. 'The Interpretation of the Pictish Symbols', *Archaeological Journal* **120** (1963): 31–97

Thomas, [A.]C. 1972. 'The Irish Settlements in Post-Roman Western Britain: a Survey of the Evidence', *Journal of the Royal Institute of Cornwall* (new series) **6**: 251–74

—— 1981. *Christianity in Roman Britain to AD 500*, London, B.T. Batsford

—— 1984. 'The Pictish Class I Symbol Stones', in Friell and Watson (eds), 1984: pp. 169–87

—— 1990. '"Gallici Nautae de Galliarum Provinciis" – a Sixth/Seventh Century Trade with Gaul, Reconsidered', *Medieval Archaeology* **34**: 1–26

Thomas, F.W.L. 1879. 'Dunadd, Glassary, Argyllshire: the Place of Inauguration of the Dalriadic Kings', *Proc. Soc. Antiq. Scotland* **13** (1878–9): 28–47

—— 1886. 'Ancient Valuation of Land in the West of Scotland: Continuation of "What is a Pennyland?"', *Proc. Soc. Antiq. Scotland* **20** (1885–6): 200–13

Thomas, G. 2001. 'Strap-Ends and the Identification of Regional Patterns in the Production and Circulation of Ornamental Metalwork in Late Anglo-Saxon and Viking-Age Britain', in Redknap et al. (eds), 2001: 39–48

Thompson, H. 1993. 'Iron Age and Roman Slave-shackles', *Archaeological Journal* **150**: 57–168

Thomson, D.S. 1968. 'Gaelic Learned Orders and Literati in Medieval Scotland', *Scottish Studies* **12**: 57–78

Trench-Jellicoe, R. 1997. 'Pictish and Related Harps: their Form and Decoration', in Henry (ed.), 1997: pp. 159–72

Triscott, J. 1980. 'Aldclune: Defended Enclosures', *Discovery and Excavation in Scotland 1980*, Edinburgh, Scottish Group, Council for British Archaeology: pp. 82–3

Turner, R.C. 1995a. 'Recent Research into British Bog Bodies', in Turner and Scaife (eds), 1995: pp. 108–22

—— 1995b. 'Gazetteer of Bog Bodies in the British Isles', in Turner and Scaife (eds), 1995: pp. 205–20

Turner, R.C. and Scaife, R.G. (eds) 1995. *Bog Bodies: New Discoveries and New Perspectives*, London, British Museum Press for the Trustees of the British Museum

Turner, V. 1994. 'The Mail Stone: an Incised Pictish Figure from Mail, Cunningsburgh, Shetland', *Proc. Soc. Antiq. Scotland* **124**: 315–25

Tweddle, D. 1992. *The Anglian Helmet from 16–22 Coppergate*, The Archaeology of York, vol. 17: The Small Finds, fasc. 8, London, Council for British Archaeology for York Archaeological Trust

Underwood, R. 1999. *Anglo-Saxon Weapons and Warfare*, Stroud, Tempus

van der Sanden, W. 1996. *Through Nature to Eternity: the Bog Bodies of Northwest Europe*, Amsterdam, Batavian Lion International van der Veen, M., Hall, A.R. and May, J. 1993. 'Woad and the Britons Painted Blue', *Oxford Journal of Archaeology* **12.3**: 367–71

Wainwright, F.T. 1948. 'Nechtanesmere', *Antiquity* **22**: 82–97

——1955. 'The Picts and the Problem', in Wainwright (ed.), 1955: pp. 1–53

—— (ed.) 1955. *The Problem of the Picts*, Edinburgh, Thomas Nelson; repr. 1980, Perth, Melven Press

—— 1959. 'The Inchyra Ogam', *Ogam* **11**: 269–78

Watkins, T. 1980. 'A Prehistoric Coracle in Fife', *International Journal of Nautical Archaeology* **9**: 277–86

Watson, J. 1994. 'Wood Usage in Anglo-Saxon Shields', *Anglo-Saxon Studies in Archaeology and History* **7**: 35–48

Watson, W.J. 1926. *The History of the Celtic Placenames of Scotland*, Edinburgh, William Blackwood & Sons; repr. 1993, Edinburgh, Birlinn

Way, A. 1849. 'Notices of a Remarkable Discovery of Silver Ornaments in a Tumulus at Largo, in Fifeshire', *Archaeological Journal* **6**: 248–59

Webster, J. and Backhouse, J. (eds) 1991. *The Making of England: Anglo-Saxon Art and Culture, AD 600–900*, London, British Museum Press

Welsby, D.A. 1982. *The Roman Military Defence of the British Provinces in its Later Phases*, Oxford, BAR British Series 101, BAR

Whimster, R. 1981. *Burial Practices in Iron Age Britain: a Discussion and Gazetteer of the Evidence, 700 BC–AD 43*, 2 vols, BAR British Series 90, Oxford, BAR

Whittington, G. 1974. 'Placenames and the Settlement Pattern of Dark-Age Scotland', *Proc. Soc. Antiq. Scotland* **106** (1974–5): 99–110

Whittington, G. and Soulsby, J.A. 1968. 'A Preliminary Report on an Investigation into *Pit* Placenames', *Scottish Geographical Magazine* **84**: 117–25

Williams, J.E.C. 1974. 'The Court Poet in Medieval Ireland', *Proceedings of the British Academy* **57**: 85–136

Wilson, D.M. 1966. 'Some Neglected Late Anglo-Saxon Swords', *Medieval Archaeology* **9** (1965): 32–54

—— 1968. 'Anglo-Saxon Carpenters' Tools', in M. Claus, W. Haarnagel and K. Raddatz (eds), *Studien zur europäischen Vor- und Frühgeschichte*, Neumünster, Karl Wachholtz Verlag: pp. 143–50

—— 1970. *Reflections on the St Ninian's Isle Treasure*, Jarrow Lecture 1969, Jarrow, H. Saxby

—— 1973. 'The Treasure', in Small et al. (eds), 1973: pp. 45–148

—— 1976. 'Craft and Industry', in D.M. Wilson (ed.), *The Archaeology of Anglo-Saxon England*, Cambridge, Cambridge UP: pp. 253–81

Wilson, P.R. 1991. 'Aspects of the Yorkshire Signal Stations', in V.A. Maxfield and M.J. Dobson (eds), *Roman Frontier Studies 1989: Proceedings of the XVth International Congress of Roman Frontier Studies*, Exeter, Exeter UP: pp. 142–7

Wise, T. 1979. *Saxon, Viking and Norman*, Men-at-Arms Series 85, Oxford, Osprey

Wooding, J. 1996. *Communication and Commerce along the Western Sealanes, AD 400–800*, BAR International Series 654, Oxford, Tempus Reparatum

Wooding, J.M. 2001a. 'St Brendan's Boat: Dead Hides and the Living Sea in Columban and Related Hagiography', in J. Carey, M. Herbert and P. Ó Riain (eds), *Studies in Early Irish Hagiography: Saints and Scholars*, Dublin, Four Courts Press: pp. 77–92

—— 2001b. 'Biblical Narrative and Local Imagery on the Kilnaruane Cross-Shaft, Co. Cork', in Redknap et al. (eds), 2001: pp. 253–9

Woolf, A. 2001. 'Birth of a Nation', in G. Menzies (ed.), *In Search of Scotland*, Edinburgh, Polygon: pp. 24–45

Woolf, R. 1976. 'The Ideal of Men Dying with their Lord in the *Germania* and in *The Battle of Maldon*', *Anglo-Saxon England* **5**: 69–81

Woolliscroft, D.J. 2001. *Roman Military Signalling*, Stroud, Tempus

Yorke, B. 1990. *Kings and Kingdoms of Early Anglo-Saxon England*, London, Routledge

Young, H.W. 1891. 'Notes on the Ramparts of Burghead, as Revealed by Recent Excavations', *Proc. Soc. Antiq. Scotland* **25** (1890–1): 435–47

—— 1893. 'Notes on Further Excavations at Burghead', *Proc. Soc. Antiq. Scotland* **27** (1892–3): 86–91

Youngs, S. (ed.) 1989. *'The Work of Angels': Masterpieces of Celtic Metalwork, 6th–9th Centuries AD*, London, British Museum Publications

# Index